THE ARENA

THE ARENA

INSIDE THE TAILGATING, TICKET-SCALPING,
MASCOT-RACING, DUBIOUSLY FUNDED, AND POSSIBLY
HAUNTED MONUMENTS OF AMERICAN SPORT

Rafi Kohan

LIVERIGHT PUBLISHING CORPORATION

A DIVISION OF W. W. NORTON & COMPANY

INDEPENDENT PUBLISHERS SINCE 1923

NEW YORK   LONDON

For Arielle, my home-field advantage

CONTENTS

BEFORE WE BEGIN

(Or: Preface)

Picture a city, any city. Imagine a TV camera scanning the horizon. There are the buildings—the high-rises, the landmarks— all framed by the region's geographic signatures: its mountains, its bodies of water, its deserts. We know where we are. Now imagine another overhead shot, taken from some aerial advantage, from a satellite or a blimp. Slowly, we focus on a particular building. It's round or square or even ovaloid.

Oh, yes. We know where we are.

There's the grassy expanse, the bustling sidelines, the athletes who squirm with nervous energy beneath an exploding fireworks display. Nearby, cheerleaders bleat in bursts of faithful incoherence, smiling eagerly at a face-painted and beer-brave crowd.

Some fans wander the concourses, examining the concession stands, weighing their options, deciding if they really want a hamburger wrapped in a pizza topped with bacon. (They do.)

Elsewhere, beneath the surface, an operations manager monitors the proceedings, making sure the smoke machines, pyro turbines, and giant American flags are escorted on and off the field.

The grounds crew fixes a divot.

A fan leaps the guardrail, races onto the playing turf, is chased and whisked away by security.

The crowd goes wild.

The national broadcast comes back from commercial break.

It is almost game time.

———

For one year, from January 2015 to February 2016, I traveled the United States visiting sports stadiums—all manner of arenas, domes, ballparks, and football-specific pleasure palaces (*ahem*, AT&T Stadium)—for the purpose of writing a book, this book. The idea was to go beyond the ball games and architectural blueprints to explore the inner workings of these steel and concrete structures that hover over our towns, imposing their will on landscapes and skylines, to better understand our relationship to them—psychologically, economically, politically, culturally, historically—as individuals, as cities, and as a society.

It seems fair to warn you now that this isn't a book about sports; it's more like a book *around* sports. While reporting, I didn't care about wins and losses. I didn't hang out in locker rooms, hobnob with coaches, track statistics, or build a case for advanced analytics. Instead, I spent my time in the concourses and service tunnels, the parking lots and production booths, the groundskeeper clubhouses, sprawling concession warehouses, and cramped mascot rooms, as well as countless other corners of American stadiums that aren't necessarily hidden but are almost assuredly unseen.

When talking about sports and fandom, the personal is unavoidable. For many Americans, stadiums serve as storage units for emotional memory, as touch points of interpersonal connection. They are where we take our sons and daughters, where traditions and allegiances are passed down like heirlooms, and where tailgates become family reunions. Stadiums are empty vessels that transform into volatile petri dishes. They are concrete monuments and fluid social spaces. And on game days, they gather us together.

In an era that has become both highly individualized and impenetrably siloed, with on-demand everything, sports venues serve as one of the last places in which to experience a live, collective cultural event. But even that aspect is changing. There is a trend within stadiums toward "neighborhoods"—luxury clubs, tequila bars, kids' areas, celeb-chef-driven restaurants—that offer something for everyone, "a product mix." As Joe Spear of the sports architecture firm Populous remembers one client telling him, "I don't want ten thousand of anything." In this way, even our cultural common areas are becoming subject to society's splintering. But we haven't totally drifted apart yet. Communalism can be a hard habit to kick.

This book attempts to stitch together a variety of disparate stadium experiences—of the fans and the functionaries who populate our most loved and loathed arenas—into a kind of tapestry. Each chapter is meant to stand on its own, but together they should also provide a patchwork view into the microcosmic, compartmentalized, and often unconsidered worlds of modern American stadiums, highlighting idiosyncrasies and commonalities alike. Because while every stadium experience is different, they are also all one. This is their composite picture.

THE ARENA

1
TAKING THE OATH

(Or: The Old-Timers)

By the time I meet the Mayor of Lambeau Field, he's already had a few. Then again, who in this town—in and around this facility—on this day—has not? It is the 2015 home opener for the Green Bay Packers, the NFL's most successful franchise, and the Sunday-night affair is as good an excuse as any for a town that never needs one (all 104,057 of them) to throw back cold beers and grill up some brats.

Many have been tailgating since the team-run parking lots opened, five hours before the 8:25 p.m. kickoff. Others, in unaffiliated parking areas, have been at it since six a.m., while some—the RV crowd—have been holding a hops-and-malt vigil in the former Kmart lot, just off Lombardi Avenue, since Friday. (On game days, the whole town turns into a massive makeshift parking lot, with vehicles covering every available blade of grass on nearby front lawns.) How long the Mayor presided over his own tailgate, how many hours or days before entering the stadium, is unclear. But it doesn't seem to matter. Time is a flat circle, after all, like a crushed wheel of cheese.

I spot the Mayor, who bears a passing resemblance to *Breaking*

Bad's Walter White, because of a message spelled out in big block letters on the wall behind his seat via painted-yellow refrigerator magnets—JONES IN FOR A TD—referring to wide receiver James Jones. Because there are few actual chair seats in Lambeau Field, mostly metal benches (eighteen inches per spot), many fans choose to stand, spilling frequently in and out of the aisles, trying not to tumble into those veteran supporters who bring their own seat cushions and clip-on seatbacks for a touch of comfort. It is perhaps an illusion, but as I glance at the field, at the players, everything seems slightly washed out, in a favorite-pair-of-blue-jeans kind of way appropriate for Lambeau, which isn't the oldest stadium in the league,* but is unquestionably the most historic. There is nothing flashy here, hardly any advertising visible around the bowl, which is painted in a green and gold color scheme, an almost uniform sartorial choice for crowd members as well (although an usher tells me that will change come deer-hunting season, when bright orange infiltrates the stands).

The Mayor—whose position is as unofficial as it is unelected—works at the post office when not at the game, "but I am *always* the Mayor," he assures me. Wearing a yellow polyurethane foam top hat made to look like cheese, a gold sash covered with Packers patches, a yellow-shirt-and-Packers-tie combo, and a green sport coat—picture Willy Wonka if the candy magnate had a lactose fetish instead of a sweet tooth—the Mayor pats his pockets furiously, scrunching his goateed face in officious consternation. "My cards," he says, turning to his adult son, Rob, on his way back from a beer and nachos run. "You maybe gave them all out?"

Rob doesn't respond, busy negotiating the last steps and human obstacles that occasionally stagger into his path as he hunts for equilibrium and high fives. Halfway through the first quarter, the crowd

---

* That title belongs to Chicago's Soldier Field.

is bubbling, Green Bay out to an early lead against the "Legion of Boom" Seattle Seahawks, the same team that knocked Wisconsin's beloved Pack out of the play-offs the previous season.

"I have one," I say. From beneath his top hat, the Mayor gawks at this reveal like I am David Copperfield.

"Oh, you got one!" He pauses, furrows his brow. "How'd you get that?"

Like I said, he's had a few.

As for the Mayor's magnetic missives, they have been a game-day tradition since 2003, he tells me. His favorite sign to date: R-E-L-A-X, a response to superstar quarterback Aaron Rodgers's locker-room message to overwrought Packers fans, following a slow start to the 2014 season. "But every year I go through a Lambeau virgin," he explains. "I bring somebody that has never been." For those games, the sign invariably reads, LAMBEAU VIRGIN.

I confess: today is my first in Green Bay, which delights the Mayor.

"Oh!" He looks at me meaningfully. Says, "We might have to have you recite the Lambeau Oath."

At this, Rob looks up from his nachos. He hands his father a small point-and-shoot camera, which houses an image of the Oath lyrics. "Oath of the Lambeau Field Virgin," Rob shouts, for all who care to bear witness. "He is going to administer the Oath!"

———

It makes sense that Lambeau Field, which rises like a shrine from Green Bay's modest family neighborhoods, would have an oath. Unlike so many modern-day NFL facilities, whose tenants' past glories are often overwhelmed by that new-stadium smell, this is a place twice baked with legacy and lore.

By taking the Oath, I can tap into a tradition that dates back not just to 2003, when the Mayor started making his signs, or to 1957, when Lambeau opened its doors, but as far as 1919—when a semipro team was formed at the *Green Bay Press-Gazette* offices, named for a meat-packing plant—and every year in between.

Hell, this is *Lambeau Field*, football mecca, the place to which so many fans make pilgrimage, regardless of their team allegiance; the place *Sports Illustrated* called "the NFL's answer to Boston Garden or Yankee Stadium [the old one]—hallowed ground where dynasties were born." It is here that Hall of Fame coach Vince Lombardi stalked the sidelines under the brim of his fedora, leading the Packers to an unfathomable 98-30-4 record and five championship seasons in nine years. It is here that Brett Favre took up the "Titletown, U.S.A." torch—a nickname Green Bay bestowed upon itself twenty-five days *before* the 1961 championship game—a quarter-century later and soon added one more. And it is here that a team enjoyed so much generalized success, it invented a new form of celebration, the Lambeau Leap, in which a scoring player launches himself into the crowd's eager arms, following a touchdown.

But there is more to it than winning. Historic stadiums have become rare birds across our country's sports landscape. For decades, a fetish for the newest and shiniest (and most revenue-generating) raged, razing important buildings in its path, like Tiger Stadium, Yankee Stadium (again, the old one), and even the Boston Garden. Suddenly those that remain, like Lambeau, are no longer facing extinction. Something clicked in our collective consciousness, a new sort of fetish, the novelty of the old. Perhaps sensing some irrevocable severing from the past, we have become nostalgic, not wanting to give up those last lines of connection.

The significance of Green Bay's stadium, in particular, had been on my mind earlier that day as I drove up Route 41 from the Milwaukee area. I kept thinking about what a bartender at Bryant's Cocktail Lounge had told me about his first trip to Lambeau Field. He said, "When I saw that G, I understood what it's like to go to church."

The religious metaphor isn't a new one, of course. A professor emeritus at Amherst College, Allen Guttmann writes in his 1978 book, *From Ritual to Record*, that modern sports tend to "become a kind of secular faith." Bob Trumpbour, who teaches in the communications program at Penn State University, argues much the same in *The New Cathedrals*, positing that the sports stadium has taken on serious symbolic import, often serving as "the most visible and recognizable structure in many communities," taking the place of "the beautiful cathedral, the ornate train station, or the huge skyscraper" as a signature civic building. But symbolism alone doesn't make a place sacred. As German sociologist Henning Eichberg puts it, "there is the 'normal' space, which can be 'seen'; and there is a 'holy' space, which is experienced," delineating the physical and the spiritual elements of a stadium, "the visible and the evocative."

As I motored north along Route 41, cornfields and open prairies were soon overtaken by a congested series of roadside billboards. Pro-life and GOT GOD? signs were interspersed with those promoting adult superstores and fireworks depots. My favorites proclaimed WE SELL SILENCERS! and JESUS DIED FOR THE SINS OF THE WORLD. Although I was nearly tempted to pull off the road by an advertisement offering ALL THINGS JERKY and another that simply read CHEESE in big bubble letters, which felt borderline divine given the region, I stayed the course, my GPS trained toward a temple of a different sort.

Before long, off in the distance, I caught my first glimpse of the big green G, unmistakably the same one that so affected my barman. The G is plastered to the backside of Lambeau's south end zone scoreboard, a beacon to weary highway warriors, game-day migrants. According to at least one Lambeau tour guide (mine, a few days later), it is the biggest G in the world, "as far as we know."

But to really understand Lambeau, I needed to spend my day out in the parking lots with the unwashed masses, the team owners, the NFL's most profoundly invested fan base.

————

"Give him a little sip of that, come on. Let him try it," Rasta pleads with his Lot 1 Mom, the second woman he's introduced as his mother in the five minutes we've been together. The woman, late-middle-aged, hands me her cup, containing some sort of caramel apple alcoholic drink. Says, "He calls me Mom. I guess because I'm old."

"In Lot 1, we are a family," another Mom adds with regard to this cross-generational parking-lot party.

Confabbing with this new Mom, who stands behind a table of treats that wouldn't be out of place at a smutty bake sale (boob cake and penis lollipops; all proceeds benefiting her grandson's diabetes), I point at Rasta. He is outfitted in an elaborate Packers getup including green and gold argyle knee-highs, matching Mardi Gras beads, and a pair of Groucho Marx–like aviator sunglasses that feature the top half of a helmet and a dangling face mask. He poses for a photograph, balancing two cans of Busch Light. Who's he? I ask her.

"Him? He is my designated driver."

I don't understand. "*Him?*"

"Yup." She nods.

"I like that your designated driver is double-fisting," I say.

Ears burning, Rasta turns toward us. "One love, yo! Life is good."

For Green Bay fans, life always seems to be good around Lambeau Field. The stadium stands as a physical reminder of the deep historical connection between town and team. "It all goes back to our ownership structure," Packers president Mark Murphy tells me later that week, when we meet in a team conference room high above the stadium's sparkling new atrium. "We are community owned."

This one-of-a-kind arrangement—the team is literally owned by its fans; the only publicly owned, nonprofit organization in all of major American professional sports—began in 1923, when the Packers held the first in a series of five stock offerings. (The most recent was 2011.) Green Bay was trying to keep its fledgling football club alive, and survival was no guarantee. "I hate to toss around the term miracle," says Cliff Christl, who came on as the Packers official historian in 2014, after nearly four decades as a sports journalist (he is also the mind behind the Packers Heritage Trail, a self-guided walking tour that memorializes important moments and places in local Packers lore), "but essentially it is."

Remember: at the time, this wasn't big business. After games, the team would take up a collection so players could be paid. Across the country, small-town squads were falling off the map as quickly as they formed. The Packers, which Christl describes as "perpetually on their deathbed," had close calls as well. Like when the team had to stage an intrasquad Thanksgiving game in 1949 to stave off bankruptcy. Earlier, Curly Lambeau, the franchise's first head coach and stadium namesake, considered turning the Packers into a traveling team. In the 1950s, things started to stabilize, beginning with the team's third stock sale, which raised $100,000, along with a mid-decade infusion of TV money. But the true turning point came with the construction of Lambeau Field. "No question whatsoever," says Christl, who attended the first-ever game at what was then called City Stadium and hasn't missed many since, "that stadium saved the franchise."

———

With the sun out, the temperature pushing seventy, and cars pouring into town, there is a welcome-to-Bonnaroo vibe around Lambeau Field, the home opener only hours away. Beanbags and footballs fly through the barbecue-smoke-filled air. Musically, an ever-changing soundtrack wails from innumerable portable speakers and a variety of live bands, including a bluegrass ensemble on the other side of the stadium that keeps inviting Seahawks fans to join in on their go-to ditty: *Da Bears still suck. Da Bears still suck. They really, really, really, really, really, really, suck.*

Amid the revelry is Scott Schwartz, the ringmaster of Lambeau's Lot 1 party, just outside the Oneida Nation Gate. Two hours before the parking lots opened, he was already here, as he has been for the last twenty-five years, setting down traffic cones to reserve his spots. "Right now I'm happy," says Schwartz, swigging from a barrel-size beer mug. "But for two days, I didn't sleep well. This morning I was inconsolable. I was an absolute prick for the first fifteen minutes setting up."

Dude takes his tailgating seriously. And why not? According to Christl, tailgating is a local tradition that both predates Lambeau Field and dovetails seamlessly with another beloved Green Bay pastime: drinking. Even Prohibition couldn't slow the town's taps. "There were speakeasies all over," says the historian. "I was told once that one of the reasons the mob never moved in here was because it was so wide open. They couldn't get a foothold. It was just generally accepted that Green Bay wasn't going to obey the Eighteenth Amendment."

That independent streak is crossed with a fierce loyalty when it comes to the green and gold. "I think in 'twenty-three, the first stock sale, the franchise became community property, and that has never changed," Christl says of fans' intense identification with the club. Take, for instance, Justin Sipla, another Lot 1 regular. For every home game, he drives five and a half hours from Iowa City, where he teaches neuroscience and human anatomy at the University of Iowa medical school, a job he accepted solely on the basis that it was closer to Lambeau than his previous position, in El Paso, Texas. "And I got to redo my contract," he laughs. "I don't have to work Mondays after Packer home games."

But enough chitchat. It is time for Sipla and Schwartz to lead today's first oration of "Tim the Diehard Packer Fan," a poem by Paul Gilmartin about a man who belches himself to death in order to help the team win a Super Bowl, immediately followed by a recitation of the Wedge of Allegiance, both Lot 1 rituals. Before heading off, Schwartz points me toward Gary Platt, another regular and something of a legend, even if no one's penned a poem on his behalf. Having attended his first Packers game in 1961, Platt has missed only two since the '77 season, which is even more impressive when you consider the Packers split their time between Green Bay and Milwaukee from 1933 to 1994. Of the Ice Bowl, the infamous 1967 game that featured a wind chill of nearly minus-fifty degrees, he says, "I don't remember it being that cold."

I talk to another old-timer, lounging in a nearby lawn chair, whose van appears to be a decommissioned mail truck, painted blue and adorned with a Packers logo. The van man tells me he's had season tickets since 1960, the last year such seats were available without a waiting list. Today the waiting list stands at an ever-growing 119,000 and is the stuff of legend. Tickets can be inherited, they can be won or lost in a divorce, but they very rarely turn over. Parents put down the names of newborns, and those babies still might never hear their numbers called.

"I also got stock," my van man says proudly, which makes him one of the franchise's 360,760 owners. Not that he ever stands to benefit. If the Packers were to be sold, all proceeds would be turned over to Green Bay charities and community organizations, according to the team's Articles of Incorporation.* But that isn't likely to happen anytime soon, my van man insists. "Even if a hotshot owner would come in, I don't think it would happen. Even if somebody offered the team five or ten million dollars, I don't think they would sell it," he says, sounding as adorably disconnected from the financial markets as Dr. Evil. Perhaps sensing his figures are woefully low, he reconsiders, then shakes his head. "They would say no."

---

* Previously, the bylaws stated all proceeds would go to a local American Legion post.

The clock ticks closer to kickoff. Shadows lengthen as the sun dips behind Kroll's restaurant, across South Ridge Road. In the parking lot, a Journey cover band croons as a couple of dudes play Wisest Wizard—a drinking game that involves duct-taping your empty beer cans together to form an unwieldy wizard's staff. Out on the street, a group of tandem bicyclists hop from spot to spot, a tailgate on the move. They ride past a man helping his female companion into a cheese bra, but there is some trouble with hand-eye coordination. She scolds him and tells him to hurry—"My boobs are sagging!"

Someone shouts, "I'm so happy to be here!"

Perhaps that's what happens with a championship pedigree, when winning is a given. Or maybe it's just an extension of midwestern self-deprecation, the same impulse that led Packers fans to adopt the term *Cheesehead*—and literally wear cheese on their heads (and boobs)—when folks from Illinois directed the name at them as an insult.* It's hard to take yourself too seriously, to intimidate opposing fans, when wearing dairy on your head. (I try it and feel immediately ridiculous.) But even if Packer backers don't instill fear in others, neither are they intimidated by opposing fans, comfortable with who they are, confident in the Lambeau mystique.

One of the first—if not *the* first—football-only stadiums in the United States, Lambeau Field ranks among the NFL's top home-field advantages, a place where fans take quiet pride in their ability to win cold-weather games like the Ice Bowl. Visiting teams dread late-season contests on Lambeau's "frozen tundra," even if the frigid turf

---

* The term also had derogatory connotations when used by Germans against the Dutch, I am told.

is more bark than bite.* Why bully opponents when your stadium does it for you?

———

In 776 BCE, a footrace was held at the ancient Greek site of Olympia, the sole athletic event in a brand-new religious festival honoring the god Zeus, what we now know as the Olympic Games. As Allen Guttmann writes in *Sports Spectators*, "earth removed in the process [of leveling ground for the track] was formed into an embankment for the spectators," but it would be another couple hundred years before the first Olympic stadium was constructed.

The term *stadium* comes from the Greek *stadion* or *stade*, which refers to a single length of the racetrack (which was also the length of the stadium)—at Olympia, it measured 192 meters, although the length wasn't uniform and varied from site to site—as well as to the venue itself. Fast-forwarding through history, we come across other landmark structures, like the Panathenaic stadium in Athens, built in the fourth century BCE, upgraded with marble about five hundred years later, and refurbished for use in 1896's first modern Olympics. But none was more important than Rome's Flavian amphitheater, an engineering marvel that essentially gave birth to the contemporary conception of stadiums.

Built by the emperor Vespasian and his son Titus, the Flavian amphitheater—perhaps more easily recognized by its other name, the Roman Colosseum—opened in the year 80 and became known for the gory spectacle of its gladiatorial games, combat events that began more than three hundred years earlier with a religious aspect, before taking on more secular overtones on the arena floor.

---

* Lombardi had a heating system installed under the field in the 1960s—though it failed during the Ice Bowl—and a more modern and functional system has since taken its place.

The Colosseum, which could accommodate impressive crowds of fifty thousand (still only one-fifth the size of the Circus Maximus, a hippodrome built for ever-popular chariot races), is undeniably the Roman Empire's most famous attempt at stadium building, but it wasn't its first. In fact, the evolution of Roman stadiums over the preceding century closely mirrors that of modern American ballparks, starting in the mid-1800s. In 65 BCE, for example, Julius Caesar erected a wooden amphitheater for a combat show celebrating his election to the aedileship, per Guttmann. But such wooden structures, typically dismantled after events, had an unfortunate tendency to collapse too soon and kill their occupants, prompting the construction of something more permanent.

Likewise, in America's Gilded Age, temporary wooden ballparks tended to be rickety assemblies, according to Trumpbour, and a team could be evicted from its home midseason if politicians found a better use for the land. Players would often help construct seating areas and maintain the grounds, while any sort of outfield enclosure was intended far more as a deterrent to gate-crashers, field runners, and curious wildlife than as a boundary demarcation.* But even in semi-permanent wooden structures, the conditions weren't exactly safe, as the grandstands were apt to collapse *and* go up in flames, just as soon as someone dropped a lit tobacco product. Owners did not love the liability, but they didn't mind the money. In the early days, it wasn't uncommon for an owner to also be the operator of a streetcar company, who might view the club as a loss leader, building a ballpark along his streetcar line just to get fares to and from the games.

Brick, steel, and concrete sneaked into ballpark construction materials at the tail end of the nineteenth century. But it wasn't until Harvard University built a home for its football team in 1903, thanks

---

* The first enclosed field in baseball history is often credited to William Cammeyer, who was behind Brooklyn's Union Grounds.

to a gift from alumni, that America had its first permanent steel and concrete stadium.

Pro baseball wasn't far behind. In 1909, both Philadelphia's Shibe Park and Pittsburgh's Forbes Field cut the ribbon. And over the next few years, a slew of ballparks followed, including Comiskey Park (Chicago), Fenway Park (Boston), Ebbets Field (Brooklyn), and Tiger Stadium (Detroit), until the New York Yankees brought up the rear in 1923 with Yankee Stadium. (The Bronx Bombers were the first major-league club to call its home park a stadium.)

Built into urban neighborhoods, the ballparks of this era were one-of-a-kind structures, with signature elements and strained contours, features that were essentially reverse-engineered, based on space constraints. (These organic quirks stand in contrast to the recent trend of "retro" ballparks, whose design can sometimes feel like heavy-handed marketing gimmicks, or in the words of veteran Boston sportswriter Bob Ryan, "a lot of phony baloney.") Today only two baseball venues from that time period remain in existence: Boston's Fenway Park and Chicago's Wrigley Field, which opened in 1914—then known as Weeghman Park, for Chicago Federals owner Charles Weeghman.

Having avoided the wrecking ball, unlike all the others, these venues are central to the identity of the Red Sox and Cubs organizations, while fans see the ballparks as time capsules that preserve the past even as they showcase present-day competition, wherein future histories are sure to be written.

———

From the top row of the press box, Wrigley Field peels open before you. The white foul lines race into the distance. A thick clutch of ivy pads the brick outfield wall. And off in center (slightly off-center), the vintage green scoreboard, part of a 1937 refurbishment of the park, is recessed above the jam-packed bleachers, which boomerang to a peak at the scoreboard's feet. To many, these features, along with the iconic marquee, are the physical attributes that define Wrigley Field, that most strongly tether it to a bygone era. But nobody here has a finger on the pulse of the past quite like Rick Fuhs, aka Quick Rick.

In the press box, I sit next to Fuhs, perched in the top row. It has been a long day for Fuhs, a grounds crewmember for almost four decades, now in the back half of a day-night doubleheader. To his right, a small desktop fan works against the heavy July air.

"This is the original score panel from 1937," Fuhs says of the electronic box resting before him, about the size of three sheet cakes stacked on top of one another. The buttons on the box, oddly glassy and ovoid, like someone's long-ago estimation of futurism, relay electronic signals to the otherwise all-manual scoreboard, updating balls and strikes. It is an in-game assignment Fuhs has held since 1987. Despite the long day, he is fully engaged, his hands hovering just over the box as if it were a Ouija board, waiting for the spirits to speak.

Sometimes it does seem like Fuhs has supernatural help when updating the count. It's like he knows what's going to be called before the pitch is thrown. That is how he earned his nickname. In his mid-fifties, Fuhs has white hair, a creased forehead, and a slightly sunburned complexion, yet manages to give off a youthful impression. It reminds me of a Skip Rozin quote I find in Michael Benson's *Ballparks of North America*: "While it would be an exaggeration to suggest that time stops at Wrigley, evidence indicates it moves slowly there." Others, older fans and ushers, have called this phenomenon "Peter Pan syndrome," claiming Wrigley keeps them young.

As if to prove the point, Fuhs tells me about the time he met Curt Hubertz, the man who designed the electronic part of the center-field scoreboard. "We had a problem, and he said, 'I know what's wrong. I have the parts in the garage. I'll come down and fix it for you,'" recalls Fuhs, eyes still aimed at the field. "I asked, 'How are you going to get into the scoreboard—climb a ladder? It's not easy.' He said, 'Oh, I'll get in there.' He was ninety years old!"

And he did.

According to Ed Hartig, affectionately known as the Rain Man of Cubs history, the scoreboard is off-center because the whole ballpark is off-center, based on its original design. "In 1922, they actually moved the ballpark, the grandstand," Hartig says. "They cut it into pieces and slid two-thirds of it more south and west," which allowed more space for bleachers.

During games, a handful of grounds crew guys hole up in the three-story center-field board, which looks like a fire escape inside, changing by hand the inning-by-inning results and out-of-town scores. It is a place of honor, per Hartig, but Fuhs is happy to be at a distance. "Those guys got the harder time out there, flipping the plates," says Fuhs, who had the opportunity to work the interior of the scoreboard before. What he remembers most is the sweltering heat. "And it smells like rust," he says. "Rust and steel." Another advantage of his position in the press box: indoor plumbing. Because those inside the board aren't allowed out after first pitch, they make use of a funnel and rubber hose, which runs through a PVC pipe.

I ask Fuhs about his scoreboard style, how he reads the umpires so fast. "I like to get into a rhythm," he says, detailing certain tics and movements of the men behind the plate. As he talks, he also demonstrates how to operate the box, which retains vestiges from when football was played at Wrigley.* Fuhs shows me how to enter the uniform number of the next batter—"Rizzo, forty-four," he says—and how to add balls, strikes, and outs, then how to clear the board at the end of a half-inning: "Hit these two at the same time."

There was one umpire with whom Fuhs could never find a rhythm: Tim McClelland, most famous for his role in 1983's "Pine Tar Game," when he nullified a go-ahead home run and called out

---

* The C on the console stands not for "Chicago," Fuhs explains, but for "Cardinals." The NFL team originally played its games in the Windy City.

George Brett at Yankee Stadium. "He would stand there for literally three, four seconds, and *then* call a strike, so I'd have the ball up already," remembers Fuhs. Was the ump just screwing with him? Turns out, yes, as Fuhs discovered when he got to meet McClelland before a game. "I said, 'Why are you so slow?' He said he wanted to mess up all the media and the TV personnel and radio." Fuhs pauses. "Well, he said the F-word, but I didn't want to say it."

Things have changed over the years. When he first started, Fuhs could get five or six friends into the games and no one would object. That was back when a Cubs ticket wasn't such a hot commodity. Fuhs also has a new chore this season: trimming the outfield ivy. Intrigued, I start peppering him with questions. But Fuhs is tired, the doubleheader catching up to him. He tells me to meet him back at the ballpark on Friday morning, ahead of a weekend series against the crosstown rival White Sox, when the ivy will need to look its best. He'll show me how it's done.

———

Earlier, for game one of the doubleheader, I have plans to connect with longtime bleacher regular and Bleed Cubbie Blue blog editor Al Yellon. When I arrive at Wrigley, minutes after the gates open, Yellon is already settled into his usual spot, in the far-upper-left-field corner. From there, he presides over a group of fellow regulars that can range in size from three or four to a dozen or more. At this early hour, the only other person present is Miriam Romain, who also writes about the Cubs. They instruct me to sit a couple rows down, leaving a gap of empty benches between us, lest I squat in someone else's spot.

"Everyone is real territorial," Yellon, who sports a shaved-bald head and well-groomed goatee, says of the bleacher scene, where tickets are general admission and personal pastimes date back decades. He has been sitting in the bleachers since the 1970s, having spent twenty-seven years with a group of regulars on the right-field side, before being displaced by 2005 renovations. That's when he moved over here. "I knew a couple of guys who had been here since the park opened," he says of the old crew. "They'd tell stories about watching Babe Ruth play. Pretty cool."

Bleacher seats are some of the most sought-after in Wrigley Field, but it wasn't always that way. When the park first opened, Charles Weeghman referred to outfield dwellers as "two-bit" fans, because tickets only cost a quarter. It also wasn't uncommon for overflow crowds to be placed on the grass and handed a rope to serve in lieu of an outfield wall, which they'd adjust forward and back to help the home team. Longtime Cubs owner Phil Wrigley had a policy of holding back twenty-two thousand tickets for each game—including all bleacher seats—so folks could always walk up and buy one. It wasn't until the mid-1980s that the team started selling bleacher season tickets, a result, Yellon says, of near-riots during the Cubs' 1984 play-off run. Bleacher tickets for opening day, on the other hand, were sold in advance following the 1978 season, when three thousand anxious fans lined up by eight a.m. and started climbing the walls to get in.

"The bleachers by nature have always been a different crowd," says Hartig, the historian. In the 1950s, fans would toss tins of chewing tobacco to outfielder Hank Sauer, who loved the stuff and stored extra chaw in the ivy. Years later, Yellon says, old-timers would gamble in the stands. But the most famous bleacher creatures in Wrigley history are the Bums. Known for ruthless heckling, wearing yellow hardhats and no shirts, the Bleacher Bums emerged in the 1960s. They lined up at six in the morning to get into games, poured beer on their bare chests, and organized races along the outfield wall, occasionally tumbling onto the field.* The Bums also popularized the practice

---

* In 1970, the Cubs installed a chain link fence to serve as a basket, to catch any falling Bums.

of throwing back opponents' home run balls and the accompanying cheer, "Throw it back! Throw it back!" The tradition remains so beloved, it sometimes feels like Cubs fans *want* the other team to hit a long ball, just so they can fling it back. (When I ask Yellon what he would do if he catches a home run, he unzips his backpack and pulls out a beaten-up baseball—a decoy! He'd pull the old switcheroo.)

With the Bums long gone, it is a drinking culture that permeates the outfield crowd these days, which hardly distinguishes the bleachers from the rest of the ballpark. One frequent criticism leveled against Cubs fans is that Wrigley Field is little more than the world's largest beer garden, with baseball in the background. From the two weeks I spend in Wrigleyville, as the ballpark and its environs (a heavy mix of bars and residential housing) are unofficially known, the reputation is deserved.

Sitting in the upper deck during another game, I meet Dave Andersen and Ed Bourke, both local mortgage brokers. Bourke admits there have been games he's left hammered, with a vague idea which team won but without knowing the score. Andersen mentions that White Sox fans fancy themselves the more serious supporters and try to flaunt that fact. "But I'm not here to go to school, I'm here to have a good time," he says.

Amazingly, it was less than twenty years ago that historic sports venues like Wrigley were considered endangered species and revenue liabilities. For Alison Miller, the Cubs' senior director of marketing since 2012, it didn't take long to learn that the ballpark was an irreplaceable asset. "We have two brands: the Cubs and Wrigley Field," she says. "Candidly, when our team sucks, we market Wrigley. We market this beautiful ballpark." But people didn't always get so misty-eyed about Wrigley Field, a place Cubs president of business operations Crane Kenney correctly calls "an accidental relic." According to Hartig, Wrigley "didn't have this mystic awe until the 'eighties." That was when the stars aligned, as legendarily colorful broadcaster Harry Caray joined the organization shortly after the Tribune Company purchased the team, using the expanded reach of its WGN superstation to beam its new product to Chicago and beyond.

"From a broadcasting perspective, he was always on the air saying 'beautiful Wrigley Field.' He sold fun for us. He sold Wrigley Field for a long time," explains Miller. "Anytime we show Wrigley Field in any of our campaigns, we're very conscious of continuing that kind of lure of Wrigley."

The idea of selling Wrigley as a place of leisure was actually presaged by Phil Wrigley, an inveterate innovator in baseball's typically stodgy landscape. During World War II, Wrigley was behind the All-American Girls Professional Baseball League (immortalized by 1992's *A League of Their Own*). Years later he installed a rotating system of coaches, who would alternate managing the team. In some ways, Wrigley simply took after his father, William Wrigley Jr., who was a visionary believer in the power of broadcast and had up to five radio stations carry Cubs games at once in the 1920s. The club would later become the first to televise every one of its home games. (Other owners feared television would suppress attendance.) According to a 1958 profile in *Sports Illustrated*, Wrigley created ad campaigns that showcased the ballpark as a place to have a picnic with family and friends. "We are aiming at people not interested in baseball. These are fans we want to get," he told the publication, essentially confirming what White Sox fans still charge about the Wrigley crowd.

The cultural conception of Wrigley Field isn't just about getting sloshed, though. For some fans, it's about tapping into the traditions of the past, like the Bleacher Bums, those lunatic layabouts, or giving in to other forms of nostalgia. Miriam Romain, Yellon's friend, can't visit Wrigley without thinking about the stories her father would tell when they came to the park together, before he passed away, stories from when he was a kid. "He would set the stage, set up the infield, and the history would come alive."

For others, Wrigley Field is about sunshine in a city that doesn't take good weather for granted—about escape and playing hooky, à la Ferris Bueller. And for others still, it's about the rituals. As Andersen tells me, "If I'm going to come to Wrigley, I want to piss in a trough," referring to the bathroom situation in a good many men's rooms. Yeah, it's gross, he admits. Maybe less sanitary, and maybe you get a little of someone else's splash on you. But so what? "Haven't died from it yet."

About the troughs, Miller says, "That's a funny one. We've done a lot of research, and it is commonly talked about among our fans as this rite of passage, bringing your son in for the first time to use the men's restroom at Wrigley."

———

Perhaps more so than in any other venue, it has been crucial that Wrigley-goers enjoy more than just the game. For over a century, the Cubs—long known as the Lovable Losers—have been defined by their defeats, their futility. As of my visit in 2015, the last time they won a World Series was 1908—six years *before* the construction of Wrigley Field. Along the way, they turned losing into a creative art.

Some say the Cubs were jinxed. In 1945, a local tavern owner and his pet goat were barred from Wrigley Field during the World Series, even though the man had two tickets (one for himself and one for the goat), allegedly because the animal smelled. Miffed, the man cast a curse on the Cubs, predicting they would never again win the World Series. Following the Cubs' loss that year, the man sent a telegram to Phil Wrigley, saying something to the effect of "Who stinks now?"

Over the years, attempts to break the curse proved unsuccessful, while further misfortune continued to befall the club, like the 1969 late-season collapse, during which a mysterious black cat approached the Cubs on the field at Shea Stadium. In 1984, Cubs infielder Leon Durham flubbed a ground ball to help give the Padres the pennant, a play remarkably similar to Bill Buckner's World Series error for the Red Sox two years later. (In a spooky twist, zoom lenses have revealed that Buckner was wearing a Cubs batting glove under his mitt.) And most recently, in 2003, an unassuming superfan in headphones and a ball cap—Steve Bartman—blocked a defender from making a key catch in foul territory during a play-off game while going for the ball himself, opening the floodgates for yet another flop. Quick Rick remembers watching the Bartman game from the press box. "It was an eerie feeling," he says. "The whole place was just real quiet after that."

In some ways, failure only enhanced the team's charm, although Yellon rejects the notion that curses and collapses have given Cubs fans character. "Don't buy that for a minute," he says, adding that he sensed a serious mood shift in Bartman's wake. "People got angry after 2003, and it took a while for it to go away." (As of this writing, Bartman, who was mercilessly taunted and threatened and is rumored to have fled Chicago, has never broken his silence on the incident.) Yellon does allow, however, that the team's tortured past helped create a community of commiseration—and occasional fan anxiety—which former players have said they could sense on the field, making them tense, heightening the chance for a new addition to the team's catalog of errors.

But what happens when the Cubs start to win?*

Fan identity, like all identity, is fluid, in spite of how passionately we may believe otherwise. Just consider Harry Caray singing "Take Me Out to the Ball Game" from the broadcast booth during the seventh-inning stretch at Wrigley Field, a tradition carried on after the announcer's death by celebrities like Will Ferrell, Bill Murray,

---

* In 2015, led by a veteran pitching staff and exciting young position players, the Cubs made it to the National League Championship Series before being eliminated. In 2016, the team broke its hundred-plus-year championship drought, winning the World Series in a dramatic seven-game, come-from-behind series.

and Eddie Vedder, among many others. Talk to Cubs fans, and they'll tell you this is one of the keepsake moments that make Cubs games so special.

What they won't tell you—perhaps because they don't know—is that the practice began at Comiskey Park, when Caray called White Sox games, at the suggestion of the great Bill Veeck, the team's owner at the time. (They also won't tell you that the beloved Caray used to be razzed by Bleacher Bums, when he was with the St. Louis Cardinals. Fans chanted, "Harry Caray, quite contrary, how does your ego grow?")

When the Lovable Losers wear the crown, an identity crisis of some kind is not beyond the pale. For precedent, we only need to look to Fenway Park and Red Sox fans, who endured a championship dry spell similar to that of the Cubs, battling the Curse of the Bambino amid a long run of heartbreak, dating to 1918. In 2004, that changed when the Red Sox stormed back from a three-games-to-none series deficit against the hated Yankees—a feat never before accomplished in baseball history—to steal the pennant and win the World Series. Bill Simmons and Mike Francesa, experts on the Red Sox and Yankees fan bases respectively, talked in a radio segment about how Sox fans were pathological, convinced they would never win. Bob Ryan has observed the Fenway faithful not only through his reporter's notebook, but also from his paid-for seats in section 19. He tells me Boston fans—who in the eyes of the sporting public have become no less obnoxious than arrogant Yankees supporters—were always elitist, even in their depression. "Prior to 'oh-four, it was this idea that nothing bad ever happened to anybody else, only them. It was all about self-pity," he says.

So what was a suddenly successful fan base supposed to do when much of its identity was invested in the inevitability of losing? Struggle to construct a new one (or cling desperately to the old). Despite an impressive run of success for the Red Sox (and other local teams) over the last decade-plus, Boston fans often insist on circling the wagons and painting themselves as underdogs and victims anytime they're criticized. Ryan says, "People here are in general denial. They don't get it." As an example, he brings up Deflategate, the 2015 scandal involving quarterback Tom Brady and underinflated footballs, not because the Patriots were cheating—there is no doubt the NFL bungled that situation—but because it was just the latest instance of possible Patriots misconduct. The local reaction was manifest in the many FREE BRADY T-shirts around Fenway Park. "They've taken up the predictable posture of defense," Ryan says. "The prevailing theory is that it's basic jealousy, and they're so wrong."

To offer a brief counterpoint, I remember grappling with the 2004 baseball play-offs for different reasons. As a Yankees fan, it was my belief not only that my team would win but that the Red Sox would lose—two equal and opposite forces, the yin and yang. When that script was flipped, it was like having a younger brother who could now put me in a headlock, upending my understanding of the universe. Sadness crossed with anger crossed with a bizarre sense of betrayal.

For another counterexample, we head back to Lambeau Field.

———————

Cliff Christl clearly remembers a time when the Packers weren't the biggest fish in Green Bay's small pond. That was the east-west high school game, a rivalry that precipitated the most contentious issue in the lead-up to the construction of Lambeau Field—not how much the facility would cost but on which side of the river it would reside. "Between us, I'm still bitter over the fact they built it on the west side," Christl confides. So what was it that finally united all those Packer backers?

Simple: winning.

In Lambeau's first ten years, Vince Lombardi's dynastic turn at the helm came to symbolize all that was right and good about

Green Bay's small-town values. He won so damn often, the league named its championship trophy after him. A decade after the coach left town, Allen Guttmann deemed this deification "the Lombardi phenomenon," writing: "despite his harshness and even brutality, the Green Bay Packers—if we can trust the published accounts—seem almost to have worshipped him." His shadow still looms large over Lambeau, where you're liable to find Lombardi lookalikes haunting tailgates, like Elvis impersonators on the streets of Las Vegas. The first question I field from a sizable portion of fans, after it is discovered I'm visiting from New York City, is if I have seen the Broadway play *Lombardi*.

Bottom line: the man represented *winning*, and this was a town of *winners*, by association. Until it wasn't.

By 1987, it had gotten so bad that respected sportswriter Frank Deford argued in *Sports Illustrated* that it was time for the Packers to find a new home. One of the main breaking points, Deford contended (and others I spoke to have confirmed), was race, as the small town started to show small-mindedness. In his article, Deford cites a statistic that only one out of every three hundred people in Brown County was black, reporting that people of color often felt "uncomfortable" in Green Bay, especially visiting players.

Suddenly there were layers. Did Green Bay's fans not want to associate themselves with a loser, or was the issue that the players no longer looked like them? Perhaps they could abide one of these things, but not both at the same time?

Another theory Deford presented was that, as the league expanded in popularity and more money poured in, players were becoming celebrities, and that didn't jibe with Green Bay's provincial sensibilities. They were like fans of a garage band watching in proprietary horror as their beloved hit the big time.

According to Christl, there is incredible pride among the denizens of Green Bay that "this city of 100,000 has a pro football team, and a stadium that is on everybody's bucket list." But pride can be myopic. People can be overbearing (as Aaron Rodgers discovered in 2015, when he suffered a calf injury during a January play-off game and was greeted by 100,000 amateur medical opinions). And small towns can quickly suffocate.

It remains a consideration for the current Packers front office. In reference to the team's general manager, Ted Thompson, Packers president Mark Murphy says, "Ted really does take that to heart. Because if you do anything wrong, people will know." The GM has a term for those he thinks can handle the Green Bay fishbowl: "Good Packers."

Obviously, the team didn't relocate following Deford's article. And within five years, a hotshot young quarterback named Brett Favre was giving Titletown new hope for another ring. The issues largely disappeared. Star black players in the 1990s, like Reggie White and LeRoy Butler, were as celebrated as their white counterparts.

Had the city advanced its thinking?

Perhaps.

Or maybe there's just nothing more important than those Sunday scores.

———

On the Friday morning of the Cubs–White Sox series, I arrive at Wrigley Field's cramped grounds crew clubhouse, accessible via a back-of-house passageway but also equipped with a front-facing door that deposits you in deep left field. I'm here for my ivy-trimming lesson. Quick Rick isn't yet ready, his face covered in a beard of shaving cream.

This used to be the Cubs' locker room, Fuhs tells me, dragging a blade across his face, careful of his cleft chin. Before that, the grounds crew holed up in a barn under the left-field grandstands. "We called it a barn, because they kept the horses there," he says, which I agree is a good reason to call something a barn. (The horses were used to haul team luggage down to Union Station ahead of road trips.) With a dripping razor as a pointing stick, Fuhs indicates where former players like Ron Santo would be, by which locker, and Ernie Banks, and Billy Williams. Narrow and dimly lit, the clubhouse conditions are claustrophobic just with the grounds crew guys. It is hard to imagine a whole ball club squeezing in.

With less than two hours until first pitch, Cubs players are scattered around the outfield grass, casually stretching and playing catch. We won't be doing a full trim today, Fuhs says, swiping at a spiderweb connecting two ivy leaves. ("The old guy who used to trim it, he'd say that's his website.") Typically, Fuhs works on the wall while the team is out of town. The process is a two-day task. First, he goes along on a scissor lift, shearing the top, keeping it level. On the second day, he focuses on the distance markers and door areas, ensuring all the numbers are legible and the lines are clean. Because of the big White Sox series, he gave the ivy a quick once-over yesterday, taking advantage of a team off day. "It took me two hours, wasn't that bad, just little shooters," Fuhs says of the runaway branches that can mar the ivy's eye-pleasing blanket of green.

Under the guidance of Phil Wrigley and Bill Veeck (then with the Cubs), the ivy was planted in 1937, part of the same renovation that modernized the center-field scoreboard. They are the original ivy plants that still grow today in Wrigley Field; they have never been uprooted. When the brick outfield wall was replaced in recent years, the ivy was simply plucked from the brick and laid on the ground, beneath a protective material. (Purdue University grew backup ivy, in case something went wrong.)

In the early parts of the season, the wall looks bare, as Chicago's long winter slowly retreats. As spring blooms, the ivy experiences two stages of growth—a primary leaf coming in the middle of May, a secondary leaf a month or so later. And once it gets hot, "it just grows like wildfire." Fuhs's favorite time of year is autumn, when the leaves change colors. Burnt oranges and mustard yellows and burgundy reds. It isn't impossible for the ivy to still be on the wall in late October, should the Cubs make a deep play-off run.

When balls hit the plant, they can snap—and kill—a main stem. Fuhs tries to remove those stems, along with anything showing contagious and unsightly leaf spots, as part of his trimming chores. When bald spots emerge, he strings longer shoots to cover the empty areas: ivy comb-overs. Handing me his gardening shears, customized with bits of padding to avoid blisters, Fuhs searches for a troubled-looking shooter as an example. He finds one, tells me to cut it. I pocket the snipped branch, a souvenir.

Not counting the time White Sox fans allegedly poured bleach on the outfield wall, murdering a whole section of ivy, the most damage to the plant occurs when players jump into it while attempting a catch. If a ball gets lost in the ivy, Wrigley ground rules state that the fielder can throw up his hands, indicating a ground rule double. But if the player attempts to retrieve the ball, play continues.*

For many fans, the ivy is the defining characteristic of Wrigley Field. Walking out of the concourse and into the seating bowl, it is the feature that instantly draws your eyes. Fuhs remembers visiting Wrigley as a kid, the smell of fresh-cut grass. "Now I'm immune to it," he says. But despite his proximity to the plant, Fuhs says he'll never take the ivy for granted. We stop trimming and look around at the panorama of the ballpark. Barely ten yards away, ace pitcher Jon Lester is warming up his arm, slated to start tomorrow's game. Fuhs says, "A lot of times when no one is in the park, I'll come out here, just sit with a cup of coffee." He listens to the birds chirping, the elevated trains rolling by.

---

* In 2008, Jim Edmonds was going for a catch against the wall when not one but two balls appeared out of the ivy.

———

Nostalgia aside, the reality is that Wrigley Field has been evolving for as long as the ballpark has been in existence, whether it was the addition of an upper deck, the bleacher renovations, or the realignment of seats in the post-football era. (In 1968, Phil Wrigley even considered installing artificial turf but balked at the cost.) Some changes have been made out of necessity, like when it rained concrete during the 2004 season, and some are "elective surgery," as Carl Rice puts it.

Rice, whose official title is vice-president of Wrigley Field restoration and expansion, is overseeing what will be the most intense period of renovations in Wrigley Field history—a five-phase overhaul that will effectively leave the Cubs with an all-new building, right down to the concrete and steel. There will be new concessions and bathrooms, upgraded clubhouses and batting cages, more premium spaces, adjoining offices, and a team-run hotel. Phase one began after the 2014 season with the construction of remodeled bleachers and the installation of two large video boards, the first such boards ever to appear in Wrigley Field. "You're going to get a new building in an old footprint," says Crane Kenney, team president, when we meet in his suite during the first Cubs–White Sox game.

The renovations have not been without controversy.

When phase one wasn't finished in time for opening day, the Cubs took grief, as fans showed up in hardhats, poking fun at the team's mismanaged timeline (and also paying homage to the Bums). The invective grew in volume when those fans were also greeted by Soviet-style bread lines to get into the bathrooms, forcing many to relieve themselves in empty beer cups. But the biggest issue leading up to the renovations wasn't so much a ballpark issue as a neighborhood one—a battle between the Cubs and adjacent rooftop owners, who over the last two decades have turned their altitudinal advantages over Wrigley Field into thriving game-day businesses.

Watching a Cubs game from neighboring rooftops is actually a pastime that began during the first game ever played at the ballpark in 1914, when many fans were shut out due to limited capacity. The practice picked up steam again in the mid-1980s, just as the Wrigley Field leisure brand was being sold over the airwaves and Ryne Sandberg was giving Cubs fans a reason to cheer. But the rooftops weren't moneymaking propositions yet. It was dudes in lawn chairs with coolers of beer. The first rooftop businesses were licensed in 1998, the same year Sammy Sosa and Mark McGwire captivated the nation with their home run explosions. Lawsuits and accusations of product stealing followed, resulting in a 2003 settlement. The rooftop owners agreed to give 17 percent of gross revenues to the Cubs for the next twenty years.

According to Kenney, it wasn't a sustainable arrangement. He says the rooftops had too much local influence, as the deal played out, that the tail was wagging the dog. "We just needed to eliminate that," he says. "I don't have any personal animus, even though it appears I do, with the rooftops. We need to control our perimeter."

To accomplish this, the Cubs proposed installing view-blocking signage in the outfield (to go along with the video boards) as part of renovations. The ensuing negotiations—and litigation—were ugly, occasionally devolving into "raucous fuck-you, fuck-you kind of stuff," according to Tom Tunney, who is the alderman for Chicago's 44th Ward, which encompasses Wrigley Field, and who has been at the center of many Cubs-related storms. Rooftop owners cried foul, citing the 2003 agreement. The Cubs stuck to their guns and even began buying up some of the rooftop businesses. Many believe the Cubs chose the location of signs carefully, which Kenney doesn't deny. "Well, if we own a rooftop, we probably won't put a sign in front of [that] rooftop."

"The fact that we screwed them," Tunney says of the rooftop owners, "was just painful, painful, because I don't think it was fair."

He contends that the owners suffered from a lack of cohesion, calling them "swashbucklers" and independent types. He also describes them as longtime locals, folks who invested in the community when everyone else thought Lakeview—as the neighborhood is known— was a slum. These days Lakeview is thriving along with Wrigley, the relationship symbiotic but fraught, forever caught in the gravitational pull of Chicago's contentious political vortex. "People move here because of Wrigley, and they live here in spite of Wrigley," says Bennett Lawson, Tunney's chief of staff. Those are just the ups and downs of being shoehorned into a living, breathing neighborhood, or as Tunney puts is, "trying to squeeze a major-league experience into a very minor-league setting."

A similarly heated battle brewed throughout the 1980s over the installation of light towers—a fight that locals have never forgotten. "They remind us," sighs Lawson. At that time, Wrigley was the last ballpark to remain dark, to have never played a night game. Neighborhood activists and baseball purists found easy allegiance, forming CUBS (Citizens United for Baseball in the Sunshine) even if Wrigley's lack of lights was more happenstance than philosophical. In 1941, lights were going to be installed at Wrigley Field, not to play night games (a noise ordinance prevented the team from starting an inning after eight p.m.) but so they could complete doubleheaders without being called for darkness. The team had even purchased the steel. But when Pearl Harbor was bombed, the Cubs donated the towers to government shipyards.

In the aftermath of the war, Phil Wrigley seemed to change his mind on the issue of illumination. Of night baseball, he said, "We'd kill the neighborhood." Some felt the owner was an aesthete and just didn't want to spoil the park's beauty, while Bill Veeck believed his innovative former boss didn't want lights because he hadn't been the first to have them. At one point, stockholders threatened to sue for lights (the Cubs were a stock company until the Tribune Company purchased the team in 1981), but Phil Wrigley owned more than 80 percent.

After a half-decade of courtroom clashes and threats to move, with the noise ordinance off the books, lights finally flicked on at Wrigley Field in August 1988—in what *Sports Illustrated* described as "a final defeat for the citizens of Wrigleyville"—although the first night game suffered a typical Cubs fate: it was rained out.

———

The talk inside the ballpark in 2015 is not about the rooftops. It's about what's now blocking their view: the enormous video boards.* Those giant additions, more so than any previous upgrade made to the park, have wrenched Wrigley Field—kicking and screaming— into the twenty-first century.

For an old-school fan base, the change is as jarring as when the Cubs first reintroduced advertising to the seating bowl in the early 1980s (there had been none since 1937), with the addition of Bud and Bud Light signs on the center-field scoreboard. (Distraught fans hurled objects at the ads until they were removed.) Bob Ryan shares a similar story about the installation of Fenway's first electronic scoreboard. "They booed it," he says. "They literally booed an inanimate object."

The Cubs are aware of this impulse (although there likely aren't hurl-able objects big enough to prompt the removal of these boards) and have tried to be mindful of the purists. "*Incremental* is a big word," Kenney says in reference to both the video boards and the new ads popping up around the park. "We definitely want to crawl, walk, run. Make sure it's not unsettling to our fan base."

In addition to replays, stats, and advertisements, the team is using the boards to introduce nostalgic and historic elements, like footage

---

* The left-field board measures 3,990 square feet, while the right-field board is 2,250 square feet.

of Harry Caray singing "Take Me Out to the Ball Game." Some may appreciate this process of slow introductions, although one longtime Cubs supporter says it is this exact process that has ruined the park, "boiling frog style."

On the video boards, fan opinion is decidedly split. Donna and Dale Mulford, two diehards visiting from Kansas, physically shake every time they walk into the friendly confines. They think the additions are great. Dave Andersen doesn't mind the boards, either. (In fact, he was always jealous of Comiskey's famous exploding scoreboard, another Bill Veeck creation.)

But plenty of other Cubs fans feel the new technology is crashing their century-old party. Tony Messina, at a game with his two young sons, calls the boards "eyesores," adding: "One of the things that Wrigley has is you feel like you're back in the thirties. When you start seeing all the digital scoreboards, it kind of loses that." *Chicago Tribune* architecture critic Blair Kamin has written that the new boards are a distraction, especially at night, when they "overshadow the old scoreboard [in center], disrupting the carefully calibrated sense of place that makes the ballpark a national treasure."

Kenney concedes they're still fine-tuning the boards, which is good news for the neighborhood, per Lawson, the alderman's chief of staff. "The Jumbotron, you can see it from Lake Shore Drive," he says. "And the speakers, at first you couldn't even hear inside the park, they were so loud. Now it's loud in some areas and not others."*

My favorite fan reactions come from two members of Al Yellon's bleacher crew: a late-middle-aged insurance salesman, Dave, and a woman named Jessica, who wears large-frame glasses, a NO LIGHTS IN WRIGLEY FIELD! T-shirt, and a pink hat from the 1990 All-Star game, her curly black hair spilling out the sides. Together they're the Statler and Waldorf of Wrigley Field.

---

* The unbalanced volume levels also overpower the ballpark's old-school organ, I find.

"Don't get me started," Jessica says, when I ask about the renovations.

Dave shakes his head sorrowfully. "This used to be a sacred place. Now it looks like a flea market, and they're not done."

Jessica, who has had season tickets since the 1980s, now lives in New York City and tries to attend at least twenty games per season. For the 2014 campaign, when Wrigley was celebrating its hundredth anniversary, she felt even more urgency to make it out to the ball games. Her motto, on behalf of the Cubs: "Come enjoy it, before we destroy it!"

Dave says he probably gets to thirty games a year at Wrigley, though he isn't even a Cubs fan. "Baseball is my passion," he says. "When I walked in this year, my whole body slumped. This used to be an icon—past tense!"

Jessica says, by way of explanation, "We're purists."

I wonder aloud why Jessica doesn't just abandon Wrigley Field, as a fed-up purist, just leave and never come back.* Was that a consideration?

Her answer is emphatic: "No! I was against interleague play! I was against lights!"

In this way, I realize Jessica is no different than Donna or Dale or any of the other folks who so fiercely love Wrigley Field. It is the beautiful tragedy of all their passion, of a fan base that both clings to the past and looks so desperately to the future, when "there's always next year," as the faithful saying goes.

———

The Cubs are not *trying* to destroy Wrigley Field. In fact, the whole idea is to maintain its essence, that which makes it special. But

---

* Emotions run high around Wrigley, and folks can be prone to dramatic gestures, as a 2012 headline in *The Onion* so perfectly captured: "Wrigley Field Supporters Propose Tearing Down Rest of Chicago."

how does one preserve the past while stepping into the future? How does one safeguard a ballpark's soul? "That's the big question," Kenney says, "and the one that keeps us up at night."

For answers, I ditch the friendly confines and head to Fenway Park, a facility on the other end of a decade's worth of renovations. Consensus is the Red Sox did a skillful job of navigating history and modernity, introducing new amenities without losing sight of historic elements, retaining the building's core character (an even more impressive feat when you consider the certainty that the park was a goner as recently as 1999). The man behind the Fenway face-lift is Larry Lucchino, former president and CEO of the Red Sox (he stepped down after the 2015 season) and something of a ballpark master, having previously given us Oriole Park at Camden Yards, the single most game-changing baseball venue of the last fifty years, and Petco Park.

Lucchino is sitting in a Fenway conference room, fidgeting in a rolling chair, restless. We aren't there more than a minute when I ask how important Fenway is to the franchise, how the identity of the team would change minus the ballpark. Lucchino doesn't speak but gets up from his chair and motions for me to come hither. He leads me to another conference room, one that overlooks the field, and points to a quote by Martin F. Nolan he had painted above the window shortly after the team's ownership group—led by Tom Werner, John Henry, and Lucchino—purchased the franchise in 2002. He instructs me to read the quote aloud.

It begins: "The ballpark is the star."

Growing up in Pittsburgh in the 1950s and '60s, Lucchino fell in love with Forbes Field, the Pirates' home since 1909 and one of the first permanent concrete and steel ballparks. In 1970, Three Rivers Stadium replaced the old park, yet another indistinct multipurpose concrete doughnut populating U.S. cities around that time. "I saw what was lost and what was so-called gained," says Lucchino.

That appreciation for signature charm has informed his career as a sports executive and charged his Fenway tenure. "I always thought we and the Cubs had a special obligation as the caretakers of the last two turn-of-the-twentieth-century ballparks to treat them with real thoughtfulness and planning and care," says Lucchino, who made his staff take a Hippocratic oath about Fenway: *Do no harm.*

And yet it seems so abstract. What, after all, is the soul of a building? Is it the people who come and fill the stands? Is it the memories they bring with them? The traditions passed down from generation to generation? What about the history? (Only in Wrigley did Babe Ruth famously call his shot; only in Lambeau did Bart Starr plunge into the south end zone to win the Ice Bowl; and only in Fenway did Ted Williams wield his weapon, both during the game, from the batter's box, and beforehand, when he would shoot pigeons fluttering over the field—true story.)

In Bob Ryan's opinion of Fenway, "What makes the ballpark the ballpark are the contours," referring to the jigsaw dimensions that torment outfielders, what John Updike termed "beguiling irregularities," as balls race away at unpredictable angles, occasionally Plinko-ing off the in-play Green Monster ladder, used for years to fetch balls from a net above the thirty-seven-foot left-field wall, which can turn line-drive homers into singles and lazy flies into home runs.

Or what about the quirks? Like those uncomfortable wooden seats at Fenway, many angled away from the game, possibly obstructed by a pillar? "It's part of the charm of Fenway Park!" says Jonathan Gilula, another Red Sox exec. And he's right—fans refuse to give those up.

Whenever Lucchino takes charge of a ballpark, the first thing he does is talk to the users, from clubhouse workers to groundskeepers to the fans. "Don't think you're the repository of all wisdom," he says. But in the end, there is only so much qualitative analysis that can be done. It comes down to a mix of softer sciences, like instinct— "You have to be sensitive to the emotional feel and pull of a facility.

You have to know when you're in a special place," he says—and neurotic attention to detail. "You get those right, and the bigger picture follows."

At Fenway Park, the small touches go a long way. According to Gilula, it's about "respecting the past, celebrating the past." He says this obsession permeates the ballpark completely, down to font types and colors like Fenway Green, Autumn Red, and Midnight Navy, as dictated by Fenway's "style guide." Even the digital menu boards are programmed to reflect those fonts that have been in the ballpark historically.

He continues, "We put LED fascia boards up, and we made the fascia boards look like old incandescent dot matrix boards, because that's what was there before. In center field, we have a new state-of-the-art LED board. We could have gone twice as big. Well, you know what, that LED screen, it fits almost within the framework of the old structure, which only had a small board." And like all of Fenway's video boards, it is programmed to resemble the Monster scoreboard, mimicking the aesthetic of its hand-operated panels, with fake rust and digital bolts and rivets.

"Subtle things," says Gilula, adding that it's not just how the boards look but how they function. "We resisted the urge to do a lot of spoken word during between-innings breaks, like commercials. And there aren't a lot of prompts, like, you know, these big hands that are clapping, telling people when to clap. We believe we have a highly intelligent fan base. There's nothing like that here. That's intentional, but it's hard. You have all these new toys, these new shiny toys, and you want to take more full advantage of them. But again, respect."

This restraint also keeps the boards from acting like a turned-on television at a dinner party, sucking the room's energy, draining attention away from the field.

The best compliment the Red Sox can receive is that a certain addition looks like it's been there forever. Many say that about the incredibly popular Green Monster seats, and there's a reason why. "Those seats fit within the volume of the net that used to hang there," explains Gilula. "If we did twenty rows [for which there is enough demand], would they say that? I doubt it."

A similar test is applied when considering companies for corporate sponsorships. New for an upcoming series, for example, is a Clean Harbors ad on the center-field wall. At a meeting earlier that morning, the team was still trying to decide whether it fit into Fenway. (Their conclusion: it does.) Some ads are in color, while others are only green and white. What the partners have to understand, according to Gilula, is that they're bringing their brand to Fenway Park, not the other way around. Everyone pretty much gets it. As he says, "They're not going to want to be the ones who have their name associated with the sign that denigrated Fenway Park."

———————

Carl Rice admits Wrigley Field will "lose a little bit of that historic charm"—the bullpens will no longer be in foul territory, along the outfield, for instance—but Kenney says he's convinced the team won't mess with the ballpark's "ultimate character, its soul."

When I run into *Sports Illustrated*'s Tom Verducci at Turner Field in Atlanta, I ask whether he thinks Wrigley can remain "the genuine article," as he wrote in a hagiographic essay during the venue's one-hundredth season. Verducci replies, "To me, no matter what they do, they can't touch the soul of the place. I think the soul is genuine." (Though he says the second video board feels excessive.)

According to Kenney, what will change most is the outboard side of the facility, leaving "great integrity" around the seating areas and playing field. This is likely an idea he borrowed from Packers president Mark Murphy, from Lambeau Field—one of the many iconic structures the Cubs studied ahead of the current construction. When Lambeau underwent its own modernization, the Packers determined they needed to protect the original seating bowl, the first sixty rows, above all else—that the bowl was the soul.

On the day of the Packers home opener, I find there to be something aesthetically soothing about the pure bowl arrangement, a symmetry that stretches in all directions. The club areas and luxury suites and end zone towers that have risen in recent years, both for added revenue and to help keep in the noise—Green Bay has worked hard to shed its reputation as a quiet crowd—succeed in making the building feel more monumental but do little to taint the bowl itself. The bowl exists free from frills. A plainness of design reflective of a simpler time, when one didn't need video prompts or Wi-Fi networks for in-game distraction, when the field *was* the focus. Even the championship years affixed to the scoreboard, along with the names and numbers immortalized by the team's Ring of Honor, seem modest in their size and fonts, appropriately midwestern.*

Standing in section 314, still waiting for the Lambeau Mayor to administer the Oath, to welcome me to the fold, it's clear how much history can be trapped inside a single structure like Lambeau, how it can signify so much to so many. As Danish scholar Niels Kayser Nielsen writes, a stadium is not only where a "city celebrates itself" but also where a "city and its inhabitants inherit themselves"—where they become who they are, who they have always been. For now, the crowd is loud and happy, although it will get tense in the second half, when Seattle takes a third-quarter lead. On some level, they all have

---

* In our meeting, Murphy confesses there was hesitation within the organization whether to even put those championship years on the scoreboard, for fear it might seem boastful. Ultimately, the Cheeseheads psyched themselves into it because "it is not like we are making it up. We actually won these. It is factual." With perhaps a wink of irony, Murphy adds, "We take great pride in being humble."

to know what is riding on this game, on every game—the collective identity and (humble) pride of a team's unlikely hometown, of a region, an entire state.

Bob Trumpbour talks about "the invention of tradition" at American stadiums. All traditions have to start somewhere. It is only with time and repetition that these rituals grow roots. Walk into Lambeau, and you can feel the individual baggage of so much fandom hanging like a heavy fog. The physical space is weighted down with memory, history, expectation. It is all so personal—there can never be a replacement. Just look at the new Yankee Stadium. Like the Packers, the Yankees will always have a trophy case full of championships. But never again will they play in a champion's home; the House That Ruth Built was demolished by 2010. As much as in private memory, tradition wraps itself in physical spaces, seeping into the walls, the cracks in the concrete.

In a new home, there are no ghosts.

It is easier to turn away.

As I wait in section 314, there is some sort of holdup with the Lambeau Oath. The Mayor klutzes around with his digital camera. He takes off his glasses and squints at the small screen. Not used to being defeated, he nevertheless gives up, shoving the device at his son. Says, "You got to make it bigger."

"You can't read that?" Rob takes the camera. "You should have it almost memorized!"

The Mayor sags his head. "I know."

At last, the zoom feature is discovered, and the gadget is operational. Ready to proceed, the Mayor clears his throat, as the stadium once again fills with noise, the Packers now on a defensive stand. "Repeat after me," he says, with all the power of his pretend post. "I, state your name—

"Do solemnly swear . . .

"To uphold the standards of the Packer Nation . . .

"To worship the hallowed ground that is Lambeau . . .

"To honor and cherish the players and coaches that came before . . .

"To lose my voice at every game I attend . . .

"To wear cheese as an accessory . . .

"And if I am of age . . .

"To drink *Wisconsin* beers . . .

"Until the cooler is empty . . .

"So help me God."

I conclude my repetitions: "So help me God."

The Mayor looks me in the eye, gives an approving and surprisingly sober nod.

"All right," he says, "you have been sworn in."

2

SUPER SUBSIDIZE ME

(Or: The Newcomers)

Outside the fans wait, visible through glass doors, nearly frothing. The mad rush is about to begin.

Inside AT&T Stadium, the Dallas Cowboys' home in Arlington, Texas, since 2009, workers engage in last-minute prep, fluffing fresh trash bags into bins, finalizing assignments from the vending station, stocking their trays. The energy is eerily quiet, the spit-shined floors reflecting the yellow-gray light of overcast November skies. I wonder if the concession stand workers shouldn't be wiping down the surfaces one last time—because everything inside "Jerry's World," nicknamed for team owner Jerry Jones, must sparkle always—and be battening down the hatches.

The stadium has a Black Friday feel. Expectant.

A man wearing an earpiece and EVENT STAFF polo hollers a sixty-second warning: "One minute, here we go!" Another event staffer spots me standing in the middle of the vast open space of the main concourse, just inside from the West Plaza opposite a row of pregnant glass doors. The staffer approaches. "First time?" He points toward a nearby I-beam, next to a binocular rentals stand. "Stand by the pole. They come rushing in."

A beer vendor takes my place in the middle of the concourse. In the seconds before the doors erupt, I think about Mark Williams, the lead architect behind the Cowboys' new home. He had told me this was one of his favorite ways to experience a stadium. "Being in the building and standing there as the doors open. It just blows you away, the looks on their faces. It's literally going into—what you want to call it—a utopia fantasy land, just a dream world," he'd said. "In these buildings, things happen."

And then: the doors open. Fans come surging in—speed walking, jogging, sprinting. They swirl around the beer vendor like he's a rock in a river. They don't want beer. Nor binoculars. Not yet, at least. The fans keep pouring in, cellphones raised, filming their entrances, hurrying to claim spots among the first-come, first-served standing-room crowd—the party passes, as Jerry has named this seatless ticket option. Some spirit seems to have possessed the faithful, both the Cowboys' supporters and the not-insignificant number of opposing fans. As they rush in together, men and women (but mostly men) throw their arms in the air, letting out manically joyful cries. A father pulls his young son by the hand, almost skipping, as they scream in unison, over and over: "Whoooo! Whoooo! Whoooo!"

To be fair to all the shrieking patrons, the mammoth $1.2 billion stadium—which measures three million square feet under its retractable roof, is tall enough to house the Statue of Liberty, has a capacity of eighty thousand (expandable to over one hundred thousand), features the world's longest single-span roof structure (thanks to two arches that run a quarter-mile each), and is perhaps best known for its seven-story-high, sixty-yard-long center-hung video boards that weigh more than a million pounds and draw eyeballs like moths to a flame—has that effect on people. Nearly impossible to digest all at once, it is like what you would get if a stadium ate another stadium. It demands a reaction. Even if only: *Whoooo!*

It isn't just the sheer size of the place, either. AT&T Stadium, whose other nickname is the "Eighth Wonder of the World" (although technically that sobriquet first belonged to Houston's Astrodome half a century earlier), has set the standard for modern sports facilities across seemingly every front. The venue has upped the ante on luxury amenities (in-stadium parking, anyone?), lured mega-events like Super Bowls, Final Fours, and NBA All-Star Games (not to mention high-profile performing artists like George Strait and Taylor Swift), and monetized just about everything. At Jerry's World, there's never an opportunity to get bored, thanks to the deejays, live bands, pyro shows, drumming teams, go-go dancers, and hyper-choreographed cheerleader routines that serve as an ever-jangling set of shiny keys, treating the crowd like kittens with ADD. The stadium has been rightly dubbed a "humming cash factory," as in 2014 Cowboys revenue hit an estimated $620 million, the highest ever.

Locals are proud that this giant building, which hovers over the landscape like a crouched and futuristic Ninja Turtle, has helped "turn Dallas into the center of the sports world," in the words of *The New York Times* (even if the truly local bristle at the omission of Arlington by name). According to Arlington mayor Jeff Williams, there are eighty or ninety private jets sitting at the municipal airport on a typical Sunday—an indication, he insists, of the stadium's magnetism to the nation's elite, many of whom can be found in the owner's suite, where celebrities, politicos, and other luminaries are frequent guests of the Jones family.

More than games, these are events.

Fans can even buy matchup-specific T-shirts, memorializing relatively meaningless regular-season games. (When the building first opened, the team sold gear that said OURS IS BIGGER, with typical Texas bravado.) But to do so, you'll have to wait your turn, as a mob line forms by the entrance to the team's pro shop, perhaps the only bottleneck in the spacious stadium or its outdoor plazas, where folks refill their beer cups before the game and participate in what might be the most popular fan activity: selfies.

Fans want shots with the stadium in the background, of course. But the center of self-photographic activity is *Sky Mirror*, a fifteen-million-dollar sculpture by artist Anish Kapoor, one of the ever-growing collection of original pieces of modern art that decorate the stadium, inside and out. Kapoor's stainless steel disklike sculpture, located in the East Plaza, is perched above a pool of water and angled toward the ground, reflecting the sky on one surface and earthbound patrons on the other. (From the side, it looks like a celestial magnifying glass, as if God were frying Cowboys fans like ants.) It is the perfect sculpture for this selfie crowd, as everyone stops in the artwork's reflective scope, delighting in their likeness.

Just in case fans are dissatisfied with their photographic chops, the Cowboys have set up a green-screen kiosk, where folks can purchase pictures in which they're superimposed onto the stadium-related background of their choosing.

And why not? When you're here, there's no question this is the place to be. Even when no event is scheduled, folks show up at the stadium doors—every day, about fifteen hundred people pay to take tours (art-specific tickets are also available). That is the magic spell Jerry Jones has cast with his new stadium. People just want to be here, like those standing-room patrons, so many of whom have no shot at seeing the field and may catch only a sliver of the video board.

Out in the East Plaza, I notice an older gentleman dressed in what might be considered a throwback Cowboys hat and jacket, except he probably didn't buy them vintage. He is sort of smirking and nodding, resting in the shadow of the Kapoor sculpture, possibly overstimulated. To his right, a teenage dance troupe performs a kind of collective shimmy-twerk, their movements projected onto a big screen. How does he feel about all of this? I wonder. About his team, and its push-the-envelope owner, who would rather err on the side of too big than too small, of too much than not enough?

The old man shrugs. "Typical Cowboys," he says.

———

It all started with a motorcycle crash. A loose patch of gravel on a lonely country road.

Flashback to 1994, to a man named Robert Cluck. In his mid-fifties at the time, Cluck wasn't what you would call a biker. He was a cautious man who had carved out a safe little life as a respected ob/gyn in the midsize city of Arlington. In nearly twenty-five years of private practice, he had delivered thousands of babies and looked forward to at least another decade in the doctor's smock. It wasn't exactly a midlife crisis, but when all of his friends started cruising around town on motorcycles, Cluck decided he'd buy one, too—a big old Harley-Davidson, with serious giddy-up.

It was a beautiful spring day, perfect weather, the first time he took the bike for a spin. Riding with his friends, Cluck quickly gained confidence, working his way up to forty miles per hour. Never speeding. Still, with the warm Texas air roaring by, the doctor was digging his new toy. On an uphill climb, it happened—not that any of Cluck's friends could do anything but watch and scream. Leaning into a right turn, Cluck tore through some gravel. His back wheel slid out. He tried to correct the bike but only succeeded in wobbling at full speed toward a metal guardrail.

He slammed into the barrier, the metal stabbing through his shoulder, but the hit wasn't flush enough to halt his momentum. Arm all but severed, Cluck kept falling, tumbling down the hill, grasping at trees, weeds, anything, finally coming to rest in a lake. His friends pulled him to shore and called for help (at least one was a cellphone early adopter). As he waited for the helicopter, Cluck remembers staring at the open wound of his shoulder with detached medical curiosity. More than once he lost consciousness in a pool of his own blood. En route to the hospital, he came to and overheard the medic tell the pilot that someone on board was in the process of dying. The good doctor looked around the helicopter cabin, but no one else was there. *Oh, crap*, he thought, *he's talking about me.*

Incredibly, Cluck would survive, but his practice wouldn't. His right arm was ruined, his career as he knew it over. After suffering through blood-loss hallucinations, he nearly lost his mind. Having poured himself wholly into his practice for a quarter-century, he stared down a suddenly void future, sure of only one thing: he needed something else to do with his life before he went crazy.

After an early stint playing at the Cotton Bowl, the Dallas Cowboys moved to Texas Stadium, in Irving, in 1971. By 2001, the end of the team's lease was within sight, and Jerry Jones was committed to building a new facility for his franchise. Never shy of the media, Jerry didn't keep the decision to himself, and Arlington resident Robert Rivera was paying attention.

Rivera had always been a big sports fan. In 1991, at eighteen, he ran for city council on a platform that called for Arlington to purchase the Texas Rangers, after learning the club was thinking about skipping town. Following that political defeat, the precocious teen didn't give up. Instead, he formed an organization called Home Run Arlington and successfully advocated for the city to help build a new ballpark, largely funded by a voter-approved half-cent sales tax. Ten years later that debt had been retired, and Rivera, who works full time as an investment banker, had risen to the position of chairman of Arlington's Convention and Visitors Bureau. When Rivera saw the Cowboys on TV talking about needing new digs, he was shocked to learn other North Texas communities were already discussing how they might accommodate the team, but not Arlington. Nobody in city hall seemed interested. Nobody, that is, except a newbie city council member, barely two years in office. As it happened, this council member also sat on the Convention and Visitors Bureau board of directors. His name was Bob Cluck.

Together Cluck and Rivera cofounded an organization called— you guessed it—Touchdown Arlington and modeled it after its winning predecessor, Home Run Arlington. The group's early mission was twofold. One, to announce to the wider North Texas region that Arlington was interested in building a stadium for the Cowboys. And two, to drum up grassroots support to set the stage for a citywide ballot initiative. But this was going to be a different kind of battle, Rivera quickly discovered. The day after the group announced its intentions, an article ran in *The Dallas Morning News* describing the Arlington mayor's displeasure with the idea.

And it wasn't just the mayor. Some folks took issue with the idea of subsidizing the *über*-wealthy Cowboys and balked at the fact that building a football stadium would require the use of eminent domain. Some felt the Cowboys would never really consider Arlington a potential landing spot, only using the city as leverage to secure a better deal elsewhere. And some objected because they didn't like Jerry Jones. The ostentatious Cowboys owner had provided no shortage of polarizing decisions, but this particular distaste dated back to his earliest days with the club, when the Arkansas businessman bought the team and promptly fired legendary coach Tom Landry— a transgression some fans will never forgive.

There was so much resistance that even those who supported the idea would do so only in secret, fearing the potential political fallout of participating in a loser—and a divisive loser at that. "We were definitely out there," remembers Rivera, who now sits on the city council. The group pressed on through the summer of 2001, without gaining much traction. And after September 11, they went dark.

In 2003, there was no doubt Touchdown Arlington had been a flop. It was recommended to Rivera that he remove the group's name from his résumé while applying for a position with a community organization. During that year's mayoral race, which Cluck entered, he was attacked for his involvement. Rivera remembers one mailer in particular that essentially said, "This guy wanted to bring the Cowboys here. You trust him to be your mayor?" Apparently, the citizens did trust Cluck—or at least were willing to forgive an early political indiscretion—and he won the election.

Arlington's new mayor never gave up the idea of bringing the Cowboys to town, though. From a distance, he watched with great interest as discussions with Dallas County—which included a potential hotel and rental car tax—and then the city of Dallas itself picked up over the next year or so. Publicly, Jerry made noise about returning the team to its namesake city. He even hired Allyn Media, a public relations and political media firm that helped elect Dallas mayor Laura Miller. But Cluck held out hope he hadn't missed his window, and when he read something in the paper about discussions stalling out, he sensed this was his shot.

"Nobody knew I was going. One person, my wife," Cluck says of the secret meeting he set up with Jerry and Stephen Jones (Jerry's son and right-hand man). Though he speaks now with some bluster about that time—"I put the whole thing together . . . I called Jerry and said, I need to talk to ya"—Cluck admits he was scared when he arrived at the team's headquarters in Valley Ranch, greeted by the Joneses and a few of their attorneys, unsure if he was doing the right thing. But the Cowboys quickly put Cluck at ease, and before the appointment ended, Cluck and Jerry had an agreement: Arlington would contribute $325 million to the cost of a new stadium. "When I look back on it, it's almost unbelievable, because I didn't spend much time thinking," says Cluck. But a deal was a deal. "We shook hands on it."

In the aftermath of that secret meeting, there were some sleepless nights. But deep down, Cluck says he just knew it was the right thing for Arlington. Plus, didn't they have that half-penny sales tax available, since the ballpark was paid off? Sure they did! And actually, the more he thought about it, Cluck didn't have any doubts at all. The same way he had always been certain in his doctor's gown, always decisive, playing his part in a miracle. Now all he had to do was win the support of the city council—they were still in the dark on his handshake agreement—and then of the Arlington electorate.

Surely they couldn't all hate Jerry as much as they used to, could they?*

It would take a miracle, all right.

————

According to Stephen Jones, who calls me from the nearly complete construction site of "The Star," the Cowboys' new training facility and headquarters in Frisco, "Jerry always had the mantra as the leader of the organization that you're never standing still." Leaving Texas Stadium, the team approached AT&T Stadium with a singular vision from the very beginning: it needed to be a physical manifestation of the Cowboys brand, a total distillation. Not just the building as a whole—every nut, bolt, elevator button, and piece of floor tile had to scream *Cowboys!*

Even before the team knew the zip code of its new home, the Jones family, led by Jerry and his wife, Gene, was working with the architecture firm HKS, specifically Mark Williams. "They met with us weekly for years," says Williams. "Not every owner chooses to do that." Another big picture concern was elevating the fan experience—both for folks in the stands *and* for those at home. Due to the popularity of the NFL and the international reach of the Cowboys, Williams

* They could.

believed AT&T Stadium had the potential to be "the most viewed building in the world." Think about football broadcasts, how the TV cameras pan over South Beach for a game in Miami or the snow-capped Rockies for a game in Denver—establishing shots. "Well," the architect says, "there's no reason the stadium shouldn't be that, so that when it shows up on TV you know immediately—boom!—that's the Cowboys."

In other words, he needed to build an icon.

Easier said than done. In the history of stadium building, not much has changed over the last two thousand years. Which isn't a condemnation of sports architecture so much as it is a testament to the genius of the Roman engineers behind the Colosseum. "It's basically the same building," Williams says of the Colosseum and modern football stadiums. According to pretty much every architect I speak with, the Roman Colosseum—which was constructed via cranes and had numbered gates, tickets, reserved seating, sophisti-cated crowd flow, vomitories (the tunnels leading from concourse to seating bowl, not a place to throw up during feasts), a hydraulics sys-tem that provided water to all levels, and even a domelike awning to provide some shade—just nailed it.

But in perfection, Williams saw opportunity. And necessity. Drawing a crowd on game day is harder than ever. With rising ticket prices crossed with inconveniences like traffic, staying at home with a high-definition TV, a stocked fridge, and an always-available restroom can be pretty appealing. To combat that, Team Jones recon-sidered everything. "The only given we had in the whole process was that the field was one hundred yards long," says Williams.

For inspiration, the Jones family toured buildings across the globe, and not just sports venues, seeking out iconic structures like the Eiffel Tower and the latest in modern architecture in Manhattan skyscrapers. They had input on every decision, in every part of the stadium, from bringing over the roof design from Texas Stadium (a late-game audible, so to speak) to what sort of food they would serve (together with the Yankees, the Cowboys launched Legends Hospitality, acting as their own concessionaire) to the exotic woods in the suites. "They got very, very specific on materials," says Williams, who calls the family's hands-on approach "one of the great unknown stories" of AT&T Stadium.

Take a tour of the facility (it'll run you twenty-five dollars, unless prices have gone up), and you end on the field. From there, the stands look like an imposing silver-and-blue seven-layer cake, the seating arrangement tall and stratified, the opposite of Lambeau Field's pure bowl. Some things in the stadium, says Williams, aren't so different from Lambeau or the Colosseum, or are at least in the same cone of vision. But others are "in a different galaxy," he says. "We totally reinvented the seating bowl experience, from the patron side."

Dominated by posh clubs and three hundred-plus luxury suites (with standing room as a counterbalance), AT&T Stadium pioneered a slew of new premium products to satisfy every conceivable segment of the high-end market. There are traditional suites, of course, which Williams equates to opera boxes. Lower down, only twenty rows up from the field, are the ultra-premium offerings (Jerry's suite is located on this level), with optimal sightlines and amenities straight out of a Four Seasons. Even lower, for a more immersive experience, there are field suites recessed from the sidelines (picture a baseball dugout), which literally put patrons on the same level as the players. "They are people who can spend a lot of money who want to hear [Cowboys coach] Jason Garrett praise or yell at [former quarterback] Tony Romo," says Williams.

That kind of close encounter—or the kind provided in the exclusive Miller Lite Club, where players walk through on their way to and from the field—allows fans memorable access to the Cowboys, according to Williams. Ripped from the Disney playbook, the strategy is to command brand loyalty by creating memories for kids. It is why the stadium tours all end on the field, and why Jerry lets you stay there for as long as you like, tossing a football, lying on the midfield star, or even getting hitched.* As another example, Williams tells me about a Boy Scout overnight at the stadium. The troop watched a movie and played video games on the big board, sleeping in tents out on the turf. "I guarantee you one of them will own a suite someday," he says.

———————

The reality is that Jerry Jones was probably never bringing his team back to Dallas. There just wasn't enough money. Margaret Keliher, who was Dallas county judge at the time—essentially, a chief executive—tells me her interactions with the Cowboys never left the starting gate. Even so, there was tremendous pushback on the potential hotel and rental car tax. National conventions threatened to stop hosting in Dallas, rental car companies considered moving their offices outside county borders, and outlying towns complained of shouldering the burden for another city's gain.

Discussions with Laura Miller, Dallas's mayor, went further, despite the fact that she had made her name as a journalist by opposing sports subsidies. The problem was, preparing Fair Park, the leading site candidate in Dallas, would have cost $140 million-plus. And unlike Arlington, Dallas didn't have a half-penny in its sales tax. It would have had to borrow all the money. Explaining this to Jerry Jones, Miller asked if the $140 million could be deducted from the overall subsidy amount for which the Cowboys were asking. "And he said, of course not," remembers Miller. The Cowboys wanted what they wanted, and what they wanted was $325 million. "There just wasn't ever any real negotiation."

———————

* The Cowboys don't necessarily encourage the practice, but one team employee tells me it is not uncommon for couples to arrive with an undercover priest—or some other officiant in tow—to conduct an impromptu on-field ceremony after tours.

The Cowboys couldn't wait forever, and Jerry knew it. It was 2004 now, and to stay on track for a 2009 opening, the stadium initiative needed to be on a ballot that year. The clock was ticking, and talks were getting nowhere. Then came a phone call from Arlington's newly elected mayor. Bob Cluck wanted to talk to Jerry.

———

Taxpayers haven't always subsidized sports stadiums in the United States. Before World War II, with rare exceptions, team owners paid their own way. According to Penn State professor Bob Trumpbour, politicians held more power than team owners in those early days—it was a time of "honest graft," he says—so a franchise couldn't extort a municipality by threatening to leave (now a go-to strategy). Instead, even minor transgressions against local officials, like not providing game tickets upon request, could result in serious political retribution. Plus, without TV money, the biggest markets were by far the most attractive. "The real game changer in my mind was when the Boston Braves moved to Milwaukee," Trumpbour says of the team's 1953 relocation.

Suffering from poor attendance back east, the Braves, who headed to Wisconsin less than a year after baseball owners approved the idea of relocation in general, moved into a publicly funded stadium built for the sole purpose of luring a baseball team and immediately drew record crowds. Other American cities took notice. They too wanted to become "major league," as civic boosters and local politicians viewed securing a professional sports team as a way of putting themselves on the map. Team owners were paying attention as well, as the move to Milwaukee "legitimized stadium subsidies," per Trumpbour. Cities could recoup their investment via tax receipts, rent payments, or stadium-related revenue, and teams gained tremendous profitability in their new paid-for homes. Leverage shifted away from cities, which became either desperate to attract a team or terrified of losing one. That psychology only deepened as baseball relocation and expansion continued through the 1950s and '60s and into the '70s, as the Dodgers moved to Los Angeles, the Giants to San Francisco, and so on.

In the early-1980s, former Raiders owner Al Davis won another victory for team owners when he broke from NFL ranks and began a court battle against the league, in which he eventually earned the equivalent of free agency for franchises, while moving his club to L.A. Though Davis was viewed as a black sheep in the NFL family, he opened the floodgates and argued as much at a 1985 owners' meeting, saying, "franchises' leverage in the superstadium game had made a quantum leap," as Trumpbour writes.

The 1980s also saw the rise of public-private partnerships in stadium construction. But even if some teams were now contributing to capital costs, their profitability continued to skyrocket as local governments—or as Allen Guttmann calls them, "gratefully bilked municipalities"—abdicated their share of stadium-related revenue, from things like concessions and parking, thanks to sweetheart leases signed with pro-team tenants. Canadian scholar Bruce Kidd terms this the "socialization of risk and the privatization of profit," and it was especially important to football franchises, since certain types of earnings—like from luxury suite sales and sponsorships—were exempt from the league's revenue-sharing program. By the time NFL teams started abandoning bigger cities for better stadium deals in smaller markets, "it was very clear the owners dictated what was going on," says Trumpbour.*

---

* Congress inadvertently tipped the scales even further in the owners' favor in 1986, when lawmakers tried to eliminate public stadium deals, which were often funded via tax-exempt bonds (providing yet another form of subsidy), by passing the Tax Reform Act. But a loophole in the bill actually encouraged cities to strike deals that were *less* favorable, in order to still qualify for tax-free borrowing. As Neil deMause and Joanna Cagan write, the loophole essentially forced "cities to fund only facilities that were guaranteed money losers." And: "Congress had created a monster."

When I interview Neil deMause, coauthor of *Field of Schemes*, he explains that he started reporting on the phenomenon of publicly funded stadiums in America in the mid-1990s, thinking the United States was going through a fleeting burst of stadium madness. "We thought it was this moment that we were capturing," he says. Two decades later his career as a stadium chronicler and critic is going strong. "What is remarkable is how little has changed." According to deMause, Toronto's SkyDome—which opened in 1989; it is now known as Rogers Centre—marked the start of the current cycle of stadium building. "That was really the first one that had so much, both so much public money, and then so much—this isn't just a stadium. This isn't just for sports. This is also an . . ." He trails off. "An amusement park?" I ask. "Yeah, exactly."

Sports subsidies are problematic for a number of reasons, says deMause, not least of which is that local governments can't seem to help outdoing one another with bad stadium deals. Often those decisions are made both with a figurative gun to their head, as teams threaten to move, and over the opposition of polls via special interest politics, with lobbyists and political contributions but without public referendums. When such an issue *does* go to a vote, "it winds up being the worst kind of political campaign, completely dominated by money." And folks shouldn't necessarily trust the sticker price, either: Judith Grant Long, a stadium scholar, has discovered that subsidies are on average 40 percent more expensive than taxpayers are first led to believe.

I ask deMause about the worst stadium deals in America. He sighs. "I always tell people, every unhappy stadium deal is unhappy in its own way." Marlins Park in Miami, for instance, will cost Miami–Dade County well over $2 billion to pay back $500 million in bonds, thanks to interest and balloon payments. (Worse, Marlins brass misled the public ahead of the stadium deal by claiming poverty, while they were actually in the black.) And Paul Brown Stadium in Cincinnati was built after the Bengals threatened to skip town if they didn't get a football-only facility. ("Keep Cincinnati a Major League City" was the pro-stadium side's campaign message.) In addition to providing construction costs and a bevy of revenue guarantees, the local county agreed to cover operation and maintenance, as well as some capital improvements. Unfortunately, the county's debt responsibilities have been higher than its ability to pay, and it has been left holding the bag. The debt has eaten into its general fund, caused budget cuts in other public-sector areas, and even forced the sale of a public hospital. DeMause lists another couple examples, then stops. "They are all so awful. I don't think you can just single out one."

According to Roger Noll, a professor emeritus at Stanford and something of a grand poobah when it comes to stadium economics, "the early 2000s were the golden age of being an owner of a sports team," in terms of subsidies. But observers like deMause don't see the practice going away anytime soon. Teams are just finding new and more creative ways to hide the subsidies, with tax breaks and kickbacks, subsidized operations and maintenance costs, and state-of-the-art clauses, which are the gifts that keep on giving.*

This one-upmanship has created a stadium arms race. As Stephen Jones was told by NFL colleagues upon completion of AT&T Stadium, the Cowboys had "made a lot of stadiums antiquated overnight." But it is a cycle of mathematical absurdity—after all, not *every* team can be in the top third or whatever upper-tier fraction is promised by a state-of-the-art clause. Instead, the one-upmanship allows owners to insist on better amenities in perpetuity, lest they fall behind the cutting edge, in which case, they argue (i.e., threaten) that

---

* Paul Brown Stadium has a clause that guarantees the county will purchase for the Bengals "holographic replay systems" if and when such systems are invented. Compare that to the time when Shibe Park in Philadelphia accepted a hand-me-down scoreboard from the Yankees, and you'll see how far we've come.

they won't be able to afford to field a competitive team. The irony is that almost none of these teams would be building such lavish facilities if they didn't have public contributions, because stadiums cost a lot more than they need to.

"They are Taj Mahals," explains Noll. "Monuments to the ego of the owners." Geoffrey Propheter, a young economist who has focused on the effect of subsidies on stadium opulence, agrees. "There are two people contributing [to the cost], and only one of those people controls the design, so there is an incentive for owners [who also control the revenue] to add on all of these luxury amenities that have nothing to do with the actual game," he says. Or put another way: subsidies are "making the sports facility cheaper for a private owner. And what do you do when something is cheaper and you want it? You buy more of it."

When I meet Bob Cluck, still in office at the time (he served twelve years as mayor, then was voted out in May 2015, due in part to a lack of promised development around the Cowboys' stadium, which became a key campaign issue in Jeff Williams's mayoral victory), he strikes me as a pleasant and possibly even Magoo-ish grandfather type. But over the course of our talk, there are times when his eyes dim, when he tells me certain stories off the record, and it becomes clear that he's a man who knows how to get things done.

Over protests from the city manager, Cluck convinced Arlington's city council to unanimously approve his deal with the Cowboys in the summer of 2004, sending it to voters in time for the November elections.

Then the real work began.

Initial polls showed the initiative falling well short with the public. But this is often the case, according to Mari Woodlief and Jennifer Pascal of Allyn Media. "They're usually the angriest," Woodlief says of stadium campaigns. "They always start out losing. It's your job to figure out how to make them win."

One of the leaders of the opposition was an electrical-engineer-turned-law student named Warren Norred. Norred had actually been an original member of Touchdown Arlington, one of the few, though he was never in favor of building a stadium. He wanted a seat at the table to serve as a voice of reason during the process, but eventually he abandoned his Trojan horse strategy. In his mind, the city was dead set on handing over $325 million to Jerry Jones, no questions asked, even though there didn't seem to be any other suitor cities. "All we had to do to win was outbid everybody else, because that's how capitalism works," says Norred, who in a delicious twist can see AT&T Stadium from the front window of his law office on Abram Street. ("We call it the Silver Roach," his wife and managing paralegal, Annette, says.) "But it looks to me like we are giving all the money we *can* give to Jerry. I'm out."

Allyn Media created direct mailers and TV spots touting potential economic benefits, while the Cowboys paraded cheerleaders and big-name players at rallies around town, trying to turn out what Norred derisively calls "low-information voters." The city even held a series of debates, every one of which Norred claims to have won. But it didn't matter. The tide was turning.

The opposition was severely outgunned. On the advice of campaign leaders, Jerry Jones made himself scarce during this time because he inspired such strong and split emotions, but he still footed the five-million-dollar campaign bill. About the financial disparity between the pro- and anti-stadium sides, Norred says, "They spent I think fifty thousand dollars on one billboard. I sent some outrageously good emails."

According to Woodlief, the Cowboys would have lost the vote if they hadn't poured so much into it. Norred estimates his side would have won if they'd had only a quarter-million dollars, one-twentieth the Cowboys' budget. This figure fits neatly into a stadium-campaign theory devised by deMause. His rule of thumb for many years was that the pro side had to outspend the anti side by thirty to one to guarantee a victory. ("More recently, it is like one hundred to one," he says, due to the nation's growing skepticism around stadium projects.)

Even with its shoestring budget, the opposition still could have won in Arlington. As the football season unfolded, polls showed a neck-and-neck race, and the pro-stadium side would surge or falter depending on how the Cowboys fared on Sundays. "It was so close going into the election, we thought a win or loss could depend on how [the Cowboys] played," says Woodlief. And don't think Jerry Jones wasn't relaying that message to his coaching staff. Says Woodlief, "They knew." After three straight October losses, the Cowboys had one final chance to create a surge before the November elections. It was a home game on Halloween against the 4-2 Detroit Lions.

Overcoming a first-half deficit, the Cowboys won the game.

Behind all the spectacle and slick packaging of the campaign, beyond the few-points spike of a Cowboys win, at its core, the election fight "was about selling an economic development project to voters in Arlington," according to Pascal. The stadium would become an economic engine for the city, the pro side contended, and ancillary development, like shopping and retail, would flower around the new facility.

Time and again such an economic argument has been used to justify building stadiums on taxpayers' dime. It is the frequent flip side to the public subsidy coin (*yeah, it'll cost you something now, but soon you'll make it all back—and then some!*), and it is often a winning argument. The only issue is that, in the overwhelming majority of cases, the argument isn't true. As Robert A. Baade, an economist at

Lake Forest College has written, "the history of stadiums has been written in red ink."

Sports stadiums are almost never good economic drivers. And many stadiums, especially those surrounded by a sea of parking lots, have been shown to have net *negative* effects, sucking the economic life out of a community. About this, Noll says, "there is complete consensus." Football stadiums in particular have proven to be poor investments. Noll suggests thinking about them like shopping malls. "A football stadium is used ten to twelve times a year," he says. "But you would never build the Mall of America if it was going to be open once a month."

So where do all the rosy forecasts come from? They come from economists and economic consultants, typically ones contracted by the team or pro-stadium city. (A firm hired by Arlington projected the local economy would benefit to the tune of $238 million annually.) In *Public Dollars, Private Stadiums*, authors Kevin J. Delaney and Rick Eckstein invoke the sociologist Lee Clarke, who has a name for these type of impact statements: "fantasy documents." Part of the problem, according to deMause, is that there is so much gray area that economic consultants, who rely on assumptions and multiplier effects, can draw whatever conclusions they want. He explains how an expert witness might use the same logic in two different cases—one in which he's testifying on behalf of a team and the other against a team. Says Trumpbour, "You have to look at who is paying the piper, because generally they dictate the tune."

What these projections also miss are things like leakage (dollars spent at a stadium that are not re-spent within the community, going instead to a national concessionaire's home office, for instance) and substitution effect. While many of these studies look only narrowly at the economic activity in and around a stadium, substitution effect draws a wider circle, looking at a region more macroscopically. For example, if people go to a ball game, they're likely doing so in lieu of seeing a movie or dining out elsewhere in the city. Folks have only so many entertainment dollars to spend.

None of this is to say there isn't value in having a sports franchise. It is just wildly overstated from an economic perspective. Allen Sanderson, an economist at the University of Chicago, actually finds impact studies quite instructive; he takes whatever number they spit out and moves "the decimal point one to the left." Suddenly $100 million is $10 million, and you're probably getting closer to an honest figure.

Heading into the Arlington campaign, Norred had done his homework. He knew all the arguments against stadium building, the dubious economics of the endeavor. But even if the academics were wrong, "if all of that is just hooey," the fact was, "all we had to do was give Jerry $200 million and we could have gotten the team," he says. This is the thing that still irks him: "I'm right!" he insists. "I'm as right as the day is long." Norred even approached Cluck before the city officially inked its Cowboys deal and offered his support for the stadium at that lower price—"I know how these things go, and it's unlikely my side is going to win," says Norred—but the mayor wouldn't budge.

Norred wasn't the only one advising Cluck to lower his offer. As fate would have it, Laura Miller vacations at the same California hotel as the man who represented the Cowboys in the stadium deal. When he disappeared from the beach one day, she knew something was up. "I called Cluck on the phone," Miller recalls, "and I said, 'Listen, I know you're getting ready to do a deal.' He said, 'Yes, it's imminent.' I said, 'I just want you to know nobody else is in negotiations. No other city has an offer. Cut a better deal!'"

What she didn't know when Cluck blew her off over the phone, and what Norred didn't know when he gave Cluck the same advice, was that the mayor and Jerry had already shaken hands, and Cluck was of the mind that a man's word should mean something ($125 million, in this case). "I felt like I was putting my credit on the line," Cluck says of his initial meeting with the Cowboys. "It was a good subsidy. I thought that was a fair price."

To Cluck's credit, AT&T Stadium hasn't turned into a horror story for Arlington, like so many other stadium deals. The city's contribution was capped at $325 million (half of the initial projected cost), which is a good thing, since cost overruns are par for the course in stadium construction. What's more, out-of-town tax dollars have been flowing into the city treasury, and this too was part of the economic argument, because the Cowboys would draw fans from all over North Texas, not just from Arlington. Thanks to its half-cent sales tax, as well as a couple of other small taxes on hotels and car rentals, Arlington is on pace to pay off the stadium debt by 2021, according to Mayor Williams, well ahead of schedule, with about half of the money coming from visitor taxes. Cluck points to Arlington's record tax revenues— even higher than projected, thanks in part to Jerry finding so many ways to monetize and use the building beyond game days—as a good gauge for the project being a win for the city. But economists call tax revenue an unreliable indicator. Of course, tax revenues went up, they say—you raised the dang tax rate!

In many ways, in spite of all the futuristic bells and high-end whistles, and in spite of all the promised development, Jerry's World is no different than any other stand-alone stadium surrounded by parking lots. Victor Matheson, an economist at Holy Cross, would refer to such a facility as a "walled fortress," trying to capture all economic activity instead of interacting with the community.

Roger Noll says there does seem to be something different about AT&T Stadium, although it might be dangerous for others to try to duplicate it, due to Jerry Jones's unique genius as a salesman. "We may have to use the Texas variable," he laughs. And while there is no doubt that the stadium is extremely successful for the Cowboys, Noll stops short of calling it a win for Arlington. "It probably is a wash, at best."

Folks like Cluck and Williams and Robert Rivera are confident Arlington did the right thing. They see the money coming into city hall, and they see the pride on people's faces, people "who enjoy being seen as something other than a little town," says Cluck. "Plus," the former mayor adds, "there's the fun factor."

Norred remains unconvinced, and he doesn't seem to be having much fun. He talks about opportunity cost, wondering what else the city might have done with its resources, or how residents' lives might be different if they had more disposable income, with lower taxes. "They only see what's in front of them. But there is also what's unseen," Norred says, describing what Propheter would call a "counterfactual frame of mind." AT&T Stadium is a success in the eyes of city hall, Norred believes, because "city bureaucrats handle more money, they have a bigger empire. But what am I getting out of it? Not a thing."

Over the last century-plus, sports facilities have cropped up across the United States like an untreated case of chicken pox. The most recent building boom—which began in the early 1990s and lasted into the mid-2000s—was the most prolific to date. John Bale, author of *Sports Geography*, has asserted the United States suffers from "stadium mania."

Stephen Jones calls AT&T Stadium "a generational project," predicting the Cowboys will be playing there until he's dead and buried and beyond—but that would be breaking from national trends. With a build-first-ask-questions-later mentality, stadiums have become disposable. "The cycle for replacement," Bob Trumpbour writes, "has shrunken from fifty years during the 1960s to a more recent standard of between twenty to thirty-five years." According to deMause, this is a direct result of the seemingly constant availability of public money, which alters the economic calculus for owners. "In most cases, you would be stupid to build a brand-new stadium" without some form of financial assistance, he says.

In popular culture, the issue of sports subsidies seems to be having a bit of a moment, gaining attention from more mainstream outlets in recent years, like *The New York Times*, *The Wall Street Journal*, *The Atlantic*, *Forbes*, *USA Today*, and CNN, among others, while newer-school media like Deadspin and *Vice* hammer the topic constantly. John Oliver dedicated a segment on his HBO show to stadium subsidies, and even Malcolm Gladwell has weighed in (on a podcast with Bill Simmons), wondering why league commissioners don't show more leadership in stopping wealthy owners from shamelessly plundering public coffers. (The thing Gladwell misses is that the commissioners, whose jobs are to maximize profits, *are* showing leadership by acting as enforcers, offering big events, like Super Bowls, as "rewards" for new buildings and passive-aggressive encouragement to get with the program—or else—because subsidized stadiums mean more money for owners, which means more money for the leagues.)

The leagues aren't going to alter their behavior, and they will hold all the leverage as long they have monopoly power, deciding which cities get teams and which don't (controlling a limited supply with infinite demand). Until that changes—and it won't, short of a national legislative solution—communities simply need to have realistic conversations around the topic of stadiums. "First, get it out of your head that it is an investment activity. It is not," says Rodney Fort, co-director of the Michigan Center for Sport Management at the University of Michigan. Like an opera house, a public golf course, or an arts district, "it is consumption."

Which isn't to say there aren't intangible benefits—things like civic pride (i.e., wanting to be "major league"), Bob Cluck's "fun factor," and quality-of-life concerns. "I am big on quality of life," says Fort. As Noll puts it, "It is an amenity. As long as you realize that, you really can't argue with somebody for being in favor of it. What you can say is, don't feed me a line about how this is going to make me rich, because it's not."

If communities decide, after an honest accounting, that this is how they want to spend their money, so be it, says Fort. As long as the money isn't a diversion of other funds (as is happening in Cincinnati, due to overly optimistic forecasting, or as can happen by introducing a new lottery game to cover stadium costs, when lottery proceeds typically benefit education and infrastructure, for instance) and doesn't unfairly burden unintended segments of the population (like a sin tax, which disproportionately affects lower-income folks), Fort says any complaints are just sour grapes. "You hear the exact same thing," he says. "'What about streetlights and the buses? We can spend it on that!' And the answer is, apparently not. If you could have spent it on that, and you had the will to spend it on those things, you would have. We wouldn't be having this argument."

When I ask Noll what he thinks the future holds for stadium subsidies, he says teams can no longer brazenly insist on large up-front sums from local governments, as they once did, and predicts it will soon only be in smaller metropolitan areas that we'll see major public contributions—places like Oklahoma City, where they love their Thunder and are happy to pay for them to be there. It makes less financial sense for owners to be in smaller markets (despite the trends of the last century), according to Victor Matheson, due to basic supply and demand. (Bigger markets have more people and therefore more potential buyers.)

As a result, smaller cities may have to overpay to attract or keep a team. In those cases, blackmail will still work, says Matheson, "because it really does make sense to move." It is why the Rams left St. Louis for Los Angeles, where the team owner is going to privately finance a multibillion-dollar mixed-use development with a stadium as centerpiece, while turning down several hundred million in subsidies from his former host city. It is also why *The New York Times* wrote a piece about how St. Louis won by losing the Rams, since they would have been paying beyond their means. "People eventually learn," says Noll. "In the long run, people will get it. In the short run, they may buy some snake oil."

DeMause isn't so sure. "I think people are getting more skeptical, and I don't think it matters at all," he says, noting team owners and politicians always seem to find a way to win. As an example, deMause mentions Brooklyn's Barclays Center, which he classifies more as a real estate deal than a stadium deal, since the arena is only a fraction of a larger development. "I think [Barclays Center] was kind of groundbreaking in that sense," he says. "There is a definite benefit to throwing enough crap into the deal that it muddies the waters. At a certain point, it gets so complicated that people just throw up their hands."

Or at least most people do.

———

Norman Oder is a self-described "watchdog journalist" living in Brooklyn. In September 2005 he started a blog that tracked real estate developer and then–New Jersey Nets owner Bruce Ratner's multibillion-dollar Atlantic Yards project (now known as Pacific Park), a proposed series of residential and office towers, of which the Nets' new home, Barclays Center, to be designed by world-famous architect Frank Gehry, was going to be the centerpiece. A complicated, belabored, and at times vicious decade ensued—years filled with lawsuits, lobbyists, political posturing, construction delays, racially charged neighborhood quarrels, a financial crisis, eminent domain battles (and buyouts), and enough twists and turns to make your head spin. (At the end of 2008, an opponent group was declaring, "Victory is in Sight"; shortly thereafter, the Nets were sold to a jet-skiing, karate-chopping Russian billionaire.) By the much-hyped 2012 grand opening for the arena, headlined by hip-hop superstar Jay

Z (who then owned a small fraction of the franchise), nearly everyone involved seemed to be left embittered, angry, and thinking they got the short end of the stick—and Norman Oder has chronicled it all.

A soft-spoken yet relentlessly meticulous reporter, Oder doesn't consider himself part of the heavy opposition that faced down Atlantic Yards—although Ratner and company surely view him that way—but a curious observer who became engrossed with what he saw as a complicated project, sold to the public under the slogan "Jobs, Housing, and Hoops." Oder felt the project deserved some scrutiny, or at least more than legacy media outlets were providing. "The interesting thing for me is I went from being, I think, a fairly mainstream journalist with professional skepticism or whatever to being perceived as this kind of outlier radical, just because I follow the story and keep asking questions," says Oder, who alleges Atlantic Yards/Pacific Park has been plagued by "dishonesty and misdirection."

To Oder, it's all about accountability. He sees a laundry list of transgressions of which the developer is guilty, from bypassing the local approval process known as ULURP (Uniform Land Use Review Procedure)* and overriding zoning regulations to renegotiating the key rail yard deal multiple times with the Metropolitan Transit Authority for better terms, to an architect swap that a *New York Times* critic called "a stunning bait-and-switch," to shifting percentages and definitions of promised affordable housing, to a yawning time line for completing the project, to selling a majority stake to Chinese investors as a kind of bailout. Asks Oder, "Is it finding fault to point out that they're not doing what they've promised to do?"

---

* Instead of going through ULURP, Atlantic Yards was kicked upstate to Albany, to the Public Authorities Control Board, which has been described in a *New York Times* editorial as "a shadowy entity controlled by the governor and the leaders of the Assembly and Senate" and been disparaged by others as "three men in a room." See "Mr. Cuomo's Housing Wrecking Ball," *New York Times,* February 3, 2016.

And he's a journalist observing from a distance. For those involved with the arena fight on the ground level, things really got dirty.

Marty Markowitz, who served as Brooklyn borough president from 2002 to 2013, was on the front lines, a local politico who claims to have masterminded the whole thing. "It didn't come across my desk," says Markowitz, who gets heated easily and speaks in a colorful Brooklyn accent. "I generated it!"

To Markowitz, who had his heart broken as a twelve-year-old when his beloved Dodgers fled to L.A., attracting the Nets to Brooklyn would be the suture on a fifty-year open wound. Early in his first term in office, he sensed an opportunity when the team across the river seemed to be floundering financially, with turmoil in the owner's box. But who in Brooklyn would have the money and desire to buy the Nets? He could think of one name: Bruce Ratner. An initial call to the developer went nowhere. "He said, 'Marty, I don't build arenas, and I don't buy sports teams,'" recalls Markowitz, but the borough president was persistent. Eventually Ratner agreed to make an inquiry, but only to get the pestering politician off his back.

Markowitz was thrilled. He knew this opportunity was once in a lifetime, and he remembered how crazy fans had been for the Dodgers. It was a no-brainer. Bring a team to the borough and unleash Brooklyn's passion. And he unleashed the passion, all right. Markowitz first received a taste of the project's divisiveness while eating at Blue Ribbon in Park Slope. That was where he got the news that a deal for the Nets had been approved, that the team was Brooklyn's. First Mayor Michael Bloomberg called to congratulate him. Ratner called right after. "Of course, I gave a big scream," he says, "and some of the people in the restaurant applauded when I announced it, and other people booed me." The mixed reaction took Markowitz by surprise. "I thought Brooklynites everywhere would celebrate it," he says. "But I was very, very wrong."

The issue of eminent domain became a major lightning rod,

since the proposed site, at the intersection of Atlantic and Flatbush Avenues, wasn't wide enough to accommodate an arena. A stretch of Pacific Street to the south would have to be commandeered.* New York's highest court ruled in favor of property seizure in the case of Atlantic Yards, but there was genuine debate as to whether that area ought to be considered blighted. Markowitz recalls the Atlantic Avenue corridor being "really unkempt, ugly," but such a narrow view ignored larger trends, as surrounding Brooklyn neighborhoods in every direction were growing and thriving.†

In Brooklyn, those who were to be booted refused to leave. Others who lived nearby raised a variety of concerns as well—they feared an ensuing traffic nightmare ("carmaggedon") and what would happen to their street parking (already impossible to find in New York City). They wondered how the scale of the project might dwarf their brownstone neighborhoods, and how the presence of an arena and its attendant crowds might create quality-of-life issues, like noise, congestion, and general chaos. They questioned whether the community benefits agreement (CBA) the developer had signed with local groups had any teeth. There were multiple problems with the CBA, according to critics. One, the agreement didn't have a government signatory to ensure it was enforced. And two, many of the groups were newly formed, without any track record (but with financial backing from the developer). Some felt Ratner used the CBA to "divide and conquer neighborhood groups," deMause and Cagan write in *Field of*

---

* Ironically, Barclays Center now sits just across the street from a site that was denied to the Dodgers by the powerful city planner Robert Moses, when the team was trying to build a new stadium in the 1950s. Moses wanted the team to build in Queens—what would become Shea Stadium—to expand his highway system.

† In yet another irony, the Dodgers' move to L.A. precipitated what might be the most famous example of sports-related displacement, as the last holdouts of an idyllic community of mostly Mexican-American families were evicted from Chavez Ravine, identified by the city as a "slum," setting a precedent for bulldozing private homes in the service of stadium construction.

Schemes, "by offering carrots on specific issues rather than discussing the overall scope of the project." In popular narratives, this conflict was often cast along class and racial lines, as African American–led organizations that signed the CBA were pitted against white opponents, who symbolized the widespread gentrification of Brooklyn. (In reality, people of all colors both supported and opposed the project.) More broadly, many citizens resented the use of public subsidies for a sports team* and the way the whole development was being jammed down the city's throat, without voter input.

In Markowitz's mind, it is the most vocal opposition groups, like Develop Don't Destroy Brooklyn, that still stick out. "I used to joke that they would rather have Osama bin Laden at that location, and I don't think I'm very far wrong," he says. But I can hear the hurt in his voice as he continues, "There were some folks whose opposition I didn't agree with but I respected. They raised interesting questions and did so in an intelligent way. They didn't call me a fat horse and pig. They didn't call me a corrupt motherfucker. They didn't tell me, 'Drop dead, up your *fucking* ass!'

"Even local stores that in any way tried to show their support, they threatened to close them down," he says. "I even had people, one or two individuals, they put out, 'Here's Marty Markowitz's home address, go urinate there.'"†

Markowitz suffered a political blow as a result of his involvement, losing significant support from Park Slope and areas right around the

---

* According to deMause—whose latest book, *The Brooklyn Wars* (New York: Second System Press, 2016), details how rampant development over the last two decades has reshaped the borough—the size and muddiness of this project have made it nearly impossible to nail down a figure for the subsidies, which could be considered both direct, in the form of cash and discounted land, and indirect, via things like tax breaks. He says, "You can come up with anywhere from a couple hundred million to a couple billion dollars, and I can absolutely justify that as being a realistic number."

† Public urination was an early issue for the neighborhoods surrounding Barclays Center.

arena when he ran for reelection, though he won anyway. For his role as a kind of pro-development mascot, Oder calls Markowitz a "nasty clown." He adds, "Marty was supposed to answer to the public. In some ways he did; in many ways he didn't."

So were the local fears founded? It probably depends who you ask. Despite the early urination epidemic, the neighborhoods have not been thrown into chaos. As *The New York Times* put it several months after the venue opened, complaints "have shifted from warnings of existential threats to gripes about everyday irritants." Traffic isn't a major issue, partly because of heavy police presence during events and partly because fewer people are driving than anticipated.* Still, there have been noise complaints and side street congestion, with loading-dock issues and idling town cars, and parking hasn't gotten any easier. "Everything's mixed," Oder says, adding that many Brooklynites are happy to have the arena. At the same time, he says, "I think the impact is quite unpleasant for a small number of people who thought it was going to be quite unpleasant."

As for the bitter fight and hardball politics that preceded the opening of the arena, the legacy is unclear. While Markowitz has said this battle will go down "among the most contentious developments in America's history" and Oder refers to Barclays Center as a "tainted building," both Bloomberg and Ratner have contended that the details will soon be lost to time. As Ratner told *New York* magazine, "No one will care what we had to do to make it happen."

I ask Oder if he takes such proclamations personally, if they fuel the fire of what has become his life's work. "Yeah, that does stick in my craw," he says. What's worse, he knows that they're likely right.

---

* While fewer cars coming from places like New Jersey may be good for traffic, it doesn't help the initial economic argument made on behalf of the project, which relied in large part on capturing tax dollars from Nets fans who live beyond the city limits.

"Time passes, people don't remember, people leave, [but] there's so much fundamentally troubling about this that to let it go, and to let it fade away, and to let them be the arbiters, massagers, the re-writers of history would be very wrong." For Oder, this is far from over. As housing towers finally rise around Barclays Center, he continues to monitor the project via his blog and is also working on an ever-lengthening book manuscript. He says it is a "fool's game" to predict what plot twists are on the horizon for Atlantic Yards/Pacific Park, as it proceeds into the foreseeable future. But he will be there to track them, whatever they may be.

––––––––

As the Nets prepared to ditch the Garden State and move into Barclays Center, the NBA franchise devolved into something of a dumpster fire, winning a total of fifty-eight games in its last three years in New Jersey, with the worst attendance in the league. Brett Yormark, CEO for the Nets and the new arena, wasn't worried about the past, though. Others may have seen his team's lack of success or personality, but the veteran marketer saw only opportunity. "Leaving from New Jersey provided us with a complete blank canvas," Yormark says. "We looked at it as a totally new chapter. A new beginning."

Whereas retro baseball parks, with their quirks and nods to bygone eras, often attempt to reconnect patrons to the past, and even the progress-at-all-costs Cowboys tried to preserve some franchise history at AT&T Stadium, Yormark knew nostalgia for the Nets—if such a thing even existed—would gain no purchase in modern-day Brooklyn. The team was moving only twelve miles, he says, "but it might as well have been the other side of the country." What he had to sell to prospective fans was a whole new identity, a new brand. And that brand was Brooklyn.

If AT&T Stadium is a pure reflection of Cowboys ownership—and it is—Barclays Center used the Nets' new home market as its only input. It was all about Brooklyn, Brooklyn, Brooklyn—the borough, with its historical authenticity and contemporary cultural cool, as a package-able product. "That's been the epicenter of really every decision we've made, both team and arena," says Yormark. "How do you embrace Brooklyn? How do you make Brooklyn the biggest part of your identity?"

Minority Nets owner and celebrity figurehead Jay Z, who grew up in nearby Bed-Stuy, provided initial credibility for the arena. The organization also made a big deal about its local hiring practices and food program, featuring popular Brooklyn vendors. But what really set the tone, according to Yormark, was the team's first ad campaign, heading into the 2012–13 NBA season. The tagline, visible on billboards and at bus stops all around town: HELLO BROOKLYN.

It was both an introduction and a stake in the ground, as the team tried to insinuate itself into the borough. It was also barely about basketball. As Yormark puts it, they envisioned the Brooklyn Nets as a "lifestyle brand." They wanted cool kids to wear their hats and cool kids to come to their games. (Imagine the team's joy when Justin Bieber wore a HELLO BROOKLYN T-shirt on *Late Night with Jimmy Fallon* or when Jamie Foxx did the same during *Saturday Night Live* promos.) It was about becoming hip in the city's hippest borough and also possibly deflecting attention from the team's uncertain on-court product.

This lifestyle brand would permeate Barclays Center, from the nightclub vibe at the superexclusive bunker suites in the Vault, to the arena's embrace of hip-hop as soundtrack, with renowned deejay J.Period serving as musical supervisor, to a motorcycle-riding, cigar shop–owning, dreadlocked arena announcer (David Diamante), to the herringbone-patterned wood court and black and white uniforms (Jay Z has been widely credited for the team's color scheme, although Gregg Pasquarelli tells me his firm, SHoP Architects, first pushed the idea), to the clientele itself, chicly dressed in skinny jeans, beanies, peacoats, and slim puffers. It would waft through the arena like the signature scent Yormark pumps into the concourses. (He bor-rowed that idea from Disney, although the concept dates back to the Colosseum, which perfumed its air.)

The success of this branding effort—which coincided with a splashy public relations push in the lead-up to the arena's opening—came as a relief to Yormark, in part because he had spent eight years trying to convince talent agents and promotional companies that Barclays Center was "going to be this hip, cool venue that they had to be a part of," and in part because he was finally controlling the mes-sage, shifting the story from the metro pages, after a decade of local battles, to not only the sports pages but also the entertainment and business pages.

The coup de grâce came on opening night, in a moment that solidified the convergence of sports and entertainment at Barclays Center. In the first of eight sold-out concerts—all of which are now commemorated by a banner hanging from the arena rafters—Jay Z appeared on stage wearing a custom Brooklyn Nets jersey, officially unveiling the never-before-seen uniform design. "That was huge," recalls Yormark. "At that moment, he launched the Brooklyn Nets identity, and it went worldwide."

The accolades started pouring in. *The Village Voice* named Bar-clays Center best sports venue for 2012 and 2014, best stadium dining experience in 2013, and best large music venue for 2015, while *New York* magazine celebrated the arena in its annual "Reasons to Love New York" list. Big events like MTV's Video Music Awards and the NBA All-Star Weekend descended on Brooklyn, and the arena, once a PR nightmare, now seemed an unmitigated success, as Barclays Center ranked among the nation's top-grossing venues and even announced the future arrival of a new pro-team tenant in the New York Islanders.

Although critics like Oder have questioned the arena's financials, as profitability seems to be lagging behind projections, raising the point as yet another example of Barclay's behind-the-scenes murkiness, the publicity was a success. There is no question Yormark's marketing had thrived in the short term. The arena opened with a bang, and the Nets even enjoyed a few play-off seasons before returning to their losing ways. But with so much focus on being cool, could Barclays Center, like any trend, eventually go out of style? (The risk seems especially poignant in a high-metabolism city like New York, where hipness shifts shape by the hour and relevancy is a frantic hamster wheel.) One NBA executive tells me he prefers arenas that don't yell and scream at their guests. "I didn't quite get Brooklyn," he says. "We have a phrase, 'too hip for the room.' It's like they were really going to make this *über*-hip. Now the question is, Is it timeless? In ten years, are you going to go, 'Yeah, that's where the Jay Z Club *used* to be'?"

———————

Walk anywhere in or around Barclays Center, and the building's design drips with a kind of big-city cool, it's true. But achieving this trendy troposphere wasn't a given for Brooklyn's new venue, especially on the heels of our country's financial crisis.

It was the last workday before July Fourth weekend in 2009 when Gregg Pasquarelli got the call. Bruce Ratner needed an architect. The developer's partnership with Frank Gehry had fallen apart due to the recession—he could no longer afford to finance the entirety of Gehry's design, which included tall towers connected to the arena—and he was under intense pressure to deliver something of similar quality, since Gehry's design had been such a big part of the Atlantic Yards sales pitch. (Ratner's initial post-Gehry plan was to plop down a replica of Indianapolis's Conseco Fieldhouse in the middle of Brooklyn, which raised the ire of basically the entire city.) Could Pasquarelli help?

Pasquarelli had never worked on a stadium before, but he was intrigued by Ratner's only piece of direction: do something cool. The SHoP architects spent all weekend coming up with three designs, all of which Ratner loved. But none would work. Why not? That was the catch: the developer had already bought the steel (based on Conseco) and couldn't alter the interior structural design. And why had he done that? That was the other catch: if he wasn't in the ground by the end of the year, the bond financing would no longer be tax-deductible, costing him hundreds of millions. So basically, the SHoP guys surmised, Ratner wanted a skin job (i.e., an external, largely superficial design). They didn't do skin jobs. Ratner said, "No, think of it like a couture dress." To which Christopher Sharples, another partner in the firm, replied, "I think your budget only allows for a leotard." They left it at that.

But later that day, literally scribbled on a martini napkin over drinks, the architects had an idea. They called Ratner and offered to share their thoughts, but on one condition: if he liked it, they wanted the whole thing—the skin, the interior, and the public space. "The juices were flowing," says Pasquarelli, "and I think we found a way to do a skin that would not be a skin, that would become spatial and performative, and that's what made it interesting to us."

Ratner agreed. They were hired.

What the architects came up with was a facade that would fold into the building, "changing the space fundamentally." "I don't think anyone's ever made a facade like that before," says Pasquarelli. They got to work immediately, forging 11,499 individual pieces of uniquely shaped steel, weathering the metal through fifteen wet-dry cycles a day, for four months, which added ten years of rust patina. (The ribs that hold these panels tuck into the arena and become lighting pieces.) The exterior design, which also curls into an oculus above a public plaza, emphasized the horizontal aspects of the building, sinking it more naturally into the Brooklyn skyline. But while the scale-like weathered steel pays homage to the borough's postindustrial past, Pasquarelli says the design isn't nostalgic. "It's got a grittiness, but that's clearly a contemporary building."

Inside, the architects sought to resist the Conseco constrictions as much as possible. By the main entrance, they created a large open vomitory so the scoreboard could be seen from beyond the front doors, for example. More than structural changes, they wanted to create a mood. "I don't understand why so many arenas look like shitty shopping malls with all these stupid colors and all this distraction," says Pasquarelli. "The reason I love sports is because it is unscripted. You don't know what's going to happen. Our whole idea was to make it super dark." With black seats, dark gray concrete, and even painted-black steel, they envisioned, in essence, a black box theater with a basketball court as its stage.

Pasquarelli kept thinking about the old Bugs Bunny boxing cartoons, in which a small well-lit ring was at the center of a giant dark stadium. He also pulled inspiration from the nearly vertical upper deck at old Yankee Stadium, the way it held noise, with fans almost on top of the field. (In new ballparks, the upper decks are more elliptical and pushed way back, to create better views for lower-bowl patrons.) "New Yankee Stadium fucked it up, totally," says Pasquarelli, a Yankees fan. "We lost all home field advantage." (Unfortunately, at Barclays Center, the second level isn't cantilevered over the lower bowl as it was at the House That Ruth Built, and multiple levels of luxury suites push the upper deck even farther from the action so the steep seats don't feel as close as they could and instead give some people vertigo.)

All in all, Pasquarelli was thoughtful about the fan experience— the way he wanted the court to be the center of attention—since he's a fan himself. But while architects can inform, they cannot dictate. And at Barclays Center, it is often everything beyond the seating bowl on which the fans focus, like the bar scene at the arena's 40/40 Club outpost or the all-you-can-eat perk for certain ticket holders, who gorge themselves on fish tacos from Calexico, white cheddar brats from Brooklyn Bangers, hot pastrami sandwiches from David's K Deli, and much more. I have such a ticket for a game in early March (face value $125, bought online for $40) and manage to blitz my way through more than $105 worth of food, per arena prices, before wanting to unzip my pants and pass out. Sitting next to me is a father-son duo who have also made a last-minute ticket purchase. It is the son's eighteenth birthday, and they're both geeked about the lower-bowl seats. But sometime in the first quarter, they disappear, and I don't see them again until the fourth, sitting by a closing concession stand in a club area, munching burgers and fries. The father smiles sheepishly when I ask if he's been here the whole time. "Yeah, pretty much," he says.

That's the thing about the patrons at Barclays Center—for the most part, they aren't real fans yet. Even Yormark, with his slick marketing plan, knew he couldn't create diehards overnight. By definition, the Nets lifestyle brand was inorganic, a boardroom creation, and a fan base has to evolve naturally. "I often tell my ownership and my staff, we have a casual fan base. It's a new fan," says the CEO. "They expected us to proactively prompt them to cheer versus just feeling that here is the moment where the team needs you." It is getting better, he says, but it will take time. The roots need to grow on their own.

***

The Cowboys have more of what Yormark would call a "legacy fan base." And yet there is almost no home-field advantage at AT&T Stadium, either, where the game often seems secondary. Troy Aikman, the Hall of Fame former Cowboys quarterback, called out Dallas fans, saying they come "to be seen," not to cheer, viewing the games as social events. (Such a charge isn't new: Roman poets made the same point about certain spectators almost two thousand years ago.)

In other words, it is a *scene,* and not just for those folks pulling up at the valet gate. The tailgate parties outside of AT&T Stadium are like nothing I've ever seen. You'd think every Cowboys fan moonlights as a deejay, there are so many turntables and blaring speakers. Walking past a row of tailgate tents, the music seems to change by the step—classic rock, pop, electronic dance music, old-school hip-hop, new-school rap, mariachi, country. Just a crazy cocktail of sounds. And speaking of cocktails, there is former Cowboys wide receiver Roy Williams. He has a tent set up, offering free samples of his MVP Vodka.

I stop to talk to a man named Jose Olivares, entranced by his Cowboys-skinned karaoke machine, which he purchased in Monterrey, Mexico, and holds more than a million songs. Olivares, who has been coming to Cowboys games since 1984, says it never used to be like this. The new stadium has turned out a new crowd. "I feel like some of them aren't real Cowboys fans," he says. "They just come to party, you know? A lot of the youngsters."

Local good-timers aren't the only ones drawn to AT&T Stadium. "It is a big problem. We walk in, and we are like the visitors in our own home," Olivares says of the opposing fans who regularly flood the stands. Which makes sense, both because Jerry has fashioned his facility as a global destination and because the Cowboys have priced out so many former ticket holders. (Even those who can afford season tickets often look to offload their seats to make back some money.) At one point it got so bad that Tony Romo was forced to use a silent count on offense, because visiting fans were too loud. And forget any home-field edge—in its first seven seasons in the building, the team has a losing record at Jerry's World. Some Dallas devotees would probably settle for a home security system, as Cowboys fans have become assault victims in their own stadium.

According to Mario Whitmire, a former season ticket holder and the owner of Tailgate Tavern, a nearby bar that opened the same day as AT&T Stadium, there is no longer a sense of community at Cowboys games. "I had sixteen tickets together, on the fifty," he says. "I knew everybody twenty rows down and twelve seats apart on both sides. If someone missed a game, it was like, 'Oh, I hope nothing's wrong. Hope everything's all right.' That's the way it was. I'd sit on the aisle and people would walk up. 'What's up, Mario?' Shake my hand. That's the way it was."

And that was lost?

"Instantly," says Whitmire, who gave up his tickets but still occasionally attends games. "Because half of them, maybe seventy percent, didn't take their seats." It was just too expensive. In addition to the seats themselves going up in price, the Cowboys were also charging a personal seat license fee. (PSLs are licenses that fans must buy in order to gain the right to then purchase season tickets. They have become common practice across the NFL, as an additional source of stadium funding.) Whitmire's seats—some of the best in the house—would have run him $150,000 a pop, he says.

"It's a corporate deal now. You go sit in the seats, and you see different people all the time. It's all corporate, man," he says, referring both to the lack of emotion in the see-and-be-seen crowd and to the fact that so many ticket holders use the purchase as a business expense and often give their seats away. This is a lesson deMause says he's learned about new stadiums: "They aren't built to be better for fans. They're better places to sell you things, and they have a lot of stuff to sell you."

There is no doubt the fan experience is night-and-day different than it was at Texas Stadium, from the percentage of opposing fans at games to the over-the-top creature comforts to the giant video board—which folks admit they can't take their eyes off of, even as the action happens just below it—to the cutting-edge in-stadium technology. (Both AT&T Stadium and Barclays Center are considered leaders in the tech space for their extensive Wi-Fi networks, which allow for constant tweeting and snapping, and for their pioneering venue-specific apps.) According to Mark Williams, architecture firms like his are merely responding to changing generational demands. "Some people spend a *lot* of money to buy a seat and never sit in that seat," he says. A fan "may not want to see the field. He may want to be in the building. He may want to have full access on whatever handheld device he has. He may want to be in the tequila bar. That's a much different priority. So I could say that's stupid or that's genius, I don't know. What I do know is that's what people do."

But even if this is in some ways a dumbing down of the sports experience—there's a reason AT&T Stadium puts basic football rules on various screens around the stadium, under the heading "NFL 101"—and even if Jerry Jones has gone too far in the eyes of some, blurring the lines between fans and nonfans, home and away, and sports and entertainment, while shamelessly commodifying any emotional connection people may have to his team, there is no denying that the events themselves are flat-out *fun*.

At the game I attend, the Cowboys lose a close one. But you wouldn't know it from the live postgame concert in the West Plaza. In front of the stage, hometown and rival fans shake their hips to a cover version of "For the Love of Money" by the O'Jays (seriously), as marked-up booze flows from the bars behind them in the Miller Lite Corral. There a middle-aged man in a backward hat and sunglasses lightly bites his lower lip, looking for a dance partner. A younger woman, likely overserved, leans into a garbage can, holding her own hair like a champ, and vomits. Sure we lost, everyone seems to say, but why ruin the party?

Honestly, I have more fun at AT&T Stadium than at any other venue I visit (though Lambeau is close), and I think that's due in large part to the fact that the Cowboys go to such great lengths to please, whatever happens on the field. More than an hour after the game ends, the band is still rocking, and it appears the good times may last all night. No one wants to leave Jerry's World.

3
ALL THE TICKET MEN

(Or: Beyond These Walls)

O n a little patch of gray sidewalk, on the corner of East Fourth Street and Huron Road in downtown Cleveland, Ohio, directly across from Quicken Loans Arena, the ticket men are looking for business.

"Ti-*ckets*! Ti-*ckets*!"

"Guys need tickets?"

"Tickets-tickets-tickets!"

"ANYBODY SELLING TICKETS?"

Before the Cavs game, the crowd seems to be changing by the minute, a kaleidoscope of characters, and they're not just scalpers. A short man with a long gray beard, a yellow poncho, a maroon turban on top of a wool winter hat, and a digital camera and a tambourine looped around his neck, appears out of nowhere. He shakes the instrument intermittently and asks passersby to take a picture with his sign, which reads: WELCOME JIMMY DIMORA SQUARE. He explains the sign is a local political statement about recent renovations of Public Square. (The man uses the name of Jimmy Dimora, a former county commissioner serving twenty-eight years in federal prison for racketeering and other charges, to invoke the general idea of corruption.) I agree to be photographed.

Tires squealing, a T-shirt seller—a "hit-and-run guy," as such merchants are described to me, because they're more likely to be unlicensed or have knockoff gear, or both—pulls up on a bicycle, wearing at least five T's himself, with a backpack stuffed with merchandise. He starts yelling, in reference to LeBron James (aka King James), the hometown hero, "The *KING* has *reTURNED*." Another man drops a duffel bag to the pavement, unloads a handful of T-shirts, and lays them on the ground. These read: BOSTON SUCKS. (The Celtics are the Cavs' first-round opponent in the 2015 NBA play-offs.) The man repeats the phrase as a sales pitch, over and over—"Boston sucks!"—as passing fans try not to step on his wares. One young fan, wearing a visor with curly Sideshow Bob hair spilling over the brim, walks past without stopping. But to himself, he mutters, "Boston *does* suck," as though he'd never considered the possibility.

The ticket men keep up their calls, many of which I have come to learn over the past few days, each distinctive, like birds in the field—"Ti-*ckets*!"—occasionally roping a vaguely interested potential client into a tête-à-tête, with varying degrees of success. The tambourine man *shake shake shakes* as one seller, new to me—with the play-offs starting, scalpers are coming out of the woodwork—sees me writing in my notebook. He approaches. Peers over my shoulder. Says, "What are you writing, the scalping rules?"

What are they? I ask.

"Ain't none." He turns away. "Make them up as you go along."

———————

When I arrive in Cleveland, almost a week before the Cavaliers' first postseason game, I have one goal: embed with the scalpers. I don't have any local connections but am confident, heading into the NBA play-offs with the LeBron-led Cavaliers considered a favorite to win the title—and baseball season just under way—that this is the place to be. In 2015, there may not be a more tortured sports city in America, no population hungrier for a winner, as Cleveland's teams haven't captured a championship in any sport since 1964. According to Cavaliers CEO Len Komoroski, that collective memory goes deep. "The identity of Clevelanders, a large part of it, is wrapped up in their teams," he says. "This is a really hard-core fan base."

Over the past half-century, this prideful city of diehards has become the butt of the joke, and not just on the playing field, where the default mode of futility is occasionally punctuated by spectacular failures, as heartbreaking as they are legendary. In the 1980s, there was "Red Right 88," "The Drive," and "The Fumble," all shorthand terms for devastating play-off losses by the Browns. In 1997, in the bottom of the ninth inning of the seventh game of the World Series, the Indians held a one-run lead—and blew it. Even worse, that loss came on the heels of Browns owner Art Modell doing the unthinkable, absconding to Baltimore with his football team, betraying an entire city. And in 2010, it was like a bad acid flashback when LeBron James, the best player in basketball—who grew up in nearby Akron, Ohio, no less—went on national television and told the world he was heading to Miami, to South Beach, ditching his hometown for greater glory in sunnier climes.

Cleveland is used to such kicks in the nuts. As its sports teams came up short, so did the city itself, suffering through decades of postindustrial decline, job loss, and depopulation. For years, downtown was dominated by the asphalt graveyards of surface parking lots, with the occasional wig shop and prostitute along the main drags. The Cuyahoga River that snakes through town is the same body of water that was so polluted it famously caught fire in 1969 (not the only time, by the way), cementing the city's reputation as "The Mistake By the Lake."

In a dying city, there is little reason for optimism, but a hard kernel of hope persists. Such is the blessing—and the curse—of being a sports fan, when you can always wait till next year.

In 2014, it seemed like that next year was imminent. After a four-year absence, during which time scorned locals watched LeBron win two rings for another city, the King announced he was coming home, thrusting Cleveland back into the national spotlight. Cavs season tickets flew off the shelves, while breathless (and dubious) estimates claimed LeBron's return would mean $500 million a year to the local economy.

It was the LeBron Effect, they said. LeConomics! The LeBronomy!

The excitement climaxed in late October, at the season opener, LeBron's welcome home party. The downtown streets flooded with fans, as scalpers sold pairs of lower-bowl seats for $5,000 and asked upward of $600 apiece for nosebleeds. Sean O'Donnell, the general manager of Flannery's, an Irish pub with sightlines of Quicken Loans Arena, says that night was one of three times in his two decades at the bar that he was scared to be working. "You couldn't drive down the street," he says. "It was pandemonium."

It is the same impulse that led title-starved fans to fill the Indians' home ballpark, Progressive Field (then called Jacobs Field), for 455 consecutive sellouts, from 1995 to 2001.

Given a reason to believe, this city doesn't hold back.

———

"Are you going to interview the undercovers, too?" veteran street vendor Tom McCarthy asks, nodding toward the newly renovated plaza outside the center-field gates of Progressive Field.

We are standing at the corner of East Ninth Street and Bolivar Road, by McCarthy's merch station, a sanctioned sidewalk outfit held together by bungee cords and metal spring clamps, basically kitty corner to the stadium, in the hours before a mid-April Indians game. Ticket scalpers flutter up and down the block, as I strain to identify the cops. Where are they? I ask.

"Oh, come on," he says, unable to believe I'm so green.

McCarthy has allowed me to fall in with his crew, which deals in hats, T's, hoodies, peanuts, water, and pistachios, for my first two days in Cleveland, but he's perhaps questioning if I have what it takes to make it on the streets.

"You're going to get a demerit."

Point them out, I say.

"No, I can't."

McCarthy's peanut seller, a guy named Art with shaggy brown hair and varying levels of enthusiasm, says, "They're coming over." I spot them now, the undercovers—off-duty Cleveland police officers employed by the Indians—one in black, one in red. As they cross the street, the scalpers, who aren't allowed to sell tickets this close to the stadium, scatter like pigeons.

Not that there is much business to be had. It is only the second home series of the baseball season, and while opening day—a veritable city holiday—sold out in eleven minutes, interest has dried up. The team is off to a horrid start, and foot traffic in Cleveland's Gateway District, which contains both Quicken Loans Arena and Progressive Field—the two venues only a block apart—is slow.

Whatever the crowds, McCarthy is always here, always on this corner.

In his mid-forties, the vendor resembles a young Gene Wilder, with hair shooting out from either side of his head and eyes that turn on like a lightbulb. Despite a slightly impish personality—he's a ballbuster—McCarthy is no clown. For twenty-one years, he's worked every Indians home game, occasionally forced to protect his turf, a prime piece of stadium-adjacent real estate. One summer about five years ago, he lived here in a motor home, taking day trips to the southern suburbs to visit his wife and twin toddlers.* "I heard things," he says of potential encroachments to his corner location. "I wasn't going to let it happen. Twenty-one years I've been here."

Over that time, McCarthy has become part of the game-day tapestry, just like Phil Priester, the hot dog guy on East Ninth who staked his spot years before the ballpark opened, and the horn musicians across the street, now blowing "Take Me Out to the Ball Game" on repeat. "People walking by only hear it once," McCarthy says of the tune, shaking his head. "But when you're sitting here and you hear it for an hour and a half?" The vendor makes a gun of his thumb and forefinger and blows his brains out.

Neither is McCarthy a fan of the hit-and-run guys. His crew offers only officially licensed products. Other street merchants may have a mix of legit gear and knockoffs, but that is a risk, since Homeland Security comes sniffing around on occasion, checking for counterfeits, which they seize. "Doesn't help my cause," McCarthy sighs. His objection isn't on ethical grounds; their shadiness simply makes his shadiness look bad. "Running a nice little operation, nice and clean," he says, hand to heart, then reconsiders: "Well, maybe not *one hundred* percent clean."

Talking to fans is the fun part of the job, per McCarthy. He loves haggling, always willing to cut a deal, hoping to win repeat customers. This strategy jibes with his overall philosophy of building allies, developing relationships with other regulars beyond the walls, like the traffic controllers who rest at his stand, and Brickstone Tavern, a neighboring bar that opens its bathroom to McCarthy and his men— a vital resource for a street-side operation. "I figure it's better to have people on your side than people against you," McCarthy says as we

---

* McCarthy has a license to sell near the stadium, but only those with permits for East Ninth Street specifically have protected spots. Everyone else is first-come, first-served, and he technically sets up on Bolivar.

drag a ticketless fan toward a thickly built scalper named Big Mike, no officers in sight.*

"Hey, Mike," McCarthy calls out. "You have a single?"

Big Mike looks up, recognizes the fan, pale skin and red beard. "I talked to him already," he says. "He could have had one."

McCarthy makes a face. "What do you mean? Give him one. Give him the one in the front row."

Big Mike doesn't budge. "I talked to him already."

For all his years in the business, McCarthy says the most valuable lessons he's learned about negotiation have come not from the streets but from watching reality television, shows like *Pawn Stars* and *Storage Wars*. He says the key is to negotiate from power, not pride. "These people out here, they want to make it a game of ego," he says of the fans. "Like, 'I'm smarter than you.' I've seen people walk away from a deal over a dollar, because they want to make it a pissing contest."

McCarthy tries to cajole his friend, while sounding sympathetic to the fan. "Maybe he'll buy something another day, man, all right?"

Big Mike acquiesces, hands over a ticket.

"All right!" says McCarthy.

But Big Mike isn't pleased. "Next time turn the lights on before you *fuck* me," he shouts to the customer, who hurries away with a cheap ticket and a very punch-able grin.

———

The basics of scalping are fairly simple—just buying and selling. All across the country, the ticket game is pretty much the same, as Mike and a scalper named Nook explain to me. Guys show up

---

* While McCarthy tries to keep any involvement he may have in the ticket game under wraps, the undercovers clearly suspect he is running some sort of sideline. At one point, I follow the cops into Brickstone as they post up at a window, pointing at McCarthy. The vendor is delighted to hear that I spied on his behalf. He hands me his card. "Call me next time, man! They've been itching to get me."

at sports stadiums and concert venues without tickets but with wads of cash (ideally) and possibly a hand-drawn cardboard sign scrawled with the universal scalper message: "I Need Tickets." "You might buy a ticket at $150 and sell at $175," says Nook, or you might buy five seats for twenty bucks and flip them for ten apiece. As one scalper told me earlier, "Sometimes you can make more money when it's bad." It's all about working the margins. "It's like the stock market," Nook says, rubbing the scruff on his face. But it's a commodity with a shelf life. "When you don't sell it, you bought that ticket forever."*

Ticket scalping isn't a new trend in the United States. In *Sports Spectators*, Allen Guttmann describes such street-level sellers outside a 1908 regatta in Poughkeepsie, New York, while author Kerry Segrave explains in *Ticket Scalping: An American History, 1850–2005* that the term dates back even further, to the nascency of American railroads, when semi-used tickets would be pawned off at reduced rates. Big Mike is fifty-seven. His scalping career began more than two decades ago in Atlanta, where he lived for a time (and where his daughter and grandchild still live), when a stranger passed him an extra World Series ticket, before the Braves took on the Blue Jays. Mike sold that ticket for two hundred dollars and was hooked. "I gotta do this again!" he remembers thinking. Nook is thirty-four and a sometimes scalper. (He also works construction.) He started coming down to Indians games in 1999, but only to watch the others hustle, since reselling tickets was then outlawed in Cleveland and could lead to jail time.†

---

* In Boston, around Fenway Park, where I also spend time with scalpers, they call this "grinding." My main contact there, a thirty-year scalping vet named Jimmy Downs, tells me the key is doing volume—just buying and selling, buying and selling—never falling in love with a single seat or holding on to a ticket for too long.

† There is no federal law against scalping. Regulations are state by state and can on occasion seem bizarrely antiquated. In Indiana, for instance, it is illegal to charge more than face value for any boxing or unarmed sparring match, while Wisconsin prohibits profiteering from events at its state-fair park. In Ohio, it is up to municipalities to regulate or ban the practice. Change came to Cleveland in December 1999, when then–

Still, he couldn't believe how much money the sellers were pulling in. "They were getting fifty, a hundred fifty, two hundred dollars a ticket," he says. According to Mike, the Indians' sellout streak was the halcyon days for Cleveland scalping, when he'd make five hundred dollars on a bad night.

Of course, some bad nights can be worse than others.

Nook says his worst came in June 2000, during an early foray into the ticket business (he decided to get in the game not long after it became semilegal), when he dropped $450 for fifty Indians tickets and couldn't move a single seat. That wasn't nearly as bad as Mike's worst night. He lost a thousand dollars at a college football game, which would be bad enough. The kicker was, he drove to Atlanta expecting a bonanza. He was so pissed, he didn't even stick around to see his family. "It's like I drove, threw out a thousand dollars, drove right home," Mike recalls. "It was a *long* twelve hours back."

Road trips are actually a great way to hunt for profit, since a scalper can always chase big events around the country, especially during the winter months, when things dry up in Cleveland. Some guys follow concerts or hit up boxing matches in Vegas. During college bowl season, Mike loves cruising the southeast, while the NFL play-offs offer another favorite stretch of fertile games.

On such trips, scalpers often travel in groups, splitting gas and other costs. Mike tells me about the time he and two other local guys were heading east for a play-off game between the Pittsburgh Steelers and New England Patriots. It was the middle of the night, and

---

city councilman Michael O'Malley saw cops seize his friend's extra Browns tickets because he was trying to sell them cheaply before a game. O'Malley proposed new legislation, adopted in April 2000, that made reselling tickets at or below face value kosher in Cleveland. The ordinance has since changed. Now scalpers can resell tickets for any price but must do so within designated "permissive" zones. The zones were established in 2008, to counteract what the city believed were "aggressive sales tactics" on the part of scalpers, and to discourage "sidewalk turf disputes," which Big Mike and others tell me had a tendency to turn violent.

they were in a rental car, the only licensed driver taking a nap in the backseat, when a police cruiser going the opposite direction pulled a one-eighty on the highway, sirens screaming. Frantic, the scalpers roused the licensed driver, a dude named Sheets, who is not a small man. With sleep in his eyes, Sheets squeezed into the front seat, just in time to pull to the side of the road. The cop strolled up, shined a light in his face. Said, "You know how fast you were going?"

Sheets said, "No."

Which was the truth. But still—Mike nearly lost it. "Sheets gonna say no!"

Somehow the cop was cool. He leaned into the car, and said, "Look, I don't know which one of y'all was driving, but *he* wasn't driving. Just slow down."

This past winter Mike says he was planning to spend the cold months in Atlanta, logging some quality time with his grandkid. Instead he stayed in Cleveland, parking his Lexus, a 1990 model with 317,000 miles, on the snowy streets. (After the incident with Sheets, Mike took his road test.) And all because of one man: LeBron James.

"When he announced he was coming back," says Mike, "I was like, I *got* to stay. I'm thinking new Lexus. Seriously! Buying a new house. I'm thinking it'll be that big."

———

Even if the return of LeBron James isn't worth $500 million a year to the local economy—and it's not*—it is amazing how much one man can mean to a city.

Consider the scene when he went to Miami in 2010: distraught

---

* Economist Victor Matheson has called this "the worst economic-impact estimate ever," since the figure failed to account for any kind of substitution effect, assuming it would all be *new* money, and that initial spending in and around the arena caused by LeBron's return would then also be re-spent within the Cleveland region, for a multiplier effect.

fans on the streets, burning his jersey, number twenty-three. That happened right outside Flannery's, on the corner of Prospect Avenue and East Fourth Street, the pub's general manager tells me. He compares the emotional experience to having your girlfriend leave you, as the city suffered a collective loss of confidence, chased by depression spiked with rage. "That whole next week," he says, "everyone was just moping around."

It was the inverse when LeBron returned—jubilation. And many folks did indeed have dollar signs in their eyes. The Cavaliers organization, for one, is directly enriched by him, as attendance returns to capacity levels, sponsorship deals soar, jersey sales skyrocket, and the team threatens to go deep into the play-offs. Online ticket brokers like Mark Klang of Amazing Tickets stand to benefit, as do the brokers on the street, the scalpers like Big Mike, who were expecting a serious payday—if not a total return to the cash-printing days of the Indians' streak. Remembering how business fell off when LeBron left, Mike says, "Bad isn't the word. It was terrible!"*

The bars and restaurants and T-shirt shops in the immediate vicinity of the arena have also seen profits rise, as crowds returned to the area. Flannery's has been nearly doubling its staff on game nights, while nearby bar owners have reported game night revenue jumps between 30 and 200 percent over the previous season. In this way, there is no doubt that, whatever the actual number of new dollars LeBron brings to Cleveland's economy (and that number is not zero), he profoundly impacts spending choices, redistributing money toward downtown, toward the Gateway District.

---

* For local scalpers, LeBron has been a reliable source of income since his high school days, Mike tells me, when tickets to the teen sensation's varsity basketball games could fetch up to a hundred dollars.

To truly understand the economic landscape of downtown Cleveland, we need to rewind to 1990. That was when Cleveland's Gateway project, which aimed to revitalize a jigsaw-shaped piece of the city via the simultaneous construction of a new ballpark and arena, was pitched to the public. At the time, the would-be district had no housing units, no hotel rooms, and only six full-service restaurants.

Tom Chema, who served as executive director of the Gateway Economic Development Corporation, a nonprofit created to oversee the project—a project largely funded by a countywide sin tax*—says the original idea was simply to save the Indians, who were threatening to skip town. The concept of a sports complex that interacts with a wider district emerged only out of political necessity, a ploy to garner support, but it was a happy accident. "The objective of the way we put this together," Chema tells me over lunch at Flannery's, now devoid of burning jerseys, "was to integrate the buildings into the fabric of the city, not to have them be some destination, so they cause people to spend some of their money outside the four walls of the buildings. That was all very intentional. But it was an evolutionary intentionality."

Since the sports complex opened in 1994, the formerly derelict district has changed dramatically. East Fourth Street is a bustling brick-paved block jam-packed with bars, restaurants, coffee shops, and more. The city's historic arcades are once again showing signs of life. Both within Gateway and beyond, downtown is enjoying a residential boom, with an occupancy rate over 97 percent. Many stadium advocates point to Cleveland as an early model of how a city can successfully weave sports facilities into rundown areas, sparking revitalization. Even stadium-critical economists don't dispute that this can be an effective strategy, so long as it is done intention-

---

* The sin tax, it ought to be noted, was voted in by the suburbs, against the wishes of city residents.

ally. In this way, stadiums can be useful political instruments when included in larger development plans, according to Stanford's Roger Noll, especially in cities that could use a boost. "Having the government commit successfully to a twenty-year redevelopment project is a considerable political accomplishment," he says, "and including sports will get you twenty to twenty-five percent of the electorate. It adds to the coalition."

Still, Matheson says folks must not confuse local neighborhood effects, which can occur, as they have in Cleveland, through targeted revitalization efforts, with region-wide economic development.* It is why he lambasted the $500 million estimate. Likewise, *Field of Schemes* coauthor Neil deMause says it is worth considering how much credit stadiums and their tenants deserve in terms of revitalization (because they will claim all of it), when they are planted in already up-and-coming neighborhoods, as happened in Brooklyn with Barclays Center and in Denver with Coors Field.

According to Tom Yablonsky, executive vice-president of the Downtown Cleveland Alliance and perhaps the person most responsible for the city's housing boom, it is important to take a longer view of downtown Cleveland as well. As far back as 1985, Yablonsky was championing historic adaptive reuse as a tool for redevelopment, focusing at first on the Warehouse District, which served as a template for areas around the new sports venues.† In other words, he says, downtown was on the way up, and Gateway accelerated an ongoing process.

John Grabowski, a history professor at Case Western Reserve

---

* Cuyahoga County is still paying the debt service on Gateway and will be doing so into the foreseeable future.

† While the Gateway Corporation anticipated being left with a moderate endowment for additional economic development projects, the group was forced to drain its funds as a result of cost overruns, thus making Yablonsky's tax-incentivizing efforts all the more vital.

University, also gives credit to the Gateway facilities for anchoring the city's renewed focus on downtown. He is undecided, however, as to whether the project has proven to be a good thing for Cleveland at large. "Is it lifting all boats? I don't know. I'd argue it requires more nuance," he says, conceding that it has done wonders for Cleveland's image, from a public relations perspective. Grabowski also admits it might not be bad for local citizens, so conditioned to Cleveland's unique brand of pessimistic failure, to see their city making such an investment, taking a big swing. "People need entertainment and people need something to believe in," he says. "However fictive it might be in terms of its economic impact, it embodies some degree of loyalty to a community, some degree of hope."

This season, LeBron's first back in Cleveland, there has been no shortage of hope, and no shortage of demand. The Cavaliers even instituted a monthly lottery, holding back individual game tickets, in an attempt to cut out speculation. Some call this a war on brokers (although such an effort is probably overstated, as the team continues to work with ticket men like Mark Klang, rewarding the loyalty of those who stuck it out through the lean years). Unfortunately for Big Mike and others of his ilk, the street ticket business ain't what it used to be, in spite of the Cavs season opener, which Mike calls "the biggest ticket in Cleveland history."

In 2010, the year LeBron left, it was estimated that 60 to 70 percent of the secondary ticket market in America—an industry now valued around five billion dollars—existed in front of event venues. By 2015, that number had dipped to 15 or 20 percent, as sites like StubHub exploded, redefining the ticket resale experience, while turning average fans into amateur brokers. (StubHub, specifically, grew 30 to 40 percent year over year from 2010 to 2013, according to Glenn Lehrman, a company spokesperson.)

Outside Quicken Loans Arena, where I meet Big Mike for game one of the Cavs-Celtics series, a Sunday afternoon affair, the talk isn't so much about StubHub as it is about Flash Seats, the team's proprietary digital ticketing platform that blends the primary and secondary markets. (Flash Seats is part of Veritix, a Dan Gilbert–owned company.) Here is how it works: To buy tickets, a fan must first have a Flash Seats account. On game day, ticket holders swipe a unique form of ID to get into the building. The fan is then issued a seat locator, as she enters. Should a fan want to resell her ticket, she can do so within Flash Seats' secondary marketplace—essentially the team's own StubHub. For the current season, Cavs CEO Len Komoroski says the team achieved 95 percent digital adoption, and they expect to have all paper tickets off the street by next year, which is bad news for scalpers.

From the Cavs' perspective, going digital has many benefits, from eliminating will call to thwarting broker bots that buy up tickets the instant they go on sale, thus elbowing out real fans, to monitoring secondary-market activity, on the lookout for unapproved resellers. The Golden State Warriors have a similar system in place, in partnership with Ticketmaster and its secondary platform, Ticket Exchange. But such environments can be monopolistic, or so alleged a 2015 lawsuit by StubHub against the Warriors, especially when fans are forbidden to post extras elsewhere or risk having their ticket privileges revoked. Lehrman says StubHub could have gone after the Cavs instead of the Warriors, although they're hoping the Cleveland marketplace will open up following the 2015 merger of Outbox AXS—which is the ticketing platform for AEG (a StubHub partner)—and Veritix.

The StubHub lawsuit was ultimately dismissed, but to many fans there is a general ickiness to the idea that a team can control both primary and secondary markets. Beyond the fact that it gives teams the power to create false demand—whether they do this or not, folks are suspicious—it feels like double-dipping, as teams take hefty fees on secondary market transactions.

Like a handful of other scalpers, Big Mike has a Flash Seats account. He simply operates within the system. To avoid fees, he still buys extras on the street—or in advance, through his Rolodex of clients—but instead of sending payment online, he deals in cash, transferring tickets from the sellers' accounts to his own. (Fans can transfer tickets as often as they want.) Next, a Cavs employee—an inside man—prints yet-to-be-used seat locators from the box office and brings them to Mike outside the arena. The locators can then be sold, just like paper tickets. (At first, Mike was going to the box office himself, but he got tired of being written up for trespassing.) Guys like Nook, who don't have an account, are cut out of the Flash Seats loop. Instead they can "middle"—essentially act as a middleman— by connecting ticket-hungry fans with scalpers holding seats. After a successful transaction, the scalper tips out the middleman. Or not. And a fight ensues.

None of the ticket men, even those with accounts, have much love for Flash Seats, which makes street sales that much harder, or for Cavs owner Dan Gilbert, who they call the biggest scalper of all.

According to an aggrieved hustler named Paul, "Motherfucker is a crook!"

———

With about three hours until tip-off, there is a surprising stillness in the Cleveland streets. Ticket sellers outnumber fans on this side of the arena. (On the other side, the Cavs are throwing an official pregame party, featuring a concert stage, carnival games, and beer trucks.) The scalpers hover in and around the zone, looking listless, like zombies, until fans appear. Then they come to life, all shouting at once, occasionally charging up the block to intercept any potential customers, looking over their shoulders to see if the undercovers are watching.

In general, the relationship between the scalpers and the under-covers seems well established and (for the most part) amiable. The cops yell at the sellers to keep the sidewalks clear, as the scalpers push the boundaries of the zone, seeing how far they can go. (Serious violations result in misdemeanors.) As the fans start rolling in, an undercover passes through the zone. He says to the ticket men, "No breaks today, just so you know."

An alpha in the hustler hierarchy, a big man named Bill, shouts right back, "Might as well handcuff me now, because you *know* I ain't going to stay in the zone."

The undercover stops walking. Turns to Bill. "Would you like to make a couple sales first? Or you don't want none? It will happen."

"I'm just giving you the heads-up," he says, nonchalant. "I'm *not* staying in the zone, so you might as well take me now."

"Okay," says the undercover. "So we catch you, then you go."

"When you catch me, I go." Bill nods.

"You go."

It is agreed, and the cop moves along.

―――――

In reality, Bill isn't going anywhere, not with business so slow. Even as energy picks up closer to tip-off, with fans literally hanging out the windows of nearby bars like Flannery's and Harry Buffalo—even as the tambourine man shows up, along with the hit-and-run guys—tickets just aren't moving.

The first round of the play-offs is never a big earner, Mike says. It's the later rounds when scalpers can make serious scratch. Still, today is worse than anticipated. It's like fans were expecting an expensive ticket and therefore stayed away. The vultures start to circle. Vultures like John, a hobbyist broker, dressed in a *Field & Stream* pullover. He stands to the side, monitoring the online Flash Seats market on his phone, waiting for the scalpers to lower their prices.

He tells me the street market can crash close to game time, when sellers must decide whether to unload their tickets cheaply, or eat them. (Many opt to eat them, preferring to price-enforce rather than devalue their product.)

A bit of a voyeur, John likes watching the scalpers work. He gets a rush buying off the street, treating the sidewalk like an Arab souk. "I don't want to pay more than twenty-five dollars," he says, citing the online price, right around forty dollars, with ninety minutes till tip-off. But for now, the street market stands its ground. Scalpers want seventy dollars for uppers. Vulture John must wait.

———————

Among the couple dozen scalpers out for today's game: Donald Biggins, who tells frequent stories of his childhood friend Steve Harvey; El Rasheen Dozier, who is concerned I might misspell his name; Big Mike's brother Garland, aka G; a nattily dressed scalper named Mark, wearing a sweater vest and Bluetooth earpiece; and a veteran who goes by Downtown Ronnie and tells me most scalpers are suckers. "You can tell them Downtown Ronnie said that," he says as he steps out of the zone and heads toward the arena, looking neither way to cross the street.

Kenneth Taylor is another top-of-the-food-chain scalper, like Bill. He wants me to know that he's famous, from appearances in *Draft Day* and a documentary called *Losing LeBron*. He insists that I Google his name. "Put that in your phone. Kenneth S. Taylor," he says. Such Internet searches are how he seals the deal on sales, since most people's main concern when buying tickets in the street is that they could be fake. "Everybody always say, we don't know who we buying from. Just put my name in Google. It's the worldwide web! So it's legitimate."

Mike tells me that counterfeit tickets are almost never a problem in Cleveland, since scalpers don't want to shit where they eat. Issues arise during big events, like the NBA finals and the NCAA tournament, when out-of-towners pour in looking for a quick buck. Police confirm that it is outsiders who are likely to pass off bad tickets. For this reason, a contingent of local scalpers, led by Big Mike, are working on a proposal to City Hall that would require all street brokers to acquire a license, so fans know from whom they are buying. As Kenneth says, trust is paramount. And a single bad experience can hurt all their bottom lines. It is why they will even turn in their own, as they did with El Rasheen, when Kentucky was in town for the NCAA tournament last month. "He sold counterfeits," Mike says. "Because we usually right here, right? He was on Ninth and Carnegie, past Tom [McCarthy]'s stand, way over there. So the guy in the orange [Kenneth] happened to see him way over there. We told the cops on him."*

As with any underground business, there are going to be some unsavory characters. "You see him?" Mike says, pointing at a scalper, a regular, who has a box cutter hanging from his pants pocket. "He killed three people. Even my brother been in prison—but no violent crimes. There was one dude, vehicular homicide. He was high. This one right here, in the gray, child molester."

Because of a criminal record, a habit of some kind, or the simple fact of being out of the documented workforce for an inexplicable amount of time, many of these men see selling tickets as the best—and maybe only—way to make a living. Indeed, scalping seems to be a catchall occupation for those who've washed to the margins of society, either by action or by accident. It's a job that requires a lone wolf mentality. And with money on the line, conflict can occur. Mike tells

---

* El Rasheen also got in trouble for selling fakes in Pittsburgh, in 2008. And in 2014, Bill was found guilty of "theft by deception" after hawking bad tickets at Ohio State. But scalpers aren't the only ones with blood on their hands. Oftentimes they wind up on the wrong side of a rotten deal, like when Nook unknowingly acquires a used ticket before the play-off game and then has to refund the man who buys it from him.

me about the time a scalper took a swing at a fan. At another game, Sheets had an argument with a potential customer that ended when he got hit in the face with his own cane. There aren't a lot of robberies, but they can happen. Nook was recently held up at gunpoint, and believes he knows which scalper set him up.

With certain sellers, a level of menace can underscore some of their interactions. Like when two frat-brother types approach Bill and ask what their tickets are worth.

"You selling?" he asks.

"No, just curious," they respond.

"Well, Curious George fell off his bike and broke his neck."

"Just asking," the bros say, scurrying away.

"And I told you."

Big Mike scans the sluggish scalping scene, about an hour before tip-off. He says guys are more apt to act erratic when things are slow. Before one Indians game, he tells me, when no one was buying, a single man came looking for a ticket. "About ten scalpers started running at him, and he turned around and ran." Mike giggles, still in disbelief. "He got scared. The man ran! I guess he thought they were coming to jump him."

———

I begin to understand the danger and desperation that can exist on the streets after the last Cavs game of the regular season. That's when I hang with Maurice Reedus Jr., a local legend better known as Sax Man, who sets up his amp on a walkway between Huron and Prospect. A staple of the Cleveland scene since 1996, when he started performing downtown, Reedus is the reason other musicians, like those outside Progressive Field, are able to play for tips: the Street Performers Ordinance, i.e., the "Sax Man Legislation," passed in 2013, stopped cops from hassling street buskers.

Aside from complaining about Cavs fans' lack of appreciation for music, the sixty-two-year-old Reedus is pretty sanguine. "I'll come downtown when ain't nobody here. It ain't about no money," he says, putting his lips to his horn, beginning a rendition of the jazz standard "Misty."

Moving on, I talk to a postgame hustler in the roses racket—he attempts to guilt passing fans into buying flowers for their dates. He asks why I'm taking notes. I tell him.

"There's too many people on this block," Roses says, looking at his competition: merchants with sacks of glow sticks, vuvuzelas, and other cheap plastic crap; promoters handing out free admission cards to a gentlemen's club called Diamonds. There is something aggressive about this guy, his demeanor. Roses has a scraggly gray beard and booze on his breath. "There are too many people here, but I'm still going to try. I'm the best of the best," he says.

Roses doesn't do well.

"Roses, roses! *Fresh roses!* How many roses do you need?"

He is practically shouting. His movements are jerky as he chases after fans in the yellow glow of parking lot lamps, or backpedals to stay in front of potential customers on the sidewalk. But no one wants a flower. He comes back. Tells me he's homeless. Tells me how brutal life on the streets can be—how a guy he knew froze to death this winter, "sitting on some steps, drinking a pint of wine." He is no longer optimistic that he's going to sell much of anything tonight, and the reality is starting to sink in.

Roses reaches into his pocket and pulls out a knife, a gleam in his eye. "This is cutthroat, man," he says, slurring his words, inches from my ear. "This is about who's eating good, who's drinking good, and who's sleeping on the street. Friendship? He said it's about friendship?"

I'm not sure to whom he's referring, but I nod along.

"Nah. Cutthroat. He comes over and does this—"

Roses slides his knife along my back, holds it there. He is giving off a last-grizzly-before-winter sort of vibe, desperate. But I know he's telling the truth. Telling his truth. In this moment, I think about what Cleveland State University professor emeritus Dennis Keating calls the "dual city": a place where stadium-centric downtowns thrive, along with white-collar areas, while lower-income neighborhoods don't grow, left to wither and die. I think about how this might apply to Cleveland, where the school system is crumbling, where the poverty rate is 36 percent, and where more than half the adult population isn't working.* New stadiums don't create divided societies, I know, but I wonder to what extent such choices exacerbate these conditions (while also sweeping them under the rug)—to what extent they factor into the life of a man who sells flowers on the street, or one who decides ticket scalping is the best way to make a living. I think about all this with a knife to my back.

Roses laughs. "Write that down," he says. "That's serious."

———

With about thirty minutes till tip-off of game one, things start to pick up for the scalpers, a last-minute semirush. The ticket men hustle to flip as many seats as possible, trying to convince buyers that the market is burning. Mike, too, is in full sales mode: "Sir, you guys need tickets?"

Vulture John is circling, but the scalpers are still not willing to come down to his price point, to play his game of chicken. I witness a few sales, like when a middleman named Steve walks into the zone with a buyer in tow and announces, "He wants two for a hundred." (Though Steve often works with Mike, another scalper steps in and completes the sale, accepting cash for seat locators. Mike sees, isn't

---

* Really, the city's dualistic nature may have been captured perfectly by *The New York Times*, which named Cleveland to its list of "places to go" in 2015, then the country's most distressed city barely a year later. See "52 Places to Go in 2015," *New York Times*, January 11, 2015; and Karl Russell, "In an Improving Economy, Places in Distress," *New York Times*, February 24, 2016.

pleased, and screams, "Steve!") But it isn't enough to make up for the day's lack of action.

With ten minutes to go, Bill says, "This shit ain't selling!"

The market is flooded.

Three o'clock comes and goes. The streets get quiet.

Sheets is muttering about how dead it is. Mark holds his head in his hands. Big Mike offers me a ticket and tells me to go in, to enjoy the game. He'll try to join me, he says. "I'm stuck with tickets. I'll be out here awhile."

At this point, guys are fighting for scraps, and tensions run high. Bill and another scalper start jawing at each other. The cops come over. Say, "Can't we just be nice?"

One scalper jokingly tries to sell to the undercovers. At 3:18 p.m., another says, "Why we standing out here? It's over."

The cops seem to agree. Ready to head inside.

Before they leave, the cops put Bill in charge.

———

Cops weren't always so cordial with the ticket men in Cleveland, especially when scalping was outright illegal. That was when police held all the power. When they could throw on the cuffs, turn a blind eye, or demand a piece of the action.

Big Mike used to have an arrangement with a local officer who would confiscate tickets from Indians fans trying to offload extras and pass them his way, for a cut. (Phil the hot dog guy tells me a similar story about how, before he had his own cart, he used to get kicked out of the municipal lot by one cop during Browns games whenever his employer's envelope wasn't thick enough.) This isn't just a Cleveland phenomenon. In Buffalo, Mike says he and his brother were blatantly shaken down for a hundred dollars, a so-called tariff to work in a policeman's area. Meanwhile officers in St. Louis were recently busted for using seized World Series tickets.

Both Mike and Nook tell me Chicago is a scary place to scalp, because the cops are vicious. ("Wrong place to hustle, bro," says Nook.) But the most stories of police corruption and brutality come in Boston, where I spend a week with the hustlers at Fenway Park. Unlike Cleveland, there are no restricted zones here, and scalpers float around the stadium, haunting every nook and cranny and alley of the area's irregular streetscape. On Brookline Avenue, between Yawkey Way and the bridge that cuts over the Massachusetts Turnpike, I meet a hulking ticket man named Jimmy Downs, with gray-white hair sticking out the sides of his Red Sox cap. He has been scalping since 1985, when he was fifteen, along with his buddy John Green, aka Greeno, a short wiry guy with a thick Dorchester accent.*

Before 2000, scalping was illegal in Boston, as it was in Cleveland, and in those years Jimmy says he was arrested about twenty times. Greeno has lost count. The last time he was booked, he says, it took the precinct fifteen minutes to print out his rap sheet. "The booking guy came back, like, 'Jesus! What the fuck did you do?'" The scalpers wouldn't do jail time; it was just a fine.

But the real punishment came in the streets. "They'd jump out of nowhere and tackle you," Jimmy says of the old undercover cops, his voice low and gravelly. "I used to hide tickets in the sole of my shoe. It was so dangerous. Cops would search you, and if you had them in your pocket, you'd get arrested. So you'd hide them, you know? Have them down your pants and everything, but they'd go down there, looking around."

"It was really cat and mouse," Greeno remembers. "They'd be hiding on rooftops. They went to great lengths to get us. It was crazy."

And when they caught you, there was hell to pay.

"They beat the shit out of us," explains a scalper named Charlie,

---

* Greeno insists that if I quote him on only one thing, it is this: "Mark Wahlberg is a scumbag."

who started out here in the early 1980s. "I have a scar on my neck from fighting with three of them in old Kenmore Square. They body-slammed me."

A uniformed cop once cracked Jimmy in the mouth with his walkie-talkie, he tells me, breaking his front tooth. He wasn't even selling, just hanging out in a nearby parking lot. After the assault, the cop went, "*Get the fuck outta here!*" Jimmy remembers. "I go to walk away. He goes, *Run!*"

"They were just animals," Jimmy adds. "Back in the day, it was a shadowy business. It happened in the shadows, and they would fuck with us. They had no problem just hitting us. They had that power, and they took advantage of it."

The cops knew the hustlers had no recourse—they couldn't go to the press or to the courts. "If you busted their balls and brought them in on a trial, you'd never work out here again," says Greeno. "Back in the eighties—'85 to '95, them ten years—cops were corrupt out here."

"They were so corrupt," says Jimmy.

One officer, Jimmy charges, had interests in certain sausage carts around the ballpark and would chase off all the others. Jimmy claims the same cop had a partnership in a nearby liquor store as well. The cop would confiscate merchandise from vendors and sell it out of his own store. Everyone knew what was going on, Jimmy says. The cops weren't subtle. It was good old Boston arrogance. They would shake down bars and nightclubs for cash—in 1988, seven officers were convicted of extorting such bribes around Fenway—and rip off tickets from scalpers, handing them over to a couple hustlers who worked under their protection.

It was rough, but it was worth it, especially for teenagers, who were suddenly making fast money, pulling down six figures a year. Fenway was always reliable, and the Larry Bird Celtics offered a cash cow through winter. "Then came the drugs, the gambling, the broads," says Greeno. "We were fucking rock stars for like twenty years. Piss through your money. Think it will never end. Going out, make a thousand a night, blow it, wake up broke, and do it again."

But those nights are over.

It all started to unravel on April 10, 2000, when an injunction came down against the city, following the July 1999 scalping arrest of a veterinarian who was trying to unload his extras and subsequently sued the city. As a result of that suit, which challenged the idea that individuals couldn't resell their own seats, the law was changed so that tickets could be resold at face value or less. Cops could still arrest legitimate hustlers, but for all intents and purposes, scalping became legal. That opened the floodgates, as wannabe scalpers, previously scared to wind up in cuffs, flocked to Fenway. The cops didn't bother the hustlers anymore. They cared more about crowd control.

Previously, established scalpers would take it upon themselves to run off newcomers, since they bled for their turf. But now what could they do? They could steal a sale, yell, be an asshole—but that was about it.

Business was still good for a few years, as the Red Sox–Yankees rivalry reached peak vitriol, as the Sox captured their first World Series title in eighty-six years. But slowly the air started to let out. After 2004, fans weren't as feverish. ("Winning the World Series? It killed it," says Jimmy.) And then came the Internet.

For guys like Jimmy and Greeno, times have gotten tougher. "You can't make that money that you used to. And forget it if you picked up a drug habit or a gambling habit, or both, along the way," says Greeno. "Now you're just living to feed your habit."

Jimmy yearns for the days when he might have taken a walkie-talkie to the face. "I liked it when they were arresting us," he says, "because it kept all the riff-raff away. I was willing to take two or three arrests a year, I didn't give a fuck! Got twenty of them. What's the difference if I get one more?"

A car pulls up to the curb on Brookline. Jimmy hops in the passenger seat, as Greeno hides behind me. "I owe him money," he whispers about the driver, his dealer. "Owe him a small outstanding tab."

The car pulls away. Greeno reappears. Says, "Believe it or not, we want to get the fuck out of it. I got a daughter, a seven-year-old. I'm still battling demons here or there, but not like I used to. I've seen at least thirty people die. People we've known and other hustlers, from overdoses, this and that, living the high life. A lot of us are gone. A lot of old-school guys are gone. People like me and Jimmy, we're fucking dinosaurs."

He says it again, "The minute I can get out of this business, I'm getting the fuck out of it."

———

Not all scalpers take such a dim view of the lifestyle. On the backside of Fenway Park, at the intersection of Van Ness and Ipswich, I meet another old-timer named Steve, with pale watery eyes and a vintage Suzuki motorcycle parked across the street. Steve is a sweet guy, with no regrets from his four-plus decades of scalping and a whole arsenal of amazing tales.

In perhaps the most Boston origin story of all time, Steve started scalping at the age of twelve, before a Boston College football game, when a priest offered him five tickets so he and his friends could get in. "I sold every one of them," Steve says. Having gotten a taste, he returned to the priest and asked if the man of God had any additional seats—for more friends. "He goes, 'How many do you need?' I go, 'Give me twenty!' I ran around the corner. I said, 'This is my business now.'"

During those early days, Steve discovered another easy scheme, when he was loitering by an alley on Lansdowne Street and a couple cars pulled up. "They go, 'You parking cars?' I looked at the alley. I go, 'Yeah! Just pull it all the way down,'" he says. A couple drivers even tried to leave their keys. "I go, 'No, no, no. You better not do that.'" (The same thing happened recently near the Patriots' stadium in Foxborough, when the Rolling Stones were playing a concert. Steve was walking by a darkened house when the first car rolled up. He loaded up the lawn with fifty vehicles, at twenty bucks apiece, then just walked away.)

In the 1960s and '70s when Steve was growing up, things weren't as buttoned up around Fenway. He and his friends once sneaked into the visiting locker room, when the Patriots also played at the park, and made off with all the duffel bags they could carry. What was inside? They didn't know. "We ran out, we got on the bus, got out to Brighton. We looked in the bags. They were the helmets for the game, the whole team, the Oakland Raiders!" Quite a score. But when the kids learned Fenway was looking for them, they tossed the loot into a reservoir, ditching the evidence.

A couple years earlier Steve sneaked into Fenway before the deciding game of the 1967 World Series. Not sure what to take, they spotted a cake—what was to be the celebratory cake—and grabbed it. As it happened, the home team lost, and the young scamps handed out slices at Kenmore Square to despondent Red Sox fans leaving the game, like some kind of confectionary Robin Hoods.

Steve laughs. "So we ate the cake. The Red Sox didn't need it."

———

Back in Cleveland, the scalpers have a couple days to lick their wounds before game two. But no one is optimistic. On the morning of the game, I phone Scott Merk of Merks Tickets, who tells me game one was rough for brokers as well. He predicts tonight, a weekday game, will be even worse. "This is a bloodbath," he says.

It isn't that the scalpers made no money on Sunday, just not as much as they expected. (Big Mike, for example, had forecast a thousand-dollar day but instead pulled in five hundred.) The shaky start to the play-offs seems emblematic of the fragile state of scalping. With the intrusion of the Internet and digital ticketing, it is a fading—and possibly dying—trade. No doubt many folks would say good riddance, considering the ticket men to be parasites feeding off the passion of the fans. But extinction would be a shame—the steamrolling of an organic element of stadium-based ecosystems, of an entire industry for street-level entrepreneurs.

There is an end-of-days aura in the air when I arrive at Quicken Loans Arena before game two. A powerful wind whips through the Cleveland streets, displacing wood chips and litter. Mike and others are already stalking the sidewalk, backs turned against the gusts, a few hours till tip-off. As the fans start to file through, the scalpers break their huddle and unleash their game-day cries.

They do not go gentle into that good night.

"Come here, man. Come here, bruh. Bruh! Come here."

"Hey, my man. You selling tickets? Just trying to talk to you."

"Ma'am, ma'am, ma'am, ma'am. Ma'am!"

Early indications are that the online ticket market is pitiful once again. Perhaps worse than Sunday. Lowers going for barely over a hundred dollars. But it's too early for the scalpers to react to that. Out here they set their own prices—or at least they can try. When a potential buyer mentions the action on Flash Seats, scalpers just turn away. It's not a negotiating tactic; it's a nonstarter. With the ability to separate from any other reality, the street market can rise and fall on its own terms—and after a few sales today, incredibly, a ticket bubble begins to form.

Bill unloads eight seats right out of the gate, speed walking between customers who show even an inkling of interest. Sheets sells one for $350, although he has to sell it through another scalper because he doesn't have a Flash Seats account. ("I'm going to go home and make an account tonight," he swears.)

When a passerby asks about two lowers, Bill tells him five hundred dollars, holding up five fingers, wide. The fan doesn't bite, but the next guy does—a middle-aged man with slicked-back hair, chomping on a fat cigar. With minimal negotiation, Cigar Guy starts peeling off hundreds, his bleached-blond date looking on. Later Bill tells me the guy would have probably paid twice as much, since he was expecting to be a hotshot. Bill simply fulfilled his fantasy.

The sales keep coming. At one point, I even start middling, the action is so intense. I ask fans where they want to sit and direct them toward different scalpers (but mostly toward Big Mike). Long before tip-off, Mark sells out of his seats. "Damn, this game like it's something real good today," he says.

"I wasn't expecting this," Big Mike agrees. "I turned down tickets!"

A near-manic joy spreads through the scalping zone, as Bill, feeling magnanimous, tips out multiple middlemen for single sales, thus avoiding the typical quarrels. It is a blissful hysteria, and really it doesn't make sense, too good to be true. As the street market froths, the online prices plummet. The vultures are dumbstruck, staring at their phones. They can't understand why the scalpers won't drop their demands. But why would they? Fans are buying, and inventory is running out.

By the middle of the first quarter, Mike is also out of tickets. Together we head to Harry Buffalo, a bar down the block. There we watch the rest of the game. Watch LeBron lead his hometown team to another play-off victory over the Celtics, closer to the next round, closer to the finals, to a long-overdue championship for a long-suffering city.

And for at least one night, things seem all right in Cleveland.

4

"AS FAR AS THE EYE CAN SEE, TOILETS"

(Or: Straight to the Dome)

"**B**aby!" Raymond Smith exclaimed, waking with a startle. "Everybody gone and you looking at the news?"

It was the morning of Monday, August 29, 2005, and Smith had overslept. He didn't set an alarm. He thought his girlfriend would wake him. The night before, they'd had a low-key hurricane party, a New Orleans tradition, when the city shuts down and there's nothing to do but drink a little, smoke a little, and wait for the coming storm. She would wake him if action needed to be taken. But he overslept and woke to a growling stomach and an empty apartment complex, on Congress Drive, in the Gentilly neighborhood. Woke to the weather on TV.

No time to eat.

"Come on!"

Smith, who had celebrated his forty-fourth birthday the previous week, hurried toward his sister's house on Franklin Avenue and Acacia Street, the rain coming, the wind blowing sideways. That's where he planned to meet his mother, his grandmother, and a few other family members. Too late to evacuate, they would ride out the storm there.

Such a scenario isn't unusual. Locals are all but immune to the false alarms, to the promises of devastating hurricanes that don't deliver. To the weathermen who cry wolf. Plus, if you don't have out-of-town relatives—in New Orleans, a city of immense wealth and immense poverty, families don't always travel far; four or more generations may live within a few blocks—evacuating can be a financial hardship.

Safe at his sister's, Smith figured he at least could eat some grits. He turned on an electric burner. He heard a noise. *Cla-click!* Just like that, the power went out. The pot wasn't even boiling yet. So much for breakfast.

Slowly the water came.

Then not so slowly.

Step by step the water chased Smith and his family off the ground floor to the attic. Hours went by. Finally a boat went by, a small motorboat, en route to another rooftop rescue. Smith flagged down the captain. The captain took Smith and his family to a nearby overpass. From there they were driven to a giant sports facility nestled like an alien egg into New Orleans's central business district. A facility already overrun with those seeking shelter from the storm.

They were driven to the Louisiana Superdome.

––––––––

The story of domed stadiums may feature Hurricane Katrina as its most tragic chapter, but that isn't where it begins. It doesn't even begin in New Orleans. The story of domed stadiums starts 350 miles to the west, in Houston, Texas. That's where a man named Roy Hofheinz envisioned an enclosed ballpark in which his baseball team, then known as the Colt .45s, could play in any weather.

Perhaps it is odd to think about it now, as the demolished ashes from dusty old domes, like the Metrodome and Kingdome, litter the stadium landscape, but in the early 1960s, the idea of playing indoor baseball was about as eccentric as putting a man on the moon.

Hofheinz didn't mind the naysayers. A visionary politician, lawyer, entrepreneur, and huckster, Hofheinz, who was affectionately referred to as "the Judge," knew it could be done. And in April 1965, the Astrodome opened as the world's first domed stadium. It was a facility unlike any before it, and not just because it had a roof overhead. Part of the building's innovation was driven by necessity, a response to the region's muggy, insect-infested, and unpredictable weather. But the indoor aspect was only a fraction of what soon made the venue, which featured a record-setting clear span of 642 feet and which *The New York Times* called "the grandest stadium in baseball," a leading tourist attraction in the United States.

The Judge had a larger-than-life personality. He was a showman, and the Astrodome reflected his whims and wishes. His office, for example, was on the seventh-and-a-half floor. For a while, he even lived in the dome, in a personal apartment, which featured a bowling alley, a shooting range, a barbershop, and per an article from the time, "a bar with stools that can be raised or lowered by remote control, for comic effect." With skyboxes and exclusive club spaces, he introduced the idea of luxury at stadiums, prompting the publisher of *Sports Illustrated* to dub the place the "Houston pleasure dome." Other innovations included a four-story animated scoreboard—a cutting-edge technological gem, which lit up with cartoon graphics and other messages for the crowd—and synthetic playing fields, i.e., AstroTurf.*

The Judge played up the high-tech angle (staffers wore silver spacesuits), but it was more than a marketing gimmick. It was a means of rebranding an entire city. In those early dome days, the

---

* Originally known as Chemgrass—and originally intended not for sports stadiums but for urban spaces and schools, to provide children places to play, so they could be more fit when they entered the Army—AstroTurf wasn't in the blueprint for the ballpark. The plan was for real grass to grow under a translucent roof. Unfortunately, the resulting glare proved detrimental to play. And when the roof was painted over, the grass died. Not even the "Earthmen," as the groundskeepers were known, could save it.

very notion of a covered stadium captured the public's imagination. Far more than their open-air counterparts, domes stood as symbols of American progress and possibility, of self-determination. They represented something essential about us as people, reflecting a kind of can-do spirit, fueled by big ideas and fearless dreamers. They were portals into a man-made future, a future where every day the temperature could be seventy-two degrees.

The idea of a domed stadium was so revolutionary, in fact, that— combined with the fledgling NASA program—the Astrodome's opening, described by a local sociologist as "the most exciting thing that has ever happened to Houston," remade the city's image almost overnight, from that of a cow town to a technology leader. So what if air-conditioning gusts within the building tended to thwart would- be home runs, and so what if an infestation of giant rats forced the stadium managers to bring in a herd of feral cats? There would be other notable domes, of course, like Montreal's Olympic Stadium, which had the first retractable roof, and Toronto's SkyDome, which had the first retractable roof that actually, you know, retracted. But the first dome cut the deepest, per Bob Trumpbour, the Penn State professor who is also coauthor of the 2016 book *The Eighth Wonder of the World: The Life of Houston's Iconic Astrodome.* "It is the building that in many ways changed everything."

New Orleans's covered stadium owes its existence to its westerly neighbor, but the Superdome wasn't so much inspired by the Astrodome as provoked by it. When former Louisiana governor John McKeithen walked into the House That Hofheinz Built, he remarked, "I want one just like this, only bigger." If that sounds a bit like a pissing contest, that's because that is exactly what it was. From inception, the New Orleans project was an attempt to outdo the Astrodome, to reclaim pole position in the rivalry that existed among southeastern cities like New Orleans and Houston and Atlanta.

Size definitely mattered, as marketing materials for the new stadium made sure to mention that "Houston's Astrodome could fit comfortably inside" the Superdome, with an accompanying illustration. And while the Astrodome bragged about its animated scoreboard, the Superdome introduced a center-hung gondola that featured six "giant" twenty-two-by-twenty-six-foot full-color television screens and pioneered instant replay.* Even the Superdome name was a thumbed nose to Houston. According to a *New Orleans Magazine* story that ran two years before the venue's 1975 opening, its name caught on "because it was a direct affront" to the Astrodome.†

There was no lack of bravado, no crumbs of modesty for the facility that some called the "un-stadium." Per an architectural brochure prepared by the dome's designers, Buster Curtis and Arthur Davis, "few projects in the history of building have set out more boldly to leap from the past to the future." If that weren't enough, the dome was also said to be the "most usable public building ever designed in the history of man." With movable stands, theatrical lighting, and a rounded-square seating arrangement known as a "squircle," the Superdome would be able to host everything from football, baseball, and basketball games to concerts, aquatics, and any manner of convention. Dave Dixon, the stadium's first executive director and the driving force who conceived of building a dome in New Orleans, envisioned the new facility becoming the permanent home to both the Super Bowl and the World Series.‡

According to Tulane University architecture professor John

---

* At first, the NFL limited the use of replays, requiring preapproval of any potentially controversial clips, for fear they may cause a riot among New Orleans's "traditionally unruly" crowd, per then NFL executive director Jim Kensil.

† Other names considered included Mardi Gras Stadium, Mardi Gras Dome, and Ultradome. Though none of those took, the artificial turf inside the Superdome did become known as "Mardi Grass."

‡ Dixon also envisioned eight high school basketball games being played inside the dome simultaneously, with whistles of different pitch. That never happened.

Klingman, the bluster wasn't unwarranted. The Superdome stood out from its contemporaries, he says, and not just for its size. Built during the midcentury multipurpose era of American stadiums—a largely failed era, defined by the proliferation of first-generation domes and concrete doughnuts, like Three Rivers Stadium, Riverfront Stadium, and Busch Memorial Stadium (which are also known as octorads, are all but destroyed, and are mourned by no one)—the Superdome strove for something grander than those cookie-cutter venues. More than a vessel in which a city could cram as much crap possible, New Orleans's stadium was intended as a statement piece, devised for the long haul. "I think it was always thought about as being a civic monument as well as a highly efficient place," he says.

Aesthetically, the dome forged its own path. While the Astrodome evaded architectural categorization,* and the concrete doughnuts participated in a style fittingly called Brutalism, which Klingman says "is basically the use of unadorned concrete as a structural material and also as a finish material"—others have called it neofascist—the Superdome grew out of the Modernist movement. "It is a pure form," he says. "The defining character is that there are no quirks."

That isn't to say there were no bumps and bruises. The stadium was built amid considerable controversy, with twenty-two lawsuits, financial shenanigans, and backroom political deals. Within the building, there were early hiccups, like holeless ticket windows, vandalism in the vast, unpoliceable concourses, a possible need for a "spit barrier" between the upper and lower levels, and an interior decor that was said to resemble "a Holiday Inn motel room blown up to fantastic proportions" (although that may have been intended as a compliment). Still, New Orleans residents took to their new dome home with the same intensity and pride they reserve for all things local, like Fats Domino and king cake.

---

* "It's not a particularly good design. It's a first attempt," Klingman says of the Astrodome.

Just look through the deep reserve of Superdome materials at Tulane University's Southeastern Architectural Archive, or the extensive personal files of old newspaper and magazine clippings kept by Bob Remy, the Saints' team historian and longtime statistician, at his Metairie home. Even before the stadium opened, homegrown media members noted that the facility had "revitalized the psychology of the city," while brochures for the dome touted "a new horizon of hope," calling it "the depository of Louisiana's belief in itself." Elsewhere in the press, writers threw out infinite facts and figures, as many mind-bending stats about the new stadium as they could muster, trying to digest the dome, to reckon with its sizable meaning. One article's author tells a story of how a friend decided to relieve himself on the roof of the dome during a tour, "because the place inspires you to perform irrational acts of frustration." And really, that rooftop piss may have been the greatest compliment of all. The Superdome emerged as an instant icon, a new community anchor, and a symbol of brighter tomorrows.

What passes for normal in New Orleans has never met any sort of dictionary definition. This is a town of extremes, where voodoo priestesses hold sway, overindulgence is the baseline for moderation, and families don't bury their dead. (They inter them above ground instead.) So perhaps it shouldn't come as a surprise that the most life-altering event inside the city's roofed-in sports palace turned out to be weather-related. Even by New Orleans's warped standards, the Superdome scene that greeted Raymond Smith and his family on August 29, 2005, was anything but normal.

There Doug Thornton, an executive for SMG, which manages the venue on behalf of the State of Louisiana, was trying to keep the dome from devolving into chaos, trying to keep people calm and fed. With the power out, the building was running on a generator. The stadium's nine thousand tons of air conditioning had gone silent. The food in the freezers would soon spoil. Aside from the National Guard's eight-hundred-megahertz radio, there was no communication with the outside world, as rain poured in through a hole in the roof, which had started shredding at six o'clock that morning, courtesy of Hurricane Katrina's high-velocity winds. As water pooled on the playing field, a general anxiety festered within the breached stadium, thick as the gathering humidity.

Initially, the plan had been for the dome to host fewer than a thousand people during the storm—several hundred seriously ill patients, and that was it. According to Bill Curl, who served as the stadium's spokesman for more than three decades, the phrase they tried to broadcast was "Not even if you can swim up." He says, "I don't think it ever got in print." Instead, New Orleans mayor Ray Nagin asked Thornton to open the dome's doors. So several hundred became fourteen thousand. That was how many people had already spent a night in the Superdome by Monday morning, when the storm made landfall, the levees broke, and the stadium population exploded again, more than doubling over the next twenty-fours hours, as conditions rapidly deteriorated and floodwater crept closer.

Inside the Superdome, this building that housed the city's beloved Saints and lifted New Orleans to "major league" status, the running water shut off. The toilets stopped working, then overflowed. Liquid from trash bins oozed onto the floor, as distraught worshipers wandered the field, praying, just praying. As Thornton tells me, a "despicable smell" of sweat and mold and human feces filled the arena, gagging him when he walked into the main bowl. "The smell is something I'll never forget," he says. But the smell wasn't the worst part. The worst part was how quickly he got used to it.

In the building where Muhammad Ali defeated Leon Spinks in 1978 to retake the world heavyweight boxing title, people were treated for dehydration and heat exhaustion. A baby was delivered. Women were raped. A man was beaten nearly to death after being accused of molesting a child. A National Guardsman shot himself in the leg while struggling with an attacker in a darkened locker room. A black market of stolen goods—like cigarettes and candy—emerged, as an atmosphere of fear rippled through the dome. Sensationalized news reports—symptoms of what *National Review*'s Jonah Goldberg would term an "unmitigated media disaster"— trickled into the stadium via battery-powered radios, as small bands of no-goodniks and tweakers were allowed to establish a disproportionate presence, terrorizing those who were just trying to survive, to achieve a degree of normalcy.

Raymond Smith and his family joined the uneasy crowd. In the stands, Smith made a bed of three stadium seats, passing in and out of sleep as time seemed to both speed up and slow down, as days turned to nights turned to days in a kind of prolonged fever dream. Waking to escort female family members to the bathroom. Waking to the sight of praying women, of a naked man assaulting an officer. To authorities wrestling that man to the ground. To the sound of that man screaming something unholy. To the sound echoing throughout the dome.

In the building where the Rolling Stones set a world record for attendance, where the NFL hosted the first-ever indoor Super Bowl, Thornton and the National Guard fought back the flooding of the generator, the stadium's sole power source. On the concrete engineering-room wall, they marked the rising water levels every half hour with Sharpie tabulations, like prison inmates scratching time served, wondering when the building would plunge into total chaos.

Thornton saw no end in sight. By midweek, the mayor was forecasting another five or six days in the dome, which Thornton knew wasn't feasible. At an early-morning briefing on Wednesday, the National Guard chaplain, a man named Walter Austin, who had been keeping tabs on morale, confirmed Thornton's intuition. He reported,

"We are about to lose this place." Conditions were getting worse, if that was possible. People were restless. Fires were being lit throughout the building, as desperation filled the dome. Finally, about twelve hours later, word came that FEMA buses would arrive the next day.

In the building where New Orleanians had always believed they would be safe, in a building designed to withstand sustained winds of 150 miles per hour and gusts of 200 miles per hour, where they could hide their ball games (and themselves) from Mother Nature, Thornton and a handful of remaining SMG employees hunkered down in the overnight hours in a lonely office space, flanked by two National Guardsmen. They called this the Vigil. Thornton didn't sleep. He waited for daybreak, waited for the buses, knowing how close they were teetering toward the edge. Beyond the office, the noise of the stadium provided an eerily familiar sound. If he closed his eyes, the sound was almost like a game-day rumble, like the sound of a milling crowd. But the sound kept getting louder, picking up urgency. "I'll be honest with you," Thornton says, pausing to choke back tears, still shaken by the total helplessness of his position, seemingly abandoned by the government, tens of thousands left for dead, "I was frightened."

In the building whose very construction had been "an exercise in optimism," according to former New Orleans mayor Moon Landrieu, morning finally came. And so did the buses—eventually, after more delays. Smith couldn't wait to escape this cauldron of filth and death. Officially, there were ten fatalities at the dome, including an apparent suicide, but Smith says that number seems low, based on the bodies he saw. Perhaps he counted the dome itself as one of the dead. The building was destroyed, and folks felt unmitigated relief to be leaving. Saying goodbye to all that, some evacuees tied lengths of cloth to a goalpost and set it ablaze. "They lit that son of a bitch on fire," Smith recalls. They wanted this place to burn, this cesspool. They wanted to burn this building down to the ground.

This building, which had meant so much to its community, which took on new meaning as it took on water and became a warehouse of suffering.

This building, where nothing would ever be the same.

————————

Barely a week after leaving the Katrina-ravaged Superdome, this onetime sanctuary that had all but become a crime scene, Doug Thornton was back inside the stadium for a remediation tour. Although Thornton remembers thinking "it would never be rebuilt," when he first evacuated—how could it?—he kept an open mind as he walked the empty concourses, analyzing the damage from inside a hazmat suit, putting aside the feelings of depression and rage that plagued him for months following the storm.

Jeff Duncan, a sports columnist for the *New Orleans Times-Picayune*, who contributed to the paper's Pulitzer Prize–winning coverage of Hurricane Katrina and its aftermath, was also on the tour that day. What jumped out to him was the trash. "It just struck me how desperate people must have been, how miserable they must have been, because literally every square foot was covered in refuse and debris," says Duncan, who trained an eye on Thornton for any hints of a reaction. But the SMG executive held his poker face.

It wasn't until September 30, weeks later, that Thornton received word that the dome could likely be saved. Based on some napkin math, it would cost more than $200 million and take two years. But that provided a much-needed glimmer of hope for Thornton, a man desperate to reclaim some sense of purpose. After getting the green light from the governor, Thornton focused on nothing but the rebuilding project, trying to fix what the storm had broken—within the stadium, sure, but also within himself. Says Bill Curl, "Please don't use the word, but he was obsessed."

"When you get knocked down to the lowest point, there's a natural instinct that God gives you to reclaim what we had before," Thornton says. Every day he reminded himself to look for little signs of noticeable progress. "You hang on to the small victories when you get them, and you reclaim another piece of territory, and over time you can rebuild."

Unfortunately, complicating matters, the New Orleans Saints didn't share the same dedication to the dome. Team owner Tom Benson had been trying to secure a new revenue-rich stadium for his team for years, and the storm provided the perfect escape route for the Saints, now shacked up in San Antonio. Despite some revisionist history (a statue of Benson now stands outside the Superdome), there is no question that he wanted out—not just out of the stadium but out of the state. "They were looking for an excuse to leave," Duncan recalls.

Benson didn't even wait for the clouds to clear when he started telling staffers, "We're a Texas team now." "Literally, it was a day or two after the storm," says Duncan. Benson even fired top business executive Arnie Fielkow, who went on to serve on the New Orleans city council, because he was advocating for a return. Any doubts Duncan had about the team's intentions were erased at the NFL owners' meeting that fall, when Saints general manager Mickey Loomis told him the city was crazy to pin its hopes on NFL commissioner Paul Tagliabue. He remembers Loomis saying of Tagliabue, "He has no power, he works for the owners, he works for us. He's not going to do anything."

But Loomis was wrong. With the backing of the league's other owners, who would have to approve the move (and who understood the PR implications of letting the Saints leave after Katrina), Tagliabue had plenty of power. The Saints would return to New Orleans on September 25, 2006. That was the day the dome was set to reopen, for a nationally televised game against the Atlanta Falcons, thanks to Thornton's around-the-clock work and an NFL-assisted fast-tracking of the recovery timetable, via political string-pulling.

Not everyone was thrilled that the dome became the city and state's chief priority, even if a speedy rebuild was New Orleans's only chance to keep the fleeing Saints. One critic was Thornton's wife, Denise, who committed her time to rebuilding on the neighborhood level and didn't understand why a sports stadium should be prioritized over personal homes. In fact, the couple nearly divorced over the difference of opinion. But Thornton was convinced the Superdome had to lead the recovery charge, and not just because the project was so clearly his post-Katrina coping mechanism. For one, he argued, the dome was a central element of the New Orleans economy, which for decades had stilted itself on tourism, conventions, big events, and the corresponding hospitality industry.* Beyond that, it was a hugely symbolic gesture at a time when many people were still debating whether to return to the city at all, whether it was worth saving. "It was the poster child for disaster," Thornton says of the Superdome. "It was seen on every news clip. The minute you turn that roof white again—that roof that was ripped off—people are going to believe the recovery can happen."

And on September 25, 2006, Thornton was proven right, at least for one night, as fans descended on the dome, with or without tickets. Duncan remembers the stadium feeling like a mini–Super Bowl, with performances by Green Day and U2 and swarms of media members. Bill Curl describes it as an emotionally charged family reunion, as folks in the stands, who hadn't seen one another in nearly two years, reconnected. "By time, we had reached a point where you didn't

---

* This type of consumer-focused, pleasure-driven economy is worthy of a deeper sociological discussion for the ways in which it widens inequality by carpet-bombing the employment landscape with low-paying service gigs and by incentivizing governmental agencies, such as the police, to treat nonconsumers like enemies of the state. But: I'm on a word count.

even ask. You looked in somebody's eyes, and they told you if they had a tragedy or not." Curl pauses. His voice breaks. "So there was a lot of hugging, a lot of crying."

The Saints won that night, on the back of a dramatic first-quarter blocked punt by special-teams-player-turned-local-legend-turned-tragic inspiration Steve Gleason. (In 2011, Gleason received an ALS diagnosis.) His block resulted in an ear-splitting touchdown for the home team, and the refurbished Superdome burst with happiness, with hysterical celebration. "The place came unglued," says Curl. It was an emotional outpouring that couldn't help but reverberate throughout the city, as a team once known as the Aints started to do the unthinkable. They started to win. With a new superstar quarterback in Drew Brees and an offensive-minded coach in Sean Payton, the Saints transformed into one of the NFL's most exciting teams. The Superdome, the birthplace of the Bag Heads—dedicated yet forlorn fans that hid their faces inside grocery bags—became one of the most hostile environments for visitors, as decibel levels reached 120 and higher and opposing players wore custom earplugs to block out the noise.

"The national narrative was, you know, the Saints are lifting the city," says Duncan. "But I think it was actually inverted. I think the city was lifting the Saints." When fans started showing up at the airport to greet the team plane after road games, the players had to realize they were part of something bigger, he says. Either way the Saints were rising just as the city was being reborn. Once again the team was part of New Orleans's cultural fabric—as vital as brass bands, beignets, second lines, and streetcars—and a long-simmering love affair between the city and the Saints hit the fireworks phase.

The remarkable run culminated in a Super Bowl victory in February 2010, the first championship for a formerly hapless franchise. A feeling approximating pure joy washed over the city that night, according to writer-photographer Amy K. Nelson, who was in New

Orleans on assignment. Beneath the gnarled branches of live oak trees, which were slowly regaining their roots after Katrina's nuclear-dumpsite-like effect on plant life, and beneath the eternal canopy of power-line-draped Mardi Gras beads, the city bled together in the streets. Prim and proper old ladies embraced young men inked with tattoo sleeves. The seersucker set high-fived those from the service sector. And no one went home until six in the morning.

It was tempting to say that the city—and the stadium—had been not only reclaimed but redeemed. The calamity washed clean. But nothing is ever so simple. Especially not in New Orleans.

"Dude! *The dome?*" Chuck Simpson says, pouring charcoal and wood chips into his well-worn sidewalk grill, contemplating the meaning of the stadium.

It is hours before an early November matchup against the Tennessee Titans, and I have fallen in with the Saints supporters, taking advantage of New Orleans's open-container laws, a little breakfast booze. While every NFL stadium has a whiff of bacchanal, with face-painted fans and daylong drinking, New Orleans is a city that believes deeply in the power of communing, of coming together around big events like Mardi Gras and Jazz Fest, and I have been told that home games here can feel like Carnival. Sure enough, there is a festive mood, as drum lines march to their own beat, costumed fans go full-on masquerade, and tailgaters set up in the city's limited parking lots, on every available side street, and underneath the highway overpasses that graze the northern tip of the Superdome.

A middle-aged man dressed in camo Saints shorts, Simpson is on the corner of Julia and Rampart Streets. He interrupts his train of stadium thoughts with loud cries to passersby of "Who dat," which functions as a kind of all-purpose call, like *aloha* or *shalom*.

"Who dat!"

"Who dat!"

Along with an old Navy buddy named Scott Mitchell, and another pal, Mickey Lanclos, Simpson is readying what appears to be a month's worth of meat—chicken, country ribs, sausage, and boudin. Finally finding the right words, he says, "On Sundays, there are three kinds of churches in New Orleans. There's Catholic, there's Baptist, and there is *the dome.*"

As if to accentuate Simpson's point, to demonstrate the stadium's inalterable place in city history, Lanclos fetches a yellowed newspaper out of his pickup truck. It is the front page from the day after the dome reopened in 2006. The headline reads: REBIRTH. REJOICE!

On the opposite side of the stadium, under the Route 90 overpass, a man named Derrick Campbell, who is part of a group called the Violet Tailgaters, tells me he calls the dome the "People's Champ." Explaining, "Even though he never won no belt, he's the People's Champ. That's what the dome is. Even before the Super Bowl. It just brings people together."

That's the beauty of the building, according to Campbell. In a town as deeply divided and diverse as New Orleans, the dome manages to marshal a wide cross-section of folks from throughout the community and the whole Gulf Coast, because everyone— *everyone*—just loves the damn Saints. The affection is unwavering. And when the ball is in play, real-world concerns simply melt away. "I don't know where you work. You don't know what I do, but we sit right next to each other. Whatever your story is, you put it on hold," he says.

This escapism was part of the gift the Saints gave the city following Hurricane Katrina. But while the Superdome has been reclaimed, those stories of trauma remain, and some roil pretty close to the surface. Like the story of Ray Byrd, a twenty-plus-year member of the New Orleans police department, who tailgates beneath a different overpass and never rooted for the Saints before Hurricane Katrina.

That changed in August 2005, when Byrd found himself in New Orleans East, stuck on a roof, and started getting flashbacks to his time in the Marines, to operations like Desert Storm and Desert Shield. "It was like Beirut," he says of the city. "It was like an atomic bomb hit. Even though to my eyes it was color, it looked black and white."

Byrd lost everything during the storm. Left with nothing but the clothes on his back, he transported stranded storm victims to the convention center in an eighteen-wheeler that he learned how to drive on the spot. "I was driving back and forth, sunup to sundown," says Byrd. "Trips all day long." As he went, Byrd made pit stops, anytime he saw a body, and he would tie the corpse to a pole. "I couldn't just let them float away. That is somebody's family member."

After the storm, Byrd says he had job offers from other cities, from poachers. But he wanted to stay. "I love my city so much. I can't abandon my city, my team, no. I couldn't do it." That's when rooting for the Saints took on even more meaning. When he stopped pulling for the Eagles or the 49ers or the Cowboys, or whichever team caught his fancy. He says, "After Katrina, I had to support my town."

Chuck Simpson and Scott Mitchell lived through Katrina, too, although for them, the storm went beyond the dome, beyond New Orleans. As active-duty members of the Navy, they were stationed in Mississippi, and when the base in Pascagoula flooded, they decided to commandeer a Navy van. "They had little distribution points, where the Army Corps of Engineers and the National Guard were handing out MREs [Meals Ready to Eat] and ice and water to people driving by," says Mitchell. "Well, we took that van down there, opened up the back, and said, put as many pallets as you can in there. We're going to drive down where people can't drive up."

And that's what they did for two months after the storm, covering about two hundred square miles, from Alabama to Louisiana. In some areas, they would just drive up on the beach because there were no roads. Says Simpson, "We would pull into places, in between Long

Beach and Gulfport, pull into a subdivision, and as far as the eye can see, toilets. That's the only thing left." But the weirdest visual came in the north part of Biloxi, says Mitchell. "There is this guy's house, the roof was sitting on the ground, like the walls just fell, and he's sitting on top of it. There was a Bayliner in a tree and a coffin in the road—"

"We drove around it," says Simpson.

Mitchell remembers kids running alongside the van, as if it were a Mardi Gras float, as they tossed out pieces of chewing gum. Folks weren't afraid to show their appreciation, either. Says Simpson, "I remember getting back in the van. I said, 'If one more person hugs me that hasn't had a shower, I'm going to fucking puke.'" He pauses, flips the grill cage, smiles. "Dude, it was beautiful."

———

With about an hour until kickoff, I enter the stadium, where the Saints have sold out of season tickets every year since the team's 2006 return to the city, where a banner hangs from the rafters honoring these SEASON SELLOUTS, a put-your-money-where-your-mouth-is testament to the fact that New Orleans would not let this team leave.

It isn't my first time inside. Months earlier, during the off-season, Bill Curl had taken me on a tour of the building, calling attention to a variety of little details, like the vestige outline of a baseball diamond, which can be seen on the Superdome floor. He pointed out where the six-sided gondola once hung and told stories of how they used to bring in fan boats to dry off the turf. We also visited the engineering room, which is still scarred with the Sharpie wall markings from Katrina and which must be monitored twenty-four hours a day, seven days a week. (There a woman named Patricia sat bragging about job security.)

It wasn't hard to appreciate the size of the facility from the upper levels, as we looked out on the vast expanse of the main room and seating bowl, where insect-size workers scurried below, setting up chairs for a convention. With the stands empty and no natural light, it felt like being inside a giant tuna can. But the dome feels different today. No less big but more intimate, somehow. The noise of fans filling the space slingshots around the room, amorphous, all-encompassing.

I can't help but feel a vague sense of haunting. As the legend goes, the Superdome has always held spirits inside after being built atop the abandoned Girod Street Cemetery. But the haunting feels more recent than that. As I walk the concourses, I think about where people slept and shat and cowered and died during the storm. I think about those who suffered here—survivors of robberies, beatings, and rapes—and how, for some, the dome may never be redeemed. I think about the Katrina stories from beyond the stadium as well— Ray Byrd plowing through floodwater in an eighteen-wheeler, the Navy guys delivering MREs. Each of these experiences reverberates through the halls, part of the cacophonous concerto of post-Katrina fandom. But with a game to be played, no one else seems to notice the noise. Not the fans. Not the players. Not the drunk dude being rolled out on a gurney. This makes sense, I guess. In New Orleans, even the iconic athletes are haunted by tragedy; Archie Manning, Pete Maravich, and Drew Brees each lost a parent to suicide. It is a town that is used to dealing with ghosts.

Not everyone can escape the echoes of the past, though.

In the last few minutes of the third quarter, by section 144, a beer vendor nears the end of his shift. The Saints are driving, up by a point, when Brees throws an interception in the end zone. The vendor sags his head. "Man, I was going to sell out just now," he says. "Every time the Saints score, everybody wants to drink. Now I probably won't sell but one or two."

The vendor excuses himself. Takes another run down the aisle, to see if he can't unload some of his tray, score a few more commissions, before they suspend the sale of alcohol. But we agree to meet back here after he cashes out. The vendor wants to tell me a story, he says. It is a story of Katrina.

The vendor's name is Raymond Smith.

Midway through the fourth quarter, the game still in doubt, Smith and I exit the Superdome. Understandably, he prefers not to stay in the stadium any longer than he has to. Plus, he'd like to stop by Seman's Center, a hole-in-the-wall cellphone store on Royal Street, in the French Quarter. His phone has been deactivated, which happens from time to time.

Now fifty-four, Smith appears at least a decade younger, with a cleanly shaved head, dark eyebrows, and the stubbly hint of a goatee, specked with gray. Outside the stadium, he tries to buy a smoke from a fan, to unwind after an afternoon of lugging liquid courage up and down the stands. When the fan says no, his girlfriend, adorned with fleur-de-lis sticker paint on her cheeks, hands Smith two cigarettes. She's being nice, naturally, but Smith also has a way with women, an effortlessly flirtatious grin that has gotten him into trouble before. As we walk away, Smith looks back toward his tobacco benefactor and tells her she's beautiful. She says, "Yeah, I'm beautiful. That's what they all say."

Her boyfriend doesn't seem pleased.

It is overcast but not raining, so Smith decides to hike the mile-plus to the French Quarter. Walkability is one of his favorite things about the city, he says, sparking up a cigarette. "Anywhere in New Orleans. You don't need no car. You just need rubber heels." After taking a few pulls, he pinches out the ember so the cigarette doesn't burn on its own, so he can light it again later.

Smith grew up in New Orleans's Desire Projects, but he wasn't born here, he says as we cut across Poydras Street and hang a left on Loyola. His mom brought him to the city as a four-year-old, in August 1965, just in time for Hurricane Betsy, a brutal Big Easy baptism. Smith likes talking about his mother, a woman named Julia. In today's vernacular, she might be considered a helicopter parent, but Smith didn't mind being under his mother's watchful eye. "No matter what I did. I mean, fucking women and all—Momma knew it! She said, 'If anything happen to one of y'all in them streets, I want to know who to go to.'" The memory brings a smile to his face. "There was just so much togetherness, man."

That togetherness was what helped Smith get through Hurricane Katrina, what kept him strong and sane during those days in the dome. "I was just glad I was still around my momma," he says, remembering the overrun shelter of the Superdome, which to his eyes looked like a plundered city. And yet the seeming lawlessness inside the stadium, the environment of on-edge terror, wasn't the most traumatic part of the experience, says Smith. That would be the way he and his family—and the rest of the largely African American crowd—were treated: like criminals in a war camp, not American citizens in need. "Them people didn't give a fuck about us, bro. They were nasty," he says of the National Guard and other foot soldiers of the dome. He remembers one guardsman shouting at his family, "Niggers, y'all get over there! I said one at a time," while pointing a loaded weapon in their direction as they waited in line for MREs. Smith still can't fully believe it. "To be treated that way? I'm glad I never went in the Army. Treating your own people like outsiders? Your own people!"

In this way, the dome simply served as a microcosm for the response to Hurricane Katrina, which was largely militaristic from the outset. National Guard troops, police officers, and private security forces like Blackwater were deployed throughout the city and given "shoot and kill" orders from the highest offices. They focused their efforts on protecting property from would-be looters rather than on rescuing survivors, at times using the tragedy as an excuse to abuse those (mostly black and poor) residents who were still in the city, whose only crime was staying behind—residents who were regarded as likely offenders. Many were locked up, or shot, for no reason and given no recourse, since the justice system had effectively shut down, taking habeas corpus with it. Many with power and badges didn't seem to care who they captured, and folks were forced to serve "Katrina time." (In some cases, petty charges from before the storm resulted in years behind bars.) Prison officials have denied stories of inmates being killed and disappeared, but nothing is hard to believe from this post-Katrina period, when there was no social safety net, no checks and balances, no accountability.

According to *The Nation*, the Black Lives Matter movement was born from Katrina, because the storm "forced America to confront black vulnerability and to understand how that vulnerability indicts a system of national inequality." But it is unclear how many U.S. citizens had that takeaway, when most of the country seemed to experience the storm as a "third-person event," in the words of sports journalist Bomani Jones.

This wasn't the first time a sports stadium served as a portal into a natural disaster. In 1989, the Loma Prieta earthquake rattled the San Francisco Bay Area to the tune of sixty-three deaths and six billion dollars in damages during game three of the World Series. But unlike that tragedy, in which the television broadcast cut out from Candlestick Park, like something from an end-of-the-world summer blockbuster, thus implicating viewers as witnesses, as participants, Katrina was seen as something happening to *them*, not to *us*. Still an event consumed from one's couch, yes, but more like a foreign war. Even the language used at the time reflected this point of view. Those in the dome were "refugees," a word of psychic distancing.

Raymond Smith's Katrina story didn't end when FEMA began its days-long evacuation of the Superdome, when his family, like so many others, was scattered across the country—one brother ending up in Arkansas, his grandmother all the way in California. "Nobody knew where we were going," recalls Smith, who boarded a bus bound for Houston, where he would spend the next four years.

Life in Texas was always temporary, a holding pattern. Smith says he knew he would return to New Orleans, succumbing to the city's siren song. The jazz. The Patton's hot sausage po'boys. The walkability. As one local puts it to me, "This city tugs on people, for some reason," even if those seductions so often end in a sucker punch. Folks just can't stay away. But Smith didn't get to return on his own terms. "I was forced to come back," he says as we sit in a booth at Popeyes on Canal Street, where the Saints game plays on TV, now heading to overtime.

Smith still doesn't totally understand what happened that night in Houston, that night he was attacked. But he tells me what he remembers, as much as he can piece together. He was on the street, outside his apartment complex, when a strange man started hassling him. Sensing the stranger's aggression, the inevitability of confrontation, Smith ran, hoping to avoid a fight. But the man gave chase. Smith tried to keep an eye on the guy, the would-be assailant, as he ran, but "then suddenly I don't see him," Smith says. "Boom! Boom! Still don't see nobody. Seeing stars now. Boom!" The man was clobbering him. Three hits to the head. "You know how a tree falls, when they cut it? Straight down in the middle of the street."

Smith was out cold. He believes the man left him there only for a minute and was "coming back to finish me off," when a neighbor chanced by, walking his dog. He helped Smith to his feet, though it took three tries. Still woozy, Smith hurried to his apartment and left town that night, grateful to be alive. "Left everything," he says.

Why was he attacked? Smith just shakes his head. "I don't know," he says. "Still don't know." Mistaken identity? Perhaps, but he's convinced it was a setup of some kind. This wasn't the first time in his life Smith had been jumped. The first time was decades earlier, when he was young and, in his own words, "a pretty motherfucker," with a Jheri curl down to his shoulders. That assault was born of jealousy, Smith says. Over women. It left him with a scar on his forehead but no lasting damage. This one proved harder to process. The question he kept asking, as he rode back to New Orleans, for the first time in four years, was a simple one: Why?

Back in New Orleans, Smith was reunited with his mother, whose recent lung cancer diagnosis gave him some sense of purpose upon his return, a distraction for his lizard brain, which kept asking that question with no answer. Smith served as his mother's caregiver until the day she died. On that day, he came undone. When he found out his mom had passed, he wrapped the phone cord around his neck and sobbed like a child. "I couldn't do nothing but cry. Where my momma? Baby, where my momma!"

The tears, the grief, the trauma—it all caught up to him at once.

"I was about to kill myself," he says.

Flooded out of his home.

Shacked up in the dome.

Bused to Houston.

Beaten on the street.

And now without his momma.

Smith was a man unmoored.

He knew he had to get his life together, but how? Like so many others returning to New Orleans, hoping to help the city recover, Smith would discover a rebuilding effort without opportunities, as good construction jobs were going to outsiders, not locals, to cheap laborers. Smith bounced between a few gigs—he did janitorial work at a hospital and bar security in the Quarter. Then three years ago he found himself strapping a tray around his neck, walking into the Superdome. Unlike those in the stands, Smith wasn't returning in some statement of reclamation. He was here because he needed work, because he had to survive. "It brings back memories, but you got to be strong," he says of the stadium. "I try not to mentally go there, because this is my only means of making money."

The mental effort is not insubstantial. Ever since returning to New Orleans, Smith has suffered from paranoid schizophrenia, according to his doctors—the corrosive power of *why*. "I try to forget a lot of things. Put it in the back of my mind. But sometimes, boom. Flashback. And I just stand there, staring. Wondering, is this going to happen again?" He takes a deep breath. "I just cry sometimes," he says. "I feel things, and I get full. You know? I can't control it. I just get so full. And I cry."

———

When we finish eating, Smith leads us into the Quarter, to a bar called Jean Lafitte's Old Absinthe House, on Bourbon Street, where his brother Alton works. On the way, we pass a woman talking on the phone. She pauses her conversation to give Smith a once-over. An old-fashioned eye-fucking.

I say, "You are something, man."

Smith blushes. "I didn't do nothing!"

He laughs. Says, "You know, I'm doing something I don't do. I used to stop and eat. I used to have conversations with a partner. I used to be carefree. Don't do that no more. Ever since I left the Superdome, I'm going straight home. Inside, I'm afraid. All those stupid reasons I was telling you about. Ever since Katrina. I wasn't like that before. But that's how I am."

I apologize to Smith if we're venturing beyond his comfort zone, if he'd rather go home. But Smith won't hear of it. "I'm glad somebody listening to me," he says. "I used to do this. Haven't done it in many, many years. Makes me feel like I'm a person again."

At the bar, we take a two-topper along the rear wall, against a large dormant fireplace. Both our backs against the bricks. I realize this is how we sat at Popeyes as well, so no one could sneak up from behind. Smith's brother Alton comes over and asks to bum a cigarette. Smith gives him what is left of the pinched-out stick. The other cigarette Smith has already given away, to a woman at the phone store who Smith described to me as "nic-ing," meaning she was craving nicotine.

A lazy Sunday vibe fills the darkened barroom, which is almost empty—one dude watching football, the late-afternoon games, drinking skunk beer. It's odd being on Bourbon Street during off-hours, before the hordes come to pound sugar drinks and get into trouble. In gray daylight, you notice a level of grime on the pavement that will never come clean. The bar too feels sticky—from whatever happened here last night, perhaps, or a decade ago. Smith orders gin on the rocks. I have a Budweiser. Over the speakers, Michael Jackson's "Man in the Mirror" blares at a shout-to-be-heard volume. We scoot our stools together.

Away from the stadium now, away from the crowds, I wonder if Smith ever feels resentment toward the Superdome, the symbol of a supposedly roaring recovery that has stood in stark contrast to his own post-Katrina path. I know that some protesters have marched on the dome for exactly that reason. (Politically conscious sportswriter Dave Zirin called the prioritization of the dome, disapprovingly, "a sign of how business was going to be done.") But Smith shakes his head no. "That is the main part we wanted back together, because of our Saints," he says. "We loved them even when they were the Aints. We still love them. We got to keep this thing going."

And yet Smith can plainly see that his city is rejecting him, and so many others like him, spitting him out like a foreign body. In New Orleans a widely split view of the recovery breaks down along racial lines. According to a poll conducted by the Public Policy Research Lab at Louisiana State University, about 80 percent of white residents believe the city has mostly recovered, while 60 percent of black residents disagree. Within that divide, resentment rightfully lurks. "A lot of places, like in the Lower Ninth Ward, they're still not together," says Smith. "We understand the city got to come together financially, get certain parts together, so we can get the money. Understandable. Really. But on the other hand, before you go fixing this red light down here, we got a couple of buildings that need to be fixed. Get what I'm saying?"

Smith has experienced the uneven recovery firsthand, and not just the lack of decent employment opportunities. (But that is a major issue, as income inequality in New Orleans approaches Zambia levels, per a recent Bloomberg report.) It is also other basics, like housing. Affordable housing is disappearing, in part because of growing gentrification, but also because many landlords decided not to rebuild their properties after the flood, and renters were turned out on the streets. People slept in shelters, under bridges. Smith tells me he's been homeless for two years. He's not on the streets—he's staying with friends. But that isn't an arrangement with which he feels comfortable. "I'm used to my own home," he says.

In pockets both large and small throughout the city, there is no such thing as a return to normalcy—not even by New Orleans standards—as folks are still grieving from the wounds of the storm, still trying to pick up the pieces. Amy K. Nelson, who now lives in New Orleans and covered the ten-year anniversary of Hurricane Katrina, which was marked about two months before my visit, tells me how many residents were disturbed by the event. Media outlets portrayed an uplifting narrative, one of rebirth and redemption. In the eyes of locals, she says, it seemed like outsiders were co-opting the meaning of Katrina, declaring a victory and celebrating a tragedy through which they didn't suffer. It was as if the country were closing the book on something it had never even bothered to read. But the story isn't over.

The fact is there is no simple lesson of the storm—or of the Super-dome. Great abuses coincided with great acts of courage. Individuals went above and beyond and still couldn't do enough. Doug Thorn-ton, for example, rejects the notion that Katrina is a scarlet letter, something about which the stadium ought to be ashamed. "It's part of the history," he says, explaining why he installed a Katrina photo exhibit on the loge level of the dome, before the building reopened. And he's right.

But that doesn't mean shameful things didn't happen. They did.

All these stories—from the days in the dome to the rebuilding effort to the blocked punt to the uneven recovery to the local lives still in tailspin—they all tangle and intertwine. They are all part of a muddy legacy. It is how one man's symbol of rebirth can be another man's mental prison. And even that dichotomy doesn't capture the whole story.

Ask enough people in New Orleans, and you'll hear them say the same thing about Hurricane Katrina: the real story has never been told. And I believe that to be true. I don't think it has been told, and I don't think I'm telling it, either, because I don't think it *can* be told.

There will always be more to the Katrina story, another layer of the onion, another person's harrowing and heroic experience to complicate the legacy, which hasn't been accounted for—each one an oversight equal parts inexcusable and unavoidable, each one deserv-ing of an article, a movie, a memorial.*

---

* Even Thornton, who has been the subject of innumerable Katrina pieces, has felt betrayed by the coverage, like when Anderson Cooper and Douglas Brinkley pub-lished supposedly authoritative books about the storm and didn't even bother giving him a ring. Says Thornton, "I remember reading Anderson Cooper's book and laugh-ing at times, thinking: That's not correct."

————

In overtime, the Saints lose to the Titans.

Smith and I leave the bar, say goodbye to Alton. On our way out of the Quarter, we stop at a convenience store called Unique Grocery. This is where everyone comes to cash checks, Smith says as a way to explain the long line. We stop so he can buy a pack of cigarettes.

When it's our turn at the register, the cashier says, "Yes?"

But Smith doesn't answer. He spaces out. In that instant, he's gone. He's back in the Superdome, perhaps. Back in Houston, who knows? Anywhere but here.

He says, "Ummmm . . ."

The cashier rolls his eyes. "Tell me when you're ready. Next!"

The cashier looks to me. "We're together," I say.

He replies, "I know. He need to wake up."

Smith snaps out of it. Orders his cigarettes. But he's unnerved by the episode. Furious at himself. "See what I'm saying!" he says as we walk outside. "That isn't intentional. That is really happening. I'm not playing with him or nothing. Stand up and stare, forget everything. Forget what I come here for."

He lights a cigarette.

"It's disgusting," he spits. "Make me look stupid to people. I'd judge that, too. Standing there, freezing. I'm really like that?"

A man sees Smith smoking as we walk down Canal Street. He asks if he can bum one. But Smith says no. Says he doesn't have any more. He no longer feels like sharing.

5

ED MANGAN'S BURDEN

(Or: Field of Dreams)

Around the lip of the warning track in Atlanta's Turner Field, the Braves grounds crew chugs along on a Massey Ferguson garden tractor and flatbed trailer. As one guy drives at a rate of about five feet every sixty seconds, three others ride in the flatbed, showering the upper yellow line of the outfield wall with cleaning products like Grez-Off, Zep, and Spray Nine. They wear plastic gloves and scrub with the same heavy-duty brushes used to wash the bases after game action. Trailing behind is a crewmember I will call Patterson, who douses the wall with water in their wake and has an uncanny ability to punctuate his thoughts with a lazy spray of the hose, attached to one of the nine spouts hidden in the outfield lawn.

Explaining this particular chore to me, Patterson, who is the type of molasses southerner who manages to always seem either tired or bored, says, "This is just some *bull*shit we have to do."

S-s-s-s-spray.

It is a Tuesday in early April. The Braves are in Miami to open the 2015 season and won't play their first home game until Friday, against the New York Mets. After letting the field lie dormant from

December through February—occasionally covering the infield and the hips (i.e., the grass in foul territory) during that time with warming blankets, aka sweaters, when the temperature would drop below forty degrees to prevent winter kill—the grounds crew has been prepping the big-league field, getting ready for opening day. This year they have already replaced about six thousand square feet of sod (since certain areas of the field never get enough sun during the cold months), laser-graded and reworked the infield clay, and brought the pitching mound and home plate area back to spec. (The mound must be ten inches above home plate and slope down at a rate of one inch per foot.) This week they're applying finishing touches. But while the grass and dirt are pretty much camera ready, the outfield wall is not.

New last season, the wall is already gross, streaked with black dirt and grime. Even with the cleaning products and elbow grease, the wall will never get *clean* clean. Still, the chore is required, exactly the sort of Sisyphean task with which one needs to make peace when battling nature for a living. "If we don't," drawls Patterson, "then they'll show it on TV, and they'll freak out, and we'll be doing it that night. There's always something."

S-s-s-s-spray.

After another hour or so, Patterson is ready to surrender the hose. He has to go meet a prospective game-day staffer. Of the five crewmembers here today, two work year-round. The other three work full time from February through November. Once the season starts, a few others will join the full-time ranks as well. The rest of the grounds crew is hired on a part-time basis, just for home games. They are unofficially known as "part-time Douchers," I'm told, and are a combination of college kids, genuine grounds crew aspirants, and Braves fans of all ages who want to catch some free baseball. The team always overhires the Douchers, since there is steady attrition over the course of the season. "Everyone thinks it's a cool job till they're here till two in the morning," Patterson says, adding with a shrug that it's minimum-wage work for the part-timers. "You get what you pay for."

With Patterson back in the groundskeeper clubhouse beyond the right-field wall, I ask one of the other guys, who requests that I call him Virgil, how many crewmembers they will have to begin the year. This year? he says. Thirty-one. "Well, thirty-two, if you count Ed," Virgil corrects himself. "But we don't really count Ed."

"Ed" would be Ed Mangan, head groundskeeper for the Atlanta Braves and the sole reason I have traveled to Georgia. He has agreed to let me trail him and his crew as they get ready for the season, and then again during the summer, when the games are in full swing. In addition to his role with the Braves—this will be his twenty-fifth season with the ball club—Mangan is also the NFL's field director for the Super Bowl, the man in charge of making sure the grass for the big game is as pleasing as it is playable. With that kind of résumé, I figured: who better to teach me about the art of groundskeeping than this multisport master of the craft?

Only problem: Mangan isn't here this morning. This doesn't register as a surprise with his crewmembers, who adapt to the boss's absence every year, when he heads south for spring training. Even upon his return, they tell me, his whereabouts are unpredictable from day to day, when he's more likely to be tucked behind his desk, poring over some administrative task, down in the closet-like radar room, off the Braves' dugout, checking weather patterns, or up in the front office for who knows what, than he is to be out on the field with the rest of the guys. As Patterson says drily (or perhaps just practically), "If he's not here, we don't care where he is."

Today, I am told by the public relations staffer who has been my intermediary with Mangan, the boss is out in the suburbs, in Cobb County, at SunTrust Park, which will be the Braves' new stadium starting in 2017. (This is the second-to-last season the team will play at Turner Field, which was originally known as Centennial Olympic Stadium and was constructed for the 1996 summer games.) The staffer instructs me to hang with the rest of the crew for now, but before leaving, she also warns me that Mangan is a bit uptight. No, wait, check that, she doesn't want to say uptight. Regimented, she says. He runs a tight ship.

Point is, stay off his grass.

In this way, even with Ed out in Cobb County, Mangan's meticulousness hovers over Turner Field as we walk the warning track. His present nonpresence is also tangible inside the groundskeeper clubhouse, which is basically a large warehouse where the team stores a variety of rakes, shovels, brooms, tampers, aerators, levels, watering cans, wheelbarrows, push mowers, riding mowers, rollers, fertilizer spreaders, and seemingly every other gardening gadget the guys and gals at companies like John Deere and Toro have dreamed up. If that sounds like a jumble of junk, fear not. Each instrument is carefully organized and put away in its proper place, as the boss demands.

There is no question we are in Mangan's domain, and the Big Brother vibe makes more sense when I learn that he's returned, now sitting in his large office, on the near side of the clubhouse. Next to his office is another, narrower office space, shared by the two year-round guys, the field manager and the grounds crew assistant, effectively Mangan's number two and number three. Everyone else, the hoi polloi, sticks to the far side of the clubhouse, where there is a flatscreen TV mounted above a picnic table. This is where the crew sits during games, watching the broadcast to see if they're needed.

I'm told that Mangan knows I'm here, but he doesn't come out to greet me. After an hour, I finally knock on his door. He looks up, peering over a pair of reading glasses. Though forewarned, I'm still struck by the man's unyielding gravitas, his seeming inability to smile. With a shaved head, a thick neck and forearms, and a walnut-crushing handshake, Mangan appears more Army general than farmer. As I introduce myself and remind him of my purpose, he looks at me skeptically, as though I'm trying to pass him a religious pamphlet on the sidewalk. He nods once or twice, says maybe a word, and then returns to his work. I retreat to the picnic table with the rest of the guys as they eat lunch, watching some reality show about knife forging. Hanging overhead, I notice, there is a sticky flytrap, a so-called "southern chandelier."

Later that afternoon, a delivery arrives at the groundskeeping clubhouse and manages to accomplish what I cannot: lure Mangan from his hollow. It is the team's new infield drags, which are pulled across the dirt for grooming purposes before the game and then every three innings. (The frequency of this task can vary by team and according to conditions, per Murray Cook, major-league baseball's field consultant.) While it might be a stretch to say Mangan reacts to the delivery like a kid on Christmas morning, he does animate some as he inspects the new tools, then gathers his crew to demonstrate how to use the drags.

Mangan has a very specific way he wants his guys to pick them up, just as he has a very specific way he wants them to do everything around the field. Of his crew's understanding of expectations, he says, "You'll know. Or you will not know once." For the drags, the move is a swift liquid action, involving both hands, no jerking motions, graceful. "See?" he says, showing them again. "It's simple."

Some of the guys get it right away. But one crewmember keeps trying to do it with one hand. He is struggling. He laughs at himself—Mangan is not amused. With no trace of affection, he says, "You've only been working here eight years. You'll get it eventually."

The next morning the guys are out behind home plate, painting a tomahawk into the grass. It is only ten a.m., but the sun is beating down strong. The forecast says it will be in the high eighties today, midseason weather, and Patterson is already sweating buckets as he leans over a stencil of the logo, which allows him to connect the dots of the graphic with an industrial spray gun of turf paint. You don't need to be Picasso. The key is to color inside the lines. Some of it Patterson does freehand, explaining he's done it a thousand times, since they freshen the logo before every home stand and sometimes before every series, depending on rainfall and how much has been mowed off.

The stadium is busier today than it was yesterday, when it felt a bit like a ghost town, as if the team were already moving out. Between the mound and home plate, there is a two-man team from major-league baseball setting up sensors for a new and improved K-Zone, a balls-and-strikes pitch tracker for TV broadcasts. Beyond them, the big video board in center field flickers a kaleidoscope of colors as the club identifies which panels need to be replaced.

Asked if the stencil makes the painting pretty idiot-proof, Virgil, who is holding a printout of the Braves logo to use as reference, shrugs. Says, "We manage to screw it up." As evidence, he tells me about the time they painted the foul line on the wrong side, thus making the field just a few inches smaller than it should be. (To fix the error, they simply painted it green and redid the line.) On cue, Patterson steps in some paint and smears it across the grass. Another crewmember shouts, "Oh, shit!" He hustles to a bucket of water and wets a towel, blotting the paint off the grass before it can dry. It is important to blot, not rub, he says, because if you rub, the turf could develop holes.

Catastrophe averted, the guys move on to the hip on the first base side. Along both baselines, they must paint Opening Series logos, provided by major-league baseball (MLB), as the league celebrates its own return. Ed Mangan joins the crew at about half-past noon. He takes over painting duties from Patterson, while assessing his underling's handiwork. He uses metal planks and tape measures to check the distances every which way. To my untrained eye, the lettering looks perfect, but Mangan seems displeased. He says, "That looks crooked, boys."

Because the Opening Series logos are more intricate and complicated than the tomahawk, most of the other crewmembers are assisting now as well, holding the paint hose aloft, a reference sheet, or towels at the ready. There is a sphincter-tightening mood change with Mangan in the mix. Guys who were previously calm now bark at each other with directions. At times Mangan gives rapid-fire instructions of his own, but he doesn't yell. In fact, he has a relatively soft speaking voice. When he speaks, everyone listens.

"Touch it up," he says.

"Stay straight."

"Now eyeball this."

"Use your damn eyes."

"Look at him. No, that's going to be crooked."

"No, other side."

"Straight. That's not even close to straight."

Mangan is on a roll, like a professor with a captive classroom. As he moves around the logo, he's careful to step only on the already dry sections of paint, going from one letter to the next. He contorts and twists his body, vigilant with every movement. When painting around a curling design element, for example, he squats low and shifts his body weight from one side to the other, keeping his arm steady, as if it were on a camera dolly. Feeling a bit more expansive perhaps, he says to his crew, "It's like a pool game, boys. What's your next move?" As Mangan paints, a few social media gnats from the marketing department flit down to the field and take photos of the process. Mangan just shakes his head, but I don't blame them. It's fun watching this vast series of dots turn into an intricate design, like seeing a time-lapse video in real time. And then, all of a sudden, I realize Mangan is looking at me. We lock eyes. He says, "Towel? Where's your towel? You should have a towel."

I feel the full power of this man's expectations. I find a towel lying on the turf, but it's too late. I've let Mangan down, and he doesn't look back my way. Perhaps sensing my panic, Patterson makes a face, which says: *Don't sweat it.* "He doesn't have a lot of patience," another crewmember whispers. But it doesn't help. I feel like a failure.

A few minutes later the Braves' head groundskeeper stands up. He takes a step back, appraises the logo.

He doesn't smile.

He says, "Next side."

———

I feel sorry for the children of Ed Mangan. Not for the piercing looks of disappointment he has no doubt cast their way, but because as much of a tyrant as he might be at the ballpark, he's even more demanding of the TV remote at home.

"The Weather Channel is always on," Mangan tells me, as we take a seat in the Braves dugout, when I finally wrangle a few minutes of his time. The rest of his crew is tending to the turf—mowing the outfield, sweeping the edges, watering the new grass on the hips. "They could be in the middle of a show, and I'll just get that feeling. 'Give me the remote.' 'Okay, go back to your show now.'"

In the middle of the night, he often wakes up in a cold sweat, knowing the tarp isn't on the field, thinking he hears rain. "I just sit straight up. Holy crap! Go to the window. Go to the radar." They aren't dreams about the field, he says—they're nightmares. "Anything that can go wrong. A water line blowout five minutes before first pitch. That has happened. You've got water gushing, hundreds of gallons a minute. You gotta fix that. You've got to adapt. The weather can turn on you. Change of plans."

Now in his mid-fifties, Mangan came to the Braves in 1990 with plenty to prove. As a thirty-year-old, he was the youngest field director in the major leagues. Over the last quarter-century, his relationship to the turf hasn't relaxed, not even as he's developed a reputation for being one of the most vigilant groundskeepers in the game. Mangan knows that the best-case scenario is that his hard work goes unnoticed. He doesn't mind. "If nobody is talking about me, that's good. If nobody's talking about the field, good," he says. Because if anything does go wrong, even if the mistake isn't his own, he's exactly the person about whom folks will be talking. "Everything out here is my responsibility," he says. This—Ed Mangan's burden—is just an unforgiving fact of life for a groundskeeper: No matter how many years of good service you have logged, failure is always only a botched rain delay away.

As tightly wound as Mangan can be, there is still so much beyond his control. Maybe it's the knowledge that anything can and will go wrong that has conditioned him to be overprepared—"I have a plan. Then I have a backup for that plan. And then for me, I want a backup for my backup," he says—but Mangan doesn't think so. It's just his personality, how he was brought up, as the son of a carpenter in a small town on the Jersey shore.

As a boy, Mangan used to join his father on job sites, picking up nails. That's where he learned his ruthless work ethic. "We'd get more credit for working than we did for sports," he says of his dad, who taught young Ed to never turn down responsibility and never be afraid to work hard. These are the same lessons he tries to impress upon his crew. "There's never a time you should be standing there, just dead meat, never," he says, explaining how he trains his guys to think ahead, to consider all the angles, when havoc is as unpredictable as weather patterns out of the tropics. He resuscitates his pool game analogy. "When you're shooting pool, what's your next shot? I want to leave the ball where? You don't just slam it and take your shot. That's not a pool player. That's just having fun."

As a modern-day fan, it's easy to take field conditions for granted. But groundskeepers weren't always invisible wizards behind a perfect playing surface. On the contrary, when the game of baseball was first forming in the mid-nineteenth century, taming the undulating earth of the American East Coast was top of mind, even if the idea of professionalizing the craft came as a bit of an afterthought. (It is only within the last twenty years or so that sports turf management has blossomed as an academic major at land grant universities.)

As Peter Morris writes in *Level Playing Fields*, early groundskeepers would tend to the turf as part of a bevy of responsibilities, including fire safety, crowd control, and janitorial work. It really wasn't possible to maintain perfect conditions, as teams were frequently evicted from their grounds and had to share homes with other sports and amusements, like ice skating rinks, polo matches, and horse racing tracks. Fields were so regularly chewed up and unpredictable that for many years baseball had a "bound rule," which stated that a hitter would be called out so long as a defensive player caught the ball before it hit the ground twice.

Provided minuscule budgets, early groundskeepers, who were typically seasonal employees, ran makeshift operations, spreading sawdust and igniting gasoline to dry the fields after rainstorms (drainage was a major issue) and constructing dikes with ingredients like rye bread and cheese. As for crews, groundskeepers would take what they could get: at Sportsman's Park in St. Louis, for example, a goat helped trim the grass, according to Michael Benson's *Ballparks of North America*.

Not everything was so primitive. In fact, a variety of features of modern ball fields owe a debt to groundskeeper ingenuity, such as the pitching mound, which began as a buildup of sawdust; the warning track, which replaced small hills before outfield walls that told defenders the end was near; and even basic terms like *infield* and *outfield*, which were adopted from Scottish farming and allowed for the section of the field farther from home plate to be less carefully manicured than the nearer section, per Morris. Though they weren't always effective, these crude attempts at lawn and order also helped establish the concept of home-field advantage. Baseball crowds were initially nonpartisan, but a team's familiarity with the eccentricities of its home turf provided an inherent edge, such as where to position fielders and how to avoid endemic obstacles like trees.

Before long, a more creative brand of groundskeeping emerged. The pioneers in this area, according to Morris, were two brothers, Tom and John Murphy. Like most early groundskeepers, each man was a "rugged individualist," never staying with one team for too long, always storming off or patching up a feud. Despite their caustic personalities—and the occasional incident involving physical violence, such as when Tom allegedly assaulted longtime baseball man Connie Mack's brother with a bat, nearly killing the guy—the brothers' superior skills kept them in high demand.

Working for the Orioles in the 1890s, Tom Murphy tailored the field to his team's strengths, tilting the baselines inward so bunts wouldn't roll foul, and hardening the dirt around home plate so batters could slap the ball straight down for a sky-high bounce and then leg out a hit. (This became known as a "Baltimore chop.") Around the mound, Tom would scatter soap flakes to mess up the opposing pitcher's grip when he reached down to rub dirt on the ball. Meanwhile, in right field, the creative keeper designed a purposefully ragged and sloped patch of grass that featured a maze of "runways" that only the Baltimore defenders knew how to navigate. His contributions weren't limited to the field, either. Once an opposing player made an errant throw that rolled into the Orioles clubhouse through an open door, which Tom quickly shut and locked until the Orioles scored.

It was a swashbuckling period, when anything not specifically against the rules was considered fair game. It gave rise to a storied baseball tradition of stacking the deck in the home team's favor. Legendary Kansas City groundskeeper—and Ed Mangan's mentor—George Toma (at eighty-six, he's long retired) tells me these sorts of dark arts are known as "groundskeeping by deceit." I meet him on a trip to the Midwest, when he invites me to his home, not far from the original Oklahoma Joe's. When I arrive, Toma is in the front yard, watering the lawn without a shirt on.

Known by a variety of nicknames—Sod God, Sultan of Sod, Nitty Gritty Dirt Man—Toma refuses to sit still even in retirement. Having begun his career as a thirteen-year-old minor-league grounds crewmember in Wilkes-Barre, Pennsylvania, he's never missed a Super Bowl—working the majority as the NFL's field director before turning over the reins to his protégé, Mangan, in 2000—and he still flies to Florida every year to assist at the Minnesota Twins' spring training facility. For decades, big-league teams have turned to Toma as a consultant to fix their fields when problems arise. In 2012, he was inducted into both the Royals Hall of Fame and the Major League Baseball Groundskeeper Hall of Fame, after receiving the Pioneer Award from the Pro Football Hall of Fame a decade earlier.

"When I see a bad playing field, it hurts me," Toma says, kicking his grass-stained white sneakers up onto a leather ottoman, settling into his tchotchke-filled living room. Toma tells me he learned his trade from Emil Bossard, who he calls "the greatest groundskeeper that ever lived." Toma isn't alone in this opinion. Bossard was the patriarch of baseball's most renowned groundskeeping dynasty. (His grandson Roger is field director for the Chicago White Sox, having taken over for his father, Gene.) Emil has been referred to as an "evil genius" for his ability to doctor fields to his team's advantage, like the Murphy brothers before him.

Toma carried on this tradition, even as baseball started cracking down on most groundskeeping tricks, like altering the height of visiting bullpen mounds and tossing pebbles in the base paths to discourage sliding. For years, he tells me, the Kansas City Athletics sent a spy into the scoreboard to relay signs to home team hitters.

Though accusations still occasionally fly for transgressions like sign stealing and other manipulations (the Braves came under scrutiny for allegedly widening the catcher's box in 2000, to give the impression to umpires that off-the-plate pitches were still strikes), the field of play is much more tightly regulated than it was fifty years ago. Groundskeepers can still tweak the turf to benefit their teams. Kansas City Royals field director Trevor Vance, for example, keeps his infield playing fast for 2015, when the Royals win the World Series, because the team is stacked with young and athletic infielders, Vance tells me. But the simplest way to provide a home-field advantage is the same as it ever was, according to Toma: deliver a consistent surface, day after day.

It is a privilege to sit and talk with Toma, who has the scaly arms of a lifetime in the sun and a seemingly bottomless trove of war stories, featuring the likes of Mickey Mantle (who thought Toma's outfield was too hard), Ted Williams (who couldn't get a toehold in Toma's batter's box), and Alex Rodriguez (who offered to hire Toma as his personal groundskeeper when he signed with the Texas Rangers). My favorite is from a recent Super Bowl in Tampa, when he says the NFL got a little lax with security and a couple kids from the University of South Florida sneaked in and painted, in Toma's words, "a big penis and two balls" on the field. (The grounds crew painted over the genitalia before kickoff.)

Toma has some good Ed Mangan stories, too, like the time Mangan had a fellow groundskeeper by the neck ("I thought he was going to kill him"), after the guy doused a Super Bowl field in chemicals without approval. Or the time he threw Diana Ross off the field when her Super Bowl halftime rehearsals ran long. Or the time he used a pair of bolt cutters to snip a TV wire into three-foot strips when the network left the heavy cable lying on his outfield grass overnight after a play-off game. "Eddie isn't afraid."*

But I sense some tension in their relationship. Though he claims he doesn't care, Toma was clearly hurt when Mangan neglected to call and congratulate him on his Hall of Fame inductions. And even though he admits Mangan was the best young groundskeeper he'd ever seen, Toma—who has a habit of prefacing all criticism by saying, "I'm not ripping, but . . ."—takes a couple of potshots at the man's abilities. "The ballplayers all bitch about Atlanta," he says, explaining that Mangan isn't what he would consider a "complete groundskeeper," because his infield is always too hard, like concrete. "His infield dirt is the worst in baseball. The players say they can't wait to get out of Eddie's park." Toma has told Mangan this before, but his mentee is too stubborn to do anything about it. "Eddie's Eddie. He ain't going to change," he says.

Toma's reproach of modern-day groundskeeping isn't limited to Ed Mangan. "I'm not ripping groundskeepers today," he says, "but the art of groundskeeping is being lost." When I ask what he means, he answers by listing some of his old responsibilities, when he was in charge of the fields both for the Royals and for the Chiefs. (In 2015, Oakland's Clay Wood is the only remaining groundskeeper who tends to the needs of both a football and baseball team.) He describes how he would salvage dirt from construction sites and nearby farms, how he had to screen twenty tons of the stuff by himself every winter, and how he grew his own grass and never resodded the field. "It was seed, seed, seed. Now, it's sod, sod, sod," he says, referring to the fact that stadiums buy sports turf from sod farms instead of growing their own. "They maintain the field until the grass goes bad, and then a company comes in and gives them a new field." It's like a totally different profession, in Toma's mind. "They're not groundkeepers. They're caretakers.

"I'm not ripping them," he says, "but . . ."

---

* I could not get comment from Mangan on these incidents, because the Braves did not respond to requests for follow-up questioning.

It's true that big-league stadiums no longer grow their own grass. The Atlanta Braves get their turf from an outfit known as Bent Oak Farms in Foley, Alabama, not far from the Redneck Riviera along the Gulf of Mexico or my all-time favorite restaurant, Lambert's Cafe, "home of throwed rolls." Founded in 2007, Bent Oak burst onto the sporting scene and quickly became the go-to grower for major-league teams like the Braves, Marlins, and Astros, NFL teams like the Jaguars and Dolphins, and a host of big-time college football programs like the University of Georgia, the University of Alabama, and Auburn University. While you'll easily find Bent Oak in any discussion of top sports turf providers, you can't find it on a map.

"There's a reason for that. I ain't looking to be found," says Bent Oak owner Mark Paluch, who instructs me to meet him at a nearby Pick-n-Pay gas station, surrounded by nothing but flat grass pastures and a blinking red light. There I ditch my car and join Paluch in his pickup truck. "We're only about a mile from the Gulf of Mexico," he continues, pointing out the other sod farms (mostly landscape grass) and the soybean-, peanut-, corn-, and wheat-growing operations we pass on the way to his place. "This is the last piece of fucking dirt between here and Mexico, and that body of water doesn't allow the air here to drop below freezing. I didn't pick this place by accident."

Paluch actually has two farms here, one growing Bermuda grass and the other growing paspalum. While both are warm-weather varietals, they would cross-contaminate and create an undesired hybrid if they grew too close together. Paluch takes me to the Bermuda farm, where a crew of workers is rolling up thick strips of sod, which are forty-two inches wide and between forty-five and fifty-five feet long, each one weighing around two thousand pounds. The sod is being shipped to the University of Georgia, in preparation for football season.

"They all come down to get grass from Hillbilly Willy," cackles Paluch, who at fifty-five has wind-mussed gray hair and a wisp of a mustache. He is alternately braggadocious and weirdly secretive as we drive around his property. One guy we come across, he tells that I'm a representative from MetLife Stadium—for what reason, I'm unclear. He also tells me not to take photos of certain machinery, which they have customized to their needs. One machine, in particular, I'm told not even to describe. "You don't need to write about that," he says. On second thought: "You can call it a gadget."

We drive past a shed that is filled with various other sod machines and draped with Super Bowl banners. (Unsurprisingly, Mangan relies on Paluch as a regular supplier for the big game. For the 2015 Super Bowl in Arizona, for instance, which is significantly farther away than any of Bent Oak's regular clients, Paluch shipped sod to Glendale in refrigerated trucks.) "I sleep out here," Paluch says, explaining his dedication to the turf. "I don't chase pussy, dude. I don't have any hobbies, habits of any sort. You got to live this shit." He points to the banners. "This is how I get off. Watching TV and your grass is on every channel? Oh yeah."

Paluch parks his truck. Before getting out, he spritzes himself with some sort of pink liquid from a Victoria's Secret bottle. "Alabama bug spray," he says, by way of explanation. "Works better than OFF or DEET, which you'd have to drink. Forty-five dollars a bottle and you smell like a lady, but most the guys down here are sissies anyway. Come on."

He wants to show me the grass.

Actually, not grass, Paluch clarifies, as we walk onto a patch of the stuff. "Value-enhanced athletic turf." Unlike most sports turf growers, Bent Oak grows sod only for stadiums. Paluch doesn't dabble in residential installations or even golf course grass. But what really sets his operation apart, he explains, is the manner in which he grows it: on sheets of plastic. "I'm not in the dirt business," he says. "I only grow grass on plastic."

Paluch lifts the corner of a strip of sod to reveal what looks like a black tarp or thick garbage bag underneath. The grass is *literally* grown on plastic. "You can take one percent of the grass and roll over three hundred percent," he says, emphasizing the strength of the sod, its ability to withstand the sharp movements of 350-pound linemen. "It's bulletproof. Boom. Now look at that fucking piece of felt right there." I have never seen anything like it. The sod itself is about two inches thick, the bottom as flat as a piece of floor tile.

Paluch's bulletproof sod doesn't begin life in Alabama. Bent Oak is more like its finishing school. First Paluch grows his grass the traditional way—in the earth—at a farm in Georgia. After the better part of a year, he harvests that grass and ships it down to Foley, where it is laid down on plastic and fattened up for another year by raking in sand—because the sod is sand-based, it is less likely to come apart in the rain; or as Paluch puts it, "There is no mud in it." The care programs are customized so that each field has been treated with the same cocktail of fertilizers and fungicides being used at its stadium destination. Richard Wilt, a former groundskeeper for the Miami Dolphins and Marlins who now works at Bent Oak, explains how the plastic impacts the growing process. "Typically, grass grows down, right? The roots grow down. We don't grow down. We grow up. Once the roots hit the plastic, they turn back up, and it grows within itself." That is why the sod is so dense and heavy, he says. "The root-to-shoot ratio is twenty times more than any other grass. You can make a hammock out of it."

Another advantage to growing grass on plastic, Wilt says, is that there is zero stress on the sod when they ship it to a stadium. "When we cut and roll it up, you're not hurting the grass at all. All you're doing is rolling it up. Basically moving it. Other guys that sell grass, they harvest it. They cut it off dirt, and they're cutting half the plant off." Paluch nods, because now we are hitting on the heart of his business model. "It's carpet, dude," says Paluch. "It lays like carpet, and you can play on it in the morning. When you put it down, you can play on it immediately." Because the sod is so thick and heavy, it won't slide around, he says, not even under the stress of NFL game action. Why does this matter? "Because the money is in the concerts," Paluch says with a smirk. "Not ball fields."

He's right. Of the twenty-plus groundskeepers and turf industry insiders I interview for this chapter, each one identifies the increasing number of event days at stadiums as a growing issue for field directors, who have to maintain a surface that is both aesthetically perfect and safe to play on at all times. As Steve Wightman, the retired head groundskeeper for the San Diego Padres and Chargers, puts it, "You live and die with that field. It just tears you apart when they start putting all this stuff in there, and then they expect you to have that field the way it was before the event."

Ed Mangan describes a delicate balance between using and abusing a field, because depending on the type of event—and its duration—it can be hell on the turf. Dave Mellor, who is the field director for the Boston Red Sox, tells me about the time Fenway hosted the Rolling Stones. "Most shows are here for about five to seven days," he says. "That show was out here thirteen and a half days. About the sixth day of the show, I remember a roadie said to me, 'Hey, duuuude, you smell rotten pumpkins?' I said, 'Yeah, I think that's my grass.' He's like, 'Ah, you are so fucked!'" Mellor had two truckloads of new sod ready to go, as soon as the stage came down.

"It hit me in the head like a fucking hammer," Paluch says, crediting a conversation he had with Mickey Farrell of the Tampa Sports Authority, which manages Raymond James Stadium, where the Buccaneers play. "He looked at me and said, 'Let me tell you something— the Bucs ain't my best tenant. I got to do something with these other forty-four weekends.'" After all, stadiums can make good money off of ancillary events, like motocross shows, soccer exhibition matches, and concerts. Paluch's advice to field directors and stadium operators is not to try to save the grass during such events but to "kill the son of a bitch. You'll spend three hundred thousand dollars trying to protect it. Just scrap it. Keep the three hundred thousand and kill that motherfucker. For four hundred, I'll give you this one. It's a total different concept. Swap the son of a bitch," he says.

Of course, this is exactly what George Toma is talking about, when he criticizes the state of modern groundskeeping. I ask Wilt if he thinks Toma's critique is fair. He does, without reservation. "All the legwork and grunt work are done here," he says. "Most places have more checkbook than they do patience."

Mark Paluch isn't the only one growing grass on plastic. In recent years, a variety of other sod farmers have adopted the practice, including Carolina Green Sod and West Coast Turf, which is tabbed to provide the field for the 2016 Super Bowl at Levi's Stadium. Ask Paluch about these other growers, however, and he just scoffs. "They're my best salesmen," he says. "I have no competitors."

The question no one seems able to answer—Paluch included—is when or how exactly the idea of growing sports turf on plastic emerged. Says Wilt, "Who came up with the idea of wearing a hat? I don't know."

But there is one guy who says he knows exactly how it started, Paluch's former boss at a company called Southern Turf Nurseries, Ed "Eddie Boy" Woerner. Now in his sixties, Woerner, who is based in nearby Elberta, Alabama, has always had a curious mind. He's a tinkerer and an inventor, a problem solver. When starting a sod farm in Hawaii, for example, he knew he couldn't use the native soil. "You got that lava," he says. "So we got some soil from a horse farm, we put down plastic, and we put the grass on it with a fancy irrigation system." Sure enough, it worked. Not long after that, he brought the idea back to Alabama, where he was multiplying seed stock. "If you multiply it in contaminated soil, you're going to plant contaminated soil. You want to plant pure seed, so I was growing it on plastic," he says. "I had never considered using it as a grass that is ready to play."

That changed after an encounter with George Toma in Green Bay in the mid-1990s, when Woerner delivered a couple of the sod-laying machines he had invented and Toma had been flown in to fix the field after a snow-filled season destroyed the turf. They stayed in touch. "I was on the phone with George every other week for a solid year talking about what I got to do to be ready for these kinds of events. Not just the machines but the grass," says Woerner. Toma gave him three criteria: the grass had to be green for TV, it had to hold up for the players, and it had to be mobile. By 1999, Woerner was ready. His first stadium installation of sports turf grown on plastic would be for an exhibition game at the Louisiana Superdome—indoors!—as if the challenge weren't difficult enough. "When you put grass on plastic, you have now put it in intensive care," explains Woerner. "That isn't normal for the grass. What I created is not in a textbook. There are no groundskeepers learning or studying what I did. That is not there. That's not even science. Hell, I tricked the system."

Woerner wasn't afraid to go beyond the bounds of book learning, and the exhibition game was an unmitigated success, a victory for shade-tree mechanics and garage inventors everywhere. "Old boy from the stadium said, 'That's the rug!'" Woerner recalls.

According to Toma, it was the best sod he's ever seen.

Woerner made one mistake, though. "I didn't patent it," he says. "I just assumed it wasn't patentable. See, grass isn't patentable. Plastic isn't patentable. Sand isn't patentable. But you know what happens when you put a combination in an order, that's a process patent." Woerner learned about this category of patent only recently—

surprising for a man of so many inventions. "I wish I'd patented the process," he sighs, "because if I would have, then Mark or nobody else would've been able to do a damn thing. So I could've done that, but I didn't know at the time. I didn't know about that."

———————

If we're going to talk about grass, then we have to talk about the alternative: artificial turf. I take one more road trip before returning to Turner Field, this time to Dalton, Georgia. About ninety miles north of Atlanta, Dalton is informally known as the carpet capital of the world, for its many mills, which once produced about half the world's carpets. It is also the home of AstroTurf, and I have been invited to take a tour.

"This is the original plant," Sydney Stahlbaum, AstroTurf's director of sales support, says as we pull up to a low-slung building in the heart of carpet country. Inside, the factory is filled with what appears to be a mess of interconnected instruments and engines straight out of the board game Mouse Trap, as raw pellets of polymers (nylon and polyethylene) are melted down and extruded into long strands of monofilament fiber, before those fibers are dipped in a cooling bath, stretched for strength, and sometimes crimped (either with steam or mechanically) to impart certain performance characteristics. "Yeah," Stahlbaum shouts, to be heard over the noise of the machines, which are running twenty-four hours a day to meet the demands of fall school schedules, "it might not be organized in the most intuitive or most efficient [manner], but because the machinery was just kind of set up that way, this is how it's evolved."

AstroTurf (originally known as Chemgrass) was developed in the 1960s by a company called Chemstrand, which was a joint venture between chemical giant Monsanto and American Viscose, and the green Brillo pad of a playing surface served as the first true disruptor of the sports turf industry. In many ways, it created the sports turf industry. According to Ed Milner, who oversaw early AstroTurf manufacturing and would go on to serve as president of what was then known as AstroTurf Industries,* a lot of fundamental research was being done in those years, as they developed ways to measure things that had never previously been measured, like traction and abrasiveness and shock absorbency and how a ball rolls or bounces. All the while, a single research extruder at a nylon plant in Pensacola, Florida, produced six strands of fake grass at a time, day and night.

"We were in the fibers business, that's what Chemstrand was all about. We supplied fibers to a lot of the carpet manufacturers," says Milner. Working with a manufacturer known as Mohasco (or Mohawk), Chemstrand sent its slowly extruding nylon ribbon to Amsterdam, New York, where the first Astrodome turf was "literally woven on Wilton carpet looms," producing about three-quarters of an inch per minute. "Pretty damn slow," says Milner. Soon after that project, production of AstroTurf was brought in house, to Dalton, where it remains today. "We had Wilton looms—we could weave it—but we preferred the knitting process," says Milner. "It made a stronger, more conforming fabric, and we could make about twelve inches a minute." And so by the late 1960s, knitted fields became the artificial turf of choice—tufting was another (weaker but faster-to-produce) option—as synthetic products spread across the sports landscape, especially in multipurpose stadiums.

Artificial turf has been widely maligned in the sports world since its inception. Early issues included rug burns, lumpy footing, baseballs taking circus bounces off the trampoline-like turf, and a con-

---

* Since being sold by Monsanto in the late 1980s, AstroTurf has endured a complicated ownership history, including multiple bankruptcy proceedings and what is described to me as a German Ponzi scheme (under the ownership of Balsam AG). In June 2016, AstroTurf again filed for bankruptcy protection as part of the fallout from a courtroom decision that the synthetic turf manufacturer had infringed on a competitor's patent. (The turf industry is notoriously litigious and the case may continue.) Shortly thereafter, a judge approved yet another sale of the company.

ductive playing surface that could occasionally heat to 160 degrees in the sun. Some football players contracted staph infections, while others reported showering with their sheets on the day after a game, because the sheets had fused with their open, turf-induced wounds overnight. It got so bad that Congress held hearings over the safety of synthetic turf. Some of the noncontact injuries over the years proved particularly gruesome, like when Bears wide receiver Wendell Davis got his feet stuck in the turf at Veterans Stadium and ruptured the patella tendons in both knees. (Doctors eventually found his knee-caps swimming around his thighs.)

According to Milner, the conditions were no less safe (minus the rug burns) than natural grass, despite the widespread cultural perception stoked by melodramatic headlines and the occasional vomit-in-your-mouth injury like Davis's. He says players were simply using the issue of artificial turf as leverage for collective bargaining. "That's working conditions," he says, "and that's an ideal thing to raise a ruckus about."

To some, the debate between artificial and natural grass was a debate over the soul of sports (particularly the soul of baseball). In Kansas City, there was a bumper sticker campaign to "Let George Do It," when the Royals switched to a synthetic surface. In "The Thrill of the Grass," a short story by W. P. Kinsella, also the author of *Shoeless Joe*, which was adapted into the film *Field of Dreams*, a man resists the artificial takeover of his local ballpark by leading a midnight army of fellow purists to replace the turf with grass one square of sod at a time. "Pride is lost," former San Francisco Giants head groundskeeper Matty Schwab told *Sports Illustrated* in 1970. Still, according to grass professionals like Mike Goatley, a turf grass specialist at Virginia Tech and a past president of the Sports Turf Management Association (STMA), there is a place for both natural and artificial turf, as determined by a variety of factors, like geography and usage. "I like to think of them as another tool," he says of artificial fields, adding that one point of frustration is the fallacy that they are maintenance free. "That's simply not the case."

Despite the existential crises and the other "noise in the news," as Milner puts it, AstroTurf maintained a stranglehold on market share, as competitors like Tartan Turf, Poly-Turf, Omniturf, and Wyco Turf came and went for decades, right up until 1997. That's when a new company known as FieldTurf emerged, boasting a sand and rubber-infill system—what is now known as third-generation artificial turf (basically what every artificial turf company sells at the major-league level, AstroTurf included). It wasn't just a new kind of carpet; it was meant to replicate natural grass. "There have only been two game changers in the history of our industry," AstroTurf's global director of sales and marketing, Troy Squires, tells me. "AstroTurf when it was invented, and then FieldTurf."

Today AstroTurf doesn't make a lot of money from supplying big-league fields. The vast majority of the company's client list includes high schools, parks and recreation departments, and college varsity and intramural fields. But according to Squires, no artificial turf company makes much money off of stadium installations anymore, and *that* is the problem. "When a pro job comes up, we look at every one of them," he says. "We might put a bid out, but we just don't get all that excited about it, because it's like a race to the bottom."

Turf companies have a tendency to underbid each other so drastically, he says, that they end up giving the fields away for free, or worse: paying for the privilege. "It gets really crazy at a certain level," says Stahlbaum, who tells me she knows of at least one company that has paid up to one million dollars to get its turf in a stadium. There is some cachet that comes with a pro-team installation, of course, and that can be seductive, but the reality is that a free field likely won't even act as a loss leader. "Unlike the old days, if you sold a professional-level field in a certain area, you'd sell a bunch of fields off of that," says Stahlbaum. "But now every turf company has its little market share of the high-profile, so there's less translation into more sales in that region."

An industry veteran of almost forty years, Squires also questions if companies are supplying their best surfaces when giving them away for free. "I'll be honest with you," he says. "Most of the fields in the NFL, in my opinion, aren't as good as your average high school field." I find this statement shocking, not only because of the amount of money the NFL pulls in but also because of the amount of squawking the league does on behalf of player safety, especially in the wake of so many head injury headlines. And yet others in the industry say the same thing. One turf insider tells me he doesn't believe the NFL cares nearly as much about player safety as about maintaining the *appearance* that it does. "That's the only way I can see it," he says. "They talk about injuries, all that stuff. But when it really comes down to it, if they're talking, then put your money where your mouth is, and they don't. It's weird. It's just weird."

Joe Traficano, who is the sports turf specialist for West Coast Turf, tells me something similar when we chat following Reggie Bush's season-ending injury at the Edward Jones Dome. The running back slipped on a stretch of bare concrete that borders the field. "You would think common sense would tell you that it is slick and you got cleats, and they would have [covered] it. But they got to wait until something drastic happens to make a change. And it is all about money. It is *all* about money."

One place they never stop thinking about player safety (or more specifically, turf performance and how that relates to player safety) is the basement level of the AstroTurf plant. That is the last stop on our tour and the dominion of a man named Kris Brown, AstroTurf's director of research and development. There he presides over a collection of instruments of torture. And really, that's exactly what they are—a variety of machines that brutalize the turf in imaginative ways to test for things like wear (via a spinning set of four rolling cleats, which can be adjusted for speed and pressure), infill retention (via a whirling dervish of a gadget that reaches 320 revolutions per minute), resiliency (via a machine that lightly slaps a blade of fake grass over and over and over, which I find both hilarious and embarrassing for that blade of grass), and shock attenuation (via a device that drops a seven-pound missile onto the turf, meant to mimic the weight of a human head), among other things.* "There is a misconception that something has to be soft to be safe," Stahlbaum says, since many players have complained about the unforgiving nature of artificial surfaces. As the turf silently screams all around us, she gives the example of a car dashboard. "Your car is designed to take impact and spread that across the dashboard. It doesn't have to be a pillow to play on."

I ask about the future of artificial turf, since any impending game changers are as likely to come from this basement torture chamber as from a university laboratory. Both Squires and Stahlbaum express excitement over the possibilities of a new kind of hybrid field called XtraGrass, "where you grow the natural in the artificial," says Squires. Stahlbaum chimes in: "It's interesting. It has a biodegradable backing, so as it sort of decomposes, the grass roots into the synthetic that's left over." They installed one such field at a high school outside of Denver the previous summer, which will act as a beta site for North America.

Beyond that, Stahlbaum tells me they're experimenting with a possible fourth-generation turf, which will ditch the rubber infill, largely in response to an NBC News report that highlighted a potential link between crumb rubber pellets and types of blood cancer. (When I talk to Darren Gill of FieldTurf about this, he tells me he suspects the natural grass lobby scared the whole thing up, since they

---

* I am glad to learn Brown has ditched former Houston Astros owner Roy Hofheinz's initial durability test: renting elephants to pee and stomp on the AstroTurf.

were hemorrhaging market share.) Says Stahlbaum, "We totally disagree with [the report], because the science just doesn't support it. At the same time, there are certain clients who are reluctant to accept crumb rubber, and so the need has arisen to cater to that market."

As we wrap up, Stahlbaum shows me a rectangular remnant of the original AstroTurf field from Three Rivers Stadium, from the fifty-yard line, which is fittingly lying alongside all of Kris Brown's modern tools of torment. Laughs Brown, "There's probably some Lynn Swann skin in there."

Monday, July 20, ten a.m. I arrive back at Turner Field, ahead of a three-game series against the Los Angeles Dodgers. It is still early in the day, but the Braves grounds crew is beat. The guys always wear down over the course of a home stand, when the full-timers clock fourteen-to-fifteen-hour days on average, showing up at nine a.m. for a night game and even earlier if the field is covered. (Once the sun comes up, the turf starts to cook under the sauna of the tarp, and that can kill the grass.) And then, of course, there is the possibility of rain delays or extra innings—or both.

At least a couple times a season, they expect to sleep at the ballpark.

During most home stands, the crew can recharge after Sunday games, when the Braves typically play in the early afternoon. But not yesterday. First pitch wasn't until 5:11 p.m., and then they had to stick around for a postgame event. "I think I've slept four hours the last three nights," one guy tells me, while smoothing the infield dirt. "I didn't want to get up today. It's going to be a fight until the end of the home stand."

The heat can't be helping. According to the morning news, the expected heat index is 109 degrees today, which makes maintaining moisture levels all the more critical. "Yeah, it's pretty much a groundskeeper nightmare," says Virgil. Around the field, crewmembers tend to various tasks, their daily routines—fixing the mound and the home plate area, brushing conditioner into the baselines, sweeping sunflower seeds out of the grass, hand-watering the infield and the hips. Soon the guys will move on to mowing. Virgil tells me they always try to double-cut the lawn to ensure they shear every blade of grass. This is important because if they miss, the ball can snake. "If it bounces right in between those seams, it's going to hit some [taller] grass, and that's when it shoots it right or left." Certain mowing patterns can also cause the ball to snake, he says, which is why it's important to change the grain on any pattern every week or so, to keep the grass as upright as possible. "Infield, the ball is going so fast, doesn't matter. Outfield is where you're going to get your issues with snaking."

A conga line forms on the infield as Virgil waters the skinned areas, the dirt, with a handful of crewmembers draping the hose over their shoulders behind him. They do this every day the same. Muscle memory. Perfection. I think about what George Toma says about groundskeeping, how the art is being lost, and I'm sure on some level he is right. But what these guys do is not unimpressive. High-definition TV is unforgiving, and it is impossible to predict what kind of field-related emergencies might emerge at a ball game on any given night. There can be rain, obviously—in Atlanta, precipitation usually comes in prolonged downpours out of the tropics, or in thirty-minute thunderstorm bursts, what the crew calls "poppers"—which is when the guys snap into action, spreading drying agent on the dirt or pulling tarp during a delay. It's not nearly as simple as it looks.

Just Google "baseball tarp incidents" for a bevy of bloopers, like when a Kansas City grounds crewmember was steamrolled underneath the tarp and its metal tube, or when the Pittsburgh crew lost control of the tarp amid strong winds, and one crewmember was briefly swallowed inside. Richard Wilt tells me a story from his time in Miami, when a crewmember was lifted off the ground by a gust of wind while holding a corner of the tarp, before being slammed back to earth. In 1985, Vince Coleman was blindsided by an automatic tarp in St. Louis, and it cracked the speedster's tibia, ending his season. And he got off lucky. While that automatic tarp was nicknamed the "killer tarp," some grounds crewmembers have actually lost their lives to unwieldy infield covers, George Toma tells me. "In the olden days, they were heavy tarps. A lot of army tarps, from the war. Some of them were what we call twenty-ounce tarps," he says. "Now you got six-ounce tarps that go on easy."

Easy being a relative term.

But tarps are just the beginning. Remember when flamethrower Randy Johnson hit a low-flying bird with a fastball? (The bird exploded on contact.) Well, who do you think had to clean that up? Wilt tells me about another fauna-related incident, when the Miami crew was attacked by a swarm of bees. "All of a sudden you see half the crew come running across the field, screaming. We're laughing at them because we thought they were fucking around, and then the next thing you know you hear *pop pop pop*, and they start hitting you." There was also that time a fan asked to spread his dad's ashes on the field. The crew told him no, but he dumped the urn out anyway, when he thought no one was looking. "We had to go out there and sweep him up before the game started," says Wilt.

In Atlanta, the craziest episode came after a controversial infield fly call during a 2012 play-off game, when a popup landed safely in (not so) short left field. The call went against the Braves, depriving them of a bases-loaded situation, and the fans weren't happy. A garbage shower began to rain down on the umpires, Patterson remembers, leading to a suspension of play. "All fucking hell broke loose," he tells me. "They were throwing so much garbage out here. It was crazy. Beer bottles. We were out here picking up all the trash. Finally, eventually, they ran out of shit to throw. They were throwing their shoes. From up in the 755 Club, they were throwing full ketchup bottles. That shit was coming in *hot*." Patterson still has a memento from that night. "I saved a ball," he says. "I was standing near the umpires, and someone threw a baseball, and it hit one of them in the side. I picked it up, and it said 'Fuck You' on it. I saved that."*

———

At two p.m., with Ed Mangan yet to make an appearance, the crew is back in the groundskeeper clubhouse. Virgil hands me a putty knife and a brick of packing clay. "Just don't tell anyone you did this," he says. "They told me you can't do any manual labor."

Because it is too hot for early batting practice, there is less to do on the field today. The guys take advantage of the midafternoon lull by chopping clay, a good time-killing chore they have to do once or twice a month. Lined up on either side of a wooden table, it's like a cocaine cutting operation as we break the bricks down to smaller cubes, which can then be worked into the infield dirt as needed. "Smoke a bowl and you can do this for hours," one of the guys says. "Just kidding. No drugs in the major leagues."

As we cut the clay, there are no bowls to smoke—though according to one sod farm worker, weed goes well with anything turf-related: "You can't be a grass man and not be a *grass* man," he says—but there is an easy intimacy among the crew, a kind of in-this-together camaraderie, and for a few minutes I feel like one of them, too.

Such acceptance is not a given, I know. In *Level Playing Fields*, Peter Morris describes a groundskeeper who rose to prominence in the 1880s named Billy Houston who had, according to the *Detroit Free Press*, "a mysterious method of procedure which he refuses to divulge to anybody." Houston saw his process as proprietary, because he believed it

---

* Patterson can consider himself lucky he wasn't working the Buffalo Bills–New England Patriots game in October 2016, when Bills fans threw a dildo onto the field.

was the key to his livelihood. This historical example of secrecy actually touches on a philosophical split within the groundskeeping community that still exists—a divide between those who look to share information and those who want to keep their knowledge tight to the vest, who want to go it alone. Loners versus sharers.

As George Toma writes in his autobiography, *Nitty Gritty Dirt Man*, "I have often felt that groundskeepers who do the best job tend to be loners. The mediocre ones form a club and cry on each other's shoulders." Yet he was one of the founding members of STMA in 1981, which has proven a valuable resource for turf managers of all levels, while fostering a spirit of cooperation. Both Dave Mellor and Trevor Vance count themselves among the sharers. "Some people think knowledge is power and won't share it," says Vance. "I'm all about sharing." In fact, he says sharing information might be the best defense against losing one's job. "There are thirty of us in major-league baseball, it's a small fraternity. And there are probably thousands and thousands that would love our jobs. So if I can help you keep your job—if I can make your job easier tomorrow because of what I learned today, I want to share it."

Steve Wightman, another past president of STMA, says, "I look at it this way: the whole industry is going to be better and everybody is going to be better if we share everything. But a lot of people—I don't think they felt comfortable doing that. Maybe there was a lack of confidence in their own ability."

Though I doubt Ed Mangan ever lacked for confidence, he is a legendary loner. "The rumor going around now is that when [the Braves] get fertilizer or fungicide or insecticides, he takes all the labels off, so [the crewmembers] don't know what they're putting on," Toma tells me. This is false, but the fact that Toma could believe such a thing about his former pupil tells you the essence of the rumor—if not its specifics—must have some basis. Within the Braves groundskeeping clubhouse, on his own crew, there isn't much love for Mangan. Part of the problem is that he is so clearly not a member of the crew—and not just because he never seems to be around. He doesn't even bother learning the guys' names. "For a while, he thought my name was Black, since I wore a black shirt everyday," says a guy not named Black. Another time Mangan asked for security to take a mug shot of everyone on the crew, so he could know who was working for him, since apparently normal human introductions weren't an option. "I told security, and they said, 'You got to be fucking kidding me,'" says Patterson.

"It's weird," Not-Black says of Mangan's habit of ghosting the grounds crew. "I've never had a job where the boss is like not a part of what you do." It's even worse when he is around, though, they say, because he brings the same uptight energy I witnessed back in April.

But what if Mangan has to be this way? Not because he might otherwise lose his job—that's ridiculous—but because it's just the price of his own brand of greatness? What if this is the only way he knows how to run his ship? Militaristic. Keeping his guys on edge. A kind of pins and needles strategy to ensure he never makes a mistake and, by extension, they don't either. The same way certain athletes fabricate perceived slights, to nurture a chip on their own shoulder, in order to play angry. Some seem to accept the possibility. My PR intermediary tiptoes around Mangan like he's a temperamental genius. She describes him as being "in the zone," when dealing with game time stress, as a way to justify his prickly personality, his one-sided communication, and his OCD-like need to keep an outsider like me at arm's length. That's what makes him one of the best, she says.

And yet as the afternoon wears on and the clay chopping continues, no one in the groundskeeping clubhouse gives much thought to Mangan, wherever he might be. They know what needs to be done. But unlike Mangan's, their metaphorical pool games include an occasional ounce of fun. Mostly the guys give each other shit as we chop, as in any other locker-room situation, with one dude in particular receiving a lot of grief, like a resident punching bag. "Every crew has a guy like that," per Patterson. They also swap some hard-earned insight from their time on the crew, like how to tackle field runners and streakers. "They stopped letting us do that," says a veteran crew-member wistfully. Another guy describes how he became an inadvertent streaker during a rain delay. He was getting off a tractor, when a broadcast camera caught him with his fly down, without underwear on. "All the players and the Tomahawk girls [from the Braves spirit squad] saw it," he says. After that, the field manager did underwear checks for a while. Virgil tells me how he used to make little figurines out of packing clay when he'd get bored. "Little dolphins and frogs and shit. I made my mom a pot that she could put all her spoons in." He also reminisces about a former crewmember named Big Carl who cut his finger off while chopping clay, "and just kept cutting." The guys hoot at the memory of Big Carl. "He cut it off and just raked it into the clay bin. Packed it into the mound," Virgil goes on. "Players were complaining down in the clubhouse—I think I saw a guy's fingertip."

No need to worry, though—the finger looked great on TV.

6

EXTREMELY LOUD AND INCREDIBLY GROSS

(Or: Fans Behaving Badly)

Everybody wants to feed the gorilla. Chicken, hot dogs—those are the best. Anything he can shove directly into his mouth. The gorilla is being plied with drinks, too—beer, whiskey, whatever. For beer, the gorilla favors light-colored lagers and pilsner-style brews over heavier craft ales. He also prefers bottles to cans. (Even though glass bottles are technically outlawed here, none of the authorities seem to care, in a wise display of selective enforcement.) A man dressed all in black hands the gorilla a Corona, his favorite.

Someone shouts, "How are you going to drink a beer?"

The gorilla shouts back, "Like this!"

He thrusts the bottleneck halfway down his gorilla throat and turns it bottom up, downing most of the liquid in a few giant gorilla gulps. Everyone cheers.

It is barely past eight a.m., and already the smell of weed overwhelms the musky aroma of charcoal. It emanates from everywhere and nowhere all at once. I am trailing the gorilla and his handler/wife—whose name is Marilyn, known around these parts as Jungle Jane but introduces herself to me as "Ms. Gorilla"—as they venture

through the parking lots outside of Oakland–Alameda County Coliseum, which has all the concrete charm of a prison yard or mental
facility. The stadium is home (for now) to the Oakland Raiders,* who
have a one o'clock matchup against the Green Bay Packers. Amid the
sea of silver and black, the preferred color palette of Raider Nation,
a few brave souls wear green and gold. "If there was ever a game that
I've been nervous about, it's this one," a visiting Packers fan tells
me, recalling the reception he received in Candlestick Park before
the San Francisco 49ers moved to their new stadium in Santa Clara.
"Someone spit in my face. And there was a chick knocked unconscious in the bathroom, a Packers fan. There was a pool of blood. My
mom went in there. It was bad."

I understand this fan's apprehension. With a slew of headline-
grabbing incidents that include everything from in-stadium stab-
bings to parking-lot assaults to full-on city riots—a history of
violence complemented by the intimidating visual of a front row fan
base that looks like villainy incarnate, or something out of a death-
metal rocker's bad dream—Raiders fans have become a kind of cultural bogeyman. According to Raiders-fan social anthropologists Jim
Miller and Kelly Mayhew, authors of *Better to Reign in Hell*, the team
represents a "monstrous unruly other" in the sports world's collective conscience. Even Hunter S. Thompson, who spent time with the
organization, once described Raider Nation as "beyond doubt the
sleaziest and rudest and most sinister mob of thugs and wackos ever
assembled." To prepare for my time in Oakland, I'd Googled "Raider

---

* It has basically become an annual tradition for the Raiders to threaten to leave Oakland unless they receive public subsidies for a new stadium, in spite of the fact that
taxpayers are still paying the debt service on renovations made to the Coliseum in the
1990s, when the team returned to the Bay Area from Los Angeles. Last year the talk
was about moving to San Antonio. This year it's about L.A. Next year it will be Las
Vegas (which proves to be more than an idle threat). As a local sportswriter put it,
"You'll never see a more abused set of fans." See Ken Belson, "In Oakland, Some Raiders Fans Fear the Meaning of 'Last Home Game,'" *New York Times*, December 25, 2015.

tailgate" and landed on a video in which two female fans grope a mobile stripper pole, which had been set up in the stadium parking lot, while surrounded by a crowd of man-size hard-ons disguised as human beings, screaming sensible things like, "Titty fuck the pole!"

But this Packers fan has nothing to fear, according to the man in black, whose name is Oscar and is one of the leaders of the B-Lot Crew tailgate party. "It is all love," Oscar says, offering me a drink. Another Raiders tailgater weighs in. "Those are my friends from high school," he says, pointing at a couple of Cheeseheads, currently being subsumed by a huddle of Raiders diehards, who are giving them the middle finger, while chanting "Raaaaaaiiii-ders! Raaaaaaiiii-ders!" (The middle finger, I come to learn, is a standard greeting among a certain type of Raiders fan, almost like a wave or a handshake.) "We told them, don't worry about it. You might get hassled a little bit, but it's nothing but love."

Indeed, everyone is smiling.

But there is no time to revel in this public display of inter-fan-base affection. The gorilla is getting antsy. "Gotta move, gotta move," he says.

Having started our morning over by the RVs with the Bad Boyz of BBQ—which is led by Kirk Bronsord, aka Kingsford Kirk—the gorilla, whose fan name is Gorilla Rilla (his human name is Mark Acasio), is on a tight schedule, with a laundry list of other tail-gates to hit before heading into the stadium. There he will take his place in the first row of the Black Hole, as the lower-level seats in the south end zone are known, famous for its ruthless heckling of opposing teams and an impressive collection of superfans, known by names like Violator, Dr. Death, and GrimRaider. Out in the lots, it is difficult for Rilla to get very far. Dressed in a full-body gorilla costume, ski goggles, Flavor Flav–size Hawaiian beads, a Cat-in-the-Hat-style top hat, and a T-shirt with his name on it, Gorilla Rilla is a veritable celebrity among Raiders fans, who shriek for him to stop and grace their tailgates, to pause for a picture or a hug or a shot of booze.

"Gorilla Rilla!"

"Gorilla Rilla, man!"

"Can I get one real quick?"

"Hey, Rilla! Rilla! Let me get a picture!"

"One more!"

"Gorilla Rilla!"

Without fail, he obliges, communicating his ascent with loud animal grunts and elongated vowel sounds ("Yeeeeeeeeeah, man!"), while Ms. Gorilla trails behind—or trudges ahead, depending on how long he is stopped—handing out Rilla's fan trading cards. The cards, which assert Gorilla Rilla is "the official mascot of the Black Hole," feature a variety of biographical information, like the primate's birth year—1995, which is when the Raiders returned to Oakland from Los Angeles—and other Rilla-related factoids, like his 2009 induction into Pro Football's Ultimate Fan Association. (Kingsford Kirk, who has also been inducted, tells me the association is "an elite group of superfans." It sounds like the basis for an ill-conceived comic book movie.)

Rilla is so committed to Raider Nation that he actually got married in his gorilla suit in 2012, surrounded by about a thousand of his closest superfan friends. "When we were planning our normal wedding, there was no way we could fit everyone in the church," Ms. Gorilla tells me, and she knew her husband-to-be was not the kind of guy to pare a guest list. Ultimately, she didn't mind having a Raiders-themed celebration. She even saw a silver (and black?) lining in including all of their parking-lot compatriots. "He had a lot of groupies," she says of Gorilla Rilla. "He had these girls that would walk around with him. So I was like, these women got to know that you are taken now."

Rilla speed walks by just then. "Gotta move, gotta move!"

"You are not getting very far," Ms. Gorilla shouts ahead.

But Rilla doesn't hear. He is already swarmed by a new crush of dudes, each armed with a bottle of Crown Royal.

———

According to Eric Simons, author of *The Secret Lives of Sports Fans*, fandom is a "species-level design flaw." He probably won't get an argument from Chris Sotiropulos on that point. The Raiders' director of stadium operations often finds himself counseling with season ticket holders after they have been arrested at a home game or otherwise ejected from the stands. "I think people get overly excited," he says. "When they are in the heat of the moment, I think they do things that under normal circumstances, they typically wouldn't do."

Heightened emotions are par for the course at live sporting events, where alcohol and bravado (or defensiveness or anger or any number of other booze-fueled reactions) can combust in violent bursts. In the words of a deputy from the Alameda County sheriff's office, which staffs Raiders home games in tandem with the Oakland police department, "You deal with a lot of alcohol-related stupidity."

Raider Nation has been described as "an unholy fan base of hell-raisers, gangbangers, and inveterate knife-lickers," but stadium-related misconduct is hardly exclusive to Oakland. In fact, Raider Nation is not even the most maligned fan base in the United States. (That distinction belongs to the good people of Philadelphia.)* For

---

* As the charges go, Philly fans have hurled batteries at athletes, cheered player injuries, and instigated so many in-game fights that the team once set up a courtroom (known as Eagles Court) inside old Veterans Stadium to process the ruffians as they passed through. In more recent years, local supporters have made headlines for wrestling home run balls away from elderly women, forcibly vomiting on small children, and stealing the prosthetic leg of a Vietnam veteran who performs outside of games. Of course, the most infamous incident in the history of Philly sports fan behavior—an event so cartoonish that it basically launched the whole these-people-are-animals narrative—occurred in 1968, during halftime of an Eagles game, when a nineteen-year-old kid

as long as there have been sports, there have been those who use the setting as an excuse to misbehave. In his book *Sports Spectators*, Allen Guttmann writes that there is "every reason" to believe the ancient Greeks were an "unruly mob of spectators," citing as one example the Pythian Games at Delphi, where "rowdy drunkenness was such a problem that the spectators were forbidden to carry wine into the stadium." Quoting ancient philosopher Dio Chrysostom, he describes the crowds at Alexandria chariot races thusly: "When they enter the stadium, it is as though they had found a cache of drugs; they forget themselves completely, and shamelessly say and do the first thing that occurs to them."

Really, as Guttmann maps out, if there is one through line in sports history, it is that fans are going to create mayhem, from the "tumults" in Pompeii in the year 59 (which are widely regarded as the first-ever sports riots and resulted in the city being barred from hosting gladiatorial games for a decade) to the predilection for starting fires at chariot races in Constantinople in the fifth and sixth centuries (which convinced the emperor to build the city a marble—and therefore much less flammable—hippodrome) to twentieth-century boxing crowds at Madison Square Garden (who rioted so regularly that *The New York Times* distributed battle helmets to its writers).* Justine Gubar details a seemingly endless list of weird—and often deadly—fan behavior in the United States and around the world in *Fanaticus*, a book that explores "mischief and madness in the modern sports fan." In 2011, for example, a Dallas Cowboys fan Tasered

---

appeared in a Santa Claus costume and the whole stadium proceeded to pelt him with snowballs. Philly fans get admittedly defensive when presented with this litany of misconduct, sick of hearing the same old storylines dredged up anytime some local idiot does anything wrong—incidents that they insist would fly under the radar in another city. As one fan tells me, when I attend an Eagles-Giants game, "Philly gets a bad rap. I think we do. And that is why we are sensitive when people say we are pieces of shit."

* This last tidbit comes from Michael Roberts's *Fans! How We Go Crazy Over Sports* (Washington, D.C.: New Republic Book Co., 1976).

nearby Jets fans at MetLife Stadium when they hassled him for not standing for the national anthem, while in 2013, Brazilian soccer fans beheaded a referee after that referee stabbed a player to death on the pitch. Also in Brazil, at least one person has been killed via toilet bowl, when rioting fans hurled an uprooted commode at him. Even those who attempt to clean up the spectator-driven mess are not safe. Guttmann describes an emergency worker trying to save the life of a heart attack victim during a 1976 riot at a Patriots game in Foxborough, Massachusetts. As the worker administered CPR, a rioter peed on him from behind.

While the NFL keeps meticulous track of any and all instances of fan misconduct in and around its stadiums, the league doesn't make that data public. What numbers are available are suspect: a 2013 investigation by a Seattle news station revealed that local police departments across the country often work in cahoots with the league to suppress crime and arrest stats. For those reasons, it is impossible to say whether violence at football games is on the rise, although Sotiropulos insists that fan behavior at the Coliseum has been steadily improving over the last half-decade. He credits the adoption of a strict fan code of conduct, which the team doesn't hesitate to enforce via arrest or ejection. "We are not really in the business of giving out warnings," he says. (Anecdotally, Raiders fans agree that the atmosphere at home games has become more relaxed, less edgy.)

The worst Oakland troublemakers are rarely the regulars, according to Sotiropulos, and almost never those fans you see on TV wearing the face paint and the spiked shoulder pads. The serious problems come from those who attend a single game very aware of the national perception of Raider Nation and decide to play their part in stirring up chaos, as if they were attending some kind of criminal fantasy camp. "They just come in, causing their damage, and then they might never show up to a game again," he says, adding that the team has a term for such interlopers: "one-game wonders."

With a little over two hours until Gorilla Rilla intends to be in his front row seat, he crests the ramp that cuts between the Coliseum and Oracle Arena (both part of the same complex) and that leads from one side of the stadium to the other. He pauses to take in the tent-infested parking lot that lies ahead. "Look at that," he says. "Now you get to see the heart of everything." He points back from whence we came. "That was just appetizers over there."

"Mmmmm," he growls, and then takes off in a slow sprint. I walk with Ms. Gorilla, who tells me this is where most of the Black Hole regulars tailgate. As he does every Sunday, Rilla plans to snake his way through the aisles of parked cars, makeshift bars, and at least a few piss buckets. (Some fans keep a plastic pail hidden alongside their vehicles—using a car door for privacy—to avoid long lines at the porta-potties.) Along the way, Rilla will pause at a few select locations before landing at the official Black Hole tailgate, which is a multitent party in Lot D sponsored by Bud Light, punctuated by frequent rounds of tequila shots and featuring an always-open dance floor. "I go there toward the end," he says, "because if I get there, I will stay there."

Gorilla Rilla is even more popular, in even higher demand, on this side of the stadium, which I would not have thought possible. Like a furry pinball, he bounces from tent to tent, sprinting ahead, doubling back, always pausing for picture requests, hugs. Ms. Gorilla keeps an eye on her man, making sure none of the groupies try any monkey business. After giving one woman a big gorilla hug, Rilla says, "Love you," which is something he tells many Raiders fans. The woman clearly takes it personally. She replies, "I love *you*! I really, really, really love you," and refuses to let go of his paw, while Ms. Gorilla unleashes a heavy dose of side eye.

With Rilla as the center of attention, I get a chance to chat with some other Raiders regulars who populate the parking lot, like Jay Da Nygma, who goes by the fan name Mr. Jay and whose face looks like a Raiders version of Heath Ledger's Joker, underneath a black bowler hat. Having started dressing up in 2006, Mr. Jay never misses a game, which doesn't sound like a big deal, until I learn where he commutes from: "I live in Miami." "I'm going to sound like a commercial when I say this, but it is a lifestyle," he explains. "I tell people that all the time. You can't be a casual fan. When you come here for the first time, even the most casual fans are soaked up in it. The mystique. The aura."

To prove his point, Mr. Jay introduces me to his girlfriend, who has been coming to games since 2002, which was when she turned eighteen and could finally purchase her own tickets. "I wasn't allowed to before," she says. "My brothers, they party and they didn't want me to be involved in that." Mr. Jay wants me to see her tattoo—RAIDER NATION, inked huge on her right forearm.

"If I could roll this up, I would show you mine," he says, struggling with his stiff leather jacket. Eventually he gets his sleeves to budge. On either arm, he has melon-size Raiders tattoos—one featuring an eye-patched dog in a Raiders helmet, and the other a hundred-dollar bill containing the traditional Raiders pirate in place of Benjamin Franklin, along with a host of other Raiders-related Easter eggs. "The serial numbers are the Super Bowl wins," he says, "and it says 'United Nation of Raiders.' If you *really* look closely, one of the serial numbers starts double-zero, and that is the original Mr. Raider, Jim Otto."

Since their early days, the Raiders—which were originally going to be called the Oakland Señors—have represented something far bigger than football. With their owner, Al Davis, a perpetual thorn in the NFL's side, the Silver and Black earned a reputation as outcasts and rebels, accepting players no other team wanted, players who would womanize and practice drunk. But come Sunday, those same players would explode onto the field with a "Badass brand of football," as author Peter Richmond puts it. Those players, Richmond writes, "plied their trade the way they lived their off-the-field lives: with abandon, on the edge, as one, and taking no prisoners along the way." The counterculture streak attracted fans like Alfred Hitchcock, the Hells Angels, and the Black Panthers. It also created a diverse and inclusive community, the Raiders serving as the common ground between otherwise disparate factions of humanity. Such a feeling persists to this day, when all the individual tailgates combine to form something bigger in the hours before kickoff, something like family.

For many, the games also offer a fertile mating ground, as evidenced by couples like Gorilla Rilla and Jungle Jane, Mr. and Ms. Jay, and countless other prospective pairs, who are grinding like basement-partying eighth graders to a soundtrack of 1990s West Coast hip-hop. As we move through the tents, I ask Rilla about his former groupies. He stops in his tracks and takes off his goggles so I can see the whites of his eyes. Solemnly, he says, "Dude. Yeah." He lets out a primal groan of gorilla pleasure. "I got stories, dude."

Like fan violence, sex and sports is a tradition that has roots in antiquity. Chariot races and gladiatorial games "were often used as an opportunity for sexual adventure," writes Guttmann. Some, like the Roman poet Juvenal, condemned "the tarts who display their wares," but the convenient brothels at venues like Circus Maximus were lively hubs. Today lusty fans are often caught with their pants down. The sports website Deadspin has a whole series of posts dedicated to what it terms "stadium smut," which is exactly what you think it is— X-rated videos of topless women and upper-deck sex acts.

But the menacing flip side to overly macho and sexualized environments is that they can create unsafe situations, especially for female fans, who are subjected to bullying taunts of "show us your tits!" The authors of *Better to Reign in Hell*, who are married, relay a story of a Raiders fan telling Mayhew, pregnant at the time, "If I don't watch myself, I'll rape you." In Green Bay, I talked to a woman moments after two men pulled her into a bathroom, wanting to take her into a stall and "show her a good time." They agreed to let her go only when she caressed the lead attacker's chest and said, "Give me a second. I'll be right back." After regaining her bearings—she was visibly shaking—she alerted a security guard, who detained the lead attacker and called for the police.

It is impossible to know how frequently such incidents occur at NFL games, due to the league's secrecy when it comes to stadium-based crime, but it would not be hard to believe these events are of a pattern. According to a 2015 study that looked at sexual assault around college football games, there is "a strong link between football match-ups and an increase in college women, ages 17 to 24, reporting rape," per *The Washington Post*. The study, which examined twenty-two years of FBI data and was issued on the National Bureau of Economic Research's website, found the incidence of rape increased 41 percent when there was a home football game, with a greater chance that the assailant would be a stranger.

Even without specific stats, sexual assault and domestic abuse have become major problems for the NFL, as players like Ray Rice, Greg Hardy, Ray McDonald, Ben Roethlisberger, Josh Brown, and many, many others are accused of off-field violence against women. On this front, the league is completely botching the issue, with displays of gross hypocrisy such as highly variable, slap-on-the-wrist penalties that are imposed only after a public outcry or an embarrassing revelation like the elevator footage of Ray Rice or the journals of Josh Brown;* its responses seem gauged exclusively for public relations. To many, league officials appear less concerned with

---

* *The Onion* published a 2014 article entitled, "NFL Announces New Zero-Tolerance Policy on Videotaped Domestic Violence."

victims—or with meaningfully educating its audience and athletes on the dangers of hypermasculinity, rape culture, and the necessity of consent—than with optics, à la dressing in pink for breast cancer awareness. But as long as leagues like the NFL keep finding ways to excuse, minimize, and even normalize such behavior from its players, perhaps we shouldn't be surprised when violence against women infiltrates stadium gates on game days.

The Black Hole. The name alone conjures up images of some of the most visually terrifying fans in football—an army of chain rattlers, zombie clowns, and Skeletor types whose only mission is to terrorize opposing teams in service of the Raid-ahs. It didn't take long for visiting players to learn not to get too close to the south end zone, to the denizens of the Black Hole, lest they receive a shower of batteries, beer, and chicken bones—anything that wasn't bolted down. To be sure, the Black Hole is an iconic haven of hardcores, the spiritual center of a fan base that redefines dedication to team.

When the Raiders moved back to Oakland from Los Angeles in 1995, there was no such thing as the Black Hole, not yet. The idea for such a fan section was actually born the year before, in 1994. That was when Rob Rivera, a founding member and president of the Black Hole, would get together every Sunday with a small group of friends and watch his beloved Raiders from a distance of nearly four hundred miles, as the team finished out its term in L.A. Some weeks they would catch the early games, too, and the Cleveland Browns made a big impression. "This Dawg Pound thing," Rivera remembers thinking of Cleveland's famous fan section, which would hurl dog biscuits at the field and smuggle full kegs into the stands (inside a dog house), "that is fucking phenomenal, man. And our fans are better than that! We are bigger. We are better. We are badder. So if the team ever comes back to Oakland, why don't we do something like the Dawg Pound?"

For more than a year, Rivera held informal organizational meetings in which they debated everything from a group name—the Black Hole beat out the Rats' Nest, among other candidates—to practical considerations, like "How can we draw attention to ourselves?" and "What can we do to piss off as many people as possible?" To those questions, the group decided: Get front row seats, and stand for the whole game. So for the 1996 season opener, Rivera and nineteen brothers-in-arms showed up in the first row of section 105. With them, they brought banners and hats and black T-shirts that read in big block letters THE BLACK HOLE. (While some of the guys streaked their cheeks with black war paint, dressing up was not part of the group's original mission; that evolved over time.) They also had a life-size dummy, meant to represent the opposing team's quarterback, which they would abuse for four quarters.

"It wasn't even kickoff yet," Rivera recalls. "Row two is like, 'Hey, man. Sit the fuck down!' Row three, 'Sit the fuck down!' Throwing peanuts, water bottles, everything you can imagine. We did this for the first two games. We locked arms, and we said, 'One sit down, we all got to sit down. One stand up, we all got to stand up.' And we did it, man. We did it."

By game three, the self-selection began. Those who didn't want a part of the Black Hole found seats elsewhere, while those who liked what they saw in the south end zone started to move in. "They said, that is a good-ass atmosphere, that is a mosh pit. So the mosh pit started to grow, grow, grow."

The mosh pit became a powder keg. There was nothing the ferocious fans wouldn't do to support their team. "When we played the Kansas City Chiefs, we grabbed Neil Smith's face mask, ripped it off his head," says Rivera. "When we played Ray Lewis, we had him hooked up in a pig tie, and we are swinging him around—the dummy—and yelling, *Mur-der-er! Mur-der-er!*"

The dummy, which would represent a different opposing player for each game, served as a signifier for the rest of the stadium, per Rivera. "We beat the fuck out of this dummy. And when we threw it up, the whole stadium knew it was time to rock."

The Black Hole took its role seriously. They reveled in the wins, and they were pissed off after the losses. Rivera remembers one game in 1997, a Monday-night matchup against Kansas City, when Chiefs quarterback Elvis Grbac completed a thirty-three-yard touchdown pass to Andre Rison, with three seconds left in regulation, to beat the Raiders by one. "We walk out to our tailgate party, and all the Raiders are leaving, heads down. It was a fucking funeral. But there was one car with [Oakland kick returner] Desmond Howard, and that motherfucker was jamming the beat in his SUV, having a good time." This didn't go over well with Raider Nation. "I will never forget it, dude," says Rivera. "Hundreds of motherfuckers started rocking his SUV, rocking it. And as they're rocking it, I remember hearing *dunt dunt dunt dundundundunt!* Bottles flying like bombs." Rivera says Howard's car was practically sideways, about to topple, when cops finally intervened and kept his vehicle upright. But while his car may have been saved, his status among Raiders fans was forever damaged.

It goes without saying that the Black Hole has not always been the most welcoming place for opposing fans. Miller and Mayhew come up with "ten basic commandments" for Black Hole occupants, two of which are "Fuck with opposing fans until they request a police escort" and "Fuck with the police escort until they request a police escort."

But the Black Hole has lost some of its bite over the years. With forty-five minutes until kickoff, I sneak into the south end zone seats and find an empty spot a few rows behind Gorilla Rilla. There I'm greeted with all the menace of a Comic-Con mixer, as gussied-up Raiders and Packers fans pose together for pregame photos. To my right, a middle-aged dad from New Jersey (by way of Brooklyn, he tells me) sits with his young son, no more than ten, who is a Packers fan.

According to Rivera, the Black Hole peaked in its first few seasons, which he calls the "craziest time period, and it will never be matched." He compares the fan section he created to a technology startup. "There's always the start, and that is the heart and soul," he says. "I think just naturally, you start to lose some of what it is all about." That inevitable dilution—which has coincided with a particularly ugly stretch of Raiders football (as of 2015, Oakland hadn't fielded a winning team in more than a decade)—is also coupled with the ever-tightening screws of what the NFL allows at its games. "We can't bring a dummy no more, we can't sneak our band in the parking lot. No matter what we have done, the NFL has stopped it."

That isn't to say the Black Hole is a G-rated space. Far from it. The Packers players and referees are pelted with steady (if not overly creative) insults from the south end zone, as soon as the game begins.

"Fuck you, Aaron Rodgers!"

"Fuck you, Discount Double Check!"

"Fuck you, Green Bay! Let's go! Let's go! Let's goooooo!"

Each time someone unleashes an F-bomb, the Jersey Dad to my right cringes slightly. Eventually he leans into his boy and says, "What happens at a football game, stays at a football game. That is our bond, okay?" They bump fists. "You hear things, you don't repeat."

From behind us: "Fuck you, refs! Fuck you! Fuck yooooou!"

Father and son make silent eye contact, nod.

Meanwhile, to my left, a longtime fan who introduces himself as Krash keeps squatting down below the height of the crowd. He debates whether to put on his parka, as it starts to rain. "I'm just looking for a safe place to do my drugs," he says. "Don't quote me on that." When I ask Krash how the Black Hole compares to the old days, he doesn't hesitate. "It's tamer," he says. "Definitely more family friendly, except for some cursing, but whatever." He ducks down to take a pull off his pipe, offering me a hit. I decline, explaining (truthfully) that I'm slightly under the weather and don't want to contaminate him. He laughs. Says, "Look around. We're all contaminated."

The thing that most bothers Raiders fans like Rivera is not the cultural softening at home games but the tendency of sports fans across the country to characterize Raider Nation in general—and those in the Black Hole, specifically—as a band of lowlifes and criminals.

Part of the image problem, Rivera is aware, is that Raiders fans' outlaw persona was forged in the old "Badass" days and was then complicated during the team's stay in L.A., when the defiant, truth-to-power rap group N.W.A. adopted the Silver and Black as a kindred-spirit organization, while turning Raiders gear into street wear—in 1991, *The New York Times* dubbed this trend "Raiders chic"—which created an association between the team and gang activity. In the minds of many scared (often white) Americans, that was just another reason to stay away from the Los Angeles Coliseum, where the Raiders played. In Ice Cube's documentary *Straight Outta L.A.*, which revisits this time period, sportswriter Bill Plaschke describes the pregame tailgates as something "out of *Mad Max*," with fans "playing tackle football on the pavement" and "fistfights all the time." At a game in 1990, a Steelers fan was beaten unconscious in the stands, leading to a one-game beer ban. Raiders-related offenses weren't limited to the stadium, either. In a display of true team loyalty, one fan—a man who became known as the Raider Bandit—committed twenty-four bank robberies to fund his football habit. Also not helping matters was condemned murderer and rapist Robert Charles Comer, who was executed in 2007. His last words? "Go Raiders!"

Rivera concedes that a rough element came with the team upon the Raiders' return to Oakland. "Shit, if we lose, man, stuff is going down—you could feel that in the air the first few years," he says. "Then it turned into a positive, passionate, ferocious fan base, which was what we were about from the beginning." But the stigma was hard to shed. In 2011, the Black Hole hired a PR man, hoping to shift attention toward the group's charitable works. (Community service is a core tenet of the Black Hole, as it is for many other Raiders fan groups.) "We are the bad guys, but we feed the homeless, we give blood, we do toy drives. We do all that stuff," says a fan named Vinny Sullivan. He's a member of a group called the 66th MOB. Making Oakland Better.

————

Beyond the center-field wall in San Diego's Petco Park, home of the Padres, a nondescript midnight-blue box of a building looms over the playing field. With only two breaks in the uniform building face—glass slits that serve as windows—the structure provides a solid visual backdrop for hitters during the game, to help them pick up the ball out of the pitcher's hand. Where bleacher fans might have once sat in baseball-obscuring white T-shirts, this area in dead center field is now sacred in major-league parks, known across the league as the batter's eye. Some venues use the opportunity to install a luxury club in that space, behind darkly tinted glass, like Yankee Stadium's Mohegan Sun Sports Bar. Here in San Diego, there is no luxury on offer. There is not even a bathroom.

On the second level, behind one of the glass slits, lies the Event Management Center, the command post for the ballpark—the center of its nervous system. At the head of that system is John Leas, director of security for the Padres, who came to the team in 2011 after a career of nearly thirty-two years with the San Diego police department. A white-haired tree trunk of a man, Leas has agreed to let me ride shotgun for a Sunday afternoon game in early May, to help me understand fan behavior through the sober lens of enforcement, to explore the world of stadium security, and to experience a sporting event from the other side of the law. (This is access that no NFL team would ever provide.) In ancient Greece, Allen Guttmann writes, men known as *mastigophoroi* ("whip-bearers") and *rabdouchoi* ("truncheon-bearers") were called on to keep order at the Olympic games, while in the late Middle Ages and early Renaissance periods, a *Pritschenkoenig* ("king of the whip") did the same at archery contests in Europe. Today Leas, who is perched in the back row of the EMC, armed with a pair of binoculars, tells me I can just call him John.

The hour surrounding first pitch is always the busiest, Leas explains, and that results in a torrent of calls into the staffers of the EMC, who represent a range of departments, like janitorial, guest services, event security, ballpark management, law enforcement, and fire and medical. Under two large TV monitors that display a rotating selection of security camera feeds—and a few small signs that read QUIET PLEASE—the representatives sit in the window-hugging front row, each with a phone, a laptop, and an earpiece tuned to his or her department's radio frequency. As calls come in, they field every manner of ballpark issue—from unattended bags and fire hazards to vandalism and vomit cleanup to broken toilets and clogged drains to physical altercations and missing children (a Sunday-afternoon special)—and dispatch employees from the appropriate department to handle the situation as needed. In the corner of the room sits a guard named Tyler who works for Elite Services, the private security firm that staffs Padres games. He controls the cameras and listens to all the radio feeds simultaneously, a cacophony of problems large and small, trying to intuit which camera angles will be required next.

Looking at the monitors, which display bite-size glimpses from within the stadium and from outside its walls—and which supplement the EMC's panoramic view of the playing field and seating bowl—the venue starts to feel digestible, manageable. This is imperative in an operation so large and complex, when nothing less than the safety of tens of thousands of people is at stake. It is important to not be overwhelmed by the enormity of the task—by the tangled web of constant communication, monitoring, and response—because there is so much detail, so much constantly going on. Preferring to be overprepared, Leas has put together a thick three-ring binder containing a Critical Incident Emergency Response Plan, which prescribes a course of action for almost any imaginable event, from kidnapping to bomb threats. Still, there are always situations that require game-day decisions, like when a call comes in over the radio from an entrance gate. There a couple is using a wagon as a stroller and wants to bring it into the park.

Tyler pulls up the camera feed from that gate on a big screen, zooms in on the stroller-wagon. Leas takes a look and shakes his head no.

The liaison relays the message: "That's a negative. We aren't allowing wagons into the ballpark."

Leas's reasoning: "If we allow a few of those wagons in, and then all of a sudden we have a stampede, it's going to become a challenge, because they're low profile." People won't see them in their haste to get out of the stadium, he figures, and "kids are going to get hurt."

If that kind of thinking seems a bit fatalistic, that's just what the job requires. Leas needs to envision worst-case scenarios, and the last thing anyone wants is added obstacles in a crowd crush, which can result from panics (i.e., rushing away from a perceived danger) or crazes (i.e., rushing toward something desirable) and which often turn deadly. Perhaps most famously, this happened at Hillsborough, in Sheffield, England, in 1989, when ninety-six people were crushed, suffocated, and trampled at a soccer match.* If he ever had to empty the ballpark quickly without creating a panic, should the need ever arise, Leas cites a creative solution that was employed by a nearby minor-league club: shut off a bank of lights, feign a power outage, announce that the game is postponed, and ask fans to leave.

---

* In April 2016, a jury found that those fans had been "unlawfully killed" due to police mistakes.

This leads us to the other great existential stadium threat: terrorism. After 9/11, event security was put on steroids, as rooftop snipers invisibly appeared at sports venues across the country—especially for big events, like Super Bowls—along with fire hoses at the ready to respond to the possibility of chemical weapons. (The NFL still uses rooftop snipers at its games.) After the Boston Marathon bombing, major-league baseball mandated fan screening at its venues, according to Mark Guglielmo, the Padres' vice-president of ballpark operations, although 2015 is the first year they have metal detectors at Petco, since teams had two years to phase them in.* Guglielmo says there is less of a threat level in San Diego than in some East Coast cities, "but you got to take it seriously," especially given the potential symbolism of an attack at a sports stadium. Leas was able to bolster his network of security cameras thanks to a grant from the Department of Homeland Security. "That's what paid for some of our exterior cameras," he says. "It's called buffer zone protection." The idea is to provide some advanced notice before a threat arrives. "Great concept," says Leas, "but the reality is when you have ninety to one hundred cameras going at one time, if you happen to be looking at it, great. But if you're not—"

The HD-quality cameras are impressive, though. Tyler demonstrates their zoom capabilities for me, focusing in on the Coronado Bridge, which spans the San Diego Bay to the south of the ballpark. "Unfortunately, we can see when people get up there to jump," says Leas. Which is spooky to think about. Then again, all the cameras are kind of Big Brother-ish, when you consider that there is nothing inside—or even just outside—the ballpark that the occupants of the EMC cannot see, like when Tyler zooms in on a fan in the outfield stands after he throws back a home run ball, and

---

* The NFL introduced metal-detecting wands at stadiums across the league in 2011, on the heels of the Taser incident at MetLife Stadium. Prior to that, they did pat-downs.

we can basically determine the size of his soda—"Just give him a verbal warning," says Leas—or when he zooms in on a couple of surfers parked on a sidewalk outside the stadium, sitting on a blanket, drinking malt liquor. Tyler asks, "John, you want them setting their camp up right there?"

He does not. The police are notified (technically, the sidewalk is beyond the Padres' jurisdiction), and we watch on the screen as the two vagabonds try to hide their booze beneath the blanket, when they see an officer approaching. The EMC representative from the police department gets on the radio: "Fifty-five, just to let you know, the alcohol is under their blanket."

The vagabonds look at each other in disbelief when the officer demands the bottle.

At various points throughout the day, Leas and I go mobile, leaving the EMC and hoofing it around the park. Before the game, we're moving constantly, as Leas receives a steady stream of updates over the radio and via text message, e-mail, and phone call. We stroll onto the playing field, mindful not to step on the grass. Leas points out the men and women wearing red polo shirts around the field and in the stands. These are security guards from Elite. Leas calls them "red shirts," and they're his infantry, his eyes and ears. "Per California guard law," says Cornelius Jones, who is an on-the-ground event manager for Elite, "we observe and report, so that's our primary thing."

Guards will try to separate and defuse heated situations but avoid physical intervention, if possible. For that, they radio the EMC for backup, for uniformed officers. Leas staffs the stadium on a game-by-game basis, usually bringing in about two hundred guards, using forecasted attendance figures for guidance. For today's game, he tells me, the Padres expect around 31,000 crowd members. That is what has been sold. But there are always no-shows, and there are always walk-ins. (By the end of today's game, an official attendance will be announced at 34,197, although only 28,631 will have come through the gates, which is the number that matters most to Leas.)

When fights do break out, the team tries to handle the situation calmly, so as not to arouse other fans. "If you see someone taken out of the stands, they disappear pretty quickly," says Leas. First, the disorderly fan is escorted down to "guest safety," which is just a euphemism for Padres Jail (they have three holding cells). There the fan is processed and then removed from the park: ejected, sent to county jail, or taken to a detox center, depending on the degree of offense and the fan's willingness to cooperate. More so than the day of the week, Leas says it is the opponent that typically determines how rough of a day security can expect at the ballpark. Last weekend, for instance, the Dodgers were in town. "In one evening, we had fourteen fights in the stands. That's got to be a record for us."

Leas takes each of these incidents seriously. "When a fight breaks out in the stands, that's a big deal to us. When someone runs onto the field, that's a big deal to us." The worst is when the teams clear their benches and brawl, he says, "because it takes total attention, and then it incites the crowd, especially guests who are on one side or another. They start bickering with each other in the stands." And that can lead to more fights.

Field runners are almost as bad. It is the responsibility of the field-side Elite guards to apprehend the trespasser (or trespassers), while other guards, stationed higher up in the ballpark, deploy down, almost like a rotation defense in basketball. Leas advises the players to stay away from the runners—to not try to tackle them, even though it might land them on *SportsCenter,* and to not interact with them, even via high-five. The vast majority of field runners are just attention-seekers (many turn out to be underage kids, possibly egged on over social media), but there's no guarantee that a fan can't have violent intentions, as when Monica Seles was stabbed on the tennis court in 1993. "Lately it seems their strategy is to get to center field first, to get over the fence, so that's my direct point," a field guard named Greg tells me. Leas, whose office wall is decorated with framed photos of successful field-runner apprehensions, instructs the guards to play the angles with a runner, to "vector in."

Says Greg, "We try to get them off the field as fast as possible. Monkey see, monkey do, and we don't want a zoo of people out here."

"Multiple runners, that's really hard on us," Leas admits. "And we don't want to look like Keystone Cops, either. That's where there's a bunch of people chasing, and they're just running all over the field. It looks really stupid."

Greg smiles bashfully. "Last time I got head over heels, and I fell. That's beside the point!"

A prop plane inches across the high San Diego sky, trailing a banner for car insurance. This too is on Leas's radar. "During the game it's a no-fly zone," he says, looking up, hearing the distant putter of the plane's engine. "It's a safety issue for us. He's okay up until an hour before the game." But Leas is less worried about ambush marketing than about the emerging aerial danger posed by drones. "You know, drones can be weaponized," he says. "You can put a payload on there that does like dispersant sarin and make the crowd sick and panic. I've seen weapons mounted on them, and they can be very accurate. If you take an iPad that has a forward view, it's basically like a video game, except it's real bullets coming out."

––––––––––

We exit the ballpark and circle around to an entrance gate, where fans are trudging through the newly installed metal detectors. Some claim such screening measures at stadiums are little more than security theater, but Leas insists they have practical value: "We catch knives and other weapons that you know have been coming in for years, and they're not coming in anymore." The entrance gates also serve as a de facto checkpoint for weeding out intoxicated fans, Leas says, thus mitigating potential in-stadium problems. "If they're coming in drunk, they'll never get in. And we don't give refunds." Plenty of NFL teams, including the Raiders, tell me they do the same type of sobriety screening as the Padres, although given my parking-lot experiences, a fan would have to be pretty boisterous—or completely comatose—to be denied entry at a professional football game. (The absolute drunkest fans I encounter, based on totally unscientific observation, are in Buffalo, at a Bills game. I do not see anyone denied entry.)

Of course, no matter how strictly a policy is enforced, no matter how many sharp objects are turned away at the gates, and no matter how many high-powered zoom cameras a team has at its disposal, there will be blind spots at a sports stadium. Almost always it is the parking lots—with bathrooms coming a close second—where the worst incidents transpire. In October 2015, Dallas Cowboys tailgaters purportedly encouraged one fan to shoot another in the head, and he listened. In 2013, a Kansas City Chiefs fan beat another man to death after finding the guy passed out in the wrong car. In 2011, in a reportedly unprovoked attack that has come to symbolize the random-acts-of-aggression danger that haunts sporting events, San Francisco Giants fan Bryan Stow had his skull cracked by two assailants outside Dodger Stadium. They beat him so viciously Stow was left disabled and brain-damaged, unable to care for himself. In court, the judge told the defendants, "You are the biggest nightmare for people who attend public events."

In general, parking lots pose less of a problem at baseball games than at football games, where tailgating is more of a tradition. According to veteran police officer Gary Mondesir, who works as the operations sergeant during events at Qualcomm Stadium, the former home of the San Diego Chargers,* it is imperative for officers to have a presence in the lots. "We have officers on bikes. We have officers in cars, on foot." They also use TerraHawks, which are mobile surveillance platforms—basically, vans that contain a guard tower that can elevate to twenty-five feet. The officers monitor the crowd for signs of problematic behavior. Although troublemakers make up a small percentage of any stadium crowd—somewhere in the neighborhood of one half of 1 percent—that is still hundreds of people. Plus, Mondesir says, there can be groups who show up without tickets, with no intention of going to the game. "They just show up for the party atmosphere and to cause issues." Beyond that, the officers never know what they might find. One time at Qualcomm, Mondesir tells me, he caught a couple having sex in a parking-lot porta-potty, which, he adds, "was extremely gross."

Cornelius Jones, who worked Chargers games as well, says the Elite guards are always "feeling the crowd," taking its pulse. "The best thing to do is start talking to people. You realize what kind of mindset they're in, even if it's two guys arguing." If the conflict is between friends, for instance, it is less likely to escalate. On the other hand, there can be times when the presence of a security guard serves as an instigator, and the fans turn against him, heckling and name-calling. "When you start hearing that, you need to realize, 'Okay, I need to just leave.' Get yourself out of it [and call for police backup] before it escalates," says Jones. "The biggest thing is to not get surrounded."

Over the last decade, before the Chargers' move to L.A., fan behavior had been going downhill at Qualcomm, says Mondesir. He blames the shrinking number of Chargers fans at home games, which let rival fans buy up tickets. "You get a lot more arguments, a

---

* In January 2017, after failing to secure a new stadium deal in San Diego, the Chargers announced that the team would be moving to L.A.

lot more fights," he says. Raiders fans long considered their team's annual trip to San Diego an "unofficial ninth home game," per Miller and Mayhew. (One imagines a similar dynamic will quickly develop in L.A.) Among local police and security professionals, this didn't go unnoticed. In 1999, the Raiders-Chargers game produced so many in-game fights that even the players turned their attention to the stands. The following year a Chargers fan was stabbed in his seat, which resulted in a five-year prison term for the offending member of Raider Nation. In 2011, a Chargers fan returned the favor outside Qualcomm. Though Mondesir has a grudging respect for members of Raider Nation, whom he calls "true fans," he says the yearly Raiders matchup presented a "special brand" of challenge. Even the concession stands were affected when the Silver and Black came to town. Says Jones, "Alcohol sales normally stop at the end of the third quarter. For that one, we stop at halftime." They also decreased the number of beers an individual could buy at a time.

Inside the EMC at Petco Park, I ask Patti Clayton, a police officer who has worked games for both the Padres and the Chargers, about the differences between the two sports, in terms of dealing with the fans. "Baseball games are very isolated incidents," she says, while football presents a daylong simmer of every manner of issue. "We've had domestic violence right at the front gates."

Another point of difference is the medical needs at a baseball game. Of course, there is the possibility of foul balls or shattered bats flying into the stands—these incidents seem to occur with greater frequency and bloodier consequence throughout 2015, eventually forcing major-league baseball to issue a recommendation for all clubs to extend their protective netting. But more often it is the sort of call that comes in just now to the EMC that defines baseball emergencies. Clayton answers the phone, passes it over to the representative for fire and medical, and says, "Section one thirteen, row twenty, seat one. Got an elderly female. Needs a Band-Aid."

The big excitement of the day comes sometime in the middle innings, around two-thirty p.m., when one of the players-lot valet parking attendants is found sleeping in the car of Lisa Thayer, the wife of Padres reliever Dale Thayer. Having gone up to the press box to grab some hot dogs and diet soda, Leas and I cut our lunch short and descend into the bowels of the stadium. Thayer is distressed but also worried she is making a big deal out of nothing. "The seat was totally reclined, his shoes were off. It just struck me as really weird," she tells Leas. "I feel bad. I don't want to start a problem if it was something very innocent."

Leas won't hear it.

While Thayer waits in the Padres family lounge, Leas pulls the two attendants away from the valet stand. He interrogates them, one at a time. Of the suspected napper, he asks if he's ever been accused of theft, since Thayer had left her wallet along with a load of sensitive documents on the passenger seat. The suspect, who has short black hair and a baby face—he may still be a teenager—is nervous. He explains to Leas that he worked another job last night and didn't get to bed until five a.m. He is on the brink of tears. Having spent a career talking to hardened criminals, Leas knows the difference between a dumb kid and a crook. With the kid, he is gentle. He tells him he made a mistake, and it's not the end of the world, but it's the last time he'll work for the Padres. He excuses the kid from duty and sends him home. "Go get some sleep, okay?"

As all this is happening, Dale Thayer is out on the mound, faced with a bases-loaded situation, blissfully unaware. Staring down two of the most dangerous hitters in the opponent's lineup, the pitcher escapes the jam, unscathed. The Padres go on to win the game.

One theory about fan misbehavior is that fans want to find ways to feel closer to an event, to see themselves as performers. "Fans crave involvement and attention," Gubar writes in *Fanaticus*. Danish scholar Niels Kayser Nielsen makes a similar point in his chapter in *The Stadium and the City*: "Letting its presence be known, is probably the stadium crowd's most important characteristic, not least from its own point of view." In *Better to Reign in Hell*, Miller and Mayhew quote French philosopher Jean Baudrillard in regard to postevent riots. He talks about "usurping the role of protagonists" and how fans "invent their own spectacle."

Back in the Black Hole, it is not hard to see how Baudrillard's words apply. As the second quarter winds down against the Packers, in the moments following a Raiders touchdown, the section is riddled with examples of fan performance. Rilla waves the crowd on to make noise and then pounds the padded walls surrounding the playing field, while a bearded and tatted-up Raiders fan talks voluble smack to the ten-year-old Packers fan to my right, when Jersey Dad leaves him alone to go to the bathroom.

From two rows down, with veins bulging in his neck, the fan screams at the kid, gesturing to rip off his coat like they're about to fight. He shouts, "What, motherfucker? Fuck you, little kid!" He flips the kid off with both hands. "Get the fuck outta here! Fuck your bitch ass! Fuck the Packers! Fuck you, motherfucker!" With a shit-eating grin, the fan then looks around to see who has appreciated this outburst and will give him some dap. A friend offers a high-five. Reinforced, he says again, "Yeah, fuck that kid."

After stoically enduring this rant, the kid scurries off to find his father. In the second half, the football karma gods seem to smile on the little guy, as the Packers are up by seven and threatening to score again, with about five minutes left in the game. The intensity is still high within the Black Hole, even though the outcome of the game is relatively meaningless for the Raiders, who will be officially eliminated from play-off contention after this week. But for fans this dedicated, no game is ever meaningless.

Research by academics like Daniel Wann, who teaches at Murray State University and focuses on the psychology of sport fandom, has shown there are very real benefits to being a sports fan, including higher self-esteem and fewer feelings of depression and loneliness. According to Eric Simons, "The more you identify with the group, the more benefits accrue." But fans can experience negative consequences after losses, manifesting in higher rates of car wrecks, heart attacks, and domestic violence. Studies have also shown that watching sports can increase aggression.

Ultimately, Simons argues, fan behavior is a matter of self-control, but as he makes clear throughout his book, which explores "the science of sports obsession," some changes in fans occur on an involuntary chemical level. A male spectator, for instance, can experience wild swings in his testosterone levels, based on whether his favorite team is winning or losing, as Paul Bernhardt discovered in a 1998 study. (Similar results were found in men, in an experiment conducted by a postdoc researcher at Duke University named Steven Stanton, based on which candidate they voted for in the 2008 presidential election.)

In another study, a psychologist named Charles Hillman (then a graduate student) determined that diehard fans of the Florida Gators football program "experienced extreme physiological arousal," as *The New York Times* puts it, when shown images of their favorite athletes making great plays. Hillman outfitted his subjects with electrodes and measured their heart rates, brain waves, and perspiration levels. He found that, in both men and women, the physiological jumps in activity were on par with "what the fans registered when shown erotic photos or pictures of animal attacks." Meanwhile Edward Hirt, a professor at Indiana University, found that fans of the school's basketball team believed themselves to be sexier and more attractive to would-be partners following victories.

So yes, there is still plenty on the line when Packers quarterback Aaron Rodgers throws a five-yard touchdown pass to wide receiver James Jones. But there is a flag on the play. Offensive pass interference. The touchdown is called back, and the Black Hole loses its mind, trying to make enough noise to help the Raiders on their defensive stand. A couple rows down from me, a woman wearing a Raiders fedora, with long maroon-black hair and contacts of multiple colors—one is dragon's-eye red, the other light blue, with the word RAIDERS around the edge—implores her comrades. "Wake the fuck up, Black Hole, this is when you need to be yelling!"

Jersey Dad, who is rooting for the Raiders and is now back in his seat, tells his son, "Win, lose, or draw, this is the best game we have ever been to—the best."

The noise mounts. Rodgers throws a pass over the middle.

Incomplete! Fourth down! Jubilation!

But the Packers kick a field goal to go up by ten points.

As the ball sails through the uprights, the air releases from the Raiders fans' balloon, now down by two scores with little time left on the clock. The vibe grows edgy as reality sets in. Not helping matters are the Packers fans. They suddenly seem even more present, louder, more obnoxious, as they bounce and rejoice after the successful kick, rubbing it in. A fan in front of me wearing a Raiders hunting cap looks to the stands to our right, which are dotted with green and gold. "There's a lot of cheese up there," he mutters, as another few fans flip off that side of the stadium.

Someone takes the opportunity to rip the cheese hat off a fan dressed in a green and gold serape in the front row of the Black Hole. It flies over my head. Some fans cheer the act, while others try to self-police. "Hey, that's not nice. Give him back his little hat! That's fucked up. Give him his hat." The hat is passed back down to the front row—in two pieces. Someone tore it in half.

The Cheesehead suspects the Contacts Lady of destroying his

hat, because she's been so loud, but she swears she is innocent. (She is.) They get into it.

"I was respectful all game," says the Cheesehead.

"Shut the fuck up and listen to me," says Contacts.

Another fan chimes in: "Fuck the Packers, fuck Milwaukee, fuck the Brewers, fuck all you motherfuckers!"

Jersey Dad sees what's going on. Says, "They're going to beat up that Packers fan!" He doesn't sound displeased.

The Cheesehead suspects it is time to leave. He puts on half of his hat and marches toward the aisle. When he gets there, he turns back and shouts, "Scoreboard!"

Contacts hollers back, "Pussy-ass, bitch-ass motherfucker! I'll show you. I'll fucking knock your ass out." She flips him off, gesturing that he should move along if he knows what's good for him. "Fuck you!"

Like the rest of the section, Jersey Dad is inflamed by the conflict. "It's getting real now," he says. "It is like Brooklyn right now. This is *fucking* Brooklyn right now." And then, with his son by his side, with Contacts and the Cheesehead shrieking back and forth across the length of the row, he starts chanting, "Brook-lyn! Brook-lyn!" This goes on for several minutes: the Black Hole spuming, Jersey Dad screaming, the game proceeding on the field, unnoticed. The scene serves as a reminder that the biggest danger at sporting events may not always be the unknown and unprovoked Other. More often danger lurks when we don't realize just how easily any one of us can cross that line, how easily we can transform in the heat of the moment or behind the haze of alcohol. How easily we can become monsters. As Gregg Doyel puts it in a column for CBS Sports, "The true danger is us. We are the thugs, and we are everywhere."

In the Black Hole, the game's final seconds ticking away, a kind of mob mentality takes hold as everyone seems to turn against the

Cheesehead. Throughout the fan section, people holler, curse, and glare in his direction. He is the outsider, the intruder, and he is no longer welcome. Perhaps sensing this tonal shift, the Cheesehead waits in the aisle, now silent, until security arrives, with who knows how many eyes watching from above, from some distant command room. And then with half a hat, he is escorted out of the stadium.

7
IDENTITY 101

(Or: Col-lege!!)

The road from Pittsburgh to State College is a two-lane highway that cuts through the rolling hills of western Pennsylvania. Steam and fog dip into the valleys and rise off the mountaintops, beneath a sky choked with gray. The countryside is defined by earth tones, a canvas of mud browns and forest greens. Even with the cloud cover, everything seems lush; Pennsylvania State University—where I'm headed—is a land-grant institution.

Longtime Indiana University basketball coach Bobby Knight liked to joke that going to State College, a town of around 42,000, wasn't so much a road trip as a camping trip. "There's nothing around for a hundred miles," he'd say. The old coach wasn't wrong—the view from the road is lonely landscape—but on football Saturdays, there is nothing sleepy about this remote college town. That's when State College triples in size, swelling to become the third largest municipality in the state of Pennsylvania, as tens of thousands of vehicles pour in off the highway from every direction and clog the local roads that lead to Beaver Stadium, home of the Nittany Lions. With an official capacity of 106,572, it is the second-largest stadium in the nation.

"We park more cars on a game day than Disney," says Mark Bodenschatz, Penn State's associate athletic director for facilities and operations. "We are up around 25,000 to 35,000 vehicles, and we do it on grass." Unlike so many modern football facilities, a sprawl of asphalt does not surround Beaver Stadium. To accommodate tailgaters—and the Penn State fan base is filled with staunchly dedicated tailgaters, some planning their menus months in advance*— intramural fields and animal pasturelands are temporarily converted into parking lots and RV campgrounds, which serve as staging areas for all sorts of game-day rituals.

In one intramural lot, for instance, ahead of an early October matchup, I join a large group of fans taking communion, which consists of the singing of the Penn State fight song, "Fight On, State," followed by the consumption of Jägermeister. (The communion service is repeated every hour on the hour leading up to kickoff, a scowling late-middle-aged man—clearly the organizer—tells me, while his elderly mother pours shots. He adds, "The way we used to do it, somebody'd have little crackers and pass them out.") Closer to the stadium, I witness a tailgate wedding, in which a man and a woman in full-on bridal gown exchange vows. The ceremony concludes with a Penn State cheer, while the father of the bride takes a healthy swig from his red Solo cup.

The nuptials aren't a gimmick, I'm made to understand; tailgate weddings are held regularly around Beaver Stadium, where every game can seem like a life event and everything down to the parking spaces is considered personal property. To illustrate this point, Bodenschatz tells me about one old-timer who parks in the same nonreserved spot at every home game: this man goes to the trouble of

---

* Local legend has it that tailgating took off in State College before an early game at Beaver Stadium, when traffic was so bad motorists couldn't move. Stranded on the streets, they decided to have a picnic.

bringing a lawnmower to trim his patch of pastureland, to which he owns no official claim. Says Bodenschatz, "That is his home."

If this level of dedication seems a little much for a simple football game, welcome to the world of big-time college sports, where whole communities and even regions gather around the anchor of a stadium, and where traditions—both personal and institutional, like pregame player-bus processionals and midfield marching-band performances—can feel as important as the final score (and the final score is *always* important).* "The stadium becomes a vessel," Sandy Barbour, Penn State's athletic director, says of Beaver Stadium's role as a de facto reunion hall. "We are drawing from a population that has a reason to be connected, and [that reason] is way more powerful than just geography." That reason is legacy.

Quoting Edwin H. Cady, Allen Guttmann writes in *Sports Spectators* that early on—around the turn of the twentieth century—a college football game "became 'the most vitally folkloristic event in our culture.'" Which actually may be understating its prominence and importance in the lives of many Americans.

Nowhere is this more evident than at Beaver Stadium.

As a former varsity letterman puts it to me, trying to explain the significance of football Saturdays in State College, "You have got to understand—these are Penn State people." And for Penn State people, football is not just about wins and losses. It's about the confirmation—or disputation—of an entire community's way of life.

————

The very first intercollegiate football competition is said to have taken place on November 6, 1869, between Rutgers and Princeton. But the schools were more likely playing soccer than an early ver-

---

* Green Bay is the only town whose pro team comes close to duplicating this kind of college atmosphere.

sion of football, according to Guttmann, who explains in *From Ritual to Record* that the first college *football* game—or at least a rugby-like game that eventually morphed into football, through rule tweaks and standardization by its collegian competitors—was played on May 15, 1874, when Harvard squared off against McGill.

Colleges also led the way in early stadium construction, as Harvard Stadium became the first reinforced-concrete stadium in the United States when it was completed in 1903. By the time Yale built its bowl-shaped facility in 1914—which is claimed to be the largest encircled-bowl amphitheater since the Roman Colosseum—these giant structures were seen as more than just sports venues; they were "icons representing what universities recognized were important to their image-building," as Penn State professor emeritus Ronald A. Smith has written. In other words, they were marketing tools, giant billboards to the outside world, and a way to secure status among the nation's growing colleges. Perhaps unsurprisingly, then, there emerged a connection "between winning on the field and winning in a significantly broader communal sense," Bob Trumpbour explains in *The New Cathedrals.*

In State College, football emerged in 1887. "That was the first official game," says Lou Prato, class of 1959 and a sports historian who served as the first director of Penn State's All-Sports Museum, which opened in 2001. According to the historian, the sport's impact on the local psyche was immediate. "Ever since that 1887 team, there has been something called the Penn State Way. Ex-players would come back and help coach the team. And remember, coaches were not coaches as we think of them now."

This sensibility of giving back to the university, of caring about a cause larger than oneself—a life-defining principle—continued to exist in State College, even after coaching became professionalized, per Prato. The Penn State Way was here to stay. In 1966, it took on greater meaning still when a young man named Joe Paterno was given the reins to the football team after spending sixteen seasons as an assistant. With Penn State's campus as his laboratory, Paterno began what would be known as "the Grand Experiment." Says Prato, "He believed he could produce great teams with scholar athletes." The idea was for Penn State to cultivate a holistic environment, in which athletics were not glorified at the expense of academics but would be part of a formula that elevated the institution at large. Corners would not be cut. Achievements would be earned. Greatness would inspire greatness.

Not long after Paterno led his team to a national title win in the 1983 Sugar Bowl, he spoke to Penn State's board of trustees, but not about football. He spoke about academics, about areas in which he believed the school could improve. He spoke about the need to endow chairs and fund scholarships, for better research facilities and more robust libraries. It was up to them to raise money *now*, on the heels of his team's success, when goodwill would be at its peak.

The coach was trying to use football to make the university better. Time and again he and his family put their money where his mouth was, leading capital campaigns, creating the Paterno Fellows Program, and donating millions to help build a campus library and interfaith spiritual center. According to Guido D'Elia, a Penn State alumnus and the school's former director of branding and communications, who worked with the football program from 2004 to 2011, Paterno "brought something special and raised that school from, really, a cow college to something that is Big Ten caliber." (Penn State joined the Big Ten conference in 1990.)

These were the same types of lessons Paterno offered his men on the football field, according to Bob White, who was co-captain of the Nittany Lions' 1986 national championship team and now works as the director of club and suites at Beaver Stadium. "You are part of something bigger than yourself. He got us to buy into that," remembers White. "One of the things Coach Paterno was very

Fans cram into the stands at Ann Arbor's Michigan Stadium. Also known as "the Big House," it is the largest stadium in the United States, with an official capacity of 107,601.

In the summertime heat, infield clay can feel like concrete. Here Braves grounds crewmembers water the dirt at Turner Field before a July 2015 home game. Careful not to let the hose lie on the turf, the crewmembers form a kind of irrigating conga line.

Ahead of the Cleveland Cavaliers' first playoff game in April 2015, a local ticket scalper works a side hustle by selling T-shirts outside of Quicken Loans Arena.

Much of Lambeau Field has been upgraded and modernized since it first opened in 1957. But the Green Bay stadium's original seating bowl—which contains sixty rows of metal bleacher benches—remains largely untouched.

The self-proclaimed Lambeau Mayor (left) administers the Oath of the Lambeau Field Virgin, when he discovers that I am visiting the historic stadium for the first time. (Photo by Robert Wiltzius.)

The control room at AT&T Stadium in Arlington, Texas, is used for more than just football games. "We've done everything from weddings to bar mitzvahs," says Dwin Towell, director of broadcast engineering (not pictured). "We haven't done a bris yet, but if we do, I am not putting it on the big screen."

Home of the University of Utah's football program, Rice-Eccles Stadium in Salt Lake City hosted the opening and closing ceremonies for the 2002 winter games. It is also one of the most photogenic venues I've ever seen, thanks to the nearby Wasatch Mountains.

During Hurricane Katrina, when floodwater threatened to overtake the Superdome's generator and throw the New Orleans stadium into darkness and chaos, emergency workers kept track of the rising water levels with Sharpie tabulations on the engineering-room wall.

The New York Mets go through so much beer—often eight hundred kegs a game—that the team employs a five-person crew whose only job is to walk around and monitor Citi Field's walk-in beer fridges, changing out old kegs for fresh ones.

Inside an inflatable tunnel during pregame intros at an NFL stadium. As players wait to take the field, the space becomes a powder keg of pent-up adrenaline.

On the first Sunday home game of the season, the San Diego Padres celebrate Military Opening Day. Here members from every branch of the armed forces line the infield for pregame ceremonies.

On football Saturdays at Beaver Stadium in State College, Pennsylvania, many Penn State fans offer grassroots tributes to the legacy of the late Joe Paterno, the university's longtime head coach. Paterno was fired in 2011, on the heels of the arrest of Jerry Sandusky.

At a Rutgers University men's basketball game, I assist the Amazing Sladek with his Tower of Chairs halftime act. During the performance, I am pretty sure that I am going to kill him—which would be bad for me, and worse for him. (Photo by Daniel Meyer.)

A Raiders superfan, Gorilla Rilla is a front-row fixture in the fan section known as the Black Hole. Here, flanked by members of Oakland–Alameda County Coliseum's B-Lot Crew, Rilla doesn't let his mask get in the way of a cold one.

Sluggerrr, the Kansas City Royals mascot, and his handler (aka the "Lion Tamer") walk the back-of-house corridors at Kauffman Stadium to avoid being mauled by adoring fans.

A view from the upper deck of the Silverdome in Pontiac, Michigan. It's amazing how much the stadium has deteriorated in just a few years, since the roof was deflated. It is strangely beautiful, like a postapocalyptic wonderland.

clear on when I was being recruited was: you sign on to this, you are going to have to be coming for the right reasons. It is not just about football—it is about life. It is about academics. So for me, when I got the opportunity to really put the uniform on and compete, I always knew that I had earned it, and I have always associated that with this place, the stadium."

Beaver Stadium stood as a metaphor for many in State College—not just for the players. It was the physical manifestation of Joe's Grand Experiment. Football Saturdays became the time and place to celebrate the experiment's ongoing successes, to celebrate the Penn State Way. As one student puts it to me, "This is *when* we come together. This is *how* we come together."

Using college athletics as a means to enact legacy isn't unique to Penn State. At the University of Michigan, where I also spend time, the school's football program in general—and its stadium in particular, which is informally known as "the Big House" and is the largest stadium in the country, with a capacity of 107,601—similarly reinforces a localized identity, a well-honed sense of self. Fielding Yost, who served for twenty-five years as the Wolverines' head football coach and would eventually take over as athletic director, leading the 1927 construction effort of Michigan Stadium, had a saying that neatly encapsulated this: "Who are *they* that they should beat a Michigan team?" Bo Schembechler, an iconic Wolverines coach of more recent vintage, spoke about the importance of being a "Michigan Man," and those in Ann Arbor still take Bo's words to heart. "The 'Michigan Man' thing, I think it is absolutely proper," former offensive lineman-turned-broadcaster Jim Brandstatter tells me. "You have to have a connection to the University of Michigan as a player, a student, or something like that. But more than that, it's about character. It's about integrity. It is kind of a state of mind, a way you live your life."

Naturally, winning mattered—Schembechler led his football

team to a 194–48–5 record over two decades at Michigan, while Paterno earned 409 wins, a major college football record, during his Penn State coaching career—but only if they were the right kind of wins. "Don't give me generic wins," says White. Of course, with Paterno at the helm, no one doubted the Nittany Lions were racking up the right kind of wins. Each victory was another notch on the belt of the Penn State Way, another win for the community at large, for anyone who held a Penn State degree, who had any affiliation with the university whatsoever. It was proof that you could get ahead by doing things right, that you could enjoy "success with honor," another oft-quoted maxim, inspired by Paterno.

Even the famous Penn State cheer ("We are . . . Penn State!"), which was started by the cheerleaders in the late 1970s and became a Beaver Stadium staple, came to embody the fan base's sense of pride, providing a declaration for their way of life. "This place is different. We want it to be different. That is what [the cheer] stands for. In many ways, that is what the stadium stands for—tradition," Prato tells me when we meet outside the Letterman's Club lounge, which is attached to Beaver Stadium. "We believe in honesty and fairness. We never had a major NCAA violation. We never had it! What we had," he says with a pained sigh, "was a scandal."

———————

Putting aside the economic disgrace that is big-time college athletics and the NCAA, which gets fat with plunder—along with athletic departments, their directors, and college coaches—on the backs of unpaid laborers,* it should come as no shock to learn that

---

* Student-athletes may be compensated, but they are unpaid. The legitimacy of that compensation—which is not even close to the level of economic value they provide—can rightly be called into question, when you realize how many programs place such importance on athletic glory (and the money that follows) that classes become a secondary or tertiary concern for student-athletes. Hell, the very term *student-athlete* was

college programs have always found ways to skirt the rules. In the early years, college football teams would be filled with "tramp athletes," i.e., paid ringers who were not students. The problem was so apparent that in 1905, David Starr Jordan, the president of Stanford University, wrote: "Let the football team become frankly professional. Cast off all deception. Get the best professional coach. Pay him well, and let him have the best men the town and alumni will pay for . . . with no masquerade of amateurism or academic ideals."

But that didn't happen. While tramp athletes were largely stamped out in the 1920s, a new system of winking compensation was set up, wherein alumni would promise prospective athletes a job on the side in exchange for attending their school. "If that didn't work," author John Kryk writes in *Natural Enemies*, "alumni might establish slush funds or provide athletes with bogus, high-paying jobs."

Things haven't gotten much cleaner in the near-century since, as slush funds have been replaced with what political sportswriter Dave Zirin calls college sports' "gutter economy" of under-the-table payments and illicit gifts, and as supposedly reputable institutions like the University of North Carolina find themselves embroiled in academic scandals involving "shadow curriculums," so that student-athletes don't have to distract themselves from training with bothersome schoolwork.

Even sex-recruiting scandals—one of which recently ensnared the University of Louisville, when it was discovered that a former basketball staffer was allegedly paying for strippers and student sex parties—are nothing new. In *Fans! How We Go Crazy Over Sports*, published in the mid-1970s, Michael Roberts writes, "Most schools that aspire to be high in the football or basketball rankings regard sex as

---

dreamed up in the 1950s by former NCAA executive director Walter Byers to shield the organization from any potential workers' compensation claims. Not exactly what you'd call putting the students first.

a reliable tool." Many campuses had names for those who put their prettiest faces forward (with some even displaying their school spirit between the sheets), Roberts notes, like Florida's Gator Getters, North Carolina's Sweet Carolines, and (sure enough) Louisville's Gibson Girls.*

With college programs' track record of using women's bodies as recruiting props, perhaps it shouldn't have come as a surprise when universities began to excuse their athletes of sex crimes. As Jessica Luther lays out in *Unsportsmanlike Conduct: College Football and the Politics of Rape*, sexual assault is a major problem on college campuses, especially as it relates to football programs. The issue is not limited to any one university, she writes. Instead, a systemic indifference that is baked into the college football landscape allows such crimes to continue. In the last few years, for instance, the University of Tennessee and Baylor University have both been accused of ignoring or covering up rape and sexual harassment allegations, in service of protecting their high-profile football teams and star athletes. (Baylor's head coach Art Briles was fired in 2016, as part of a school-wide cleansing of its leadership.) And yet, no college football scandal comes close— or hopefully will ever come close—to what happened in State College, Pennsylvania.

————

On Saturday, November 5, 2011—in what, as chance would have it, was a bye week for Penn State's football team—former Nittany Lions defensive coordinator Jerry Sandusky, a longtime assistant to Joe Paterno, was arrested on charges of sexually abusing multiple underage boys over a fifteen-year period, both on and off the school's campus.

---

* These groups, known as hostess programs (which the NCAA made a halfhearted attempt to curtail in 2004), would never require a member to sleep with a recruit, but there is no doubt that even the most abstinent hostess would always be selling sex.

The bombshell exploded across the sports channels and cable news stations, as media vans descended on State College and hunkered down for the long haul. In the days that followed, Penn State athletic director Tim Curley and another top school administrator named Gary Schultz would vacate their positions after being charged with perjury and failing to report the alleged abuse. Joe Paterno, who had been alerted to a locker-room incident involving Sandusky and a young boy a decade earlier (and subsequently kicked the matter up the chain of command to Curley), confirmed that he would retire at season's end, admitting in a statement: "With the benefit of hindsight, I wish I had done more." Only hours after Paterno's words rang across the nation, however, the board of trustees announced that both Paterno and university president Graham Spanier, who would also be charged in an alleged cover-up,* had been fired. *The New York Times* reported, "A gasp went up from the crowd of several hundred reporters, students and camera people who were present." That night, shock at the dismissals turned to anger as Penn State students flooded the streets and proceeded to destroy cars, tear down light posts, and throw rocks and explosives at police, while chanting the name of their now-former coach.

They also cheered, "We are . . . Penn State!"

From the outside—watching the news reports, the riots, the student vigils on Joe Paterno's front lawn—it was easy to believe that those in State College had their priorities totally out of whack, which is precisely what the Freeh Report, a school-funded investigation into the allegations led by former FBI director Louis Freeh, argued when its findings were made public the following summer.

---

* By March 2017, some of the charges against Curley, Schultz, and Spanier—including perjury and obstruction—had been either dismissed or dropped. That month, Curley and Schultz pleaded guilty to one misdemeanor count of endangering the welfare of children, while Spanier was convicted by a jury on a misdemeanor child endangerment count. The former Penn State president was acquitted of a separate child endangerment charge and of a conspiracy charge. He plans to appeal the guilty verdict, according to his lawyers.

The report found that Curley, Schultz, Spanier, and Paterno—who had died earlier that year from lung cancer, at the age of eighty-five—each played a role in covering up Sandusky's crimes. (Many have since disputed the accuracy and methods of Freeh's investigation, including current Penn State president Eric Barron, who went on record in 2015 saying he was "not a fan" of the report, describing certain aspects as "absurd" and "unwarranted.")

Before the dust could settle from the Freeh Report—and only weeks after Sandusky was found guilty of forty-five counts of child sexual abuse—the NCAA levied a series of heavy sanctions against Penn State, as the university and the regulatory body entered into a consent decree. For Penn State, there would be a four-year bowl ban, temporary cuts in scholarships, a $60 million fine, and the removal of 112 wins from the football team's record books—wins which had been the *right kind* of wins, or so everyone in State College thought—thereby knocking Paterno off his perch as major college football's winningest coach.* The sanctions also came on the heels of Penn State's decision to remove a statue of Paterno from outside Beaver Stadium, scrubbing him from the grounds as if he had never existed.

It was not an easy time to be a Penn Stater.

Locals describe the Sandusky scandal as "a gut punch," as pride by association suddenly became guilt by association, especially in the eyes of outsiders who were all too happy to gloat in this supposedly pristine program's fall from grace. "We took crap for years," says a longtime fan named Ted, who I meet in the RV lot before a game

---

* Though the sanctions were deemed "unprecedented"—and even seen as somewhat merciful, since the football team avoided a so-called "death penalty"—there is doubt as to whether the NCAA had the authority to punish the university at all, since the scandal was criminal in nature and had no bearing on the football field, in spite of a tangential relationship. Many believe the NCAA, which could be in the running for world's most cynical organization, overstepped, unable to resist the opportunity for an easy moral victory and a little bit of grandstanding. Seemingly proving this point, the sanctions—including the once-vacated wins—have been walked back in recent years.

against Army. While sipping a Seagram's Blackberry Breezer wine cooler—"I got to drink fruit in the morning," Ted explains—he tells me about the time he went to St. Louis for the national wrestling championship and rival fans refused to let up about Sandusky. "It's just a comment, so you brush it off, but they wouldn't give up," he says. Another older fan named Brian tells me the worst hazing he's experienced came in New Jersey, at a Rutgers game, when local fans hoisted tailgate flags with a stick figure of a man raping a young boy and roving bands of students went around screaming, "Fuck Penn State! Fuck Penn State!"

Or consider the experience of Maria San Román, who was a sophomore in high school on Long Island, New York, when the scandal broke. Despite the geographical distance, the San Románs had always been Penn Staters, and Maria, who would eventually become the eleventh member of her family to matriculate to the university, had been attending games in State College since she was six. And all her classmates knew it. "It wasn't fun," she recalls. "I was like sixteen, and if I wore my Penn State shirt, people would say, 'Oh, you are a rapist.' I remember going on a field trip, and one of the boys, who was an Ohio State fan, had me in tears."

I meet Maria on the Thursday night before Penn State's 2015 homecoming game against Indiana, when I stop by Gate A of Beaver Stadium. She is here along with a couple hundred other undergrads, who pitch tents on a concrete plaza and camp in the days leading up to every home football game, in order to secure the best seats in the student section. Known as Nittanyville (before the scandal, it was Paternoville), the campout formally began in 2005, ahead of a game against Ohio State, according to Prato (although some of the students tell me the tradition tracks as far back as the early 1990s). Tonight, after a drop-by visit from some athletes and coaches on the football team, the students are doing student things: eating pizza and playing trash can football, which is a game modeled after beer pong but instead features trash cans and a football, and no beer. (Officially, there is no drinking in Nittanyville, but tents have zippers for a reason.)

Darian Somers, a senior from Altoona, Pennsylvania, is the sitting president of Nittanyville. His freshman year coincided with the first post-Paterno season, in 2012, a delicate period in Nittany Lions football history. Having avoided the death penalty, the program was still on life support, as the NCAA allowed student-athletes to transfer to other schools with no delays in their eligibility. (Normally they'd have to sit out a season.) "There was this time you didn't wear Penn State shit," Somers says of the days and months following the scandal, when others questioned whether he would even still attend the university. "And then the sanctions hit." He remembers sitting in his bed, just giving the middle finger to the TV with both hands, as NCAA president Mark Emmert made the announcement. "Everybody was pissed off," Somers says. For many, the sanctions galvanized a kind of circling of the wagons, as fans came together to support those players who hadn't abandoned the school and to prove to themselves that they still had something for which to cheer. Perhaps nothing captured that sentiment better than the T-shirts that read WE STILL ARE.

During games at Beaver Stadium, where legacy had always gone without saying, fans now screamed a certain line from the Penn State alma mater, "May no act of ours bring shame."* Elsewhere in town, small cardboard signs populated storefront windows, which read PROUD TO SUPPORT PENN STATE FOOTBALL. The majority of Penn State fans didn't see this as moral equivalence, as though they were victims like the boys in the Sandusky trial. By and large, they were flailing for identity, for a reaffirmation of self,

---

* On why fans belt out this line, Somers theorizes: "I think that kind of signifies that what happened here obviously shouldn't have, but we are not a part of that. That wasn't us."

in a time when the rug had been pulled out from under them. Eric Simons, a writer whose work explores the psychology and science of sports fandom, has written that "it's entirely rational for a fan to defend his or her identity against outside attack," because fans see teams as extensions of themselves. He calls such behavior "an act of self-preservation."

Still, not everyone in State College dealt with the scandal by rallying around the football team. In a town that was once as tightly bound as the fingers of a fist, the Sandusky fallout divided the community and the school's vast alumni base. Many just wanted to move on from the stain as quickly as possible, to seek normalcy. Others felt betrayed by the university, by the trustees, believing the board had sold Paterno out for the sake of expediency and optics—and in so doing, the whole community, their way of life, along with him. As D'Elia puts it, "They killed the belief that they had something special. They said, 'No, don't believe that. That was bullshit.' *What?* When did it become bullshit?" Others still felt Paterno undermined his own life mission by not doing more than the bare minimum required by law when presented with the serial child sexual abuse under his nose.* Representing this view on the heels of the Freeh Report, Michael Weinreb, a well-known college football writer and a Penn State grad, called the findings "a fundamental violation of the very Grand Experiment."

Weinreb understood the scandal was not something from which the school could simply move on—just as the former coach's victims could not simply move on, because that's not how it works. The boys

---

* A chilling quote to read in hindsight comes from Woody Hayes, Ohio State's long-time coach, who towered over his program and community, like Paterno. Decades before anyone ever heard of Jerry Sandusky, Hayes said, "the way I see it, Nixon had to cover up to win the election. Hell, I'd have done the same damn thing if any of my coaches had done something and I found out about it. My first reaction would have been: 'Well, shoot, we've done something wrong, but we can't make it right by letting the whole goddammed world know about it.'"

in this case, who had been sexually preyed upon by a supposed pillar of the community, were forced to relive the abuse as the story of their victimization unfolded in a courtroom, on national TV, and throughout State College. We can only imagine the continued trauma they may have experienced watching Penn State football fans attempt to put Sandusky in the past and rally around the team. Any discussion of what was lost in State College after the revelation of Jerry Sandusky's crimes begins and ends with his victims, and no one really knew how to assimilate the tragedy.

Post-Sandusky, State College suffered a crisis of identity as it tried to stand up for its way of life without coming off like pedophile apologists and enablers. For many, that was too fine a line to walk, as the fabric of the community frayed, civility deteriorated, and factions formed. Traditions were abandoned—like the singing of Neil Diamond's "Sweet Caroline" during football games, because of a line that goes, "Reaching out, touching me, touching you"—and businesses were threatened with boycott for little more than the presence (or absence) of a sign in the window.

There may be no place this new division—this unhealed wound—is on greater display than at Beaver Stadium, on game days.

Named for General James A. Beaver, a Civil War hero and onetime governor of Pennsylvania who helped deliver state money to improve the university's first football field, Beaver Stadium towers over its surroundings, built completely above grade. Outside State College, the no-frills football facility—beneath the stands, Beaver Stadium is a tangle of exposed steel beams—is disparagingly referred to as the Erector Set.

Folks here are proud of the stadium's unique construction history. The nickname speaks to how the venue reached its current configuration, sort of cobbled together over the years, like a Frankenstein's monster. Between the 1959 and 1960 football seasons, the horseshoe stands that existed on the other side of campus, at what was known as New Beaver Field, were dismantled, transported to the current stadium site, and reassembled. Several expansions brought capacity up from an original 46,284, but none were more impressive than the project that took place before the 1978 season. The structure was cut into sections and jacked up about twelve and a half feet, as twenty rows of concrete seating were placed in front of the existing grandstand, covering a running track. "Nothing like that had ever been done before," says Harry West, a Penn State professor emeritus of structural engineering.

Another aerial feat of engineering came in 2001, according to Mark Bodenschatz, the associate athletic director for facilities and operations. That was when the stadium, as part of a $93 million-plus renovation and expansion project, updated its video boards, which had to be lifted into place. "The scoreboards are basically like four-story buildings," says Bodenschatz. "One of the biggest cranes in the world was here, and it took a crane to erect the crane. People came in from all over, and they were sitting, drinking, basically tailgating." Bodenschatz, who is also in charge of game-day operations at Beaver Stadium, has come to learn some other quirks of the facility. "The length of the spans of the north deck happen to have a harmonic vibration that is the exact same as our fight song beat," he explains. "People start clapping and jumping up and down, and as you jump up and down, it just goes higher and higher and higher. The deck liter-ally moves. It is the right harmonic. It is the right length and deflec-tion. Unintended. But it is a really cool thing."

Another cool thing, he tells me, is how the stadium can act as a proving ground for the rest of the university, whether it's the sociol-ogy department doing a study of tailgating habits (they discovered that 25 percent of people around Beaver Stadium never come into games) or a mechanical engineering professor and his students testing a robotic climbing system just outside the Erector Set, surrounded by higher-end donors on a game day. "Some barebones, right-out-of-the-laboratory stuff," says Bodenschatz. "This is your university dollars at work."

On the day of the homecoming game, I do not see any climbing robots or sociology experiments, but the morning carries the promise of perfect October weather—crisp air and clean sunshine.

Grassroots tributes to Joe Paterno are everywhere: cardboard cutouts of the coach; T-shirts that depict an unmistakable illustration of the man's lower legs, since he always had his pant cuffs rolled up; flowers on the relandscaped ground where the Paterno statue once stood*; bumper stickers that read 409 in reference to the wins record; cases of commemorative Paterno Legacy Series Lager from Duquesne Brewing Company; and tailgate signs that simply say THANK YOU, JOE PA. Without question, Beaver Stadium is where the Paterno legacy finds its most devoted apologists; it has remained a place of worship to the coach even as any official honors from the school have been stripped away. I ask one fan, who is serving deviled eggs off a Paterno platter, if the topic of the former coach is still divisive among Penn State fans. He shakes his head. "I think it is more of a division between the fan base and everybody else," he says. But these days, "everybody else" seems to include the university itself.

Earlier in the week, for instance, I have a meeting with Eric Barron, at which the university president bristles at the mere mention of Paterno, shifting in his seat irritably and questioning what the long-time coach has to do with Beaver Stadium. He sighs, assuring me the fan base has moved on, that it is a nonissue. "It is old news," he says, as if I'm the last person on earth to understand this point. "It is not only old news, but if you wander around the stadium, nobody says that. It's

---

* Though supposedly held in secret storage, rumor has it that the statue is being kept in one of the department of food science's meat lockers.

not there." Our meeting is cut short a few minutes later. Afterward I receive a strong-armed e-mail from a Penn State PR flack, telling me she is trying to have the rest of my interviews in State College canceled, since the president didn't appreciate my line of questioning. (None are canceled.)

All of which leads me to conclude one of two things: either Barron is extremely disconnected or willfully obtuse. Because as overwhelming visual and experiential evidence suggests, and as my friend with the Paterno platter puts it to me before the homecoming matchup, "People have *never* stopped talking about it around here." He adds, "The board won't admit they did anything wrong [in how they handled the firing of Paterno, who was let go over the phone], and it infuriates a lot of us, me included."

As game time approaches, I make my way to the luxury suites (or at least what pass for luxury suites at Beaver Stadium), where I meet up with Anthony Lubrano, a 1982 Penn State grad and board of trustees member since 2012. He was elected by the alumni in the wake of the Sandusky scandal, and he's a Paterno loyalist. Previously apolitical, he says he felt obligated to get involved after watching the university dismiss Paterno. "I just felt like somebody had to be on the inside, addressing this issue," Lubrano says, readjusting his Penn State baseball cap, which has JVP (Joseph Vincent Paterno) stitched on the side. "We were not moving on without addressing this issue."

If Joe's was a Grand Experiment, this is a Grand Battle, as those like Lubrano fight for the school to restore Paterno's legacy. Lubrano tells me a story about a former Penn State dean who went on to become president of Kent State University in the early 1990s. "When she arrived, she said, there was this general malaise over the campus, and she couldn't put her finger on it, then she realized: they had never, ever addressed the [1970] shooting. Not in a meaningful way that people could heal," he says. "If you want to heal, you have to address what ails us."

This is a sentiment shared by many in the Penn State community. According to Pat Daugherty, who runs the Tavern, a local institution of a restaurant, and as much as anyone in State College is plugged into the Penn State scuttlebutt (when the school was joining the Big Ten, he knew before it was announced; when players get themselves into trouble, he knows before it hits the papers), the mood has changed at Beaver Stadium. Even before the scandal, a new seating program known as STEP, which required season ticket holders to make a mandatory donation on top of their regular fees, began to diminish enthusiasm. For many, the extra financial burden was too heavy and tickets were abandoned. Of course, the scandal hasn't helped, either. Daugherty speculates that the trustees—at least those still on the board from 2011—wish they had handled that time period differently. He says fans are staying away not because of Sandusky but because of Joe Paterno. "What there is is: 'I'm not going up there because of how they treated Joe,'" he says. "There is a lot of that."

And it's true: the stands today—on homecoming, no less—are far from full.

"The stadium really misses Joe," Wayne Sebastianelli, the former physician for the Nittany Lions football team, tells me, as Lubrano and I begin moving between suites. Like Lubrano, Sebastianelli believes the school needs to embrace the coach's legacy. "To just sort of summarily squash that whole thing and pretend the guy didn't do anything is kind of silly," he says, adding that fandom can't be treated like some ill-performing arm of a corporation. "This is a religion for people that went to school. This is an absolute. It became part of you."

———

In her mid-seventies, Sue Paterno walks the halls of Beaver Stadium like a diplomat, greeting young fans with smiles and schmoozing the adults. Joe Paterno's widow, Sue is here today to fund-raise for the Paterno Fellows. Despite the cloud that still hangs over her family, she is ebullient, even taking the time to tell me the story of when she and a friend painted the Nittany Lion Shrine on campus orange, before the 1966 homecoming game against Syracuse, to put a spark in the hometown crowd the next day. (Her paint job started a Penn State tradition of guarding the lion before homecoming.) Still, the widow's cheerfulness is a mask. When I ask if she comes to all the games, Sue's face drops. She tells me this is the first game of the 2015 season she's attended. "It is not too easy right now," she says, turning to Lubrano. "Eventually, it will get there. Right, Anthony?"

Lubrano gives half a nod.

Along with allies both on and off the board of trustees, Lubrano is pushing for the school to once again embrace the man it has kept at arm's length since the fall of 2011, and to officially honor him (the totality of his legacy, on field and off) in a ceremony at Beaver Stadium. Additionally, Lubrano says, the board needs to formally apologize to Sue Paterno for its mistreatment of her late husband. Without that apology, any remaining trustees who were party to Paterno's dismissal would need to be removed, per Lubrano. "Sue won't accept their honor unless that is what happens."*

The reality is that the administration is in no hurry to do anything involving Paterno. "There will be a time and a place, and it is not yet," says Barron. Those in positions of administrative power are waiting for the criminal trials of the former Penn State administrators to play out in court. They aren't necessarily unwise to do so, as new revelations continue to surface, like the assertion (which

---

* As part of Lubrano's efforts to restore Paterno's legacy, he and a group of fellow alumni trustees have also successfully sued the university to gain access to the materials upon which the Freeh Report was based. "We believe collectively that we have a duty to verify the veracity of a report that continues to harm the university," he says. "We really need to understand if what he said here is true." The last time we speak, in November 2016, Lubrano tells me they are still examining the documents but expect to issue a statement shortly.

emerged in 2016, disputed by Paterno's family) that the head football coach was first alerted to Sandusky's behavior as far back as 1976, as opposed to 2001, as Paterno claimed.

To many in State College, such inaction is yet another cowardly position taken by the university. The longer the issue goes unaddressed, the more the wound festers. In such an atmosphere of distrust, conspiracy theories thrive. Lou Prato tells me he believes there was a cover-up on the board of trustees in terms of how and why Paterno was let go. Others (indeed, many others) tell me that they don't see how all the facts in the Sandusky case add up, while some question whether all the victims were telling the truth. A few of the victims, these folks have come to believe, simply saw dollar signs, an easy payday. Dig even further, and you can find those who believe Sandusky is flat-out innocent. "That is not a fight I'm undertaking," says Lubrano, who has on occasion been lumped in with such truthers. "But we all get painted with the same broad brush."

As for the stadium itself, the declining attendance and the no-shows, Lubrano says, "You want to solve that problem? Honor Joe."

In fact, Joe has been slowly creeping back into Beaver Stadium, and not just through grassroots tributes and troublemakers like Lubrano. A couple years after the scandal broke, the athletic department produced an in-stadium pump-up video that included a shot of Paterno's feet—just his feet, with the rolled-up pant legs. "People went batshit," Darian Somers, the Nittanyville president, remembers of this subtle nod to the old coach. In September 2016, there's even a pregame ceremony to commemorate the fiftieth anniversary of Paterno's first game as head coach at Penn State—but it is far from a full embrace (with no apology for Sue, per Lubrano). The whole endeavor comes off mealy-mouthed, with the current football coach redirecting questions toward the administration, and the administration hiding behind a prepared statement, while trying to cast the ceremony as a celebration not so much of Paterno but of his Grand

Experiment, the men he coached, and their achievements. Within State College and beyond, the decision generates heated debate, with many condemning the ceremony as insensitive. Even the editorial board of *The Daily Collegian*, a student-run newspaper, comes out against the decision. This, in turn, fuels a venomous response, as the battle at Beaver Stadium rages on.

———

Toward the end of the 2015 homecoming game, I excuse myself from the suites and sneak down into the student section, which was once called "the best student section in the country," by ESPN's Kirk Herbstreit. Here the mourners' grief that pervades the suites gives way to a youthful kind of yearning. The undergrads—none of whom (save any super seniors) were actually enrolled at the school when Paterno was still alive—spend all game stomping on top of the metal benches, tossing fellow students into the air after Penn State scores, and letting the Nittany Lion mascot crowd surf its way up the stands. D'Elia, who enlivened the game-day experience at Beaver Stadium during his time with the football program, calls the students "infectious." Says, "They are the ones that can cause the tipping point—the real stadium eruption." I can feel the potential energy. With space for more than twenty-one thousand, the student section is a living organism, and it consumes me, part of the mob just by being there.

After the game ends, the football team heads toward the end zone, facing the student section, locking arms on the field for the singing of the alma mater. This is a relatively new tradition started by Bill O'Brien, who coached the team for two years after Paterno, but one taken seriously. Back in the old days, Lubrano tells me, the students would just chant, "We don't know the goddamn words," whenever the tune played. But today when the singing begins, I think of Somers, who can't help but cry during the song. "It's bad," the Nittanyville president admits. "My girlfriend looks over at me, and she goes, 'You are not going to cry, are you?' No, I'm not going to cry this weekend." But without fail, the tears come. Why? "I don't know. It means a lot to me," he says. "You realize you are a part of something that is a lot huger than yourself. It is a lot bigger than football. It is a lot bigger than everything else."

Today everybody knows the words.

Midway through, I hear someone mutter, "Here comes the loud part."

And then as one: "*May no act of ours bring shame!*"

8

THE OTHER SIDE OF THE T-SHIRT CANNON

(Or: Are You Not Entertained?)

PART ONE: MASTERS OF FUN

A pungent odor fills a windowless room in the bowels of Kauff-man Stadium, in Kansas City, Missouri. It is a cubbyhole of a room, cramped with all manner of miscellanea including giant pink sunglasses, a sombrero, a homespun dreadlock wig (made from doll hair and pipe cleaners), a magic wand, a cane, and a few basic amenities tossed in for good measure: a toilet, a shower, a sink. Segments of fuzzy yellow lion parts—biceps, paws, tails—hang from a clothing rack, along with a selection of baseball uniforms. Located just behind the camera bay on the third baseline, adjacent to the visitors' dugout, the tiny room belongs to Sluggerrr, the king-of-the-jungle mascot for the Kansas City Royals.

After frolicking on the field in ninety-degree heat for pre-game festivities and player introductions, Brad Collins, now in his fifth season as the team's mascot—the man behind the mane, so to speak—slams the door and rips off his Sluggerrr head, which is not insubstantial, about one and a half feet square. The stench is immediate and overpowering, like lifting the cover off a cake tray filled with soggy gym socks. "You want the full experience," the thirty-four-year-old Collins says to me, "put it on now." He holds the sweat-soaked costume topper inches over my head. I can feel the swampy heat emanating from it. I duck away.

Collins laughs and continues stripping, revealing the moisture-wicking athletic gear he wears as a base layer, covering his head and torso with bath towels, since he doesn't want his body temperature to drop too quickly. (He's already been battling a cold, and Sluggerrr doesn't get sick days.) The scent reminds me of my old high school soccer cleats. "Yeah, hockey equipment, dirty shoes, whatever," Collins nods, adding that every mascot costume develops a unique bouquet, "based on your own body odor."

Also in the tiny room, marinating in Sluggerrr's signature stink, is Drake Fenlon, a recent college graduate and aspiring professional mascot. With the Royals, he is something like an understudy crossed with an assistant. On game days, he is known as the "Lion Tamer," accompanying Collins on his various forays into the stadium, and the only other person who gets to see Sluggerrr in a state of undress. (Though I'm granted access to the mascot room, I'm not allowed to take pictures of Collins as he puts on the costume, or even of individual mascot parts, so as not to spoil the illusion of the character.)

Face still flushed, Collins sits in a folding chair, turns a portable fan in his direction, and settles in. He is not needed anywhere until the fourth inning, when he will head out to Little K, a miniature baseball diamond beyond the left-field wall, where kids can take swings and run the bases. Little K is part of the Royals' Outfield Experience, along with a variety of other games and activities, like carousel rides, mini golf, and a playground, meant to occupy young fans who might otherwise get bored by three-plus hours of baseball.* Sluggerrr will sit for a meet-and-greet photo session (for children and adults), for however long the fourth inning lasts. "That is all people want, just pictures. I mean, we'll be out there for an entire inning, but as soon as you pass the first person on the way back, 'Hey, stop for a picture, man! Stop for a picture!' If we stop in the middle of the stands, we get bombarded. Instantly." He compares the experience to being a lone survivor in a zombie apocalypse—a fitting analogy since tonight is Zombie Night at Kauffman Stadium, a themed evening when fans are encouraged to come dressed in "family-friendly" zombie attire and makeup. This is why the mascot will travel to and from Little K on a motorized scooter. "If I were to walk out, I would never make it back there," Collins says, shaking his head.

By the end of the second inning, Collins's body temperature has returned to normal. He shows me an oversize prop iPhone he and Fenlon are working on. The idea will be to take it into the stands and either tease those who are buried in their smartphones, oblivious, or pretend to take photos of all those who are snapping pictures of Sluggerrr. Having begun his career fifteen years ago as Sparty, the Michigan State mascot, Collins remembers a time when every spectator wasn't armed with a camera phone. He bemoans the effect technology has had on his craft, on crowd work. "It has ruined improv humor for mascots. The performance art in the stands is done. Anytime you start a gag, you have people come up and pull on your tail, just trying to take a picture," he says, and it's poor form to turn down photo requests. "Then you look like a bad guy, but you're trying to get the crowd going, and it is just a swarm of people."

Sluggerrr limits his trips into the stands these days, not wanting

---

* Such hypertargeted ballpark areas, like a kids' zone, a sports bar featuring craft beer, and a posh luxury club, are often called "segmented experiences."

to turn fans away and not wanting to become a black hole for camera-wielding zombies instead of an energizing force. Plus, Collins says, slipping back into his Sluggerrr costume in preparation for Little K, "when the team is good like this"—the Royals will go on to win the 2015 World Series—"you don't want to get in the way of the game."

Do not be fooled by the man's appearance. A former college football player with an Army-like, I-mean-business crew cut, Don Costante is the Master of Fun (not a formal title) for the Kansas City Royals.

And he means business.

Officially the senior director for event presentation and production, Costante has been with the team for the better part of a decade, and it is his job to make sure the fans are forever amused at the ballpark. "We are constant conductors," Costante says of his behind-the-scenes orchestration of in-game entertainment, which includes everything from Sluggerrr the mascot and on-field hotdog races to T-shirt tosses, a spirit squad of young women known as K-Crew, and a seemingly endless array of video board prompts, skits, contests, and kiss cams, which plug any possible lulls in what is generously described as baseball's leisurely pace.

Costante confesses, "I hate dead time."

Before coming to Kansas City, the Royals' MoF served a stint with the San Antonio Spurs. While there, he put his job on the line more than once for the sake of an in-game contest or promotion. Most memorable, Costante says, was Beach Ball Mania, in which inflatables would fall from the rafters and a participant from the crowd would have to catch them on the court below, during a break in play. "The visual alone was worth it," he says. "Balls coming down and some idiot trying to catch them. And then put a clock to it, and monetary value?" It was a no-brainer. The danger was that the balls might get caught in the HVAC or drift off course, possibly hitting the players, which would trigger fines and the end of Costante's career with the NBA franchise. The night of the promotion, he was given one last chance to bail, as a Spurs executive asked him, "You willing to risk everything for this? Because if it doesn't go well, you're not here tomorrow." But there was no turning back. Costante had done dry runs for three weeks and even decided to place a penny in each beach ball to help control its movement. The contest was a roaring success—and one the Spurs continue to this day.

"There's never going to be a day, in my eyes, when the fans don't want the color and pageantry—the hype videos and the pump-up music and stuff like that," says Costante, who has invited me to spend a nine-game September home stand with him and the team, to better understand all that goes into entertaining a screaming crowd of thousands, and to see what those in the stands look like from the other side of the T-shirt cannon.* When I ask what other wacky stunts Costante might have up his sleeve, he corrects me. "Call it fan engagement," he says, explaining the one question he always asks himself when it comes to possible promotions at Royals games: "Is this something that would be relevant to a person who is not really a baseball fan?"

That's the whole point, after all: to give folks a reason to come to the stadium.

When Costante came to Kansas City in 2008, he had his work cut out for him. Back then the Royals' efforts at fan engagement were in a sorry state, light-years behind anything in the NBA, which had unleashed an unrelenting prattle of ancillary amusements and diver-

---

* Unfortunately, as I discover, the Royals will not break out their T-shirt cannons until the play-offs. As for the Sluggerrr gun, a customized air cannon that shoots hot dogs, the meat-spitting firearm may be permanently retired, after a 2009 incident in which a previous Sluggerrr—there have been three, since the mascot debuted in 1996—detached a man's retina with a foil-wrapped wiener.

sions at their arenas. They had elaborate team intros, pyrotechnics, constant background music, scoreboard-led chants, dance teams, halftime shows, giveaways, and so on. The Royals knew they needed to spice things up, and for the first few years, buttressing a lackluster on-field product, Costante was given carte blanche from upper management as he attempted to recreate an NBA environment inside the ballpark. He hired an in-game host to serve as an emcee and adopted more fan cams, because everyone loves to see him- or herself on a Jumbotron. He instructed K-Crew to stop conducting marketing surveys and instead to start waving towels and doling out high-fives. He produced comedic video segments for the big board, based on Jay Leno's "Jaywalking" bits, and others, like "Sing for Your Supper," which was essentially a karaoke battle. One video series was called "Who's Got Game?" and featured Royals players competing in other sports, which was a big hit. Even the way he used music to support video prompts was seen as revolutionary within the classically staid setting of major-league ballparks (or at least in Kansas City). "We had other teams recognize what we were doing, the energy we were creating, using our video board as a conductor, different things of that nature that they hadn't seen in baseball," he says. "We were kind of the trendsetter."

Costante is a big believer in thoughtful implementation, picking his spots. "Impact versus quantity," he preaches. He denounces venue-specific mobile apps, which can offer various perks to patrons, like exclusive camera angles, replays, in-seat ordering, and live data. These have become one of the major tech innovations for stadiums in recent years, along with advancing Wi-Fi capabilities, increasing quality (and size) of video boards, developing three-dimensional and 360-degree replay technologies, and a growing investment in broadcast equipment so venues can cut their own shows, instead of relying on TV feeds. While Costante doesn't dispute that apps can provide value for NBA and NFL franchises, he says it is dangerous to direct attention away from the baseball field during play. "We do Twitter and we do Instagram," he says of the team's in-game social media efforts. "But we are not driving [technology] in terms of check out the replays on your phone, and distract you. It would be hypocritical. We are talking about balls that can kill you."

But on most questions of fan engagement, Costante is adventurous. "In the beginning, it was 'Let's max that,'" he recalls. "And I didn't have to ask. I just did it." Not everyone was thrilled with the Royals' new anything-goes mantra for game presentation and fan entertainment, though. As Costante puts it, "I pushed the envelope to the point where I went and upset the traditionalists."

The purists.

Pushback was inevitable, he knew. But pushback from a few crusty old fans was one thing. The problems began when upper management began counting themselves among the aggrieved.

———

Don Costante isn't the first baseball man to challenge the stodgy sport's status quo. As far back as the 1890s, before teams even had permanent, fireproof homes, outlets like *The Sporting News* were clutching their pearls when St. Louis Browns owner Chris Von der Ahe simultaneously staged a Buffalo Bill Wild West show and a baseball game at Sportsman's Park, according to Michael Benson's *Ballparks of North America*. The team owner had also installed a "honky-tonk, amusement park rides, and a 'wine room,'" per Benson, but while Von der Ahe dubbed his venue "the Coney Island of the West," *The Sporting News* referred to his unorthodoxy as "the Prostitution of a Ball Park."

That was nothing compared to the antics that would come the following century, courtesy of a peg-legged showman named Bill Veeck, known as the "P. T. Barnum of baseball" for his circus-like stunts, wild promotional ideas, and complete and total irreverence for anyone else's sense of tradition and propriety. He sent Eddie Gaedel—who stood three feet seven inches—to the plate as a pinch hitter in 1951, and five days later he allowed the crowd to serve as game manager, making strategic decisions via yes/no placards.

Born in 1914 and enshrined in baseball's Hall of Fame in 1991, five years after his death, Veeck spent the vast majority of his life in and around ballparks. His sportswriter father became president of the Chicago Cubs in 1918 when he criticized the club and was dared by the team's owner to do better. It was a similarly bold sensibility that informed the younger Veeck's career, as he would go on to become an owner himself (with other people's money)—first of the minor-league Milwaukee Brewers, then of the Cleveland Indians, the St. Louis Browns, and finally the Chicago White Sox.

Along the way, he left a trail of accomplishments (or catastrophes, depending on your point of view) that spanned the gamut from the monumental and profound to the shocking and absurd. As his credits go, Veeck invented the exploding scoreboard, put player names on uniforms, popularized the idea of in-game curtain calls, and helped integrate baseball by signing Larry Doby, who became the American League's first black player in 1947. He held morning games for late-shift workers, brought in belly dancers, baseball magicians, and clowns to entertain the crowd, and had a penchant for giving away live animals (lobsters, chickens, and even a swaybacked horse) to fans. Other prizes might include a thousand cans of beer, a thousand pies, a two-hundred-pound block of ice, or nylon stockings, when the accessory was in short supply after World War II.

At heart, Veeck was a marketing man, and wherever he went, record attendance followed. Many in baseball turned their noses up at the unabashed gimmick king, accusing him of making a mockery of the game, but others saw his success and followed in his footsteps. In the 1970s, at Atlanta–Fulton County Stadium, for instance, the Braves complemented their cellar-dwelling teams with a variety of madcap promotions, which included fans racing on ostriches, a "Headlock and Wedlock Night" featuring a few dozen weddings and a wrestling match, and wet T-shirt contests during rain delays, per Benson. Meanwhile, at Municipal Stadium in Cleveland, in those same years, the Indians brought in a variety of daredevil acts, like celebrated human cannonball Hugo Zacchini and high-wire artist Karl Wallenda.*

Bill Veeck didn't come up with the idea of promotions in sports, of course—according to Allen Guttmann, Ladies' Day campaigns can be traced back to 1867. He just took it to another level. And yet for every hit, there were also some epic misses. Veeck's most famous failure—a promotion that was championed by his son Mike—came in Chicago in 1979. In an event called Disco Demolition Night, Comiskey Park hosted a doubleheader, and the idea was to have patrons bring in disco records for a bonfire on the field, between the two games. But the second game was never played (the White Sox were forced to forfeit), as the raucous crowd became inflamed, whipping records like Frisbees and chanting "disco sucks." Wanting in on the destruction, thousands soon stormed the field.†

To some in baseball circles, *Veeck* is still a dirty word.

Flipping through the pages of Benson's book, you'd think there's always been a better-than-even chance that ballpark promotions end in mayhem, starting with the Ladies' Day riot of 1897 at Griffith Stadium, in Washington, D.C. After tossing the handsome hometown pitcher from that game, the offending umpire was beaten by a horde of heartbroken female fans who charged the field, while others

---

* This comes from authors Jim Toman and Dan Cook, who founded Cleveland Landmarks Press.

† There is a theory that the mayhem was spurred on—beyond the natural rowdiness of a fifty-thousand-person crowd—by racism, as the disco demolition was "seen as a not-so-subtle attack against disco's early adopters: blacks, Latinos and gays." See Derek John, "July 12, 1979: The Night Disco Died—or Didn't," NPR, July 16, 2016.

uprooted stadium seats and smashed windows to display their displeasure. Another notorious melee broke out in Cleveland in 1974, when Municipal Stadium hosted Ten Cent Beer Night, which Benson calls "the dumbest promotion in the history of baseball." Officially, sixty thousand cups of beer were sold that night, and the Cleveland faithful were not happy drunks, shelling the opposing team's bullpen with cherry bombs and cheap swill while streakers staggered across the diamond and others mooned the athletes, before ultimately charging the field, inciting a brawl between the fans and the visiting players. The hometown team fended off the encroaching crowd with baseball bats.

"The days of doing something crazy like that—you're not going to get away with it," says Costante, who predicts we may never see another Bill Veeck type in the ever more corporate world of major-league baseball. "Everyone is trying to be innovative, but the difficulty is you have to work within the framework that is given to you." When I ask about any mishaps from his past, the Royals' Master of Fun shrugs. "We've all had something go wrong."

His lowest moment came before a nationally televised college basketball game, when he worked for the University of Memphis in the late 1990s. It was at the Memphis Pyramid, and Costante wanted to create a cool visual for pregame introductions, both for those in the stands and for the viewers at home. Because the lights in the arena could not be shut off, he decided to install six remote control smoke cartridges, which would detonate when the cheerleaders ran out onto the court through a big inflatable. There would be a huge puff of blue smoke, like a fog machine at a concert. "It worked just the way I said," he remembers, "and I tell the [cheerleaders], 'Just keep running around.' People around me were all going, 'Wow, that looks awesome!' I'm thinking, 'That *does* look awesome.'"

But after the cheerleaders completed one lap of the court, the smoke wasn't clearing. "Needless to say, one cartridge was almost too many, and I used six," says Costante, who failed to rehearse the effect prior to the game. "The smoke was so thick, and it had a horrible taste, and it just got thicker and thicker, and the cheerleaders kept running around in circles. All of a sudden, I could hear the coach go, *'What the fuck! Don Costante! What the hell did you do?'*" The game was delayed as the giant blue sulfur cloud slowly rose toward the rafters, until eventually the coaches agreed to play. It wasn't until the second half that those in the upper deck could see the court.

Brad Collins sits, eyes closed, head down, lights off. Save for the muted blue glow of a small TV screen, it is pitch black inside Kauffman Stadium's tiny mascot room, and Collins has once again stripped down to his base layer. "It feels calmer when the lights are off," he says, having just returned from Sluggerrr's fourth-inning meet-and-greet at Little K. "It's so hectic out there. I just like it calm."

During the inning-long photo session—the top half of the inning seemed like it would never end, as the visiting White Sox scored three runs—I watched as the line grew and grew, soon curling out of sight. Adults and kids giggled when they reached the front of the line, eager to meet Sluggerrr. Infants were thrust into the mascot's arms, new moms and dads entrusting their precious babies to a stranger in stinky synthetic fur. Like some sort of plushy priest blessed with benediction, the mascot made everyone so happy, so joyful, so at ease—well, everyone except for those he absolutely terrified, typically small children, whose parents nonetheless nudged their offspring toward the big yellow lion. "You see him? Is he scary? *Nooooo.* He's not scary," one mom said to her sobbing son, threatening to bring the child even closer to the beast. "That happens a lot," Fenlon whispered to me. "It's a weird job. You see a lot of happy kids, but you make a kid cry every day."

Back in Sluggerrr's room, it is hard to reconcile the animated lion with the overheated human form of Collins, now slumped in a puddle of flesh, smelling riper by the minute. "Most people have this perception that a mascot must be this wild and crazy guy," he says. "A lot of times, if you put a guy like that in costume, the personality won't translate. He's just being himself. For me, I'm kind of shy and laidback, so it is a completely different persona from who I am."

For many mascots, this escapist quality is a major appeal. "It's such a release," says Collins. "I do stuff that I could never get away with as myself," such as proposing to an attractive woman or lifting up a dude's shirt to rub his belly. "There is something freeing about it." Fenlon agrees with his ballpark mentor, adding that he recently discovered he possesses some unexpected talents, but only when in costume. "All of a sudden I can make a behind-the-head, backwards shot" on a basketball court, he says, "but I can never do it as me. Never."

The divide is psychosomatic, surely. But according to Dan Meers, who has served as KC Wolf, the mascot for the Kansas City Chiefs, since the character's inception in 1989, one might not want to dig too deeply into the mental makeup of those who wear costumes for a living. "Mascots are two peas short of a casserole," he says with a laugh, when we meet before a preseason football game inside Arrowhead Stadium, which is just a few parking spaces away from Kauffman Stadium, in the Truman Sports Complex.*

Inside Arrowhead's theater room, where Chiefs head coach Andy Reid will later give his postgame press conference, Meers and I sit and discuss all things KC Wolf, like his favorite among-the-fans gags (a Polaroid camera loaded with silly string, a fishing rod baited with a hairy plastic spider), his 2006 induction into the Mascot Hall of

---

* The two venues were built simultaneously in the early 1970s, rejecting the dominant concrete doughnut model of the era and helping set the standard for modern sport-specific stadiums. "It did break the mold," says Joe Spear, a founder of Kansas City–based Populous, one of the world's leading sports architecture firms.

Fame,* and the importance of properly hydrating before a football game. As we chat, Meers, who at forty-eight is tall and thin, with a runner's build and a soft warbling voice, sucks down Gatorades like he might never drink again.

Because NFL schedules have only ten home games (including preseason), KC Wolf takes far fewer breaks than his baseball counterpart, Sluggerrr. (Says Collins, "I always get mad at Dan, because we have longer home stands than his entire season.") Starting hours before the game, Meers slips into his wolf suit and begins making tailgate visits, before leading a pregame parade around the stadium. He then participates in on-field antics as the teams come out of the tunnel. During the game, he does endless in-seat appearances to help with promotional contests, to offer moral support when a fan proposes to a partner, or just to dangle a hairy spider over someone's unsuspecting shoulder. Proper conditioning is key for such marathon mascoting, and Meers has developed a stationary-bike training program that focuses on endurance. "It doesn't matter how much I lift, I just need to be able to dance for four and a half hours in a costume," he says. Still, once or twice, dehydration has caught up to him. "I've had a couple of IVs through the years."

There are other game-day dangers, too.

"Mascots tend to use a lot of ibuprofen," Meers says of the nicks and bruises he often endures, some unexpected, some self-inflicted. "If you see a mascot running along, acting like he's not paying attention, and then run smack into a goalpost, you probably think,

---

* Founded by Dave Raymond, who served for sixteen years as the Phillie Phanatic, beginning with that character's 1978 debut, the Mascot Hall of Fame commemorates a collection of costumed icons, like Mr. Met, the Suns Gorilla, and the Famous Chicken, aka the San Diego Chicken, who is basically the godfather of modern mascoting and isn't afraid to tell you about it. "Let's put it this way," says Ted Giannoulas, who has been the one and only Chicken since 1974, "the home run was always around in baseball, but Babe Ruth decided to make it an art."

'Wow, that looked like it hurt.' Well, it hurts almost every time. But a mascot—if he heard someone laugh—he will get up and do it again the next time he runs past that pole."

The injuries can be quite serious. In 2013, while practicing a dramatic entrance that included bungee jumping out of Arrowhead's lights before zip lining onto the field, Meers fell farther than planned and crashed violently into the stadium seats, suffering major injury. (He was hospitalized for more than a week.) No fans were around to witness the mishap, but even if they had been, they might have just laughed. After all, in the eyes of the audience, mascots can't feel pain. The characters are cartoons, like Bugs Bunny or Wile E. Coyote, and pain is momentary, some birds spinning around your head after an anvil flattens you.* The costumes help preserve this illusion, like when Meers busted up his shoulder while doing a belly flop at a corporate event. (As full-time team employees, professional mascots make hundreds of outside appearances.) "Nobody could tell I separated my shoulder, because I still have this stupid grin on my face."

––––––––

Sometime in the second half of the Chiefs' preseason game, I head to a production booth high atop Arrowhead Stadium to spy on the team's video board operation and gain yet another vantage point on fan engagement. Confronted by a quilt of possible camera angles, sliced into tic-tac-toe segments across a full wall of TV screens, lead

––––––––

* I also notice this dehumanizing phenomenon when accompanying Sluggerrr into the stands for the seventh-inning stretch and a T-shirt toss. (Collins could have taken service tunnels, but wanted me to see the craziness that ensues when he attempts crowd work.) Sure enough, fans flip out upon seeing the mascot. They charge the lion, shriek his name from all directions, like he is a teenybopper heartthrob, and grab his paws, all wanting a piece of him. With a human celebrity, there might be a sliver of shame, the realization that this is an actual person. But Sluggerrr is a mascot, and he belongs to the fans.

producer Brock Raum points to one he likes and screams: "Standby truck eight! Take truck eight! Truck eight is up." Half a second later: "Where am I going?"

"We got a good look on brown," says Brad Young, who leans back in a rolling chair, behind Raum.

"Standby brown, and effect to brown," says Raum. Pause. "Nice. Standby red."

According to the weather service, a severe storm is moving into the area. But like the white noise of a pattering rain, the control-room jargon just washes over me. Up here, there is an inverse relationship to the action on the field. As a play unspools, a momentary lull takes hold, everyone's eyes on the screens. Then, as soon as the whistle blows, the commotion begins again.

"Flag! Flag!"

A penalty marker is down.

"Flag! Camera one, give me the ref. Camera one, give me the ref. Stay on one. Take one. One is up. White. Standby white. And effect to white. White is up. Uh, we got a shot from anybody? Standby four. And effect to four. Four is up. Thank you very much, guys."

Like the inside of a TV truck, the control room looks impossibly futuristic, with glowing neon consoles and enough pulsing screens and monitors to put any sports bar to shame. Moreover, the place is a beehive of activity,* as head-down replay operators endlessly splice all available game footage for possible slow-mos and the graphics guy produces other visual content that may or may not be integrated into the feed. (He also updates live stats.) Dana Witt, a game enter-

---

* When I spend time in the Royals' control room, by contrast, baseball's slower pace of play and natural breaks create a sleepier and more laidback vibe. The most interesting tidbit I learn there is the code word *C-7*, which stands for "camera seven"—there is no camera seven at Kauffman Stadium—and is used like a control room version of *five-oh*, meant to warn everyone to shape up, to stop ogling attractive fans in the stands, because a superior has walked into the booth.

tainment manager, maintains contact with the many field producers sprinkled around the stadium, while the technical director mans the main video switcher (rumor has it that a similar piece of machinery was installed in the Death Star, in the original *Star Wars*, to achieve a space age effect), pushing buttons, following Raum's direction. At the center of all this madness, Young, who is the senior producer of game and event entertainment for the Chiefs, monitors the proceedings from his rolling chair, like a captain surveying the waters from the bow of his ship. Young is the head coach of the control room, while Raum is the offensive coordinator/play caller.

"It's like a television broadcast," Young says of the team's video board content, which includes prerecorded spots, live action, fan cams, noise prompts,* slow-motion replays, and more. (The feed also broadcasts to stadium suites and concourse TVs.) The key is to provide entertainment value while also keeping fans in the loop on the smallest game details, which can be a challenge during a football game, when compared to a home viewing experience. As Raum explains, "We don't have commentators saying, 'Well, look at number fifty-eight here coming through the gap.' We have to show replays that tell the whole story."

Identifying the right replay angle is also critical from a home-field-advantage perspective. "We are always our coach's first look," Raum says of plays that could be challenged by a coach's flag. If the ball is fumbled when the Chiefs are on defense, for instance, but the refs don't call it, they need to find a replay that makes the turnover clear. On the other hand, showing a misleading angle can be disastrous if it causes the Chiefs to lose a challenge or allows the visiting team to challenge a play they otherwise wouldn't have. "We got to get it quick and it has to be perfect."

---

* In 2014, Chiefs fans broke the Guinness World Record for loudest crowd roar at a sports stadium, at 142.2 decibels. But any video board prompts—or "pumps," as they are known—must feel organic, says Raum: "We will never put a player on the board, saying, 'Hey, fans, get loud!' People do, but it is so forced and so fake."

Beginning with kickoff, this pressure for perfection mounts across the length of the game and doesn't release until the final whistle. "When I get home, I'm going to crash. And I always do, because you're literally on edge the entire time," says Young.

There are fun parts of the job. During fan cams, the control-room guys always catch weird activity in the stands (much of which is unfit for the big boards), but the funniest thing to witness is when they put a frowning fan on the Jumbotron. "You can see him in preview, and he just looks super grumpy. But as soon as you see him on camera, the guy lights up," says Young. This is one of two universal truths about sports fans, he's learned: "People lose their minds about two things—free stuff and being on the big screen."

As with game action, the producers must remain vigilant when fans are on camera. "You want to keep them engaged, but you also don't want to force it. Because you could get people who are upset, and you start seeing middle fingers. That kind of stuff," says Raum.

Young nods. "Always on edge."

During tonight's game, Raum takes a chance on a dancing woman, who seems like maybe she's had a few. When she sees herself on the video board, she begins rubbing herself sensually. Raum can't get off her fast enough. He screams, "Oh my god! Get off this. Wow. Standby three."

Her indecency was instantaneous, but it is never smart to stay on one fan for too long, per Young. "They realize they're on camera, and they're going to do *something*. There is a timer. You can see it."

"I always just feel it internally," says Raum. "Okay, this is going to get weird."

———

I can't help but wonder how Bill Veeck would deal with fan cams and Jumbotrons, if he were alive today. Would he pan quickly across the crowd to avoid any possible middle fingers, or would he be tempted to hold the camera on a single fan beyond any internal timer just to see what happens, to see how weird it might get? Such impish curiosity was a kind of guiding force for baseball's most beloved and hated promo man, and it is the same spirit that pervades the sport's minor leagues today, where Veeck's mischievous legacy lives on.

Take the St. Paul Saints, an independent-league team and one of a handful of clubs owned in part by Mike Veeck, Bill's son. Guided by a philosophy that "fun is good," the Saints—who boast Bill Murray as a "team psychologist"—have been pushing the limits of ballpark entertainment since the team was founded in 1993. Head to St. Paul's CHS Field, and you're likely to find mimes performing instant replay, ball pigs instead of ball boys, and "ushertainers," which are ushers dressed up as various characters (French chef, coach, nerd), who will not only direct you to your seat but also taunt the other team and lead cheers. At games, the Saints have staged the world's largest pillow fight and played nine innings without an umpire (but with a judge and jury), while issuing one-of-a-kind ballpark giveaways like Michael Vick dog chew toys and bobblefoot—instead of bobblehead—dolls, in honor of the wide-stanced senator Larry Craig.

"That's what I love about minor-league ball. It is literally the leading edge of sports promotion in this country," says Tom Whaley, executive vice-president of the Saints, who tells me there can even be a trickle-*up* effect, as some ideas—like letting kids run the bases and hosting heritage nights—begin to appear at pro venues. "If you look at what's going on at the big-league level in every sport, you can pretty much trace it back to a desperate minor-league baseball owner somewhere. It's true."

And yet, no major-league team wants to be considered "minor league."

It was three or four years ago when Don Costante started to hear the grumbling from upper management, when "the tides just started changing," as he puts it. "They call everything 'minor league-ish,'" Costante says of his Royals bosses, who began to gripe about his promotions strategy, all the games and contests.

The Royals' brass isn't alone in its belief in the sanctity of a pro-level stadium. According to Mark Donovan, president of the Kansas City Chiefs and a self-described "traditionalist," there is a fine line between providing in-game entertainment for fans and creating a sideshow. When we meet in his office, inside the team's training facility, he tells me he is often mortified by what kind of ancillary activities and gimmicks get the green light at other venues around the NFL. As two particularly offensive examples, he mentions a Gatling gun that shoots T-shirts in rapid succession (which sounds amazing) and a popular halftime act featuring a monkey riding a dog like a horse (ditto).* "We sit in press boxes at away games, and I just look at these guys"—the Chiefs' PR staff—"and go, *Really?*" says Donovan.

The nail in the coffin came for the Royals' Master of Fun last year, at the end of the 2014 season, when the team made a deep and unexpected play-off run. Costante scaled back his promotions during the postseason, as many organizations do, because the natural energy inside the ballpark was electric. Having endured decades of disappointing teams, the baseball-centric atmosphere seduced upper management. Why couldn't it be like that all the time?

And so a new mandate came down. Costante's orders were "Let's cut out all the antics, and let's just go back to baseball. Let's ride the fact that our team is winning." Practically, the mandate meant that the stadium host would no longer be allowed to have a role during the game, only pregame. Aside from a few contests and games that

---

* Despite Donovan's dedication to tradition, halftime shows at pro football games were actually developed in 1922, not as some tribute to the greatness of the sport but as a way to sell dogs, as players on the Oorang Indians—an early NFL team from LaRue, Ohio—would perform tricks with the team owner's prized Airedale terriers, in hopes of growing his dog-breeding business.

were grandfathered in, due to contract obligations with sponsors, the team would phase out anything that wasn't specifically baseball-related. As for future ideas, they would need to receive approval. The MoF could no longer do what he wanted.

After leading the charge on fan engagement for the Royals, after successfully bringing the NBA to the ballpark, Costante has been forced to watch the pendulum swing the other way at Kauffman Stadium, as the organization tries to seize this winning moment to shift its whole culture. "We are going in reverse order of what everyone else in the country is doing," he says. "We are catering to the older generation."

Whaley has seen this film before. "It's a tragedy," he says, "because I assure you the Royals are going to suck at some point, and then they will revert to the fun-at-the-ballpark theme. But the minute your team starts to get good again, you are like, 'Well, that fun stuff doesn't really matter so much. We are going to market our team.'" He says such thinking is a blind spot for otherwise smart sports owners. "Bill Veeck said winning is the ultimate promotion. He knew it better than anybody. But why would you base your business success on an entirely random event—a win or loss on the field, a star player getting injured? It just makes no sense."

Costante says the Royals' current engagement strategy is not only shortsighted but also reinforces a false dichotomy: winning versus fun. He believes there is a place for both. Winning "shouldn't stop you from using technology, being creative, innovative in your approach, striving to always try to do something that is going to entertain not just the traditional person."

But it isn't all bad news for fun-loving Royals fans, according to Costante: the on-field hotdog races aren't going anywhere. "Our owner, who hates minor-league games, *loves* the hotdog race."

————

PART TWO: THE KING OF THE CRUDS

Last stop on the F train. Coney Island, Brooklyn. I get off and walk to Surf Avenue, past the original Nathan's Famous, and wait in the shadow of the Cyclone, the historic wooden roller coaster, which roars on its track overhead. This is where I'm to meet the Amazing Sladek, a circus-performer-turned-hotshot NBA halftime act who in a few short years has taken the sports world by storm.

I first learned about Sladek, who at fifty-seven bills himself as "America's oldest daredevil acrobatic hand balancer," in Cleveland, at the start of the 2015 NBA play-offs, when he performed at Quicken Loans Arena. Like many arena-goers, I figured I was immune to the various halftime routines basketball teams regularly trot out—the jugglers, the local youth leagues, the mascots and trampolines. But Sladek was different. There was something magnetic about this old man in a rhinestone-spangled jumpsuit over a blousy shirt, with a deep-V neckline, bell-bottomy sleeves, and a wide collar. I don't have the metrics, but I was far from the only person at the Q who was transfixed by Sladek, who stayed seated throughout the performance instead of hustling off to the bathroom or the concession stands.*

After theatrically gesturing toward the crowd and handspringing around the hardwood as preamble, Sladek began his act, known as the Tower of Chairs. On top of a folding table placed at center court, he methodically balanced six wooden chairs, one after another, end on end, climbing the spindles all the way to the top. Once there—because being twenty-plus feet in the air on top of a shivering stack of lumber (he doesn't use safety gimmicks; the chairs do not click together) isn't enough—Sladek grabbed hold of the two top chairs,

---

* It is not just fans that have taken to Sladek. The acrobat has become a darling of Shaquille O'Neal, Charles Barkley, and the rest of TNT's *Inside the NBA* crew, who allot him generous airtime whenever they happen to be in the same building.

one of which was staggered off to the side, and lifted himself into a ten-second handstand. All the while the arena cameras transmitted close-up shots of Sladek's strained and veined face onto the giant video board above, aka the Humongotron. I could see his sweat, his stress, his exaggerated expressions. With his dated costume and severe East Bloc appearance, he looked like he'd lived a hard life, as if he'd traveled for years in a covered wagon, going from town to town under some Soviet-like regime, finally making it to the States, to this moment, to the zenith of an NBA arena.

But I had it all wrong—well, mostly.

Sladek's real name is Gary Borstelmann,* and he grew up in North Babylon, Long Island, and that presumed Soviet backstory shatters once you hear him talk. "Ooh, that's good living, bro. That's what my dad would say. *Gooood* living," Sladek says, after gliding his Mazda Miata into a just-vacated parking spot on Surf Avenue, in Coney Island. Despite the forehead wrinkles and crow's-feet, Sladek radiates youthful exuberance in person, leaping out of the driver's seat, with forearms bigger than his biceps and calves bigger than his quads, like a real-life Popeye. Dressed in soccer shorts, flip-flops, and a baggy T-shirt from the NBA Eastern Conference Finals—at which he also performed—Sladek doesn't wear rings and prefers not to carry a phone, either, because "as an acrobat, you never know when you'll see a good handstand opportunity."

During the summer months, when the NBA and NCAA basketball are not in season, Sladek will book a WNBA game or two, but otherwise fills his schedule with outdoor fairs and other small community events, which are significantly more dangerous than arena gigs, he says, because he's exposed to the elements and has to level his table against the uneven ground with little shims of wood. But

---

* Sladek is his maternal grandmother's maiden name. The Amazing Borstelmann just didn't have the same ring to it.

summer is also when he gets some time off—to travel upstate, to go to Six Flags Great Adventure, or to meet me in Coney Island to ride the Cyclone.

Unsurprisingly, Sladek is a roller-coaster connoisseur, and he especially loves the Cyclone, which he's been riding since his parents took him and his siblings as kids. "My dad would point at kids who stood up and say they were bad kids. They were cruds." But Sladek craved adrenaline from an early age. He loved riding in the Cyclone's last car, because that was the bumpiest ride, and whenever his old man wasn't watching, he would slither out from under the restraining bar and stand, as the ride whipped around the tracks.

Being a daredevil is almost a prerequisite for riding the Cyclone, given the number of recent incidents. In 2007, a man reportedly broke his neck on the first drop and died days later. At least twice already in the 2015 season, the ride has stalled out, leaving stranded customers to climb down. Also earlier this year, a woman was awarded $1.5 million for injuries she sustained in 2008. I'm not nearly the thrill-seeker that Sladek is, and having spent all week researching the many types of back and neck injuries I will surely suffer on the ride, I get nervous as we walk up to the ticket booth. Not helping matters is Sladek's excitement when I tell him I've never ridden the Cyclone before. "And here I was thinking you were a roller-coaster guy like me! Are you serious?" He is giddy. "When you ride the Cyclone with Sladek, you'll never be the same!" he cackles, but wants assurances: "Are you committing to me that you'll do this?"

I tell him I won't flake. We purchase our tickets.

"Good," he says, a smile creeping across his face. "I'm a little wild during the trip, unfortunately."

It is an early Thursday afternoon in August, and there is no line. Take any seat you want, says the yawning operator. Sladek, of course, wants the backseat but agrees to sit in the front car, which he says is second best. "Back row next time, bro," he tells me. As the cars pull into the docking bay, Sladek is disappointed to see the new padded cushions (I am not). When the Cyclone staffer comes to lock in the restraint, Sladek puffs out his stomach, hoping to gain a little breathing room so he can stand during the ride. (I shrink as far back as the seat will allow.) When the staffer jams the bar down hard, I am relieved. Sladek says, "Oh, man," genuinely disappointed.

And then with a shudder, the cars start to move. We lurch toward the top of the track, the first drop, passing a PLEASE REMAIN SEATED sign. Even though he won't be able to stand, now shackled in, Sladek is already jacked up, as if his muscles were trying to break out of the confines of his skin. When we reach the peak, there is a brief calm-before-the-storm pause. Too brief. We're off. The initial balls-in-your-belly drop gives way to whiplash turns and more drops. The ride is superfast and superfun. I grab the bar as Sladek whoops it up, yelling and punching his arms into the sky. "Whoooo! Yeah!" Trapped inside a roller-coaster car with a madman, I can't help but laugh as he forces me to raise my arms, like him, and screams over and over and over again, "I'm the king of the cruds!"

———

The madman is not without fear. In fact, Sladek gets scared every time he does his act—"every time, bro." And yet the acrobat can't begin to count how often he's been teetering on top of his chairs inside some arena thinking not about the next chair or the upcoming handstand but what he's going to eat after the show. "I swear, it is such a strange thing," he says as we sit down at Totonno's, a thin-crust-pizza joint tucked away on Neptune Avenue, after disembarking the Cyclone injury-free. "Eating is my *passion*."

Hunger serves a key role for Sladek, especially on the day of a show, when he basically goes into starvation mode, which is part motivation tool, part vanity. "I eat the right things to give me energy," he explains. "But I don't eat a lot. I want to look my best in my jump-suit." His go-to snacks on the road are beef jerky and 94 percent fat-free microwave popcorn. "After a show, it's glutton time!" He takes his food—from some BBQ joint, Chinese restaurant, or Mexican place, most likely—back to his hotel room and spreads the bounty across the bed, while catching up on the news or watching Turner Classic Movies. That's the routine, he says, "and I love it."

Sladek does have to watch his weight. Staying under 170 pounds is ideal, he says, but staying under 180 is imperative for safety reasons: "Anywhere over 180, not only psychologically, but the feel—it is so hard getting up into the handstand, let alone balancing."

As a high schooler, Sladek was a standout gymnast—a tumbler who specialized in floor exercise. At his family home, he would scoot all the living-room furniture off to the side so he could stretch on the carpet and work on his flexibility. His parents didn't mind. Still, while enrolled at nearby Farmingdale State College, the young acro-bat had no dreams of becoming a professional, even as he competed on the school's gymnastics team. He would become a gym teacher. That was the plan.

But just as Sladek was finishing his sophomore year, something happened.

The circus came to town.

Really, it was his father's fault. A banker and pillar of the com-munity, Sladek Senior, aka Robert Borstelmann, was a Rotarian. As part of a fund-raiser for his local Rotary, Mr. B contracted the Royal Hanneford Circus to perform a show inside his son's college gymna-sium. "My dad was the one who pushed for the circus," says Sladek. "Nothing to do with me. I never knew about circus in my life. Didn't think of it as a vocation." At one of the shows, Mr. B even served as an honorary ringmaster, riding in on an elephant. Afterward, back-stage, he embarrassed his son, as he often did, by introducing him to

Tommy Hanneford, the owner of the circus, and bragging about his boy's gymnastic abilities. Hanneford offered the kid a summer job on the spot. Sladek accepted.

It was 1978, and Sladek's first gig was at an amusement park in Ohio called Americana. He proved to be a fast learner: "Within two weeks, I was jumping up and down on horses. Within two weeks, I was in a trampoline act with a finish trick called the three high." Sladek was smitten. When summer ended, he decided to stay on the road with the circus instead of going back to school. He broke the news to his parents. "I said, 'Dad, Ma, this is what I was *born to do!*'" His folks were iffy about the change in plans but supportive nonetheless. For his part, Sladek had no doubts. "All I started doing was performing. Learning these different skills and putting my skills to work," he says.

His life would take another turn the following year, when he witnessed the chair act for the first time. He had gone to see some Chinese acrobats in New York City, and the Tower of Chairs was the last performance before intermission. "I was scared watching them," remembers Sladek. "It just stuck with me. It was a showstopper! I said, 'That's for me.'"

With Hanneford's help, Sladek had four chairs made. That first set was aluminum, with safety gimmicks that clicked together so that if he were to ever fall, the chairs wouldn't collapse on top of one another. "I've had a few close calls," says Sladek, but he's never fallen. Eventually he abandoned the gimmicks, investing in a new set of wooden chairs.

Through the years, Sladek has performed on cloud swings, breakaway sway poles, in the trapeze, and in the wheel of death. He has been hired as a daredevil for numerous other feats. For a time, he did a comedy trampoline routine under the name Garvekio. But the chair act was his bread and butter, even earning him an extended stay at Manhattan's Webster Hall, where he embraced the nightclub atmosphere, performing in a rhinestone thong. "I was the king of Webster Hall," he says.

But by the early 2000s, his career had plateaued. At some point, he knew, he would need to take his act up a notch—and he did, by the end of the decade, after some friends approached him with an idea they said could catapult his career into the stratosphere. "In my old age, I decided to do six chairs," says Sladek. "If I can do it, it will be fantastic."

For a whole season, he practiced the stunt while "getting up the guts." Easier said than done, since he never once practiced with a safety harness. "Six chairs is a whole different world," says Sladek, who finally unveiled his new and improved act under the big top somewhere in West Virginia in 2010. He doesn't remember the name of that town, but he can vividly recall what it felt like to perform that day. It was hot and muggy, with a full house of people. The six chairs took him nearly to the top of the tent. "I was so scared," he says. When he made it back down, he flipped off the table, triumphant, and the crowd went wild. But he was still trembling inside, totally drenched in sweat. He remembers thinking, "Oh, my gosh, I got to do *this* every show?"

The Amazing Sladek isn't homeless, but he also doesn't have a home, exactly. He often stays at his parents' place in New Smyrna Beach, Florida. He also keeps a truck and trailer—his old circus rig—parked in a nearby campground. During the NBA season, he mostly spends his life on the road, driving from gig to gig in a Chrysler Town & Country minivan, with his chairs safely stowed in the back and satellite radio as a traveling companion. "Everyone flies," he says of other performers, which he calls "suitcase acts." "I drive because I don't trust my chairs flying. What if I get there and something happened to the chairs?"

This past season Sladek performed forty-two halftime shows all across the United States, clocking fifty-three thousand miles.* There were some grueling trips along the way, like the week in which he had to do four shows while covering three thousand miles. Other times he's had to sleep in his car on the side of the road.

But you won't hear him complain.

On January 17, 2012, the aging acrobat performed his first halftime show at the United Center in Chicago, becoming an NBA rookie at fifty-three. He's remained grateful for that opportunity every day since.

"Doing the NBA, it has changed my life, bro," Sladek says as we leave Totonno's and make our way back to the boardwalk. As a circus performer, he says, "you are always working for your next show. I never saved a nickel." In a good year, he would book thirty weeks of work, while forty weeks would be a great year and twenty would be terrible. "It is so hard out there in the circus business, man. I've never done anything else in my adult life."

The memories are fresh. It was less than four years ago that Sladek was still "humping around the country," as he puts it, on three-month circus gigs, for which he'd pull in $2,500 a week. The majority of that went to travel expenses, driving from Philly to Rockford, Illinois, then backtracking to Maine, all while living in his trailer.

These days he stays at $250-a-night hotels, when the NBA puts him up.

"It is a cut above my world," he says of his new accommodations. "I've never experienced this before. I have never touched this world, these high rollers, wherever they get their money. When I'm on the circus, on the road, truck and trailer, I'm underneath my trailer fix-

---

* Compared to other top NBA acts, like the legendary Quick Change and Red Panda, Sladek manages to perform only about half the number of dates during a season because of how long it takes to travel from venue to venue.

ing a flat tire. Here, with the halftime shows, I've got my Town & Country, driving around with my air conditioning and satellite radio, and I pull into the arena. I'm the halftime act!"

We stop along the boardwalk in front of Paul's Daughter, a beachside food stand where Sladek would often eat when he was younger. We lean against a metal rail, the ocean to our back, the Cyclone off to our right. He eyes the roller-coaster cars as they race around the wooden track, which trembles in their wake. "I love to watch it *move*," he says as seagulls squawk in the near distance. The clatter of the amusement park ride seems to give him an idea. "Why don't you be my assistant on center court for one show?" he says, gauging me for a reaction. "Would you do it? Would you be willing to do it?"

A mischievous smile spreads across his face. It is the same smile he had just before we got on the roller coaster. "You won't believe how dangerous it is. You'll see."

From the stands, everything seems safe and sanitized and failure-free, like a bowling alley with bumper lanes. The results assured. Everyone goes home a winner. But zoom out from the high-profile arenas, from the perfectly choreographed and meticulously timed halftime shows—retreat through the years, through the eyes of the Amazing Sladek—and what you'll find is a trail of blood and bodies.

"I've seen a lot of deaths," Sladek says of his thirty-plus years in the circus world. "I have three friends who were killed by tigers." There was Wayne Franzen, who was mauled by a four-hundred-pounder named Lucca while opening a show in western Pennsylvania. And then there were Chuck Lizza and Joy Holiday, who performed as part of a Siegfried and Roy–type act with Joy's husband, Ron, and a white Bengal tiger named Jupiter. "The tiger just lunged at [Lizza] and throated him," says Sladek. But the animal was not put down. Five weeks later the big cat attacked Holiday. "Same tiger killed both of them. *That* is circus tragedy."

And it's not just tigers. Sladek says another three friends were killed by elephants. Allen Campbell, an animal trainer, was crushed to death after trying to save a groom from a rampaging pachyderm named Tyke. "Allen comes in and has what they call a bullhook, a stick with a little metal hook. As big as they are, elephants don't like to be pinched." But after subduing the animal for about a second, Tyke head-butted Campbell to the ground before crushing the trainer under the weight of its skull. Says Sladek, "He did a headstand on him. They said his eyes were bulging out. His chest caved in."

Early in his career, Sladek had a close call with the human cannonball when he refused to be loaded into the apparatus. "That is the one act I will never even consider doing," he says. Instead, his best friend from college, another aspiring acrobat, took his place. "We were young. We wanted to be stuntmen. He just had the balls to go," Sladek says, wincing at the memory. "First shot ever. Missed the net by fifteen feet. He came out of the hospital in a full body cast."

But even with that sliding-doors moment, it wasn't until 1997, standing on a makeshift platform high above the playing field inside the Louisiana Superdome, that Sladek experienced his closest brush with death. He was serving as an alternate for an eight-person bungee jump as part of the Super Bowl halftime show. Among the first-string jumpers was his then-girlfriend, Wendy Bell, and her sister, Lora "Dinky" Patterson, who at forty-one years old had begun to contemplate retirement, leaving the circus life behind. "The first time I did this jump, scariest thing, one hundred eighty feet. You're free-falling until the bungee kicks in. Just trusting that the bungees are in good shape, nothing is going to snap," he says. "I had to force myself to leap off that platform, because I wasn't in control. See, with the chairs, it's so scary, but I'm still in control. *I* am the one that has to make a mistake." Thankfully, nothing snapped, everything went fine on that first jump, and every other jump, until the Thursday dress rehearsal.

"ZZ Top is playing. Blues Brothers. We jump. Everybody bungeed." When they got down, all the acrobats were on stage—all but Dinky. "Her guy was either looking the other way or let the rope slip," he says of her belayer, who had the acrobat's life completely in his hands, since the safety ropes were wrapped around a pole but never fully secured. "On the very first bungee, she split her head open on the Superdome turf."

Sladek can still hear his girlfriend's screams when she learned about her sister. Can still picture the crowd that immediately gathered around Dinky's lifeless body. There was no question of her survival. "Her brains were all over."

Sladek is unaware of any major tragedies at NBA games but says if one were to occur, it will be to him.* "I'm probably the most dangerous halftime act," he says. He embraces the danger, works the angle for all it's worth. At arenas, he'll approach fans in the front rows before intermission, resplendent in his jumpsuit, and tell them, "I'm the halftime show. I will risk my life for you today."

It's all part of the act, part of his persona.

"The fans, they know that this old man loves what he's doing," he says. "They see my stressed-out, wrinkly old face on the Jumbotron, and I become this stressed-out character. And I really am stressed out, but it's show business. So I play it up and work the crowd.

---

* While Sladek is likely right on this front, there is a history of death-defying halftime acts at pro basketball games from the 1970s and '80s, like chainsaw jugglers and Victor the Wrestling Bear, a bear that wrestled humans.

"Sometimes I get concerned," he admits. "I'm getting so old. I don't want people to say, 'We are afraid to hire this guy.' That is my biggest fear—that they're going to stop hiring me."

Sladek says bookers have nothing to be afraid of. For all the (genuine) stress that accompanies his act, he knows he won't ever fall, because he *can't* fall. "You only fall once from this act," he says. "The first fall is going to be the tragic fall." Which is why he's so religious about his daily workouts, which focus on core strength and flexibility. "Bro, I put my time in. It's the only key—one hour a day. No room for error. No days off. You can't make a mistake in a handstand—you can't."

After getting such a late-in-life start at basketball arenas, Sladek wants to work until he's sixty-five, he says. That will allow the former circus performer to put some money away for the first time in his adult life and maybe even buy his parents' Florida home so they can live for free. Beyond that, there's a chance he could go down as one of the all-time halftime greats, which is a tantalizing possibility. "For me, in my little world, in my business, circus performers, we risk our life, and we don't make shit," he says as we head back toward Surf Avenue, toward his Miata, ready to call it a day. "But I got a chance here—that is the thing. And wouldn't that be great, man? In my little world, bro?"

It sure would.

Six months pass before I am to assist Sladek on center court at a Rutgers University men's basketball game. In that time, he retreats to his parents' place in Florida to prepare for the upcoming season, flies to Brazil with the Orlando Magic for an exhibition game ("I was in fear for my chairs!"), and then hits the road again, motoring from arena to arena.

The day arrives. February 20, 2016. It is an unseasonably warm and bright winter morning when I get to the RAC, the Rutgers Athletic Center, in Piscataway Township, New Jersey, moments before Sladek—who is fresh off a performance at the NBA All-Star Game in Toronto (and is wearing the T-shirt to prove it)—pulls up at a service entrance in his white minivan. With him is his ex-wife Terri Lauria,* who lives on Long Island and occasionally joins her former lover for legs of a journey. A bouncing ball of energy that even Sladek can't match, Lauria gets out of the car and wraps me in a bear hug. "Gary promises not to be too intense today," she says as Sladek loads his folding table and chairs onto a rolling cart, careful not to let them touch the pavement. "He can get *very* particular before a show."

Inside, we are taken to the track and field locker room, which Sladek must share for the day with the Rutgers mascot, the Scarlet Knight. "Terri!" Sladek scolds his ex-wife, depositing two huge suitcases, which contain all ninety-six of his costume combinations,† alongside one of the stalls, "stop touching the mascot's stuff!" After he settles in, we head out to the court to huddle with the facilities manager, to confirm there is enough space beneath the center-hung scoreboard (Sladek needs a clearance of at least twenty-five feet), and with the arena deejay, to drop off the performer's intro script and otherwise coordinate timing for his halftime entrance.

Then Sladek turns his attention toward me.

We go to a back-of-house staging area, where the cheerleaders are gathered, practicing lifts, and a young woman stands against a padded wall, singing the national anthem quietly to herself, hand to her ear. Sladek takes his chairs off the cart and places them on a mat.

---

* For a long and complicated tangent, ask about the various women in Sladek's life. In addition to his daughter, there is Lauria, his "ex-wife/soul mate," with whom he plans to live in retirement. Then there is Patricia Murphy, his "ex-girlfriend/secretary/personal assistant," who will be his and Lauria's permanent houseguest. And finally, there is Wendy Bell, another ex, who is "the only girl that I sleep with," he says. "I see her about four times a year."

† Wherever he performs, Sladek tries to match his colors to the home team.

"The order is very important," he tells me, pointing out the numbers one through six, scribbled on each chair. Even though there are no safety gimmicks, the chairs have worn against each other in a certain way after years of performances, and stacking them out of order creates a far less sturdy tower. (This has happened, and it was terrifying, he says.)

Next, we rehearse how I am to handle the chairs—how to pick them up (by the front legs), when to bring them over (when he signals), and how I am to pass them off to him (with the chair backs facing the performer). The wooden chairs are heavier than I expected, but the first three seem like they will be easy enough, when Sladek is still relatively low to the ground. After the third, there will be a pause, as he does a handstand, and then the fourth chair will have to be held high overhead so he can reach it. The last two must be lifted via a metal pole contraption, which Sladek has designed. Having seen his act several times now, in person and on video, I had assumed the handoffs would be easy. But when I try lifting one of the chairs with the pole, the whole thing starts to swing wildly in my hands, far more top heavy and unwieldy than I anticipated. For the first time, I'm worried that I may kill the Amazing Sladek.

"Don't worry about the pole, bro," he says as we head back to the locker room. "You're strong as an ox."

But I don't feel reassured.

Sladek is giving off a different energy than the last time we met. He is less manic, more matter-of-fact. Not prickly, exactly, but edgy, for which I don't blame him. After all, he is about to put himself in harm's way, as he does every time he performs, but now with an unqualified nincompoop as an assistant.* But maybe it's not just

---

* Typically, Sladek recruits a male cheerleader or someone from an arena's hype team—a helper who is young, strong, and immune to the center-court spotlight—to assist with his act.

today's halftime show occupying his mind. Maybe he's still thinking about his Canadian excursion—his first trip north of the border as an NBA act—when he performed at the All-Star Game, on basketball's biggest stage for entertainment, even earning some valuable airtime, as the TV cameras caught the Western Conference bench applauding him. Superstar guard James Harden mimicked the acrobat's wide-armed finale gestures. And even Gregg Popovich, the typically stone-faced coach, was smiling and clapping like a kindergartner at a magic show.

Maybe he's still thinking about that—about that scrapbook moment, an unmitigated triumph, by all accounts—because he knows how close it came to not happening. How close he came to flaking on the game, to being rejected at customs, and to having to watch from across the border as his whole career, for which he'd worked so long and hard, came tumbling down, as his chairs never do.

———

He knew it would happen eventually, this moment of truth. As Gary Borstelmann, aka the Amazing Sladek, pulled up to the U.S.-Canada border on the Friday before the All-Star Game, his stomach seized into the world's tightest knot. One by one the cars crept closer to the border plaza, to the customs booths. His odometer showed how far he'd come, and there was no turning back.

Inside the minivan, in addition to his chairs and other equipment, Sladek was carrying his official NBA paperwork, as well as some newspaper clippings—profile pieces about himself, about his rise on the halftime circuit. He brought them along to present to the customs agents, if need be, to prove who he was, what he had accomplished. And also maybe to prove something to himself: he wasn't the same guy he used to be.

According to the performer, his string of bad luck and worse decisions began at a gas station in Birmingham, Alabama, in the mid-1980s. That was where he first had his truck stolen, along with his chairs. Sure, he should have locked the car doors, shouldn't have left the vehicle running—but he had been in his late twenties, flying high, still invincible. Plus, he was smoking lots of pot at the time. Drinking, too. It was harmless, a little bit of fun for transient circus folk to help pass the time. The real trouble wouldn't come for a couple years, when Sladek, always a man of enormous appetites, discovered cocaine.

Now *that* was a drug.

To support his habit, Sladek started dealing, but he messed only with the best stuff and was always happy to hook up his friends, always the life of the party, never concerned about who paid and who didn't—just that kind of guy. His blind trust in others and overwhelming generosity are still some of his most enviable qualities. But they're also his tragic flaw, as evidenced by the time he befriended a young gazoonie—one of the nomadic roustabouts hired as circus hands and assistants—who served as a horse groom during an extended stopover in Greenville, South Carolina. None of the other performers would so much as talk to such tramp workers, but Sladek thought this kid could use a pal. He let him stay in his camper and even invited him to smoke a joint in his trailer, making the mistake of revealing where he kept his stash and his cash (under the mattress). After that night's show, all his money was gone.

The downward spiral accelerated for Sladek on Memorial Day, in 2004. It didn't take a criminal genius to find the acrobat's keys underneath his vehicle's floorboard, where they were always kept. And just like that, his trailer was stolen for a second time, along with all his worldly possessions, chairs included. Everything was in that trailer, everything but what he had on him: seven hundred dollars and an eight ball of blow.

That night Sladek checked into the Commack Motor Inn, on Long Island, and didn't check out until the following September, when a drug friend set him up. Inside his motel room, Sladek was robbed at gunpoint after taking a full Corona bottle to the face. "I was picking glass out of my face for two days," he says.

Bottom finally came on October 19, 2005, when the strung-out acrobat got busted with about half a gram of cocaine. It was a sting, but Sladek still believed he could have gotten off light, since the weight would have qualified only as a Class A misdemeanor. Sladek, a former Boy Scout, didn't care about getting off light, though. He had reached his breaking point. He was sick of this life, sick of the drugs. Wanted to get clean and start fresh. Voluntarily, he led the cops back to his buddy's place, where he was now staying, and turned over his entire stash. It was enough for a felony charge. Convicted of criminal possession of a controlled substance in the fifth degree, Sladek was locked up in December 2005 and didn't get out until January 5, 2007.

This whole messy history raced through Sladek's brain as he waited at customs, as the agents looked into his car and saw the chairs. *Hey,* they said, putting two and two together, *aren't you?* Sure am, Sladek said, feeling hopeful, handing over his passport and paperwork. The agents looked at the forms and went back to their computer. Should only take a second. But something was wrong. The agents looked at each other. Sladek needed to get out of the car.

Agreeing to the All-Star Game and trying to cross the border would be a risk, Sladek knew (as it was when he traveled to Brazil, as well), but a calculated risk. Plus, he was used to risks. His whole *life* was built on risks, stacked twenty-five feet high. Ultimately, he couldn't say no. Not to the All-Star Game.

Leading up to the weekend, he envisioned all possible outcomes— what could go right, what could go wrong, and this, by far, was the worst-case scenario.

The agents informed Sladek he had been banned from Canada

because of his felony drug conviction. His heart sank, and he could already imagine the fallout when word spread through Toronto, at the Air Canada Centre, where all thirty talent bookers from around the league were gathered. *You hear about Sladek?* Of course, he hadn't told anyone about his past. He hadn't wanted the NBA to know. And now he would be humiliated on the sport's biggest stage. His arena career would be over.

The customs agents interviewed him for hours, trying to decide if a special allowance could be made. Sladek told them everything. He told the agents about his life in the circus, about his drug use, his arrest. He also told them about how, when he got out on parole in 2007, he had zero, zilch, nada, making a circle with his thumb and forefinger, to accentuate this nothingness. He told them how, unable to find work, he eventually got a job at a deli counter, slicing meat, making $8.50 an hour. How he booked a summer gig at an aquarium, where he dressed as a pirate. He told them how he saved every penny he could, squirreling it away until he could afford some new chairs. Not great chairs but decent ones that would get the job done. He told them how in 2009 he signed on with a circus for a six-week stint, thus beginning his comeback. How he increased that to thirty weeks the following year, while adding two chairs to his act and making a new name for himself: America's oldest daredevil acrobat. And how, soon after that, the NBA came calling.

He told the agents how he was ten years sober.

His only addiction was to Diet Coke.

For the first time in his life, he had a checking account, some stability, and he desperately didn't want to lose that.

The agents listened. They conferred with their superiors. They waited for word, for what they called a "determination." Finally, six hours later, it was decided that they would let him in. That allowing the Amazing Sladek to entertain their fellow countrymen at Canada's first-ever NBA All-Star Game would be beneficial to the nation, better than turning him away. A special allowance was made, his secrets safe for another day.

———

At the RAC, with the Rutgers game under way, Sladek straddles a mat, begins to stretch. I take this time to practice my portion of the act. Focusing on the pole, I repeat the process, again and again, trying to master the move, reminding myself to hook the pole onto the chair's second rung, to spin the chair 180 degrees, once the pole is aloft, and to lift as high as possible, without losing control.

Sladek had said he's always a wreck before a show, and I can feel the nervous energy taking hold. The acrobat is wound tight. "I'm so hungry," he says. As time ticks down, I grow tenser, too. I try to picture a happy outcome. I practice. I want it to be over. I can't understand how he deals with this pressure on a near-daily basis; my whole body is a clenched fist. I feel an intense love for him, but right now I also hate him.

Sladek comes over to check on me. I'm in worse shape than he thought, but it's too late. We are in this together, and I see the realization dawn on him: *Oh, shit—it's not enough that I have to perform. Now I have to coach this idiot through the damn show.* He tells me he's nervous, because he's always nervous, because he wants everything to go perfectly. He adds, "I'm, uh, not really worried about you—I think you're going to be fine. I think you're going to be perfect."

He almost has me convinced.

With ten minutes until halftime, there is a break in play. The cheerleaders sprint out, tossing T-shirts and hot dogs into the crowd, as the Jumbotron creates a strobelike effect across the court. It feels like the whole place is having a seizure. Sladek is gone. Lauria says he's in the locker room, putting on his uniform. But I suspect he's having second thoughts, maybe even sneaking out the back. I wouldn't blame him.

Halftime arrives. The players vacate the court. We walk out.

To the theme song from *2001: A Space Odyssey*, Sladek executes a couple of handsprings, as I stand off to his right, waiting behind the carefully ordered chairs. He vaults onto the table and immediately thrusts a hand in my direction. He wants the first chair. And then the second. And the third.

Everything goes smoothly, as I knew this part would.

On a roll, I immediately grab the next chair, loft it high overhead for the handoff. Which is when I realize: Sladek is not ready for the next chair. He is in a handstand. I forgot about the handstand, and now I have to keep the chair in the air, because I want to be ready, and also because I don't want to look like an amateur and therefore make Sladek look like an amateur. So I hold the chair as steady as I can, as high as I can, even as my shoulder muscles begin to quake. Finally he asks for the chair.

You would think I'd have learned my lesson after that, but you would be wrong. So relieved to be rid of the fourth chair—and now laser-focused on remembering to spin the fifth—I grab the pole and hoist it up, way too soon. The shoulder tremors resume instantly. My muscles are shaking as violently as the Tower of Chairs itself, which from the stands appears relatively steady. Up close, it sways like a street sign in the wind. Really, the whole thing now feels like an overwhelmingly bad idea. I mean, look at him up there, sweating, shifting, recalibrating his weight.

I have never been more scared for Sladek—or more impressed by him. This act is so far beyond standard arena fare—your monkeys riding dogs, your free T-shirts and tube meat. It is a true standout. A showstopper. And in a time when everything else has to be the latest and hippest, when the flashing LED ribbon boards of an arena can never flash fast enough to hold our attention, when we are all slaves to pop culture's high-speed metabolism, Sladek is a holdout—legitimately, unintentionally old school. He is a throwback to a time when it took years to perfect a craft instead of seconds to create a GIF. With his perfectly unstylish costume—which Heidi Klum will disparage when Sladek competes on *America's Got Talent* later in the year—he is an artisan. An anachronism. An analog man in a digital world.

He calls for the fifth chair.

And then the sixth, which I have trouble bringing close enough for him to grab. "Come on, closer!" he hisses. But I don't want to lose control and plunge the pole into his tower. "Closer! Closer!"* Finally, I get the pole close enough to Sladek that he can grab the top end and pull it in further. He takes the chair and shoves the pole away. I retreat, heart racing, and watch him enter into his final handstand, high above the court.

He holds it. Spreads his legs. Holds it again.

I'm desperate for Sladek to come down. And he will, but not yet.

This is when he is at his best, with the whole arena captivated, tortured into a collective hush. The old acrobat shows no signs of letting up. He knows we are all entertained.

---

* Lauria would later confirm that this exchange was in fact quite scary.

9
THE SECRET LIFE OF STADIUMS

(Or: Let's Get Logistical)

After the puck drops. After the chants of "Let's go, Devils!" and "Crosby sucks!" After drunken fans bang on the dasher boards for three straight periods, like toddlers on a fish tank. After the final horn, when the men's-room line swells with dudes in hockey sweaters, as "Glory Days" blares over the speakers. After all that, it is still only ten-thirty p.m. inside the back-of-house tool storage and workroom known as "the shop" at Prudential Center, a multipurpose arena in Newark, New Jersey. Here, the day is just beginning.

Over the last hour, the overnight changeover crew has been trickling into the shop, napping, snacking, waiting for Mike Gualano, the assistant manager of operations and head honcho for all the arena's conversions, to hand out tonight's assignments and corresponding tools (drills, sledgehammers, etc.) and to give his regular pep talk, before the team of twenty-two laborers (down from the typical twenty-six) and two forklift operators descend on the floor and seating bowl and begin the slow nocturnal work of transforming the space into something nearly unrecognizable.

"We're going concert" is how Gualano starts his pep talk, which he insists isn't a pep talk—and it isn't—though I've heard worse. ("Please don't put it on YouTube," he says of his under-fifteen-second speech.)

Ordinarily, coming out of a hockey game, the first order of business would be to cover the ice with four-by-eight-foot pieces of plastic fiberglass decking, which insulates and protects the frozen sheet. Tonight, however, a postgame marketing event on center ice—a photo op for fans—precluded the Zambonis from shaving and flooding the playing surface until now. Not wanting to waste precious minutes, the crew directs its attention to the north and south ends of the arena, where they work on the hockey seats, which angle at a different grade from those needed for basketball and concert setups. While some arenas have hydraulic capabilities, which can raise and lower seats automatically, the first ten or so rows at either end of Prudential Center collapse into themselves like an accordion.

"It's a big puzzle every night, and there's an order of operations. Only so much deviation you can do," says Frank Perrone, vice-president of arena and event operations (and Gualano's boss), while leading me on a tour of the service tunnels and storage rooms earlier in the evening. The venue can accommodate all manner of events, from dirt shows (like motocross or monster trucks) to gymnastic competitions to three-ring circuses, with little to no lag. On this weekend, for instance, the arena will host a Seton Hall basketball game on Friday night, a Devils hockey game on Saturday (tonight), and a C-pop concert on Sunday featuring G.E.M.—who is the Taylor Swift of China, I'm told—before beginning immediate preparations for *Disney on Ice*, which will have a five-day run of shows over the coming week. Even when Prudential Center was home to the now-Brooklyn Nets (and the NBA team's forty-plus event-dates), the New Jersey venue was never as busy as certain arena counterparts, like Los Angeles's Staples Center or Manhattan's Madison Square Garden. (The Garden executes overnight conversions about 275 times a year with a crew triple the size of Prudential Center's.) As with any arena, the goal is to minimize "dark days," as they're called, which are eventless dates on the calendar and therefore missed revenue opportunities.

According to Perrone, the most stressful conversions come not during the witching hour but in broad daylight, amid doubleheaders, when, say, a one p.m. basketball game is followed by a hockey game that evening. On those fire drill days, it's all hands on deck. The changeover crew doubles in size, while Perrone and Gualano will have prepped the building in advance by rearranging storage schemes for maximum efficiency, since the arena must be flipped in two hours, less than a third of the usual time. "Well, it's really more like *three* hours," Gualano admits, watching his laborers struggle with one particularly sticky section of seats, which doesn't want to budge, as the clock ticks close to eleven p.m.

He can already tell it's going to be a long night. For one thing, the crew won't be able to begin laying the floor for at least another half-hour, which will also delay taking out the hockey glass and the dasher boards and flipping the player and penalty boxes into additional front rows, all of which should be happening in conjunction with the seat swaps. For another, he's breaking in a new forklift operator tonight, who is subbing for one of his regulars, and the substitute "fork" has already proven a unique ability to lodge the machine at bizarre angles inside the service tunnel, Austin Powers style.

Such hiccups are common. While Perrone contracts nineteen full-time trade workers for the building—carpenters, electricians, plumbers, and HVAC technicians—everyone on the conversion crew comes by the work through his or her union. The laborers, for instance, are Local 3. The operators are Local 825. (The carpenters used to assist with changeovers, but that ended after they went on strike.) For most members of the overnight crew, it is a second job, a side gig. Gualano can't help but compare his circumstances to those at Madison Square Garden: "They have full-time guys, which is huge. So you know who you are getting every night."

The irregular schedule taxes the workers as well, since they can't simply flip their sleeping patterns like most late shifters. Some nights they're needed, some nights they're not. "It's rough. Your sleep gets messed up," says a laborer named Mike Vizzone, who calls me out onto the ice when the crew starts laying the floor. "Come on, bro." He gestures toward the stack of flooring. "Grab one."

I glide across the ice and reach for the stack, excited for a task to distract from my growing drowsiness. But someone stops me, another laborer. He says, "I'd put your gloves on first, or I wouldn't."

Really? I don't have gloves.

He grimaces. "Think about all the beer from the concerts. People's feet."

I look to Vizzone, who shrugs. "Wash your hands after." With that settled, Vizzone shows me how to ease the floor panels off the front of the stack, and how to push each piece across the ice and then slide the decking into an open space, alongside its floor fellows. It's like the world's easiest game of Tetris. Each piece makes a satisfying plopping sound, when dropped onto the ice, that echoes throughout the empty arena. After I slap down a few pieces, Vizzone checks in on me. "What do you think, bro? Easy, right?"

Dressed in blue jeans, work boots, and a camouflage Devils hat, he appears to be one of the younger members of the crew—in his twenties, if I had to guess. But while he's been working at Prudential Center for only a handful of months, he already considers himself a semiregular. "I do this when I get laid off, when the union gets laid off," he says. "You call here and see if they can fit you on the schedule. And like nine times out of ten, if you have done it before, they let you come back."

Another regular goes by the nickname Doc. He is short, in his early sixties, with a white chin beard and a green pom-pom beanie. Originally from Grenada, Doc is a carpenter by trade, though he no longer practices professionally. A friend helped him join Local 3, he tells me, so he could pick up arena work. "I love doing this," says Doc, who has been assigned to sledgehammer duty. He pounds long slats around the edges of the floor and pluglike pieces into any remaining cracks to make sure the big panels are sturdy and won't move underfoot. It is a good assignment, he says, although working on the basketball court is his favorite—the way the hardwood segments literally pin together on top of the decking.

"Hey, watch out!"

A conversion vet named Harry, perhaps a few years younger than Doc, jokingly tries to run me over with a piece of decking before swerving left, as two other laborers nearly have an on-ice crash:

"Wrong way, asshole!"

"Shut up, dickwad!"

But this is all just standard ballbusting, and the chatter rises as the night goes on. Harry tells me the crew has fallen into a pretty good groove of late (minus tonight's forklift operator), with all the events at the arena. "We are real busy now because of Seton Hall basketball," he says, although he knows things will soon dry up, at least temporarily. "Normally, with a concert, basketball, hockey, we keep changing. With Disney, that kind of freezes the work."

But there is a silver lining.

Per Harry, "Disney is a great show. Great show."

——————

Not everyone is such a big fan. As head ice technician at Prudential Center, Nick Kryshak is like the groundskeeper of the arena, and during hockey season, the ice sheet is the building's foundation— always present, even when it can't be seen. "Nobody seems to realize that," says Perrone. When Disney comes to town, Kryshak knows he needs to up his game. "They really do a lot of damage to the ice," he says of the show's figure skaters. "It's like having the circus here. It's just a nightmare."

In preparation for Mickey, Goofy, et al., Kryshak and his team will be at the arena early Monday morning, after the building is converted back out of concert mode following Sunday night's extravaganza. First they will need to clean the ice, since there is always spillage that seeps through the cracks of the insulated flooring, along with the usual scrapes and marks. Next they will have to paint the sheet bone-white, using what looks like a miniaturized crop irrigation system, so that the hockey paint and logos—nearly an inch below the surface of the ice—will not be visible to the Disney crowd. And then finally they will flood the ice repeatedly, to build the sheet up as close to two inches as possible, because figure skaters prefer a warmer and softer surface. In reality, Kryshak says, the sheet will never get much higher than one and a half inches over the slab, due to time restrictions, and that always creates strife.

"Figure skating ice is kept nice and soft," says Kryshak, who joined the arena staff shortly after the building's 2007 opening and has learned a thing or two about the ice and how to care for it during that time.* "They want to be able to dig in when they do their jumps and stuff, but it's not possible, and they will bitch and moan the whole week they're here. They have to realize this is a hockey rink, not a figure skating pad, and we have a team to worry about."

Disney isn't the only traveling show that puts unusual strain on the building—and the ice—as I discover early Sunday morning while chatting with Kerry Graue, my PR minder and a savant of Prudential Center event history. We're joined by Jamie Marino, one of the arena's event managers, who arrives at five a.m. after the overnight crew completes its portion of the conversion and who will be running point on all remaining concert-related operations (stage build, load in, rigging, and so on) from now through the end of G.E.M.'s performance later tonight. Graue tells me how they lay

---

* He calls himself "the scholar of the squeegees."

plastic over the ice in preparation for any dirt shows, like Monster Jam or Professional Bull Riders, when big dump trucks invade the arena. (According to Kryshak, dirt can stain the ice and stress the Zambonis.) Meanwhile the Street League Skateboarding competition involves the most elaborate load-in, per Graue, because the event requires concrete to be poured onto the arena floor, in order to build a skate park from scratch. (Thankfully, for Kryshak's sake, the show arrives in the summer months, when the ice is melted.) How do they get rid of the concrete? I wonder. "Jackhammers!" says Graue. "It takes five days to load and three hours to destroy."

But the most dreaded event is the circus.*

"The smell!" moans Marino. "It smells like elephants for months. Literally two months later, it still smells like elephants." Graue readjusts her routes around the building to avoid the most fetid passageways, she says. "It is so brutal." Other issues often emerge as well, like last year when the rollup doors jammed on the ramps, which are part of the arena's loading zone. As a result, they had to sneak the camels in and out of the building through the practice rink, which would not have gone over well with the Devils' then-general manager, Lou Lamoriello, who had a reputation around Prudential Center for being a little obsessive compulsive. "The most OCD man on the planet," says Marino. "He didn't let the players have facial hair. So camels in the practice rink? That was definitely a no-no. We had to walk them under the bleachers."

Another fun circus fact is that elephants refuse to move if they can feel the cold emanating through an insulated arena floor. Therefore Kryshak has to melt the ice sheet whenever the big top comes to town, even when there is only a month left in the hockey season. "It is like a huge kick in the balls," he says, explaining that this upsets the athletes as well, since the ice actually gets better

---

* Sorry, Sladek.

with age.* Some potential good news for the head ice technician: In May 2016, Ringling Bros. and Barnum & Bailey Circus phased out its traveling elephants, retiring the animals to a conservation center in Florida. (Less than a year later, it was announced that the famed circus would soon shutter all of its operations.)

By nine a.m., nighttime has fully bled into morning at the arena. Daylight cuts through wall-size windows on the north end and splashes into the seating bowl, across the insulated flooring, which has been chalked with what appears to be alien cuneiform. (These marks indicate rigging points.) The space looks nothing like it did a mere ten hours ago, yet the work is only half done.

A whole new cast of workers have arrived. In addition to Marino and five in-house department heads—a foreman, assistant foreman, head electrician, head carpenter, and head rigger—there are the worker bees: four loaders ("who specifically load and unload trucks," says Marino), twelve riggers (who attach and raise equipment to the rafters, like speaker towers and lighting trusses), two forklift operators (different ones, thankfully), and twenty-two stagehands, which Marino simply refers to as "hands." They are responsible for building the stage (duh) and setting up all the equipment (lighting, audio, LED walls, other production elements, etc.) before it is mounted on the stage or raised to the rafter beams, which are known collectively as "the grid."

Really, the building has not stopped moving and transforming since last night—and it won't stop anytime soon. At eleven a.m., Graue and I retreat to a pair of black leather easy chairs, emblazoned with Devils logos, that sit on the front edge of the main concourse,

---

* It's not unusual for pro-team tenants to take a backseat to secondary arena events. The San Antonio Spurs, for instance, have to vacate AT&T Center for three weeks every February for the San Antonio Stock Show and Rodeo, in what's known as their "Rodeo Road Trip," while the Los Angeles Lakers, Clippers, and Kings are displaced from Staples Center for the Grammys. For years, the Chicago Bulls and Blackhawks were forced to hit the road in November, when the circus descended on the United Center for an extended stay.

overlooking the bowl. (Each game, a pair of lucky fans is upgraded to these seats.) From here, fighting heavy eyelids, we watch as the riggers lift the cabled trusses like giant emotionless marionettes. Marino joins us for a few minutes. She points out the "audio and lighting coffins," which is how they refer to the padded trunks used for electronic equipment. Unpadded, they're just called trunks or cases, she says, and an empty "is a dead case."

So morbid, I say.

"Yeah, a little morbid," she concedes. "A lot of times they'll ask, 'Where do you store your deads?'"

From this distance, all the hands and riggers and loaders look like insects scurrying around a morgue of coffins and dead cases. Marino says she is never really amazed by any of the arena transformations, because she sees them happening. For her, the process is not the butterfly busting out of its cocoon but the internal work of the caterpillar. It is slow and methodical, far from the eye-catching time-lapse videos that exist online. It is real work. Even as a kid, Gualano had a sense that there was something happening in the stadium shadows—that there was an inverse ghost world to all the blood-pumping sporting events and high-octane shows. "I actually always wanted to do this," he says of arena conversions. "I remember being a kid, and I wouldn't see the event, I would see the *next* event, things like that. *How do they do that?* It was always interesting to me." And now, like the other off-hour workers, he's become a phantom of the arena. He says, "We set up for the events and we break them down. Nobody knows what we do."

My true appreciation for the power of these transformations—this seemingly endless ability to shape-shift—doesn't crystalize until Sunday evening, when I return to Prudential Center after a few hours of rest, in time for the G.E.M. concert. Within the now-darkened bowl of the arena, a series of draped black curtains meant to block off backstage movements and hide the empty seats of the upper deck funnels my sightlines toward the stage, which now looks fully formed. The rigging, too, has assumed an air of permanence, as if it were always meant to be there, hanging from the rafters. It is an illusion, to be sure, but a convincing one. And probably no one else from the audience even looks up, once the artist takes the stage, and the lights start spinning, and the video wall flashes, and the confetti flies, unaware of the network of wires that drip down from "the grid" like dozens of spider webs, delicately supporting this fantasy.

Of course there is more to stadium operations than just converting a building. According to Ron VanDeVeen, who oversees MetLife Stadium as senior vice-president of events and guest experiences in East Rutherford, New Jersey,* the 82,500-seat venue morphs into a small city when full. "It is a lot of people and a lot of responsibility," he says, alluding to the various departments that have to thread together during major events, like police, fire, and medical, as well as parking, concessions, and guest services. In total, the stadium—home to both the New York Giants and the Jets—brings in more than 4,500 employees on game days.

I meet VanDeVeen on the field of MetLife Stadium in the hours before the Jets take on the Miami Dolphins in a late November contest. It is ten forty-five a.m., and the gates have not yet opened. Out on the turf, the game presentation staff is wrapping up rehearsals for the national anthem and halftime show. Along the sidelines, several TV networks prepare to do live media hits, as a few players trickle out of the locker rooms for early warm-ups. Elsewhere around the stadium, employees take their positions. "This is the moment when everything is starting to come together, when the atmosphere starts to really ramp up, because once gates open at eleven o'clock, it is

---

* In April 2016, VanDeVeen was named the stadium's new president and CEO.

game time," says Brian Mulligan, the Jets' director of events and game operations, who has agreed to let me trail him all morning through the depths of the stadium.*

My day at the stadium with Mulligan starts at nine a.m., when he takes me on a tour of the service corridor. He points out the control room, the command center, the cheerleader locker room. "Always make sure we have a security guard out there," he says, "for obvious reasons." The security staff's most profound concern, though, is terror-related, especially on the heels of the attack at Stade de France two weeks earlier. "The biggest fear is what goes on outside the gates," he says of any potential terror threats and the venue's vulnerability. "But these guys are not getting inside the building." Security efforts, he says, are both visible (à la metal detectors) and not, citing rooftop snipers, heat detectors, and the "100-minute meeting," which is a briefing that takes place across the NFL, one hundred minutes before kickoff, among team and stadium officials, security staff, and law enforcement agencies, like state police and the FBI, to discuss any possible threats and to review security measures taken in the lead-up to the game, such as sweeps and lockdowns of the venue, as well as evacuation plans.

In an emergency situation or not, VanDeVeen says the goal for MetLife Stadium is "to empty like water," to flow straight down. (After the final whistle, TVs around the concourses are programmed to direct patrons toward the fastest exit.) But crowd management

---

* Shortly after noon, Mulligan will head up to a booth off the press box, where he serves as the team's point of contact for "everything that goes on *not* on the field." There he is kept abreast of any possible security issues and makes sure all league rules are followed. He also acts like a theater director ("we treat the field as a stage," he says), maintaining communication with all the game presentation people, monitoring logistics and timing for pregame intros, national anthem, halftime show, and the like, while scanning the sidelines for credentials, alerting staffers when he finds an interloper. "Really, anything that pops up," he says. "If a player gets hurt, we have somebody up here that will notify his family. It's everything. All the behind-the-scenes stuff."

isn't just an end-of-game issue; it is a chief concern from the moment the first fans arrive, as the operations folks try to keep a constant finger on the pulse of crowd size and movement, especially as it relates to ingress. To this end, Mulligan and his associates receive e-mails every fifteen minutes with updates on how many fans have scanned their tickets, as well as hourly notices on how many cars are in the parking lots. (The team also has a live dashboard, which tracks fan data and allows personnel to proactively troubleshoot based on any entrance gate imbalances.) For additional insight, Mulligan brings me outside, where we connect with Seth Rabinowitz, the team's senior vice-president of marketing and fan engagement. Although a marketing man may seem an unlikely font for crowd flow wisdom, Rabinowitz is one of the masterminds behind the Jets' loyalty rewards program, which the team adopted as it transitioned to a digital ticket environment. He's used this to successfully change fan behavior by incentivizing season ticket holders to enter the stadium more than fifteen minutes before kickoff, when the worst congestion at the gates begins.*

"We do everything we can to alleviate it," Rabinowitz says of the inevitable kickoff crush. "We went to all these magnetometers, which are faster than the old hand wanding. We have this outer perimeter where we will screen people if they have noncompliance bags, and turn them around before they get into a thicker line. We do as much as humanly possible. We have tried the carrot and the stick, and the [rewards system] is the carrot, and it has worked."

Rabinowitz shows me the venue's new ticket scanners as well. "We used to have an optical scanner—the standard Ticketmaster optical scanner, and it worked only on a 1-D bar code. You know, the

---

* The goal at MetLife Stadium and around the NFL is for fans to get into the stadium in ten minutes or less. "We hit it ninety-five percent of the time," says VanDeVeen, who goes outside and puts a stopwatch to the line before each game.

normal flat bar code," he says. "And frankly, we have a lot of after-noon games. Optical scanners don't do a great job, especially early in the season, in bright sunlight, ambient light." They also don't do a great job when fans are pulling crumpled-up, printer-smudged paper tickets out of their pockets after several hours of tailgating.

The delays would add up.

The new scanners, on the other hand, are compatible with any form of media, including mobile devices. "Operationally, it's much faster, and the reliability factor is much, much higher," says Rabinowitz.*

As we're talking, a stadium employee trips over a nearby cable protector and lands hard on the pavement. He doesn't get up. The injury appears to be serious. Other employees get on their radios and call for help. It's a small incident, in the scheme of things, but also a perfect illustration of why it's so important for the stadium staff to manage as many aspects of this unwieldy environment as possible, where accidents—or almost anything, for that matter†—can always happen. (Mulligan calls it "controlled chaos.") When a medical team arrives, Rabinowitz instinctively looks at his watch. He mutters, mostly to himself, "Minute and a half. Not too bad."

---

* Although he doesn't say so explicitly, when Rabinowitz talks about reliability, he is referring to a dirty secret about nonscans at sporting events. As one source, who requests not to be named, explains it to me, "With [optical] scanners, there are always people—not out of their own malice—who try to get their tickets scanned and it just doesn't scan and they end up getting in. It is just a fact of the industry." Many teams hold back a few tickets for just this reason, in case there are multiple fans claiming the same seat. In the old days, these extras were referred to as "squawk seats," which were "good seats left unoccupied for minor emergencies," per *Sports Illustrated*. Andy Frain, who ran a famed ushering business under the same name, invented the practice.

† During the 2015 baseball season, for example, a woman gave birth to a child at Petco Park in San Diego, and skunks invaded L.A.'s Dodger Stadium.

The biggest secret today at MetLife Stadium is hidden in plain sight, and that is: the New York Giants play here, too. With a couple hours until the Jets-Dolphins kickoff, I talk to Mike Alperstein, a facility operations director, and Stephen Sansonese, the field and site grounds manager, who are collectively responsible for flipping the building before each team's next home game. Unlike the typical conversion at Prudential Center, the majority of work here occurs away from the stadium floor,* because of all the team-specific elements that decorate the 2.1-million-square-foot facility. It is a two-day process, which can be crammed into ten or twelve hours when necessary.

On a quick lap around the stadium, Alperstein points out some of these elements, almost all of which have to be changed manually, many with zip ties and grommets, from the field wall wraps and tunnel covers to the banners of various size and shape throughout the stadium. In total, there are about two thousand total changeable elements, says Sansonese. And really, they're everywhere. There are signs on the lampposts around the outdoor plaza and gel packs on the lights that cast the exterior in Jets green or Giants blue, depending on the week. In the concourses, under each section number, on every level, there are little placards that can be unscrewed and flipped—just like the double-sided photography in the suite corridors—and on one side they read, JETS NATION. On the other, GIANTS PRIDE.

It's weird seeing all this—to know how much Giants stuff is tucked into the building. As Alperstein rolls a mechanical Jets poster, which is basically on a conveyer belt and gives way to a small slice of previously hidden Giants Blue, I can imagine how, if I were a Jets

---

* To switch between teams, the field-related work is mostly limited to the end zones, which have to be changed out by Sansonese and a crew of workers. The stadium has three sets of end zones—one for the Jets, one for the Giants, and one that is neutral, for college games. Each end zone is comprised of six Velcro panels (yes, Velcro), the two largest of which weigh about eleven thousand pounds apiece when wet.

fan, I might feel as if the stadium were cheating on me.* That's why they do such thorough walk-throughs, says Alperstein: "It's our job to make sure that there are no Giants elements in this building for a Jets game." Or as Sansonese puts it, "No blue on green days."

———————

Once they're in, the people need to eat. To learn more about the mass feeding of sports fans, I visit Citi Field, home of the New York Mets. Here my food guide is Mike Landeen, the team's senior vice-president of venue services and operations and the architect of what has become perhaps the most ballyhooed concession program in all of sports, with specialty offerings from New York City chefs and restaurateurs like Danny Meyer, Dave Pasternack, Drew Nieporent, and (new in 2015) Josh Capon. Now in his eleventh season with the Mets (which doesn't include his seven years with the team as an employee of Aramark, the concession company), Landeen had a heavy hand in the layout and construction of the ballpark, ahead of the building's 2009 opening, as he was brought in on the earliest design stages and allowed to take a pencil to the blueprints in order to achieve optimal operational efficiency. With the Mets' crosstown rival Yankees also opening a new stadium that year, mediocrity was not an option.

"I knew we were up against Yankee Stadium, and they were going to compare us," Landeen says, when we meet at the mouth of Citi Field's service tunnel on a Wednesday afternoon in mid-June, a couple hours before first pitch. "And the last thing I was going to do on opening day was hide under my desk because our food is worse than theirs. I said, 'We're going to blow them out of the water.' That

———————

* In fact, a security guard tells me a story from a recent preseason game between the Jets and the Giants, when the Jets were the designated home team, and a longtime Giants fan, with whom the guard had developed a rapport, came to the game. He pointed at the guard's hat, which was a Jets hat, and yelled, "What the hell!" The guard shrugged and replied, "That's who I'm working for today."

was my motto: 'We are going to destroy the Yankees when it comes to food and beverage'—and we accomplished it."

How did they accomplish it?

"Come on," Landeen says, taking off down the tunnel. "I'll show you the guts."

Our first stop is a beer pump room, one of five that service the field level. A walk-in fridge overflowing with metal kegs, the room looks like Scrooge McDuck's money pit, if the old bird had had a drinking problem. There is practically nowhere to move, as the barrels are stacked two high and all but blockade the door. Along the walls, active kegs are plugged with two plastic hoses—one red, one clear—pressurizing the barrels, as the golden liquid is sent through a series of tiny PVC pipes to destination taps throughout the stadium. The longest beer run at Citi Field is three hundred feet, says Landeen, which is about the max length you'd want, because beer can get funky if it sits too long in the line. For the Mets, that's not a concern. "We sell so much beer here, it's always flowing," he says. "When we're cranking, we go through about eight hundred kegs a game." To handle this volume, Landeen has a five-person crew, whose only job is to walk around and "change and manage kegs."

Like all walk-in boxes in the building (fridges and freezers), the beer pump room has an alarm that will trigger if the internal temperature falls out of its ideal range of thirty-four to forty degrees. Each keg line is also equipped with a FOB, or Foam on Beer detector, which looks a bit like the upper portion of a large syringe. When a keg reaches the dregs of its barrel, the FOB automatically cuts off the tap, thereby keeping the line full of beer (and ready to flow) until a new keg is attached. At the end of every game, the lines are dumped and flushed with a cleaning solution. "People think they just get a beer poured, and it's as simple as that," says Landeen. "There's a lot that goes behind it."

Though I wouldn't object to spending the rest of today's game here in the beer pump room, Landeen leads me down the hall to what has to be considered the backbone of the ballpark's culinary operation: the main commissary kitchen, which he calls "the hub." Here, among the prep stations and lines of commercial cooking equipment, workers are loading trays with roasted carrots, broccoli rabe, and sliced hanger steak, among other unfairly aromatic dishes, getting ready to distribute the prepared foods throughout the stadium. (But not the suites; the suites have their own commissary kitchen, as well as two auxiliary kitchens that do nothing but pump out Shake Shack burgers and milkshakes.) Standing here, surrounded by busy kitchen workers, Landeen is reminded of the day, almost eight years ago, when he sat down and purchased every piece of food service equipment in the building—every fork, every plate, every tray, even the $14,000 gravity-fed Italian meat slicers. "It was eleven million dollars in one shot," he recalls. But with first pitch nearly upon us, the main commissary cooks are in no mood to reminisce. As soon as tonight's game starts, they will shift their attention to tomorrow's needs, says Landeen. "Chopping peppers and onions, you name it, everything, prepping the entire building. And then they'll be back at seven a.m."

Long hours are to be expected during home stands, not just for kitchen staff. The food warehouse maintains an equally relentless work schedule—and that is where we head next. Filled with giant metal shelving units that support ceiling-scraping towers of heavy cardboard boxes (from a distance, the impression is of a life-size game of Jenga), the food warehouse looks like the team's own personal Costco. There are fifty-pound sacks of sugar, plastic sleeves of popcorn the size of body pillows, boxes and boxes (and boxes) of paper goods, hundreds of packages of potato rolls stacked on blue plastic pallets (all of which the team is likely to plow through this evening), and enough cases of bottled water to survive the apocalypse (or at least a doubleheader), among much else. "Just putting stuff up and taking it down—it never ends," one of two full-time warehouse workers tells me of his in-season routine, which is a Sisyphean cycle of ordering and stocking product.

Every morning at five, the first of twenty trucks will show up. (At Shea Stadium, it was only five trucks.) An early stocking crew will arrive shortly thereafter and help with those deliveries, while also replenishing the concession stands before each game, based on the needs sheets filled out by the stand managers.* At all times, the warehouse director must know how much product each stand has, as well as the building as a whole, and how that compares to preset "par levels." The last thing anyone wants is to run out of hot dogs.† "That's no good. If it's in the song, you don't run out of it," says Landeen, who knows there is always margin for error, when dealing with this kind of volume.‡

Elsewhere in the warehouse, there is a fleet of forklifts parked beside a concrete enclosure. Inside the enclosure, there is a carbon dioxide plant that supplies carbonation for fountain drinks throughout the building. (At Shea, tanks of CO_2 were lugged to individual stands.) "It's all about trying to centralize as much as possible, especially those key items you do at a high volume," Landeen says, citing beer and soda (although soda sales are actually suffering badly, as fans become more health conscious).

We continue on, walking the warehouse's Jenga aisles of card-

---

* If the team is playing a day game after a night game, the warehouse pulls an all-nighter. Doubleheaders are treated as one very long game.

† In 1926, Pittsburgh's Forbes Field suffered a "hot dog panic," when the food product ran out during a rain delay, as Michael Benson reports in *Ballparks of North America*. Per an article at the time in the *New York Evening World*, the stadium's refreshments stand manager learned his lesson and "has taken such precautions that there can never be another hot dog scandal in his park."

‡ Technically, hot dogs are not "in the song"—the song being "Take Me Out to the Ball Game"—but they are certainly a ballpark staple, and an indispensible fan food. As Danish historian Niels Kayser Nielsen writes, "With beer and hot dogs one confirms one's temporary identity as a 'stadium person.'"

board towers. What looks at first like just a jumble of junk is in fact a meticulously organized space. "Whereas Shea was simple, here there are a lot of moving parts, and a lot more ingredients.* Not every stand is getting that," Landeen says, opening one of the five large walk-in warehouse coolers—three fridges, two freezers—and showing me its contents, which neatly correspond to a schematic chart on the outside of the box, designating where to put the fresh-cut fries, the buckets of pickles, the Mister Softee mix, and the Nathan's sauerkraut. "The more variety you do, the more you have to have your shit together logistically."

——————

The history of stadium concessions in the United States begins with Harry M. Stevens, an Englishman who moved to Ohio in the early 1880s and soon began selling food and scorecards at baseball games to support his family.† Legend has it that Stevens even invented the hot dog on a cold day at the Polo Grounds in about 1901. While this may or may not be true, he was the first to bring the tube steak to a ball game. Prior to that, typical stadium fare included items like hardboiled eggs and coconut custard pies, though one never really knew what might be on offer at a sporting event. (As Allen Guttmann writes in *Sports Spectators*, at a 1908 regatta, there was "a fat man in a pink shirt mixing lemonade in a washtub.")

In 1915, Delaware North—another early concession company whose stadiums division would eventually become known as Sportservice—

———————————————————————————————

* At Shea, 80 percent of concessions sold were liquid, and only 20 percent were food. Here that ratio has completely flipped, with 70 percent being food and 30 percent liquid. According to Landeen, fans aren't drinking any less. They're just eating that much more.

† As America's oldest sports concession company, Harry M. Stevens, Inc. remained a family business until 1994, when Aramark acquired it.

was founded by three young brothers named Jacobs, while running a candy counter at a theater, likely burlesque, in Buffalo, New York. The boys' business grew first into minor-league parks and eventually the major leagues, earning its first contract in 1930 at Detroit's old Tiger Stadium (then known as Navin Field). "At that time, baseball team owners wanted to play baseball and sell tickets. They didn't care about the food service or the retail. It was a hassle," says Delaware North exec Rick Abramson. "They just wanted somebody to do it." Even better, companies would now pay for the privilege, sensing the financial opportunity of a captive audience—and they were right. To believe company lore, the Jacobs brothers, after their first year in business with the Tigers, even returned some of their profits to the team's owner because they felt they'd made *too much*.

Over the years, additional competition entered the market, and the concession business formalized. Instead of selling bagged peanuts off card tables or makeshift planks, fitted stands were built into stadiums. The standard arrangement became a commission paid from concessionaires to teams, and the importance of the food program grew, as owners realized it could be a reliable revenue stream. According to Michael Thompson, who worked on Citi Field in the planning stages as a senior vice-president of Aramark, the size of this commission increased steadily in favor of team owners over the last few decades, as concessionaires fought for market share, in their own race to the bottom (not unlike artificial turf companies). But this is another area in which Citi Field forged its own path. The Mets didn't want a commission from Aramark.

"We wanted control," Landeen says of the food and beverage program. To achieve this, the Mets considered self-operating (which is basically what the Yankees are doing with Legends, a hospitality company they founded, along with the Dallas Cowboys) but ultimately settled on a hybrid agreement, in which the Mets put financial skin in the game, while Aramark would manage the day-to-day and the team would maintain final say. "Most buildings, the team gets X percent off the top. And you know what, when the team is good, that's easy. But when the team doesn't do well, they start cutting costs, and that affects customer experience," says Landeen. "And if I'm going to be a pig and just take 50 percent off the top and say, 'You guys deal with the rest,' I can't blame them."

At Citi Field, on-field success has proven elusive for the Mets, as 2015 is the team's first winning season in the new ballpark. And yet the unique financial arrangement with Aramark has enabled plenty of *off*-field success, according to Landeen, because unlike a traditional concession outfit, the team is able to look more holistically at individual decisions, which might not normally pass bottom-line muster, like offering non-moneymaker menu items, such as vegetarian and gluten-free options, or bringing in a celebrity chef, thereby adding another hand to the cookie jar. "We're willing to take the hit to make the experience that much better, because we know it's going to elevate everything else," he says, adding that these minor hits pale in the big picture.* "If we had a conventional deal, our reputation as it stands now would be nowhere near what it is."

As is, Citi Field's reputation as a foodie-forward ballpark has made the venue a destination even in down years. Fans may not have always shown up for the competition, but at least they've shown up. "That's what we've had," Landeen says of the team's concession program. "That's *all* we've had, quite frankly. Our food is what's kept us afloat."

Citi Field didn't invent the modern food revolution at sports stadiums, with complex, higher-end products and partnerships with

---

* The hits are also easier to take as concessions become a less vital revenue stream, with the emergence of giant regional television contracts. As Thompson says of modern-day concessionaires, "We can't pay for a pitcher."

celebrity chefs and local eateries.* As best anyone could tell me, the current trend likely started on the West Coast, possibly with the San Francisco Giants. (Many cite the team's garlic fries.) But the Mets' ballpark has popularized the movement.

"That whole concept kind of took off because of Citi," the general manager of concessions at a major-league ballpark tells me, speaking on background. Per Thompson, the Mets' timing was perfect, as was their market. "The New York market is wild, you can do anything you want there," he says, noting a "Citi Field effect" from the food program's success. "The publicity was so good. Every single major-league team, NBA arenas, whatever, they were asking, 'What is this phenomenon? Why can't we do this here?' And there really was no reason, so it began this movement."

With tonight's game under way, Landeen and I emerge from the back of house and wander the main concourse. The mouthwatering smells are even more overpowering here than they were in the commissary kitchen, which is no accident. "You always had that sausage and peppers smell that makes you hungry," he says of ballpark aromas. "Here every exhaust, all the hoods from the grills, are dumping out on the concourse, so you get *all* the smells.

"From a concessions standpoint, all your basic stuff is pretty much from foul pole to foul pole," he says, describing the spine of the operation as grill stands, general hot dog stands, ice cream stands, and

---

* A parallel anti-foodie trend, it should be noted, are the headline-grabbing, Frankenstein-monster-style concoctions that try to one-up each other on the gluttony scale and appeal to the thirteen-year-old in all of us. The Atlanta Braves, for instance, offer the "Burgerizza," a twenty-ounce beef patty, topped with cheddar cheese and bacon, encased in two eight-inch pizzas. The Minnesota Twins have the "Bigger, Better Burger Bloody Mary," which is a Bloody Mary garnished with a bacon cheese-burger, and the Milwaukee Brewers have deep-fried nachos on a stick. Not to be outdone, the Texas Rangers have a whole menu's worth of crazy options, including "Fried S'mOreos" and the "Boomstick," a two-foot-long hot dog covered in chile, nacho cheese, and onions.

beer. "Those are the core four. That's where you make your money." The key, he adds, is to complement that core with more name-brand stands like Shake Shack, Blue Smoke, Catch of the Day, and so on, where quality is more important than margins. "They don't make a lot of money, but they are what makes *you*. They give you the prestige," he says. "So you got to have that balance."*

At Citi Field, the biggest cluster of prestige properties is in the plaza beyond the center-field wall, which Landeen calls the "experience area." "This is like Fifth Avenue. These are like our diamonds, and there's always activity here. So pretty much wherever you're sitting, you can see it. It gets people up. And once they start walking, they go past someplace and say, 'Oh, maybe I'll go in there.' It's almost like the mall mentality."†

During a sellout, the stadium will go through about 11,500 hot dogs, 3,900 soft pretzels, 3,800 pounds of French fries, 3,000 burgers and orders of chicken tenders, 2,650 sausage and pepper sandwiches, and 2,000 bags of peanuts, according to an Aramark representative. Today's game is not a sellout but a solid showing, with an official attendance of 24,436. And yet aside from Shake Shack, where there is always a snaking line, none of the food stands—of which Citi Field has forty-seven permanent locations and sixty-two carts, which are called "portables"—seem to have much in the way of a wait. This is surpris-

---

* Another challenge of dealing with outside food partners is upholding their standards, per Landeen, and not just the fancy ones. Take Nathan's, for example. The hot dog company has rigid policies regarding its signature product. Specifically, the slight curvature of the meat must be facedown when cooking, and face up when being served. There is even a handy reminder phrase for proper Nathan's hot dog presentation: "Frowns on the grill, smiles on the bun."

† Concession companies have long deemed baseball fans their best customers for this very reason. In a press release ahead of the completion of the Louisiana Superdome, William F. Connell, president of Ogden Leisure, explained why baseball fans spend more money at games: "The baseball fan is a transient. He has lots of time to leave his seat, and he does."

ing, considering the game is still in the first inning, and I'm told the biggest food rush begins an hour before first pitch and lasts until the second inning.* (There is also a seventh-inning run on ice cream.)

Landeen doesn't seem worried. "This building was built like a well-oiled machine. At the [2013] All-Star Game, when this thing was totally full, there was not one line, and I was walking around, like, *they're not making money!* Then numbers came in, record numbers. That's how the building is designed. The amount of cooking equipment and firepower we have—it's amazing. We were cranking, and the numbers were outrageous."

(Over the course of All-Star Weekend, Citi Field went through 37,000 hot dogs, 28,357 bottles of water, 15,000 pounds of French fries, 13,700 soft pretzels, 12,500 burgers, 10,000 pounds of ice, 7,800 bags of peanuts, 7,000 pounds of pastrami, 3,000 pounds of chicken tenders, 1,700 orders of nachos, 700 pounds of shrimp, and 250 gallons of ice cream.)

It's almost easier to handle a full house, when the concession stands just keep cranking. To deal with midsize crowds, Aramark has developed a computer database that spits out cooking projections before every game, from Sunday sellouts to rainy Tuesday affairs. The system crunches the numbers based on ticket sales, buying patterns, hourly sales trends, weather, opponent, day of the week, and so on. (Before the database, which is only two years old, a concession manager would go with his gut, like baseball scouts before the emergence of sabermetrics.) Each stand receives a printout telling its workers what to cook when—maybe ten pretzels now and twenty in half an hour—based on that historical data. Naturally, the projec-

---

* Multiple people who have spent time as concession workers—in Kansas City and St. Louis, specifically—tell me they often advise friends not to buy food until the middle innings, since concession stands are instructed to sell reheated meat, which was cooked for the previous game but went uneaten, before they prepare fresh product. But maybe that's just a Missouri thing.

tions are just a baseline tool, and staffers have to adjust on the fly, because surprises are inevitable, like when the temperature drops unexpectedly and then everyone wants hot chocolate and coffee.

The team also has what is known as a "heat map," which is a live seating chart that outlines where fans are located, based on scanned tickets. If there is an imbalance, concession employees can be pushed toward whichever area of the park has heavier traffic. "With food, with security, with everyone, we move people around all the time, based on what's coming through, what we think is gonna happen," says Landeen. "There's a lot of history, and you learn. Sometimes you learn the hard way."

In total, Aramark brings in about thirteen hundred employees to staff a Mets home game, just for food service. That number includes four hundred–plus cooks, all of whom are trained in the off-season, as well as three levels of chefs—a head chef, six chef managers, and a team of about fifteen chef supervisors who monitor assigned areas, checking that cooking specs are followed, quality is up to snuff, and all stands meet sanitary guidelines.*

The vast majority of these thirteen hundred Aramark employees, who come from a rotating pool of two thousand people, are part-timers. As a result, they work the stadium and arena circuit, cobbling together gigs between a variety of local venues. It's not

---

* Food safety is a major concern at stadiums, as ESPN's *Outside the Lines* made clear in a stomach-churning report in 2010, with fewer than ten active venues (out of more than one hundred, Citi Field not among them) registering zero violations. Health concerns were raised again for the Mets in May 2014, when first baseman Lucas Duda and then–Philadelphia Phillies manager Ryne Sandberg claimed to have gotten food poisoning from Shake Shack. But such one-off incidents were nothing compared to the conditions health inspectors found later that year in Kansas City, at Kauffman Stadium, with "cockroaches in vending areas, mouse feces on the same tray as pizza dough," mold in ice machines, and a soup ladle resting inside a trash can, per ESPN.

glamorous—nearly half of the regular concession workers will not return for a second season, which is understandable given the relatively low wages and hot, grueling nature of the job—but the building's overall employee retention rate is high (86 percent through the first three years, per Landeen), and certain food-related posts are supremely coveted. Perhaps none more so than that of the stadium vendor.*

Stadium vendors are like the cowboys of concessions, independent types who show up later than all other workers, must provide their own bank, and can make as much money as they want, via commissions and tips, depending on which product they're selling and how hard they hustle. On the worst games, vendors might take home minimum wage, if that figure is higher than their commissions for the day, but vendors don't lug around heavy trays, barking for your attention, in the hopes of a minimum-wage payday. According to a Citi Field source, the highest-earning vendors can pull in five hundred dollars a game, from commissions alone.

Which item a vendor hawks is largely determined by seniority, and there is a definite product pecking order, with best sellers like beer at the top of the list and hit-or-miss propositions like cotton candy at the bottom. For a brief period in the late 1990s, there was a market inefficiency when veteran vendors didn't appreciate the earning potential of bottled water, and newbies were able to make a killing. Otherwise younger vendors have to be strategic, by selling lemon chills on a hot day, for instance, or cotton candy on a kids' day. At many parks, you can recognize the lifers by two things: a foam shoulder pad so the strap doesn't cut into the vendor's skin, and a weight belt, especially for the beer guys.

---

* Unlike Shea Stadium, which relied heavily on its three hundred vendors, Citi Field deploys only a third as many. (The decreased number is due in part to Landeen's desire to get fans out of their seats.)

To earn tips, the easiest trick is for vendors to jangle their change, as though fumbling with the coins, when breaking a bill. "Eventually, the [fan] says, 'Ah, fuck it, keep it,'" according to a friend who spent years as a stadium vendor in Chicago. "Some people are more egregious than others, but everybody does it." Beyond that, there are infinite strategies to solicit a tip—smile, make a joke, make a good peanut throw. "Everybody tips for a good peanut throw," he says, adding that, in his experience, middle-aged women are the worst tippers, dudes with dates were solid, and big groups of guys are the best, because "they want to impress each other."*

There are other ways for vendors to take home a few extra bucks as well—illicit ways. My friend tells me about the scams that went down at Wrigley Field, where vendors would conspire with commissary workers. "At the end of the day, the commissary would reimburse you for products you brought back, because you didn't sell them," he explains. "So for your last load, you'd bring back an empty container but leave sixty bucks or a hundred bucks at the bottom of it. The commissary person would look in and say, sixty returns, or fifty-two returns, so they reimburse you for a full load," which could be valued at a few hundred dollars. Alternatively, the insider could send you out with overstuffed loads—a few extra (and unaccounted-for) sodas or hot dogs, per tray—which would add up over the course of a game. "You could double or triple your earnings," he says. The lucrative scams would live for a game or two, as word of mouth spread that there was a willing insider, before the bubble burst and management traced the financial shortfalls back to the guilty commissary worker

---

* At Citi, I watch a vendor pour two tallboys for a fan and his friend. The fan tells the beer man to keep the change. In response, the vendor shouts, "Subway!" When I ask why he yelled this, the vendor says the tradition dates back to the Polo Grounds, when vendors would exclusively take the train to the game. Therefore, yelling "Subway!" when tipped was a way of saying thanks—or so he says. I choose to believe him.

(but never individual vendors), who would get fired. Eventually a new insider would emerge.

Vendors have always managed to game the system, by watering down drinks, bringing back refilled lemon soda bottles (since the liquid was basically clear) as returns, or filching a peanut or two from individual brown bags, in order to create additional units, which they would sell. Concessionaires fought back in various ways. They invested in volume control devices, like the AutoBAR, which attached to a liquor bottle and dispensed exactly one ounce of booze, and began keeping detailed accounts of all inventory, including paper cups (which is why a stadium stand charges full price for an empty cup). According to a 1966 article in *Sports Illustrated*, one concession manager went so far as to spy on his employees via peepholes.

To combat theft at Citi Field, the team does bag checks at the end of each game, per Paul Schwartz, executive director of venue services. "We're busting people constantly," another stadium informant tells me. "Occasionally we'll find a kingpin who's got hundreds of bills stuffed down their underwear. But usually it's not much, a few bucks." But you never know what you'll find, says Schwartz. "One day we opened an employee's bag, and there was the head of a pig in there." The animal part wasn't stolen, he clarifies, just memorable. "Somebody came in with a pig head and left with a pig head."

Sports fans will be excused for not feeling great sympathy toward team owners and concessionaires who endure the minor grifts of their workers. Fans believe they're the ones getting gouged at the stadium, with menu prices that produce serious sticker shock. And they aren't wrong. Team owners are always trying to "capture" fan dollars. It's why Tom Benson, when he bought the New Orleans Saints and was touring the Superdome, did a double take when he came across a third-party vending machine and demanded it be removed, per a stadium source. It's why owners install as few water fountains as possible—and hide them in out-of-the-way locations. When Dodger Stadium opened, it had zero fountains for fans (team officials insisted the 221 bathroom faucets would suffice), until the health department ordered their installation, per *Sports Illustrated*. "In Indianapolis, they actually granted a waiver so the Colts could have fewer fountains," Penn State University professor Bob Trumpbour tells me. "Think about that. I think it is appalling."

If you ask those in the business why there is such a markup for stadium food, they will talk about labor and material costs, about commodities and futures, about a "push to quality," which raises the base price of many ingredients—and your eyes will glaze over. But hope may be on the horizon for those who can't bring themselves to spring for wallet-breaking stadium grub; the Atlanta Falcons will offer street-level pricing at their new stadium, when it opens in 2017, including two-dollar hot dogs and five-dollar beer. The idea behind this scheme is meant to address the biggest customer complaint, according to Thompson. "Pricing, pricing, pricing," he says. "It's like the all-you-can-eat areas, which started rolling out after 2008, when everything fell apart. It was about building confidence in the fan that you were addressing his need. You understand the pinch on the family. So this may just be an experiment, or it may be a wave of the future."

As for the prices at Citi Field, the team just makes sure they don't charge more than the Yankees.

The bowels of these various sports facilities—their service tunnels, secret compartments, and hidden corridors—actually hearken back to the Roman Colosseum. In this respect, as in many others, the ancient venue provided a recognizable model. Known as the hypogeum and located beneath the arena floor, the Colosseum's basement passageways represented what was most likely the world's first back of house, while serving as an "underground staging area," with an elevator system of sixty capstans and a secondary system involving "cables, ramps, hoists and counterweights."* In the confined, stiflingly hot, noisy, and darkened space of the hypogeum, workers coordinated scenery changes, hoisted equipment into place, and orchestrated dramatic entrances for wild animals. In a precursor to walkie-talkies, they communicated via musical instrument (horns, organs, drums), as otherwise it was too loud to be heard.

The modern-day equivalent of one of these underground workers might be a man like Jack Holmgren, who will be the "stage manager" for pregame intros, according to Brian Mulligan, when we return to the field at MetLife Stadium, about an hour before kickoff of the Jets-Dolphins game. For now, Holmgren prowls the eastern sideline, behind the southern end zone, talking occasionally into his headset, as players go through warm-ups on the field, stretching, lunging, fetching the high-arcing footballs that soar through the air to a stadium soundtrack of pulse-quickening electronic music. "It's big theater," Mulligan says.

At twelve-thirty p.m., the players head back to the locker room.

Fans scream for their attention, for autographs.

But they do not stop. There is no time.

As soon as the athletes are inside, out comes the pregame equipment—the smoke machines, the pyro turbines, the inflatable tunnel (basically a bottomless bounce castle) through which the players will emerge. Everyone is moving quickly now, hustling in a dozen different directions. "It's going to be chaos here pretty soon," Holmgren warns me, while wrangling the eighty or so player alumni—here for the Jets' so-called homecoming game—who are going to be announced individually to the crowd and need to be arranged in a predetermined order, based on the pregame script.

With so much happening, I figure it would be best to stay out of

---

* Tom Mueller, "Secrets of the Colosseum," *Smithsonian*, January 2011.

the way. As the cheerleaders dance out to midfield, Holmgren heads into the tunnel. The alumni follow him in.

I do not.

Not at first.

But after the homecoming intros, there's a brief lull. In that lull, I notice the turned-on smoke machines at the far end of the tunnel. Along with the bright autumn sun, this creates a cool visual effect inside the darkened space, with each ribbed segment of the inflatable catching a strip of diffused daylight—an irresistible photo op. I walk into the tunnel, not wanting to overstep, knowing I shouldn't be here. To my surprise, no one stops me. So I go further, all the way to the end, where Holmgren is standing. He sees me, says nothing, too busy listening to the voices on his headset. I snap a few pictures, mission accomplished. I turn to leave, but it's too late.

The Jets players have left the locker room.

They're coming right for me.

As they pour in, I stay put, and the tunnel fills like an alternate universe in which there are no humans, only superhumans, dressed in pads, cleats, and helmets—armored, at an advantage. The fog limits visibility. I press myself against the side of the tunnel, trying to become two-dimensional to avoid being trampled. Through the wall, I can feel the reverberations, as someone at the other end works the inflatable like a speed bag.

The energy is intense, the tunnel a powder keg as adrenaline and aggression build. It's hard to make out much over the loud nonsensical screams, the hyena bursts of hysterical, unprovoked laughter, the slapping palms and plastic claps of pounded shoulder pads. The players try to psych themselves up as they wait for release.* The noise

---

* I like to imagine that this scene is not so different from what might have taken place in the *krypte esodos*, "a vaulted entrance tunnel" at Olympia, which "helped bring the athlete's full attention to the job at hand," while waiting "for the herald to call his

starts to blend together—the music from outside, the tens of thousands of cheering fans, the screaming from within.

One player shouts, "Whoooo-hooooa!"

Another says, "I see y'all right here, man! Bam, bam!"

Again, he says: "Bam, bam!"

"Gonna be *great* today, fellas."

"Awwwwwwww-yeah!"

Almost every player is shouting now, but none are listening. Each is in his own world, in his own head. Calvin Pryor, a defensive safety, hops in place, shimmies his shoulders, then starts revving the gas on the handlebars of an imaginary motorcycle. And then, after the players have whipped themselves into a proper frenzy, a siren wails, accompanied by a sizzling hiss, like the sound of a giant piece of butcher paper being ripped in half. This is the pyro, the flame towers, and there is a brilliant flash of white light.

With that, the athletes rush the field.

As I watch them tear out through the smoke wall, between the shooting flames, I realize this, too, is part of Mulligan's "controlled chaos." There is a meticulousness to this on-field, big-theater spectacle, with Holmgren presiding over the introductions like a chaperone on a field trip, with a headset and a checklist. No different from the entrance gate logistics outside MetLife Stadium or the many FOB-protected beer lines zigzagging through Citi Field—it's all about the invisible details. But while Holmgren couldn't look more bored by the screaming war cries of these athletes, I'm completely infected by the drug of this display, this adrenaline-fueled exhibition. And when the last player runs out on the field, I buzz with some kind of contact high, not ready for it to

name," as Stephen G. Miller writes in *Ancient Greek Athletics* (New Haven, Conn.: Yale University Press, 2004).

end. With the tunnel empty, I walk over to Holmgren, hoping to share this moment with someone, to receive confirmation of this fog-machined fever dream.

Holmgren seems surprised to see me, his eyes flickering with urgency.

He says, "You need to get out! This is deflating now."

I sprint for the sideline then look back.

All that is left is a puddle of plastic.

10

SEX. WAR. AMERICA.

(Or: For God and Country)

hree fighter pilots from the Black Knights squadron, which is
based at a naval air station in Lemoore, California, aka "the
middle of nowhere," stand in an outdoor plaza just inside the
VIP Gate at San Diego's Petco Park on a bright Sunday morning in
early-mid-April.

They are not alone.

Over the next hour, the plaza will fill with an orgy of servicemen and women, from the Marines, Navy, Army, Coast Guard, Air
Force, and California National Guard. "Members from each branch
of the Armed Forces," says Mia Taravella, the Padres' coordinator of
military affairs, who is frantically trying to check in and keep track
of all those who will be participating in today's elaborate pregame
ceremonies. It's Military Opening Day, which the team celebrates
on the first Sunday home game of the season, a local tradition that
dates back to 1996. As a visual buffet of GIs in dress uniforms people the plaza—for those in civvies, there is an abundance of patriotic
apparel—the place starts to feel like a military mixer. Or perhaps

more accurately, a middle school dance, as everyone sticks to his or her own kind.

The fighter pilots are no exception.

Dressed identically in black baseball hats, heavily tinted sunglasses, and olive-green flight suits, the naval aviators have tucked themselves into a shady alcove off to the side and are emitting a kind of relaxed cool-kid vibe, a more swaggering, cocksure energy than those in black berets and peaked officer caps. But appearances can be deceiving, as the pilots have plenty on their minds. After all, they're in charge of the pregame fighter jet flyover—or at least the land-based portion, communicating with those in the cockpits—which will feature two F-18 Super Hornets cruising about a thousand feet above the ballpark, at a sensible and FAA-approved speed of 250 knots (or a little under 300 miles per hour).

"We're trying to time it so they'll fly over right at the end of the national anthem," a pilot who goes by the call sign Paco explains, after he and the other aviators synchronize their watches, using the website for the Naval Observatory's master clock. The effect, when executed correctly, can be dramatic, as the planes roar across the sky and the stadium shakes.

But even with the time hack, coordinating a perfect flyby can be challenging, according to one of the other pilots—his call sign: SOBB—because some national anthem artists ham it up toward the end and hold certain notes for unpredictable lengths. At the last flyover he worked, for example, "the dude on the radio was literally singing along," so the pilots knew exactly when the song would end. Such an impromptu performance shouldn't be necessary today, however, as the Navy Band Southwest, which delivers an unwavering, to-the-second rendition each and every time, is scheduled to play the anthem. "We're confident they're going to be on time," says SOBB. "So if timing gets jacked up, it's our fault. We don't want to screw it up."

The most important thing is to establish early radio contact with the planes: "What you really don't want," warns J. J. Quinn, a retired rear admiral and current military adviser for the team, tall and broad with a square jaw and square sunglasses, "is you don't want the anthem to be done and then wait forty-five seconds for the airplanes, because it's just not right. It loses the drama."

In addition to Paco and SOBB, there is also Grimacé—pronounced *Grim-ah-chay*—who is the youngest of the three aviators and the newest to the Black Knights, having joined the squadron after it returned from its most recent deployment, a nine-month stint aboard the *USS Nimitz* as part of Operation Enduring Freedom. Though he's yet to have his call sign sewn onto his flight suit, the nickname, like all their nicknames, will stick.

"Nobody picks their own call sign," says Grimacé, who is here with his wife, Lauren. "You get it for doing something stupid or for how you look. You always get one you don't really like."

"I love it!" Lauren says of her husband's call sign.

Grimacé sighs, says, "It's like Mexican Grimace. I guess I smile like Grimace does, the McDonald's character."

Lauren bursts out laughing. To her, the explanation never gets old. "From the moment I heard it, it's just perfect," she says. "Whoever thought of that is a genius."

SOBB says his call sign is an acronym and comes from a prank that was pulled on him (in retaliation for one of his own). "It's not a very PC prank," he admits. "Someone put some of their personal items into my oxygen mask. I flew with it for about a week. So it stands for: Suck on Biff's Balls." As for Paco, his call sign is short for Paco Muchos Gatos, which is the name of a fake wrestling character on *Conan*, whose costume consists entirely of live cats and cat pelts. "He's got a couple cats," SOBB says of Paco, "so we make fun of him for it."

Paco heads inside to the production booth. The remaining aviators fight some last-minute nerves. As a distraction, they tell me about their time in the military, about their sea-duty-shore-duty rotations, about the gelatin-like substance inside the piddle packs, into which they urinate when flying long missions (I asked), and about the go-with-the-flow attitude required of their families. "I'm just along for the ride," says Lauren, who married Grimacé almost a year ago, in a courthouse ceremony, when the pilot received unexpected orders to head to Japan. "It was rushed. We kind of had to do it."

But they were already planning a wedding?

"Yeah," says Grimacé.

"No," says Lauren.

"Well," says Grimacé.

"We hadn't gotten engaged yet."

"We were planning on getting engaged," say Grimacé. "We definitely had a nontraditional timeline, although it's kind of common in the military."

"Get on a plane. Leave everything behind."

A few minutes before noon, a woman who works for the Padres approaches the aviators. The men straighten up, as if talking to an admiral. She thanks them for being here, asks if they'll be jumping out of the plane today.

"We're doing the flyover," Grimacé says, confused at first. "Wait, there's a Frog team?"

There is indeed. Before the national anthem, there will be an aerial demonstration by the U.S. Navy parachute team, otherwise known as the Leap Frogs, which consists of active-duty Navy SEALS. Weren't the pilots told?

"We were not," SOBB says flatly. "We might need to clear those guys out."

"Well, we're excited, because you guys bring the show," she says, enthusiasm intact. "Glad you could be here! Thank you."

Stone-faced, the aviators watch the Padres lady walk away. Lauren breaks the silence. "Frog team is here," she says, knowing this changes everything. Just like that, there is even more at stake for today's pregame—even more reason they need to nail the timing of the flyby; they have to outperform the Frog team. Grimacé explains: "For like the last five years there's been an ongoing battle for who has the coolest job in the Navy. It's always been aviation, and now the SEALs are trying to steal our thunder. It used to be *Top Gun* was the movie everybody liked. Now it's *Zero Dark Thirty*."

––––––––––

San Diego is a military town. With more than 100,000 active-duty Navy and Marine Corps members (and about 24,000 Department of Defense civilian employees), the city is home to "the largest concentration of military forces in the world," according to the San Diego Military Advisory Council's 2015 economic impact study. No professional sports franchise has a more robust—or more earnest—relationship with the armed forces than the Padres.

Though it wasn't always this way.

In 1995, the organization now known as "The Team of the Military" was doing little to engage the vast number of active-duty and retired servicepeople in the San Diego area. That was also the year Larry Lucchino, fresh off his success with Baltimore's Camden Yards, started to make his mark as the Padres' new president. It didn't take the executive long to realize his baseball club was underserving a giant segment of the local population, and he saw an opportunity. "An opportunity and obligation," as Lucchino tells me. "It's an issue of distinctiveness," he says. "You've got to understand, Pittsburgh is not San Diego is not Baltimore is not Boston. These cities are different, have different traits and elements of pride. And in San Diego, the military traditions and presence were large."

A conversation began between the Padres and a soon-to-be-retired Navy captain named Jack Ensch, or Captain Jack, as he affectionately became known around the ballpark, as the first-ever director of the team's new military affairs department, the only such department in all of sports. "We did the mating dance of employment, and I came on board," says Ensch, whose decorated Navy career included 285 combat missions over Vietnam, the last of which ended when his plane was shot down, leading to seven months as a prisoner of war. "I went through my own little personal hell. As you can see, they kept part of me over there," he says, showing me where his left thumb used to be. "Tony Bennett left his heart in San Francisco. I left my thumb in Hanoi. But I was lucky," he says, and means it. "I was on my fourth combat cruise. If I'd been shot down the first time I went over there, it would've been seven years, not seven months."

Ensch had credibility with enlisted men and women, which is exactly why Lucchino hired him. The Padres wanted to build a program with integrity, and Captain Jack was the perfect man for the job—not that he necessarily had any clue how to begin. "I just started doing things," says Ensch, who at seventy-seven is no longer employed by the Padres but consults for other major-league clubs like the Arizona Diamondbacks. "The way I looked at it was, if I was still in the military, what would I like that organization to do for me? So that's what I did."

Some of it was common sense, like increasing the team's military discount, which had remained static for more than a quarter-century. Ensch also orchestrated initial outreach efforts, including player visits to military bases. As the years went on, the program grew, with things like on-field reenlistment ceremonies, complimentary tickets for those returning from long deployments, designated home games (every Sunday) to honor different branches of the armed services (as well as veterans and military families), and the creation of a so-called Flight Deck area, beyond the right-field bleachers, which features a large-scale model of the USS *Midway*, a Military Honor Wall paying tribute to major-league and Negro-league players who served, and a shrine to former Padres announcer and fighter pilot Jerry Coleman.

Unquestionably, Captain Jack's most popular innovation has been camouflage uniforms—"Fans support the players by wearing their jerseys. So I said, 'Why don't we support the military by wearing *their* uniform?'" The Padres debuted "the cammies" in 2000, and the tradition has since been adopted by every team across the league.* Still, there may be no initiative of which Ensch is prouder than the Padres' POW passes. "When we got back from Vietnam, MLB issued a lifetime pass to us," Ensch says of his fellow prisoners of war. "So I got the idea, what about World War II and Korean POWs? They didn't get anything like this." He pitched the idea to MLB, but the league balked, citing administrative burden. Undeterred, Ensch implemented the program himself, on behalf of the Padres. "You'd be surprised the number of appreciation letters we got that said, you know, 'I may never come to San Diego, but I got this thing in the mail, and I can't thank you enough.'"

Ensch wasn't surprised, though. As a veteran of a deeply unpopular war, he saw how returning soldiers could be greeted† and understood all too well how much a simple gesture like this could mean, knowing that someone had your back. "In naval aviation, we call it, got your six—your six o'clock," he says. "I've got you protected."

With about fifteen minutes until first pitch, Military Opening Day pregame ceremonies at Petco Park are under way. The Leap Frogs have already jumped out of their plane (and effortlessly run-landed on the grass behind second base, precisely where they were

---

* While other clubs reserve the camouflage for national holidays, like Memorial Day and the Fourth of July, the Padres have been wearing theirs at every Sunday home game since 2008, after getting the jerseys authorized as an official alternate uniform.

† Says Ensch, "I think we, as a group, represented the only victory that anybody saw come out of that war—getting the POWs home. So we were treated like heroes. But we weren't heroes. I don't consider myself a hero. I was doing my job, just like the poor grunt who was over there in the jungles, fighting his ass off, and comes back, walks down the San Francisco airport, and gets spit on and called a baby killer."

aiming). On the field now, men and women from every branch of the military file along the infield dirt, lining the diamond, hoisting all fifty state flags. From where I'm standing near home plate, I can't possibly count how many service members are present, but I know it's a lot of sixes.

As the ceremony continues, Taya Kyle, the widow of Chris Kyle, aka the American Sniper, will toss out the ceremonial first pitch, flanked by her late husband's former SEAL teammates; an eleven-year-old named Natalie will scream "play ball!" into a microphone after receiving a video message from her father, Chief David Gates, who is currently deployed overseas; nine Vietnam vets, including Jack Ensch, will take the field in honor of the war's fiftieth anniversary; an opening video, which was filmed this past off-season at Marine Corps Air Station Miramar and features camo-clad Padres players and flight-suited fighter pilots shaking hands and saluting one another, will roll on the big screen; and U.S. Navy Vice Admiral Mike Shoemaker will ring the ballpark's Mission Bell, to indicate the start of the game. There will be so many patriotic gestures—one after another after another—it will be hard to keep up.

For now, the Navy Band Southwest strikes up "The Star-Spangled Banner." I turn my eyes to the southern California sky, excited for the impending flyover. The horns carry across the stadium's speaker system, the cymbals crash, the song picks up steam. It's a perfect blue sky day. Up in the production booth, Paco is passing messages between Matt Coy, the Padres' senior director of game-day presentation, and the rest of the aviators on the ground. SOBB is somewhere along the third baseline, communicating with the pilots in the air, possibly singing. Grimacé is also on the radio, stationed in the right-field upper deck, where he can spot the incoming planes before the others, and I hope he doesn't freak out too badly when the anthem concludes, with a few final drawn-out notes, and the big blue sky remains pristine. Empty.

The planes are late.

"Where are they?" whispers Taravella, the military affairs coordinator.

Five seconds go by.

Ten seconds.

Twenty seconds.

In what is almost certainly an attempt to buy time, a voice comes over the PA: "And now, here they come, let's hear it for the flyover by two F-18 Super Hornets from Naval Air Station Lemoore, California."

Only then, after a full thirty seconds, do they appear: two insect-size aircrafts from the first-base side of the stadium. But they're so high, and the noise so muted—a distant rumble, like a far-off summer storm—I wonder how my bones are ever supposed to rattle.

And then they're gone.

———

I reconnect with the aviators in the last rows of section 129 during the early innings of the ball game. Paco and Grimacé are drinking beers, while SOBB has two small children (presumably his own) on his lap. Still in their black hats and flight suits, all three guys seem surprisingly serene, undisturbed by the mistimed flyover and being shown up by the SEALs.

Not quite as Zen are the aviators who were actually in the planes, the four men who spent all week practicing the flyover route in the cockpit of a Navy flight simulator, replete with 3-D representation of the San Diego skyline.* The pilots are shown on

---

* According to Ian Lundy, a Navy public affairs specialist, flybys—which require the blessing of both the Department of Defense in Washington, D.C., and the local FAA office—are never stand-alone events. To qualify for military support, some form of training must be incorporated into the actual flights.

the Jumbotron walking into the stadium and come straight to the seats, where an informal debriefing begins. And they are pissed. Specifically, at an air traffic controller who held them at the last minute for a commercial airliner.

"With zero warning, it was busy airspace. He's like, *sorry*," reports one of the pilots. "Actually, he said, *Unable*."

"*Unable*, right at the very end," commiserates another, who was so upset about the delay he forgot his game ticket in the jet. (The Padres let him in anyway.) "I'm like, 'We've been telling you we're pushing at this time for the last twenty minutes.'"

The land-based crew of aviators tries to soften the sting for their Black Knight brethren, seeing how mad they are, how badly they, too, wanted the flyby to be great. They explain how Paco handled the delay on his end, relaying word of the setback to others in the production booth, and how they were able to slow down the band just a bit. "It worked out," says Paco. "I mean, if you guys got there maybe five, ten seconds earlier, it would've been perfect."

"It wasn't that bad," nods SOBB. "Song ended, pause, then okay, a little intro, flyover from two jets, blah, blah, blah. It worked out."

"It worked out," Paco says again.

"It worked out," adds Grimacé.

It's hard to pin down exactly when stadium flyovers officially began in the United States. According to Maurer Maurer's *Aviation in the U.S. Army, 1919–1939*, domestic flying exhibitions skyrocketed in popularity after World War I. It was an exciting time for the country's fledgling Air Service, as the military flying program was then known, and the goal of such exhibitions or "circuses"—which included aerial acrobatics, tactical demonstrations, and "sham battles"—was "to arouse interest in aviation, win public support, and collect information for further development of military and civil aeronautics."* Unlike today's aviators, post–World War I pilots were given a long leash in terms of midair shenanigans or "stunting"—i.e., acrobatics in noncombat situations—which were neither permitted nor necessarily discouraged. To a certain extent, American airspace was the new Wild West.

By 1968, when the Super Bowl received its first-ever aerial, these exhibitions had morphed into the flyovers we know today, which must abide by local FAA regulations with little room for deviation. Still, before more recent restrictions, aviators could be "more maverick, more aggressive," per J. J. Quinn, who piloted his share of flybys during his Navy days.

"We did some stuff," says Quinn, who believes an ideal flyover should be just above a stadium's light towers. "I mean, we've flown below flight deck level whenever we did a flyby on a shift, things like that. We've broken the sound barrier and busted windows. It's easy for me to say, I'm not the one getting the flight violation,† but back in my day, we lived by a different set of rules. You do what you need to do and then beg for forgiveness. We had a lot more forgiveness."

According to Quinn, the tipping point came at a Naval Academy football game about fifteen years ago. "I'll tell you what happened. I actually watched it," he says. "It was a reserve pilot from the Marine Reserve over at Andrews Air Force Base. He did a flyby, and he got

---

* In this regard, not much has changed in the near-century since. As Jennifer Bentley, chief of public engagement for the Air Force, which supports more flyovers than any other branch of the military, explains: "The whole point of our flyover program is to showcase the Air Force to the American public, to the taxpayer, and to be able to demonstrate our modern warfare, our modern weapons systems, to help with recruiting, to help with community support, and for funeral flyovers, for things [of that] nature."

† In recent years, several pilots have been grounded—or even lost their wings—as a result of disobeying altitude limitations on flybys.

so low he was actually *inside* of the stadium, okay? He got down in there, came up, and did kind of a hard left turn and almost clipped the left side of the stadium. Frankly, it was too much.

"He just went too far, and they should have smacked him upside the head or grounded him for a month. But no, there was an immediate overreaction. Okay, you can only go a thousand feet over the stadium. You can only go this fast. Well, you know, that makes for a boring flyby." Quinn swallows hard. "We're living within the rules now."

———

Within the rules or not, patriotic displays and militaristic tributes are nothing new for modern—and not-so-modern*—sports fans. From flyovers and field-length flags to surprise soldier homecomings and countless in-game breaks to salute the troops, American stadiums in the twenty-first century have grown lousy with a distinct brand of jingoism—a conflation of sports and military—especially in the years after the attacks of September 11, 2001, when the country went to war.

"It was the amping up of something that was already there," Dave Zirin, a journalist who covers the intersection of sports and politics, says of the nationalistic noise at U.S. stadiums post-9/11. There was an uptick of military appreciation games, in-venue recruitment efforts, and all manner of aerial demonstrations (flyover and otherwise), which prior to the government's 2013 sequestration had become so commonplace as to border on excessive.† No venue was safe from the flag waving, as ballparks across the country replaced "Take Me Out to the Ball Game"—that seventh-inning staple—with "God Bless

---

* In ancient Greece, athletic contests were held to honor war heroes, while early U.S. stadiums were often named in "memorial" to fallen soldiers, as sports historian Ronald A. Smith points out in an essay in *The Rise of Stadiums in the Modern United States.*

† On more than one occasion, the Leap Frogs have dropped in on a Little League game.

America" or "the second national anthem," as Zirin refers to Irving Berlin's famous love letter to the country. "Sports and the military have always had a very healthy, very symbiotic, and very mutually beneficial relationship," he adds. "But all of a sudden, it amped up to such a degree, it became omnipresent."

To some sports fans (myself included), this ubiquitous form of stadium-based patriotism came to feel almost perfunctory, as if teams were telling us to eat our vegetables. At times, the displays could seem so heavy-handed as to reek of outright opportunism, as if billionaire businesses were making cheap and easy plays for civic credibility.

But a stadium has always been a powerful place for messaging and manipulation. "As long as there have been sports, there have been politicians attempting to use [them] as a way to connect with people," says Zirin. As Allen Guttmann writes in *Sports Spectators,* in the Roman Empire "the hippodrome was the place for whatever interaction occurred between the emperor and the populace." And: "The emperors often used the circus to present heirs to the throne." The first instance of a U.S. president doing a press event with a sports team was Andrew Johnson, with baseball's Cincinnati Red Stockings, in the late 1860s, per Zirin. In Nazi Germany, Adolf Hitler understood a stadium's potential perfectly, as evidenced by his attempt to construct the world's largest sporting facility, which would have seated four hundred thousand and was meant to make all those inside feel dwarfed by its size. In fact, the giant stadium was to speak such volumes, the dictator referred to the would-be venue as "words of stone," as he tried to write his own legacy.*

Even modern technology hasn't blunted the power of a stadium, as live sporting events represent one of the few remaining communal

---

* Reportedly, when Hitler was told that the stadium wouldn't meet Olympic standards, he replied, "That's totally unimportant. The 1940 Olympics will be taking place in Tokyo. But after that they will be held for all eternity in Germany, and in this stadium. And it is we who will determine how the sporting field is measured."

spaces in a society so often splintered by laptops and smartphones. As Zirin puts it in *Game Over: How Politics Has Turned the Sports World Upside Down*, sports are "the closest thing to common language we have as human beings," and he goes on to warn that it "is a cultural arena that we ignore only at our collective peril."

Add sex into this already potent combination of sports and war, and the results can be both quintessential and bizarre. Award-winning writer Ben Fountain wrote a whole novel inspired by the 2004 Dallas Cowboys Thanksgiving Day halftime show, which featured Destiny's Child, a rifle-flipping U.S. Army Drill Team, a pelvic-thrusting college marching band, the Cowboys cheerleaders, and frequent fireworks. *Billy Lynn's Long Halftime Walk*, about a soldier who is temporarily home from Iraq to be honored at a game with his squadron, had Fountain watching the video of that 2004 halftime show over and over again. "Just seeing the display of militarism, American exceptionalism, pop music, soft-core porn all mixed together in this kind of crazy to-do—I started feeling like it was its own kind of voodoo," he says of the halftime show. "Something significant was going on right under our noses. It's tapping into *something*, and it's tapping into all the things that were on display."

Sex. War. America.

"It isn't nothing," he insists. "In its own goofy way, that halftime show was expressing some very basic things about human nature."

The combination can also contribute to a reductive understanding of America's wars and the experiences of its veterans. Boston University professor and retired Army officer Andrew J. Bacevich describes military tributes at stadiums as "the distilled essence of present-day American patriotism," which "leaves spectators feeling good about their baseball team, about their military, and not least of all about themselves." But there are no shared costs of war, as the ceremonies are symbolic and actual participation optional. The scales of sacrifice remain unbalanced. Bacevich writes, "The message that citizens wish to convey to their soldiers is this: although choosing not to be *with* you, we are still *for* you (so long as being for you entails nothing on our part)."*

Or less than nothing.

In November 2015, U.S. senators Jeff Flake and John McCain released a report, entitled "Tackling Paid Patriotism," exposing the millions of dollars forked over by the Department of Defense to dozens of professional sports teams in recent years to underwrite all sorts of stadium-based military tributes. It's a bombshell. Apologists argue that these outlays from the Pentagon, which were supposedly meant to help with recruiting efforts, are no different than ad buys on a TV network. But for many, the issue is one of transparency, as teams make it seem like they're paying tribute out of the goodness of their hearts. It amounts to camouflaged propaganda, and it belies any real support for American veterans.

For his part, Jack Ensch calls the practice of paid-for patriotism "shameful, deceptive, greedy, and unethical." He finds the scandal especially upsetting on a personal level, because he's seen how hard the military, as an institution, has had to work in the years since Vietnam to rehabilitate its image. "John Q. Public will just start saying, 'Why should I bother to honor the military when they're already using my own tax dollars to honor themselves?' " he laments, adding that he was relieved to learn the Padres are not one of the teams to have taken government money.†

Others aren't so sure the Padres deserve a pass. A retired Air Force officer, writing in to *The Atlantic* on the heels of the scandal, warns against giving undue credit to teams that may not accept gov-

---

* This comes from Andrew Bacevich's 2013 book, *Breach of Trust: How Americans Failed Their Soldiers and Their Country* (New York: Metropolitan Books).

† The same can't be said for the Arizona Diamondbacks, about whom Ensch says, "Rest assured that I will let the D-backs know this is [unacceptable] behavior."

ernment money but allow their "fawning to veterans" to be under-written by defense contractors like Northrop Grumman (which was the presenting sponsor of Military Opening Day in San Diego). "I am truly split at what makes me more sick—DoD underwriting it, or the purveyors of weapon system [sic] underwriting it, who help to lobby for using their weapons."

That is, for going to war.

Zirin would say the authors of the report miss the point, since the senators don't want military tributes at stadiums to go away; they just want teams to stop accepting government money for them. "I think it does a disservice to our understanding if we are judging peo-ple's personal motivations instead of taking a step back and asking the bigger question, which is: Who is served in the end by conjoining sports with militarism?" he says. "It's about how martial a society we want to inhabit, and whether we think that sports should be some-thing that is used to express either the desire or the public relations of war and living in an era of perpetual conflict."

Regardless of who foots the bill, folks like Bacevich and Fountain would maintain that modern stadium spectacles are a painless form of patriotism* and therefore ultimately empty gestures. As Fountain puts it to me, "Patriotism is love of country, and I think real love—true love—involves a lot of pain and sacrifice. Anybody who has been married for any length of time knows that. There is a lot of giving and not much taking. And so if you really want to show your patri-otism, you sacrifice. You go through some form of hardship." What we have, on the other hand, is "puppy-love patriotism," he says. "You feel good when you're putting the flag pin on your lapel, thanking the troops, but it's not real love. It's not a demonstration of real love."

---

* An early trace of it can be found in baseball man Bill Veeck's memoir, *The Hustler's Handbook* (New York: G. P. Putnam's Sons, 1965), when he asks, only half-kidding, "Look, we play the 'Star-Spangled Banner' before every game. You want us to pay income taxes too?"

Two weeks after Military Opening Day, I return to Petco Park, for Marine Corps Appreciation Day (presented by USAA), wondering what might constitute real love in this time of stadium patriotism. With about ninety minutes until first pitch, I linger outside the ballpark's northern gates, on J Street, where three busloads of Marine recruits line up along the sidewalk.

The recruits—no longer recruits, technically—are here as part of an ongoing program, started by Captain Jack, which provides thousands of complimentary tickets to soon-to-be graduates from San Diego's Marine Corps Recruit Depot over the course of each baseball season. The free passes are small perks for the newly minted Marines in the days after completing the final training event of boot camp, which is known as the Crucible and doesn't sound fun. Spanning fifty-four hours and forty miles, the Crucible simulates combat conditions and requires the recruits to operate on limited food and sleep, while tackling a variety of grueling physical and mental challenges, with an emphasis on group problem solving. At the end, the recruits receive their Eagle, Globe, and Anchor, symbolizing their transition from civilians to Marines—and then they're invited to a baseball game.

On the sidewalk outside Petco Park, the recruits stand at attention, legs spread, hands clasped behind their backs, resplendent in their crisp olive and khaki service uniforms. This is the first time they're wearing the uniforms in public, I'm told, and the drill instructors pace alongside their platoons, providing last-minute reminders of how to behave once they get inside, where they will take over upper-deck section 325.*

For the new Marines, proper behavior is paramount during these

---

* I ask one sergeant if the recruits are allowed to cheer during the game. He replies, "They're allowed to act like Marines."

outings, in the unpredictable setting of a sports stadium, where a ball field can become a minefield. As one of the instructors says, "They've been in an environment where they see only each other and drill instructors. This is their first outside exposure in uniform." Uniforms have a tendency to elicit reactions, so "they need to know how to handle that."

Sure enough, civilian passersby gawk at this collection of servicemen. Some stop to say a few words, like one middle-aged woman who thanks a drill instructor for his service. To which the instructor says, "Our pleasure, ma'am." Next an ox of a man, on his way home from the gym, sidles up. He, too, was a Marine, he explains, and exchanges some pleasantries with the sergeants while talking trash about this boot camp coddling—going to a baseball game. The instructors shrug. They don't disagree.

Inside the stadium is no different. Civilians provide a startling contrast to the buttoned-up Marines, whose intense discipline clashes with the usual ballpark levity, the near-circus atmosphere—seriously, there's a guy on stilts—as the Marines march up the stadium ramps, ignoring the boisterous fans who dress in sloppy T-shirts with protruding beer bellies and unruly facial hair. It's a perfect snapshot of what strange bedfellows sports fans and the military can make, in any venue.* I point out this odd-couple contrast to a few of the instructors. They all nod. One says, "That's why we need military."

To help clear a path for the Marines as they make their way up the ramp, a man named Sam, who works for the Padres, rushes ahead. I jog with him. "This is one of the joys of my life," he says of his role

---

* Case in point: Toward the end of the game, I'm walking with two Marines (not recruits) down a stadium ramp, when a sunburned bro, who is carrying a tallboy in one hand and dragging an iPhone-obsessed lady friend with the other, notices the servicemen out of the corner of his eye and points at one with the index finger of his beer hand. He tosses off, "Hey! Thanks for your service, bud." After they pass, the first Marine turns to his friend and says, "Next time someone says some shit like that, I'm going to hit him with 'You're *my* hero.'"

as Marine escort, and he's not kidding. As we walk, he even serves as an unofficial hype man for those in uniform. To a few idling fans, he says, "I don't know about you, but if I saw some Marines, I'd clap!"

Like good soldiers, the fans do as they're told.

Of all the military displays at Petco Park, the Marine recruits marching toward their seats—which will happen on eight different Sundays this season—are among the most powerful, according to Taravella. "It's really cool and electrifying, because everyone stops and stares."

Encouraging respect for the troops and love for the country is often well meaning—many teams likely believe such stances to be uncontroversial, while enhancing the in-this-together, rooting-for-the-same-outcome vibe that underscores all fandom—but forcing stadium patrons to show deference toward anything (troops, flags, otherwise) can be a slippery slope. In the post-9/11 era, pressure has been growing inside stadiums—often implicitly—to participate in group patriotism. I felt it at old Yankee Stadium, throughout the 2000s, when I regularly attended games. Even among fans, there was an intense and almost belligerent tendency to self-police, to ensure all those in attendance rose and removed their caps for the anthem (and for "God Bless America"), which always made me feel uncomfortable in the stands, even as I stood and removed my cap. As it turns out, this peer-pressure patriotism in the South Bronx wasn't organic; it was sanctioned from the top, from George Steinbrenner himself. He instructed security staff to rope fans into their rows so they couldn't move around during the singing of patriotic songs.*

---

* This policy made news in the summer of 2008, when a fan was allegedly roughed up (and subsequently ejected) by a couple of New York City police officers for trying to use the restroom at the wrong time.

"It's a very scary thing, this idea that we are celebrating freedom and I'm about to be beaten for exercising my freedom to not stand," Zirin says, pointing out the obvious hypocrisy. *The New York Times* called it "dark patriotism" in 1991, after basketball player Marco Lokar withdrew from Seton Hall University and left the country following a wave of harassment that resulted from his decision to not wear an American flag on his jersey during the First Gulf War. In an editorial titled "Misusing the Flag, Again," the paper wrote that the incident "is a troubling reminder of other efforts to extort conformity in a nation built on free speech and diversity."

Unfortunately, this is a typical response to athletic dissenters. When Muhammad Ali refused to be inducted into the U.S. Army in 1967, the boxer was stripped of his heavyweight title and convicted of draft evasion. When Mahmoud Abdul-Rauf declined to stand for the national anthem in 1996, he was basically bounced from the NBA. Carlos Delgado did the same during "God Bless America," as part of an antiwar stance in the mid-2000s; when he was traded to the New York Mets, his new team asked the slugger to drop his protest, and he agreed.

The pearl-clutching mainstream sports media—and the pro-team front offices—have almost always greeted such acts with the same maxim: sports and politics don't mix. But as Zirin illustrates throughout his work, what these critics are really saying is: sports and "a certain *kind* of politics" don't mix. "I wish sports could exist à la carte and be its own kind of escapism," he says, "but nothing exists in a hermetically sealed chamber in our society. So as long as the outside world affects the playing world, I think there is an obligation to make it as open as possible and not the sort of thing where owners have a monopoly on the political messages and players get punished for daring to have an opinion."

In spite of the forces telling athletes to "shut up and play," as Zirin puts it, stadiums have often been used as political stages, from an antiwar protest at a Roman horse race nearly two thousand years ago, which included synchronized clapping and "cries for peace" (according to Allen Guttmann's *Sports Spectators*) to the 1968 Olympics, when Tommie Smith and John Carlos gave their iconic raised-fist salute, protesting the impoverished and often violent living conditions for many African Americans (and other oppressed peoples around the world).* More recently, NBA, WNBA, and NFL players have worn T-shirts or made hands-up-don't-shoot gestures in the wake of police killings to indicate solidarity with the Black Lives Matter movement. Ahead of (and into) the 2016 NFL season, San Francisco 49ers quarterback Colin Kaepernick made an even more polarizing in-stadium demonstration, when he chose not to stand (eventually taking a knee) for the national anthem, explaining he's not going to "show pride in a flag for a country that oppresses black people and people of color." While Kaepernick was forced to clarify that he wasn't "bashing" the U.S. military, after initial backlash, his protest inspired other athletes—at professional, collegiate, and even high school levels—to follow his example, raising the volume on a nationwide debate surrounding patriotism, racial justice, and a lack of accountability for police brutality. (The election of Donald Trump—and his subsequent policy decisions—have also contributed to a new wave of sports figures speaking out politically.)

Traditionally, many teams (and leagues) have sought to suppress such activity because, to them, it's a business liability. Sports may be a spectacle, after all, but they need to control the narrative. "It's like the Michael Jordan statement," says Billy Hawkins, a professor of

---

* This gesture came out of a wider movement of black athletes known as the Olympic Project for Human Rights (OPHR), which was led by Harry Edwards, an author and academic whose books include *The Revolt of the Black Athlete* (New York: Free Press, 1970). The movement was initially organized around the idea of boycotting the 1968 games. On the medal stand, Smith and Carlos were joined in their protest by silver medalist Peter Norman, a white Australian, who wore an OPHR button on his track jacket.

sport management and policy at the University of Georgia, referring to MJ's famous comments that Republicans buy sneakers, too (thus explaining his apolitical public persona). "They are trying to sell to as many viewers as possible. They want eyes watching. They want people consuming the product. And when that is challenged, when that event becomes sort of this political entity, it becomes problematic."

Still, as Zirin says, the sports world cannot be decoupled from the real world. In practice, stadiums are such effective soapboxes that sometimes an athlete doesn't even need an agenda to make a statement, to disrupt a certain narrative, to be viewed as political. Sometimes the action at the center of an arena speaks for itself, like when Jack Johnson became the world's first black heavyweight boxing champion in 1908, undermining widespread beliefs about black athletic inferiority, or when Jesse Owens's gold-medal performances at the 1936 Berlin Olympics crashed Hitler's Aryans-rule-everyone-else-drools party, or when Billie Jean King triumphed over Bobby Riggs in 1973's "Battle of the Sexes," proving for those who doubted that women deserve a place in sports.

For all the political and cultural capital of a modern sports stadium, it's not hard to see how teams and leagues have had—and continue to have—an opportunity to lead on many social issues. To give a few historical examples: In 1965, players from the American Football League forced the relocation of an all-star contest from New Orleans to Houston, when they threatened to boycott, due to the city's discrimination against African Americans. Almost thirty years later, in Arizona, the NFL wanted to be on the right side of history, when the league warned that the 1993 Super Bowl would be moved elsewhere, if Martin Luther King Jr. Day was not recognized as a state holiday. (It wasn't, and the Super Bowl was moved.) In 2010, the Phoenix Suns made a statement as an organization, when the team wore "Los Suns" jerseys, to demonstrate against an Arizona immigration law that allowed for racial profiling. And in 2016, the NBA announced that Charlotte, North Carolina, would not be allowed to host the 2017 All-Star Game, because of the state's controversial bathroom law that discriminated against members of the LGBT community.

With the power to push for progress or uphold the status quo,* teams (and leagues) ought to have an earnest discussion about what level of responsibility they might assume regarding the messages they help to convey, from love of country and military appreciation to social activism and climate responsibility,† to the hypersexualization of women and how that might contribute to rape culture and domestic violence.

As sports reporter Rachel Nichols put it on Bill Simmons's ESPN podcast in 2015, none of this is unfair to talk about, not after a league like the NFL has "worked very hard to insinuate itself into every aspect of American life." In Nichols's words, "It's no longer just a professional sports league, right? It's part of *America.* . . . This is the place, like it or not, where we all come together, where we actually care about the same thing. And it's okay to hold that game and that league to a higher standard, because they asked for it."

———

On Marine Corps Appreciation Day, there is at least one woman at Petco Park for whom none of this matters, who doesn't care what militaristic messages are being broadcast at the ballpark, who is using

---

* St. Louis's Sportsman's Park "remained the only big league arena with a Jim Crow section" in the 1940s, according to Michael Benson's *Ballparks of North America*, while the Washington Redskins—then owned by George Preston Marshall, who desired "to make them 'the South's team,'" as Zirin writes in *A People's History of Sports in the United States*—only integrated in 1962, when the franchise would have otherwise lost access to its publicly funded stadium.

† While investigating a trend of urban farms in baseball parks, I learned about a fast-growing group called the Green Sports Alliance, which aims to "to promote healthy, sustainable communities" by bringing environmentalism into American stadiums.

the stadium as means to a totally different end. I meet Erin shortly after the game begins in San Diego—after the on-field ceremonies and helicopter flyover—as the Marine recruits line up along the outdoor concourse of the upper deck, in front of a folding table, where they will exchange some sort of coupon—previously tucked into their socks, for safekeeping—for a hot dog and a drink.

Dressed in a ball cap and shorts, holding a beer in one hand and her cellphone in the other, Erin films this procession of servicemen as they move down the food line, trying to capture each face on camera but looking for one young man, in particular: her son.

"Say hi to your mommas, boys!" she calls.*

For Erin, this is the longest she's ever gone without talking to or seeing her son, who enlisted in the Marine Corps as a seventeen-year-old. "He's a fucking baby," she cries, adding that she only wants to see her boy. She won't talk to him. "He'll be embarrassed. Plus, that's not fair to the other kids, who don't get to see their mothers." But she can't hide her pride. "I made a Marine!" she says as the recruits keep coming, this collection of future warriors (soon after graduation they will head to Marine Combat Training, followed by the School of Infantry), before nodding toward the drill instructors, who preside over the line of recruits, giving credit where credit is due. "*These guys* made Marines," she says. "I just gave birth."

One of the instructors notices Erin and comes over to say hello. He wants to know which of the recruits is hers, but she would rather not say. She doesn't want her baby boy to suffer any hazing.

"We never haze," the instructor replies. "And besides, they're Marines now."

Still, she won't talk.

---

* After the game, Erin will upload the video to social media, so other Marine moms will get a chance to see their child-soldiers, who have been locked away in boot camp for the past twelve weeks, cut off from the outside world.

"Fair enough." The instructor walks away.

The recruits keep coming—some tall, some scrawny, a surprising number wearing eyeglasses, at least one with his arm in a sling, almost all looking impossibly young. Still no sign of her son. "They're just *babies*," Erin cries again. "I feel like I should tell them to put on deodorant before they leave the house."

She holds her camera steady, as the drill instructors patrol the food line, barking occasionally.

"Grab your chow and then go back to your seat!"

"You will be overly polite!"

"Overly polite!"

And then Erin sees him.

Her eyes get wide. She wants to scream but bites her tongue. The kid glances up, sees his mom—which is a surprise—and doesn't look pleased. He looks mortified, in fact, as if she's walked in on him in the shower.

Unthinking, Erin grabs my arm. By now, her joy is overwhelming, and she's trying to restrain herself from running up and giving her kid a big smooch. Incredibly, she stays strong. She doesn't say a word, though it seems to require more willpower than any mother should ever have to exert. She just watches in profound silence as her son collects his food and heads back to his seat.

11
GHOST WORLD

(Or: Life After Sports)

Walking into the visiting locker room of the Pontiac Silverdome—the onetime home of the Detroit Lions and Pistons—the first thing I see is a giant penis, complete with hairy balls. There it is, crudely drawn on a whiteboard—the same whiteboard upon which dozens (if not hundreds) of coaches have no doubt diagrammed offensive game plans and defensive schemes, the X's and O's. Next to the penis, lest there be any confusion, the artist has also scribbled four large letters: D.I.C.K.

"People are always drawing dicks," says Al Allard, shaking his head, swinging a mini Maglite through the total darkness of the locker room, illuminating small patches of rusty air vents, peeling wall paint, and decomposing ceiling tile. Though it is only noon and broad daylight outside, it feels like we have stepped into a scene from *The Blair Witch Project*. Without the flashlight, the windowless room would be pitch black. There is a faint buzzing sound, which is disconcerting, given that the building's power has long since been shut off. Allard doesn't think much of the noise. He knows there are many such mysteries inside the present-day Silverdome, America's most famously derelict stadium. As for that whiteboard art, I ask if this is a new addition to the venue's penile collection and therefore the work of a recent vandal. Allard says, "Yes. Don't know how new. I haven't been down here for a while."

Can't say that I blame him.

A large man with a small goatee, Allard is the operations manager and de facto caretaker—or perhaps crypt keeper would be more accurate—at the Silverdome. He is also one of the few people on earth who still has access to this once-vibrant venue, which stood for decades as a beacon for the city of Pontiac, Michigan, drawing more than eighty thousand people at a time to major concerts and sporting events. Today the stadium (or at least what's left of it; the roof came down in 2013, precipitating a rapid decline in conditions) sits at the center of one hundred–plus acres of empty parking lot, behind cement barricades, barbed wire, and chain link fencing, adorned with NO TRESPASSING signs. With the blessing of current ownership, Allard is leading me on a rare tour of the facility, which has otherwise been declared unsafe to enter by Pontiac's building and safety department.

"I try not to come in here," Allard says, pointing with his flashlight. "The mold. You start getting into these enclosed areas. That's that black mold. It's all through here."

Indeed, the mold is *everywhere.* The walls, the ceiling, an old bulletin board—they're all ghost white, marbled with black spots. Even before we enter the locker room, I can detect it—an almost sweet scent, a kind of rancid saccharine sweetness that catches in your nostrils and stains the back of your throat. Like fruit that went bad long ago. I try not to breathe too deeply but start to get light-headed.

"When it starts turning black, you don't want to be anywhere by it," Allard says of the mold. "That's the nasty stuff. They say it could kill you."

Really?

"Yeah."

How quickly?

"Don't know."

Let's not find out.

Leaving the locker room, we plod through a deep puddled sludge, depositing sole-sucking boot prints in our wake. Allard is just happy to escape. He spends enough time in the recesses of the stadium, he says, in the confined spaces, trying to ferret out trespassers and vandals. "I start to itch," he says of the mold's effect on him. "But that's usually where they come in from, down there. By the truck entrance."

Breathing fresh air, we walk the length of the arena floor, pausing when we reach the area that once served as midfield, the same ground upon which football greats like Barry Sanders danced through defenders. It's hard to believe such a time could ever have existed here. All around us now, the stadium is in tatters. The metal safety railings are warped, ripped, and rusted. Tall weeds sprout like small jungles from the edges of the playing field, from between the seats, from cracks in the concrete. Piles of shredded AstroTurf—from the Brillo pad generation—are folded haphazardly on top of themselves, tangled with mounds of dirty white fabric, remnants of the stadium's inflatable roof, pieces of which are also scattered throughout the gap-toothed seating bowl like oversize strips of the world's saddest confetti. Even more bizarrely, there is a large deposit of sand in one corner of the end zone, on the north side of the stadium, the result of a waterline burst. "After the water stopped running, this is what was left," says Allard. "All this sand showed up."

Elsewhere in the concourses the place is similarly torn apart, completely disemboweled. Doors are off their hinges. Frayed electrical wires drip down from the ceiling. Sleeves of unused Pepsi cups, popcorn buckets, and cardboard food trays spill out of old concession stands, littering the floor, along with uprooted toilet seats, smashed sinks, and countless glass shards from broken door panels, the handiwork of vandals desperate to get in. Some trespassers have even left little presents, petrified and odorless now, inside the stadium's toilet bowls.

None of this is a surprise, exactly.

In the months before my Silverdome visit—about two years after the roof was deflated, when the stadium effectively ceased to function as a stadium—images from inside the boarded-up venue make their way across the Internet. A photographer named Johnny Joo sneaks in and has his shots published across a slew of media sites, and a sanctioned Red Bull–produced video, which features BMX rider Tyler Fernengel treating the stadium carcass like a skate-park obstacle course, is released.

Having seen these, I come to Pontiac today with some sense of what to expect. But it's different being here in person, experiencing the vastness of the place, feeling the finality of its decay, understanding firsthand that Mother Nature has taken over the Silverdome and doesn't plan on giving it back.

Stadiums as white elephants are sadly commonplace in the world of sports. And yet the situation at the Silverdome has remained one of a kind ever since 2002 when the Lions broke their lease with the city of Pontiac in favor of Ford Field, a shiny new stadium in downtown Detroit, leaving the dome without any pro-team tenants.[*]

For a time, the city continued to book concerts, dirt shows, and other events in the Silverdome, even transforming segments of its sprawling parking lots into a drive-in movie theater. But football-size stadiums can be hard to sustain, not to mention costly to operate, especially without regular tenants. In 2006, after serving as a prac-

---

[*] The Pistons abandoned the eighty-thousand-plus-seat venue in 1988, moving to the Palace of Auburn Hills, a more reasonably sized arena for basketball crowds.

tice facility for that year's Super Bowl, the Silverdome shut its doors, seemingly for good.

The question of what to do with a sports stadium after the teams and the crowds move on is one that plagues—and sometimes galls*—many American cities. Often the decision is to demolish the venue, to start over with the land. But demolition is not inexpensive, and for some, it can be hard to say goodbye. Built in 1975 and originally known as Pontiac Metropolitan Stadium, the Silverdome was a point of civic pride for many local residents, even if the venue had terrible acoustics for concerts and beer sales were often cut off by half-time during football games, because the Lions were so bad everyone would get blotto and come to blows.

Due to twisted sentimentality or plain old mismanagement (or maybe a bit of both), Pontiac's local government became paralyzed by the Silverdome situation. They didn't demolish it and redevelop the land. They didn't sell it, although there were offers at various points. They just did nothing. For years, the stadium sat—empty, unused.

By 2009, something had to give.

With the Great Recession tearing through America's heartland and decimating the automotive industry in particular, the city of Pontiac was trapped in a downward financial spiral, dealing with a deficit of tens of millions of dollars, compounded by the closure of multiple General Motors plants, which had served as the economic backbone. According to Pontiac's mayor, Deirdre Waterman, who was elected in late 2013, the city was desperate for cash and could no longer afford to pay for the Silverdome's basic upkeep. Demolition wasn't an option, since it was beyond the local treasury's means. "Pontiac was hemorrhaging money," Waterman tells me. "Any city

---

* It is not unheard of for local governments to still be paying the debt service on a publicly funded facility after the stadium goes dark.

that had its revenue cut fifty percent, essentially, had to face a reality of fiscal emergency, so that was where we were."

What happened next has been described as a "final insult" and an "existential blow" for Pontiac's citizens, as they were forced to watch in helpless horror while a state-appointed emergency financial manager sold the dome at auction in November 2009 to Triple Investment Group, a family-run firm out of Toronto helmed by a self-made Greek-Canadian businessman named Andreas Apostolopoulos, for a depressingly low $583,000, or about 1 percent of the building's initial construction costs (and that's not adjusting for inflation). Though she doesn't want to rehash the argument as to whether the decision was correct, Waterman labels the sale "controversial and dispiriting." She says, "All the ways the Silverdome was tied to the history of Pontiac—that was one of the things that put us on the map. To lose that was very painful for the citizens, especially to lose it in the way it was lost."

The anger and resentment were visceral. Much of the fury was directed at Fred Leeb, the emergency manager and a perceived outsider who presided over the sale of the dome. He quickly became the target of violent threats and hate speech, including an anti-Semitic outburst at a city council meeting in 2010, during which he was deemed the "son of Satan." Leeb resigned from his post several months later.

To many, the decline and sale of the Silverdome were allegoric, perfect stand-ins for what was happening to Pontiac on a larger scale, as jobs disappeared and real estate values cratered. It was a dying stadium in a dying city, built on a dying industry. As former Pontiac mayor Leon Jukowski, who won election the same month the dome was sold, would later tell *Canadian Business* magazine, "The city government screwed that up. . . . There was a strong feeling that we had taken a winning situation and turned it into a travesty."

But not everyone believed the dome was dead—not yet.

With the auction complete, the Silverdome's new owners, the Apostolopoulos family, drove to Pontiac to scope out their latest investment and to figure out what the hell to do with the place. It's not like they had ever bought a stadium before. As Peter Apostolopoulos, one of Andreas's three sons, tells me, "We were not in the market for a stadium." In fact, they learned about the opportunity only when Peter's brother Jim came across an ad for the property in a Toronto newspaper. From that point, one thing led to another, and boom! Suddenly they owned the Silverdome.

"It blows you away," Peter recalls of his first moments in the dome, absorbing the facility's massive size, its bubble-like roof—held up by an air-pressure system—that reminded him of an IMAX theater, in which a person is always craning back her neck to see the whole screen at once. But it wasn't just the size. The idea of owning a stadium is so outlandish—so little kid–level sensational—it sounds like the plot of a 1990s-era PG-rated comedy. "There is a romance to it, and it was really exciting, especially when we first got in," Peter admits. Even his father, a man who prides himself on making unemotional and level-headed decisions, was seduced by the facility. "He saw something in the stadium."

As a result, the family decided to make a go of it—to see if they couldn't breathe new life into the venue—even though they knew it wouldn't be easy. The scope of the work became plain as they walked around the dome, which had received little—if any—maintenance from the city since 2006.* "What are the issues here? What do we have to fix? How can we make this work?" Peter remembers thinking.

---

* In addition to the general disrepair, a variety of stadium items had also recently gone missing, like golf carts, a boat trailer, TV sets, refrigerators, a wet bar, and other furniture, allegedly looted by former employees (with the help of security staff, per a lawsuit filed by the city).

"Your mind starts to work. And at the end of the day, you are learning as you go along."

Stadiums don't come with instruction manuals. Or at least this one didn't, as city officials provided no tutorials, no how-to walk-throughs. "They handed Mr. A the keys and said, 'Bye.' That was it," explains Allard, who left a job as a propane salesman to join the Silverdome staff as operations manager in 2010, discovering the stadium's quirks through trial and error. (More than once he put the end zones in backwards and had to roll up the turf and start again.) Despite a lack of guidance, the family committed to a full refurbishment, pouring millions into the stadium in the months leading up to its grand-reopening event in April 2010, a monster truck show branded "Domination in the Dome."

There would be subsequent events as well—boxing matches, concerts, soccer games, trade shows—but it's not easy to fill an eighty-thousand-seat stadium, and the vacant seats always overshadowed those that were filled, at least in the eyes of the press, which employed the Silverdome as an easy punch line. "It was just so big. It didn't matter what you had. If you had forty thousand in there, it looked empty," bemoans Peter. To combat the size challenge, the family had a plan to convert the Silverdome into two levels, with an open-air soccer stadium on top and multiple sports and concert venues below, but that proposal failed to proceed, since it required the anchor tenant of a major-league soccer team, which never materialized.

At some point, Peter says, the family realized the deck was stacked against them, due in no small part to a poor working relationship with Pontiac's city government characterized by mutual mistrust. Ask one of the Apostolopoulos men, and he'll tell you the city proved needlessly obstructionist, when it should have been helping the dome owners in their attempt at revival. (On this point, Peter declines to talk specifics but says, "There just wasn't enough support there from the right people.") Conversely, the city was deeply suspicious of the owners' true intentions. Many believed these outsider investors were just vulturing a cheaply purchased piece of property, planning to "let it go to waste and flip it," as one reporter put it. Adding to this tension, resentment regarding the community's loss of the stadium remained thick, so it was politically poisonous to side with the Apostolopoulos family. Local sentiment was so raw and so toxic that Allard learned not to tell people where he worked. Mayor Waterman can sympathize. "If I had a nickel for every time somebody asked me how terrible it was we lost the Silverdome," she says, "it would certainly fill my campaign coffers."

The breaking point came in the last week of December 2012, when a couple of the stadium's furnaces failed and a piece of ice the size of a church van tore through the fabric roof. A temporary patch was used to cover the gash, but it barely lasted one night. On January 3, 2013, Allard was instructed to turn off the blowers, which pumped air into the building twenty-four hours a day, thus keeping the dome aloft. For the owners, the ice incident was the last straw. "We could have continued, but you are working really hard just to break even," says Peter. "After years of constantly pushing, we, as a private family, said, 'You know what? It's not working for us. Okay, turn it off.'"

Allard understood the significance of his assignment perfectly. "I knew it was not good. It was over. Every one [of the blowers] I turned off, I had Mr. A on the phone. *'Are you sure?'* Every one, I said, *'Are you sure?'* Turned one off. *'Are you sure?* Because I can still turn that one back on. *Are you sure?'*"

But he was sure. There would be no turning back.

It took forty-five minutes for the dome to slowly sink, as the air escaped from the building. "After it settled, it just creaked and moaned a bit," Allard says of the formerly floating roof cables, which now weighed heavily on the rest of the structure, drooping just above the three hundred level, bowed like a broken trampoline. "After that, it was pretty much done."

There was talk of installing a replacement roof—a hard roof—but that never happened. Instead, conditions deteriorated at the dome, beneath the increasingly ragged fabric chewed by high-wind winter storms. In a move that many construed as a waving of the white flag, the Apostolopoulos family left the Silverdome's executive offices, their original base of American operations, and headed to downtown Detroit, where they were expanding their portfolio of stateside investments. Soon thereafter the stadium lost power.

That's when the vandals showed up.

As a Silverdome security guard tells me, "No one was breaking in. Then all of a sudden, it got bad."

Not helping matters was the media's insistence on describing the stadium as "abandoned," which has always irked Peter. "We laugh about that at the office," he says, noting that they pay property taxes, lease a couple stretches of parking lots to tenants—one to Chrysler, for stashing cars, and one to a mini-inflatable dome, used for recreational classes and leagues—and in addition to Allard, who is always on call, there is a security guard on the premises twenty-four hours a day.

Says Allard, "Someone is always here."

But considering the vast acreage that must be minded, as well as the property's single guard shack—a repurposed ticket booth located just inside the former box office entrance that serves as a largely ineffectual command center, devoid of security cameras, plumbing, or even a functioning porta-potty—it's no wonder Allard and I find evidence of trespassers all over the building. He tells me about a recent increase in attempted drone incursions, which he's promised to shoot down, skeet-style, and one memorable time when a couple guys on motorcycles broke in and went for a joyride around the main concourse. "The sheriffs have gotten to know me real well here."

At the bottom of section 311, in the corner of the southern end zone, we come across a metal barrel, which is burned orange and surrounded by charred wood. Allard suspects the container was used by vagrants, although it's not a new burn barrel, he says, since the fireworks he planted underneath the ashes as a booby trap are still intact. He seems particularly proud of this trick: "When they light another one, it will go off on them."

In search of a better view, I climb the stadium steps (Allard stays behind, fussing with the barrel) and am nearly winded when I reach the top, row twenty-seven. There I sit in a blue plastic chair, marked 35, which might once have been the worst seat in the house. (From past patrons, I learn that this area just beneath the roof was where the sound echoed and the smell of hot dogs, from all the lower levels, drifted and pooled like a boiled-meat backwater.)

Alone on top of the Silverdome, everything seems oddly peaceful. There's a clear pattern of destruction, from when the roof cables—which were made of braided steel the width of a human hand—were cut and buzzed through the seating bowl, ripping up plastic and concrete. I can hear the whooshing traffic from a nearby highway, though it sounds more like gentle wind or ocean waves. All around, remnant strips of white fabric, still attached to the body of the building, flap in the light breeze.

Sometimes, Allard tells me, when I return from my perch atop the stadium, he likes to come in on his own—even though he warns his guards never to enter the dome alone—and just listen. "I will sit up against one of the pillars down there, and I'll listen to what's going on, to see if there's someone in here." Even without the roof, sounds ricochet throughout the building, catapulting around the concourses. "If someone was sitting over there, they could hear what we were saying." The phantoms—the outside voices and road noises—add to the eeriness of the empty facility, he continues, since the sounds seem impossible to place.

Back when the dome was still inflated, full moons always made for spooky nights, as refracted moonlight coming through the translucent roof lit up the stadium interior. But it wasn't to be trusted. The light was a flickering charlatan, creating a shadow world that played with a person's vision. Says Allard, "You could see things. Guards would say, 'Oh, there was someone in there!' No, you are just seeing the pillar. It was just dark."

Nothing seemed impossible inside the Silverdome. A guard might think the stadium was under artillery attack from the flapping of a tarp in the wind. Just as easily, a guard might come across a human foot sticking out of an entrance tunnel—and sure enough, it would be connected to the leg of a struggling trespasser trying to break in. After the power was cut from the building but before moving out to the shack, a guard might see "a white figure, like a shadowy figure," standing across the way, and he might respond by locking himself in the security room, where he would wait for daybreak, shivering beneath a blanket. Allard is used to the mind fucks and mysteries of the Silverdome, the unexplained noises and visions, the way one's sense of size and scale is thrown completely out of whack.* But even he is not completely immune. When I ask about other secrets of the Silverdome, he turns kind of bashful and says, "Well, a lot of us think it is haunted.

"It's in one of the suites. It actually happened to me," he says. "Couple of the guards heard a lady scream, but I disproved that when they told me where it was. We have dampers in the mechanical rooms, and when it starts getting hot, they open and"—he makes a painful screeching noise, like metal on metal—"*rrrrrrrrruuuuh.* The only thing I can't disprove is the one suite. I don't know what it is."

Naturally, I ask if we can visit the suite, and he grudgingly agrees.

---

* "When they would do concerts, they would bring in big semitrucks, and they would look so small," says Allard. "One time my dad came up here, and he goes, 'What are all those toy trucks doing here?'"

As we head to the club level, to suite 43, he tells the story of his haunting, which strikes me as relatively harmless, as hauntings go. He'd go in to turn on the A/C, and when he walked out, the door would shut on its own. It happened time and again. "And there ain't no wind going," he says. "Just for stupidity, I went in there and went, 'Maintenance! Doing the air-conditioner!' I walked out, door stayed open. So I don't know what that means."

We get to suite 43. We go in. The door stays open.

Possibly my internal EMF meter is not properly tuned, but I do not feel any disturbances as we inspect the space, any spikes in paranormal activity. It just feels . . . empty. Like everywhere else. "Someone once paid a lot of money to sit in this suite," Allard marvels. For fun, I take a photo of the suite's thermostat, in case any apparitions later appear on the image (they don't), and then we head out, down the stairwell, back the way we came in.

As we approach the exit, Allard stops short. Some sort of clatter echoes through the concourse. "Hear that?"

Yeah. What was it?

We listen, but there's only quiet. He shrugs, satisfied it wasn't an intruder. But before we leave, he directs my attention to a luxury box on the other side of the stadium, where the sound may or may not have originated, to another phantom. Whether a trick of shadows or a reflection, it looks like a human figure slouched behind some luxury box glass, near section 231. The phantom figure looks sad, as if she's received terrible news, as if her favorite team has lost and it wasn't close. When I see it, I'm genuinely startled.

My heart starts to race. Allard laughs.

If there is a stadium spirit world, I'm not convinced it's in Pontiac. More likely it would be found in southwestern Indiana, at a thirty-thousand-square-foot facility run by a man named Jim

Sprinkle, the founder of S&S Seating, who has emerged over the last twenty years as America's unofficial stadium undertaker. He prepares the earthly vessels of expiring sports venues for their final destinations. How does one find such work? Don't ask Sprinkle. His whole operation developed by chance.

It was late summer 1996, and Sprinkle—then a booster club president for a high school in central Florida—was passing through Atlanta on his way home from vacation. When he stopped to catch a Braves game at Atlanta–Fulton County Stadium, he learned the old concrete doughnut would soon be demolished as the team prepared to move into Turner Field, which was being converted into a baseball park after serving as that summer's Centennial Olympic Stadium, and the city was giving away seats to high schools and colleges. After a few phone calls, Sprinkle was in on the action, securing six hundred for his booster club. "I hired people off the street and took out the seats," he tells me, "but the whole upper deck was remaining." And what of those? he wondered. They would be demolished, along with the stadium, which seemed like a waste. "I said, 'I tell you what. I'll make you an offer.' So I gave them an offer for the seats, and they accepted it," he says, explaining how, for twenty-five cents a pop, he took possession of twenty-five thousand seats and put himself in business.

In the two decades since, Sprinkle's company has been contracted to assist with the decommissioning of Milwaukee County Stadium, Busch Memorial Stadium, Giants Stadium, Texas Stadium, Shea Stadium, Candlestick Park, and Tiger Stadium, among many others, including a host of college venues.* While some seats

---

* Sprinkle was not hired for the Silverdome's 2014 online auction, when the stadium owners sold off anything of conceivable value—including seats, strips of AstroTurf, bathroom stalls, copper wiring, pretzel warmers, office furniture, drinking glasses, and more—and reportedly earned back almost all of (or maybe even more than) their 2009 purchase price. As you can imagine, this did nothing to assuage local resentment of the Apostolopoulos family.

are shipped to predetermined buyers, as stadium owners have slowly realized there is money to be made in the memorabilia market, the remainder becomes property of S&S Seating and travels back to Indiana. At the warehouse, a segment of the inventory is retained for selling to collectors. (Those Atlanta–Fulton County Stadium seats, purchased for a quarter, now retail for $299 a pair.) Most, however, are refurbished and unloaded in bulk to high schools and colleges— though the institutions will never know if their purchase came from Shea Stadium or a defunct Little League field. "They have no idea," says Sprinkle.

In this way, Sprinkle is less undertaker than Buddhist priest, shuttling the seats from one life cycle to the next. He has also served as witness to some amazing displays of fan love and loyalty, as their beloved home parks are about to be torn down. In St. Louis, for example, Sprinkle was struck by the Sharpie-scrawled messages all around Busch Stadium. It was like the yearbook of the most popular kid in class. "I swear to you," he says, "there were messages everywhere in that stadium. Everywhere! 'This is Larry Such and Such and I was a season ticket holder for so many years—I'm going to miss Busch Stadium so much—Love this place.' Just on and on.

"The day after the last game, we were in the stadium working, and over twenty thousand people showed up, just to walk around the stadium. It was a mass of people. We ended up firing two or three [workers] because they were selling concrete for twenty dollars."

Detroit's Tiger Stadium, which was built in 1912, provided another interesting case study. "I was impressed by the feeling you get when you walk in," remembers Sprinkle. "You could really feel the history on that stadium." And even though the ballpark had sat empty for about a decade before finally meeting the wrecking ball, Tigers fans still felt a connection to it, and many wanted the seats. In fact, says Sprinkle, "People wanted those seats *as is*," which he found hard to believe. "There were places in the stadium where pigeons would roost over the top of seats, and the pigeon droppings were six to seven inches thick, on some seats. And they wanted them as is!"

The heart wants what it wants—and sometimes it wants pigeon shit.

———

You don't have to tell Ed Emmett about the passions that can surround a stadium. As county judge for Harris County, Texas, which owns the Houston Astrodome, he often tells folks, "I could solve criminal justice and probably create world peace, but the people are going to remember me for what happens to the Astrodome." And he means it. "I was half-joking when I first started saying it. Now it's absolutely the truth."

Not unlike the Silverdome, the fate of the Astrodome has been a long-running topic of local conversation and an equally hot-button issue.* In fact, when Emmett took office in 2007—a decade after the Houston Oilers moved to Nashville and became the Tennessee Titans and almost as long since the stadium's signature tenant, the Astros, moved to a new ballpark—an exclusive-rights deal was already in place for a development group to turn the former Eighth Wonder of the World into a hotel. But funding fell through, and the county was back to square one. Not that it lacked for suggestions. Everybody had an idea of what to do with the dome. Some felt it ought to be demolished, that it was an eyesore and standing in the way of progress.† Others wanted to convert the stadium into an indoor

———

* Navigate to the front page of Emmett's county judge website, and you'll find a prominently displayed link to a landing page with a prepared statement about the stadium, among other Astrodome-related items.

† Members of the tear-down-that-dome camp included both the Houston Texans—a 2002 NFL expansion team, whose new home was built alongside the Astrodome—and the Houston Livestock Show and Rodeo, which moved out of the dome that same year to take up residency in the Texans' football stadium.

ski area, a movie studio, or a waterpark. "A lot of people wanted to make it into a casino," says Emmett, "but that is not legal in Texas, so that doesn't work." His favorite suggestion was to flood the playing field, which sits a couple stories below grade, and reenact naval battle scenes. "I thought that was kind of cool."*

But for all the talk, no money came to the table, and it became clear that if the building was going to be repurposed in any way, the county was going to have to pony up. When a bond proposal to convert the stadium into a multipurpose center went to the ballot in 2013—Emmett says this initiative was misinterpreted as being for a convention center—it failed 53–47. Many assumed that would be the last they'd hear of the Astrodome, a building that once stood for futurism but had since come to signify a link to the dusty past.

Still, Emmett didn't view the Astrodome as a teardown. The building was paid off, structurally sound, and cost the county only about $166,000 in yearly maintenance. Beyond that, it had public sentiment on its side. Even after the failed bond, an "overwhelming majority" of Harris County citizens expressed support for saving the dome, per Emmett. "Houston kind of has a reputation of tearing things down and moving on," he says, "and this seems to be where a lot of people want to take a stand. We don't want to spend a lot of money on it, but we don't want to tear it down and lament the fact that it's gone."

Though Emmett frames the subject of saving the dome as a practical matter, discussing the building as "an asset," he also recognizes that the Astrodome is more than a piece of property. It's an icon and a game-changing sports venue. "It wasn't important just to us," he says. "I think about that all the time."

---

* Not only was it cool, this idea likely has historical precedent, as Roman emperors are believed to have flooded the floor of the Colosseum and staged sea fights, known as *naumachiae*.

His conservationist instincts were seemingly validated in the spring of 2015, when the county received a special dispensation (since the building didn't meet code) to hold a fiftieth birthday party for the dome, opening it up to the public for the first time in years. "We bought a thousand T-shirts. We were ready for a pretty good crowd. Thirty thousand people showed up," he says. "They waited for hours, and nobody was complaining. They just wanted to come in and stand on the playing surface and look up, and when they looked up, that is when I started watching them." He compares this moment to a scene from *Field of Dreams.* "It was like when the brother-in-law, who is the banker, finally sees it. He goes, 'Whatever you do, don't tear this down.'* And that was kind of the attitude I detected that night."

Beth Wiedower, who works in the Houston field office for the National Trust for Historic Preservation, had a similar experience. Her organization named the Astrodome a "national treasure" in June 2013 and officially began working to help preserve it. To generate public support, she drove around the city in a twenty-six-foot box truck covered in Astrodome memorabilia. "What we found was very interesting, because we thought our message would be built around how this was the first domed stadium, an icon that was representative of the Space Age, the can-do spirit of Houston and the country, but what resonated most with folks were the personal experiences: 'I remember going to the Astros game with my grandfather when so-and-so hit a home run; or going to the Selena [Quintanilla-Pérez] concert with my mother; or attending the Houston Livestock Show and Rodeo at the Astrodome for my entire childhood.' Those were the things that really motivated people to want to save this building."

---

* This is not an exact quote from the movie—what the brother-in-law says is, "Do not sell this farm, Ray. You gotta keep this farm"—but you get it.

In this way, sports venues embody uniquely significant historic spaces, well beyond any architectural or engineering feats therein. Adds Wiedower: "This is where life happens. This is where people and families interact, and where their memories are created. And that matters because we are not just saving Mount Vernon and the White House—those places where wealthy powerful white men lived and worked. Those places are not our story."

For the National Trust, the Astrodome represents both a test case, as the organization dips its toes into large-scale stadium waters,* and an all-too-familiar situation in a demolition-crazed nation. "Without disparaging any particular city or leader in the country, our mindset now is 'Let's build it to last thirty years, and then we will move on,'" says Wiedower, who finds this personally upsetting from an historical perspective as well as a sustainability standpoint.

Given the fast churn of the modern stadium game, in which owners are constantly trying to upgrade their digs on the taxpayer dime, "we have some well-built and well-located structures across the country that are ripe for reuse," says Wiedower. She's not talking just about stadium hand-me-downs, as will be the case with Turner Field when the Braves move out to a new ballpark in Cobb County in 2017 and Georgia State University's football program moves in. On the contrary, there is no limit to what a former sports venue can become. Just look at the Forum, in Inglewood, California, which is now owned by the Madison Square Garden Company and hosts a wide range of indoor entertainment. Or the Memphis Pyramid, which has been converted into a gigantic retail outlet for Bass Pro Shops. "If we can be successful in Houston in not only making the case that these buildings are worthy of preservation," says Wiedower, "but there is a viable and economic reuse in these types of

---

* Previously, the National Trust has helped to preserve New Jersey's Hinchliffe Stadium, a significantly smaller ballpark that was associated with the Negro leagues.

structures, then we can go to stadiums and communities across the country" with that message.*

In Houston, the current plan—championed by Emmett, cosigned by the National Trust, and approved unanimously by the Harris County commissioners court—calls for the Astrodome to be converted into an indoor park—replete with open green space, exercise facilities, fitness trails, music pavilions, underground parking, and more—which the county judge points out is in line with the dome's original vision of bringing traditional outdoor activities underneath its roof. "It was never intended as just a sports stadium. This was a building, and there was a stadium inside the building," he says. To Emmett, this distinction isn't merely semantic. "The stadium will go away. And the building that housed the stadium will still be there. So sure, we're tearing down the Astros' stadium, but we're keeping the building it was in."

The Astrodome is dead. Long live the Astrodome.

But it doesn't have to end this way.

For proof of life after sports, I travel to one of the last places on earth fans might expect to find a slice of Stadium Heaven: Utah. It's late January when I arrive in Salt Lake City. Sundance season. Like so many other out-of-towners, I careen through the Wasatch Mountains, the winter sun a blinding glare off the snow-dusted peaks, and make my way toward Park City. Unlike the cinema set, however, my destination isn't the downtown strip but a winter sports wonderland known as Utah Olympic Park. Built ahead of the 2002 winter games, which were hosted by Salt Lake City and the surrounding region, the 389-acre venue held bobsled, skeleton, luge, and ski jumping events.

---

* Wiedower concedes that not every defunct venue is necessarily worth saving: "By no means are we as an organization saying, 'Let's preserve every one.'"

Nearly fifteen years after the flame went out, the venue remains in active use.

In fact, the Olympic facilities are four times busier today than they were in 2002, as the park receives about half a million visits a year, welcoming both newbies and elite athletes. In addition to serving as a year-round training base for a number of U.S. ski teams, including aerials, ski jumping, and Nordic combined,* the park is home to multiple museums, frequent international competitions, youth developmental programs, a growing events business, and a variety of outdoor sports and adventure activities, from high-ropes courses to zip lines to bobsled rides on the official Olympic sliding track.† More than a souvenir of that time when the Olympics came to town, the park is a spiritual and physical headquarters.

Such longevity is not guaranteed. Governing bodies like the International Olympic Committee (IOC) and FIFA mandate the construction of numerous venues by host cities. These facilities are expensive, often draining local treasuries, saddling communities with debt, and leaving behind unneeded and costly white elephants.‡ The horror stories are endless, so common as to be cliché. Consider Athens, Greece, where the 2004 Olympic venues were abandoned soon after the summer games, eventually coming to stand as targets for populist wrath, symbols of waste, when the country fell into a deep debt crisis. (In recent years, Athens's Olympic facilities have been used as homeless shelters for struggling Greek citizens and as camps for Syrian refugees.) In Sochi, it wasn't even six months after the 2014 winter games

---

* Other U.S. teams, like snowboarding, freeskiing, bobsled, skeleton, luge, and moguls, also train here at various times throughout the year, as do approximately thirty international teams across a variety of sport disciplines.

† I do this. It is amazing and terrifying.

‡ The Bird's Nest in Beijing, for example, reportedly requires annual maintenance fees of $11 million.

when photo essays began to appear online illustrating how the recent host city had already become a ghost town.

And yet according to Colin Hilton, president of the Utah Olympic Legacy Foundation—which manages the park, the Utah Olympic Oval in Kearns, and the Soldier Hollow Nordic Center in Midway—the key to a vibrant afterlife isn't so much what happens when the games leave as what happens before they ever arrive. "For me, Salt Lake marked the first host city to put thought into what happens after the games, what to do with the facilities," says Hilton, who spent the 1990s traveling across the country—and around the world—helping communities prepare for and run big international sporting events. "Folks in Utah did their homework."

The seeds for Utah's successful legacy efforts were planted well over a decade before the 2002 Olympics, sparked oddly enough by a baseball man, thanks to a poor showing from the U.S. teams at the 1988 winter games in Calgary. Tom Kelly, vice-president of communications for the U.S. Ski and Snowboard Association (USSA), remembers it well. "Midway through the '88 Olympics, George Steinbrenner, of the New York Yankees [who went on to serve as vice-chairman of the U.S. Olympic Committee], announced the formation of a commission to study why the teams weren't doing well," he says. A year later the Steinbrenner Commission filed its report, which found, in part, that the teams' middling performance could be attributed to a lack of domestic training facilities. This was music to the ears of a man named Howard Peterson. In charge of USSA at the time, Peterson had already been agitating for an American city to use the opportunity of hosting the Olympics as "a catalyst for legacy, and build legacy facilities," per Kelly, who adds: "It wasn't an agenda for Salt Lake. It was an agenda for the sport. [Peterson] went to the USOC and said, 'Pick a site that's going to build legacy.'"

At the time, Salt Lake would have been considered a dark horse candidate—not just to host the Olympics but even to become the American bid city. The heir apparent was Anchorage, Alaska. A call went out across the country. As Hilton puts it, "The USOC said, if you invest in infrastructure, we'll make you the candidate city for two cycles of going after the games." While Anchorage officials, overly confident that the bid belonged to them, offered little in the way of legacy planning, Utah presented a referendum to its citizens in 1989. If passed, it would allocate $56 million to build winter sports infrastructure, which would provide training facilities to top-tier athletes and recreational facilities to the wider community. Needless to say, the referendum passed—specifically, that money allowed for the construction of Utah Winter Sports Park (now known as Utah Olympic Park), a speed skating oval in Kearns (the Utah Olympic Oval), and an ice sheet in Ogden, which would be used for Olympic curling—and Salt Lake leapfrogged Anchorage.

But that's only part of the story.

With any Olympics—even winter games, which require fewer venues than their summertime counterparts—a host city is going to have to deal with certain facilities that present long-term challenges, which Hilton terms "high-labor, high-cost facilities." He explains, "Facilities like the bobsled track, the ski jumps, the speed skating oval—they don't break even."*

According to Hilton, not considering (or simply not understanding) the cost of running such facilities after the games is the most egregious oversight a host city can make. Often surprised by these post-games bills, cities must decide whether to pay up or to desert the onetime Olympic venues. It's not a happy choice. In Utah, for example, there is a net operating loss of about $3.5 million a year to run the park and the oval and to support other foundational activ-

---

* The best example of such a facility for the summer games is the velodrome, which is a stadium for cycle racing.

ity. But unlike so many former Olympic cities, Salt Lake's organizing committee, aka SLOC, anticipated the need for subsidization. "People finally had enough of seeing facilities being closed less than a year after the games, going 'What the hell do we do with this now?'" says Hilton. "Salt Lake planned for that."

On the heels of a 1998 bribery scandal involving SLOC leadership and members of the IOC, Mitt Romney and Fraser Bullock took control of the city's organizing efforts. Under their direction, SLOC ran a tight-budgeted ship. They were determined not only to reimburse the state for its initial infrastructure outlays (plus interest) but also to turn enough profit to create an endowment for running the legacy foundation, hopefully in perpetuity. "The plan was to have $40 million profit," says Hilton. "So fast-forward, we had $160 million profit. And of that, $76 million went to our legacy foundation."

In Utah, the games live on.

My kickoff interview with Colin Hilton—like almost all my meetings, tours, and appointments over the coming week—has been arranged by a woman named Kathy Hunter, a Park City resident and former SLOC employee, who I come to think of as my Salt Lake City sherpa. An indispensable resource and unflagging fixer, Hunter has agreed to help me visit a handful of former Olympic venues, to better understand the breadth of the local legacy and to see how different types of facilities have adjusted to their post-Olympic existences.

Really, she's the perfect person to show me around—and not just because of her bona fides as an Olympic insider (for the 2002 games, she managed the design and aesthetic of the city: the building-draped banners and billboard-like towers that gussied up the skyline), or because she stayed on with SLOC as the organizing committee spent a year working on legacy transition after the games, or even because she's emerged in recent years as a tireless volunteer, escorting foreign representatives around town, facilitating their visits much in the way she's facilitating mine.* More than all that, she's a uniquely qualified Olympics chaperone because no one loves the games more than she does.

Even ten-plus years later, Hunter can barely contain her enthusiasm. She's wearing blue jeans, a leopard-print scarf, a black zip-up augmented with a Tenth Anniversary Olympic pin, and a gigantic smile, like she's so happy talking about the Olympics that it hurts. I'm cynical by nature and thus initially suspicious, but no one could fake this level of fervor. "Stop me if I get too gushy," she tells me, "but it was such a magical time!" And we quickly discover we have plenty else in common, like dry skin and a crippling fear of heights. (While on a tour of Utah Olympic Park, she won't come close to the ledge, as we look out over the Nordic jump.)

We begin our Salt Lake circuit, armed with Hunter's hefty Rolodex.

At the Olympic Oval, we connect with Todd Porter, the venue's general manager, and Derek Parra, a gold-medal-winning speed skater, who set a new world record in the 1,500-meter event at the 2002 Olympics and now serves as the Oval's sport program director. "He's going to coach curling here in about an hour," Porter says of his colleague as we walk along an outer track, where a group of skaters are loosening their hips via a game of hacky sack. To Porter, the intermingling of high-performance athletes and recreational users is one of the coolest things about the Oval. "There's no division," he says. Parra agrees, adding, "Basketball—you can't go shoot hoops with Kobe Bryant or LeBron James. Here you can skate with literally some of the best skaters in the world."

Ironically, this open access to the same facilities as aspiring Olympians presented the biggest challenge after the games. "A lot of the public saw it as a high-performance building," Porter says. They assumed, "It wasn't for me. So that took a while." As we walk

* Officially, Hunter has been dubbed an "international delegate liaison."

around the venue, which features a four-hundred-meter speed skating oval—known to contain "the fastest ice on earth," thanks to a
combination of the high-altitude air and a water-purifying process of
reverse osmosis—as well as two international-size ice hockey sheets,
which double as pads for short track speed skating, Porter explains
that the venue has no such messaging problems now. Over a single
week in December, for instance, the Oval received more than ten
thousand public skaters. "And that's not counting any of our other
programs," like curling leagues and disco nights, each of which adds
to the utilitarian legacy of the local facilities. According to Porter,
it's not just that they're being used but *how* they're being used that
matters. "We're unique because for a lot of other facilities, from other
Olympics, a venue like this is a big flea market or something else," he
says. "It's not used in the sense of what it was built for."

Kristy Holt, the client services manager at Rice-Eccles Stadium,
which is home to the University of Utah's football program and which
served as the venue for opening and closing ceremonies during the
2002 winter games, has also spent a good deal of time considering
the local Olympic legacy. In fact, her master's thesis was dedicated to
the topic. "This was the obvious choice," she says of using the football venue as the Olympic stadium. But to many host cities and host
nations, using existing infrastructure (assuming they have it) isn't
so obvious, as many political leaders become Pride Blind, seduced
by the possibility of Olympic stadiums standing as "potent symbols
of architectural prowess and economic pride,"* even if these venues
often hemorrhage money.

But such appeals to vanity and ego were hardly temptations in
a place like Utah, says Donald Stirling, chief revenue officer for the
Utah Jazz, who ran sales and marketing for Salt Lake's organizing

---

* Amy Qin and Robin Pogrebin, "National Pride at a Steep Price," *New York Times,* January 4, 2015.

committee. "You gotta have a little restraint," he explains when we meet in his office. (During the Olympics, the Jazz's arena held short track speed skating and the figure skating competition.) "It goes back to the essence of men," Stirling continues. "There are some people that have made a lot of money, and there are people that have *kept* a lot of money, because they are cheap. I remember [Mitt Romney] had a phrase, 'zero-based budgeting,' and that means if the money's not there, we won't do it." So naturally, they made use of every venue they could, from football stadiums to basketball arenas to ski resorts, like Deer Valley, Snowbasin, and Park City Mountain Resort.

Every venue—preexisting or not—also had a detailed post-games strategy, which laid out how the facility would either revert back to its former self or evolve into something new. Peaks Ice Arena in Provo, which hosted a portion of men's and women's ice hockey, is now home to the Brigham Young University men's hockey team, a couple of high school teams, youth programs, and a figure skating club. The ten-thousand-seat E Center, which was the primary venue for ice hockey, is now Maverik Center, a multipurpose sports and entertainment venue.

Regarding the University of Utah specifically, Holt says, "There was a careful plan put in place of what would happen. Nothing being planned for the university was going to just sit here." The Olympic Village, for instance, which was built on the school's campus, was converted into dormitories.* The school viewed the Olympics not as a liability but as an opportunity. "It jump-started our stadium renovation [a $53 million project, to which SLOC contributed $8 million], expanded student housing, brought the [public transit] Trax

---

* This wasn't a new idea, actually. A similar Olympic Village–to–college dorms conversion took place in Atlanta after the 1996 summer games. It should also be noted that, like Salt Lake City, the Georgia capital tried to build for an afterlife by doing things like passing down the Olympic stadium to the Atlanta Braves, as mentioned previously, and maintaining modest architectural ambitions in general. Still, some venues were ultimately abandoned, like the $20 million–plus Stone Mountain Tennis Center, which has fallen into disrepair and been picked over by looters.

train—not that it wouldn't have come to the university anyway, but it was brought here expressly so people could attend the Olympics— and built the footbridge, the George S. Eccles 2002 Legacy Bridge, which allowed athletes to walk across a major four-lane road from the Olympic Village." What's more, she says, the university is ready to host the games again! "When people say 'Let's have the Olympics again,' there is no skepticism now," Holt tells me, adding that the city would be able to reuse all the same venues, which have been kept in working order, as a cost-saving measure. "And that hasn't happened elsewhere. In other cities, it has left a bad taste in their mouth."

To Bob Wheaton, the thickly mustachioed president and general manager at Deer Valley Resort—which hosted alpine slalom, aerial, and mogul skiing—and a board member of the Utah Olympic Legacy Foundation, the 2002 Olympics story is one of collective pride and confidence. "I think it brought a lot of people closer together, and I don't know how else you could get that," he says. "It's a monumental effort, but once it happens, there's a pride in ownership, pride in accomplishment, and it also raises the bar as to what people think and know is possible in a community like this. We knew, if we manage this thing correctly, look at what we're going to have left over at the end that can help the youth. We would like that to be our biggest legacy. So far, so good."

———————

Here's another way to not get stuck with a white elephant stadium: Don't build one in the first place. Or at least not a permanent one.

That's the idea behind the modular stadium movement, which has been gaining traction across the country. To learn more about modular, I book a quick trip to Atlanta, where the system first appeared in the United States, at the BB&T Atlanta Open tennis tournament in 2013. After that initial event, the venue was broken down into its component parts and trucked up to North Carolina, where a new stadium was assembled from the same pieces in time for the Winston-Salem Open. "That's the beauty of all this," says Peter Lebedevs, the assistant tournament director, while showing me around Stadium Court, as the BB&T Atlanta Open's showcase venue is known, ahead of the 2015 event. "It can go up quickly, come down quickly. And you can put it wherever you want."

Built into the nook of an empty asphalt lot in Atlantic Station, a retail complex just off the northernmost segment of the I-75/85 Downtown Connector, Stadium Court seems both out of place, with Dillard's looming in the background, and perfectly natural.

And yet the whole thing will soon be gone, disappeared without a trace.

With vomitories, video scoreboards, luxury suites, hospitality platforms, and a 360-degree seating bowl (capacity: about 3,500), it's an honest-to-goodness stadium. "You feel like you're at the U.S. Open," Lebedevs says of fans' experience at the facility, which takes less than four weeks to build and less than half that time to break down. Compared to other types of temporary structures, he adds, "This really is a stadium versus just seats. This looks like a big-league stadium."

To gain a better understanding of how the system works, Lebedevs connects me with Chris Kersey, the on-site project manager for Nussli, a Switzerland-based company that specializes in building temporary sports structures and is responsible for introducing modular stadiums to the American market. "It's basically your typical scaffolding, with our stuff on top. It's a bleacher truss," Kersey, who shows up wearing a hard hat and wraparound shades, says of the prefabricated steel modules that pin together, without a single nut or bolt, in countless combinations. He leads me down the stadium steps and underneath the stands, for a glimpse at the skeletal understructure. "It's all integrated steel, man. Steel and aluminum. It's like a big Erector set—that's all it is."

But a modular stadium is more than just oversize sets of bleachers jammed together. For one thing, it's far stronger and more structurally sound than temporary bleachers—of which Kersey says, "If you call that a stadium, an engineer would laugh at you"—and can therefore be built to accommodate more people (as in capacities of fifty thousand or more) and be left standing for longer periods of time. "This could sit here for ten years," says Kersey. "Just put it on concrete pads and anchor it in."

A modular stadium also allows a team or event to completely customize its venue, from different seating configurations and seat types (like hardback chairs, more luxurious recliners, simple metal benches, and standing decks) to outer design shells and roof covers to incorporating concession stands, bathrooms, locker rooms, and even air-conditioned spaces. Says Kersey, "We can integrate all that."

For the BB&T Atlanta Open, this flexibility has proven invaluable, as the tournament modifies its stadium specs each year. "We can take a row out, we can put more decking in. It allows us to be creative. We're always looking to change, based on feedback from our fans," says Lebedevs. "We even looked into covering it because it's so hot." But they deemed that option too expensive.

While Nussli initially hesitated to ship its modular components to the United States, where there is a glut of permanent sports infrastructure and therefore questionable demand, the company has been expanding its modular operation all across North America, from Formula One racing in Mexico City to the Pan Am Games in Toronto to tennis's Fed Cup in Hawaii. (The company's first modular project on the continent was in Canada: a twenty-thousand-plus-seat semipermanent stadium for the BC Lions in 2010.) Recently, Nussli has built the front-stretch stands for the Brickyard 400 at the Indianapolis Motor Speedway, a tennis stadium *inside* Petco Park for Davis Cup matches, horseshoe-shaped arenas for the AVP Beach Volleyball tour, and a semi-permanent soccer venue for the Charlotte Independence, as well as spectator grandstands and other event infrastructure for the FIS Alpine Ski World Championships in Colorado.

"This is the future," Kersey says, noting that modular facilities are a natural fit for one-off events like the Olympics. "They spend all this major money on these stadiums, and it's a waste." Many host cities, from Vancouver to London to Rio, have been embracing aspects of the modular concept.* Meanwhile, for the 2022 World Cup in Qatar, which will require the construction of up to nine new stadiums, Nussli was commissioned to do a series of renderings for venues that would be either partially or completely modular. Modular expansions—or "stadium extends," as some call them—involve the overlay of modular components on top of an existing structure, for temporarily increased capacity. After the soccer tournament, the stadiums won't be left to rot, as the desert country plans to disassemble the modular portions and send them to developing nations around the world, which lack sports infrastructure, in a gesture of charity and sustainability.†

What is less clear is how—if at all—major American sports leagues will make use of modular designs. "Right now I'm doing something for the Minnesota Vikings," Kersey tells me. "They're building a new stadium‡ and playing at the [University of Minnesota's] stadium, which is a horseshoe, but the NFL doesn't want a horseshoe. So I go fill that gap."

Kersey has also spoken to some baseball teams about possibly providing semipermanent ballparks in the twenty-to-forty-thousand-seat range, should they ever need an interim place to play.§ But even

---

* Modular shouldn't be considered a cure-all, however, as evidenced by numerous Olympic venues in Rio—including the legendary Maracanã soccer stadium—falling into disrepair and decay by early 2017.

† While this is a laudable legacy goal, it is important to mention that Qatar's seeming progressivism stands in stark contrast to the serious allegations of human rights abuses of the migrant workers who are building the World Cup facilities.

‡ U.S. Bank Stadium opened in time for the 2016 NFL season.

§ Populous built a temporary 12,500-seat ballpark for major-league baseball in 2016, when the Atlanta Braves and Miami Marlins played a regular season game at Fort Bragg, in North Carolina. Although the venue wasn't modular, its component parts were broken down and reused after the game.

if those projects never materialize, Kersey says it's always fun to have the discussions, in which he gets to show off Nussli's modular capabilities. As he puts it, "It's like being the guy who comes into a party with all the toys."

———

For now, American stadiums are permanent, or as permanent as anything. Whatever happens over the course of the life and even death of a particular venue—whether the home team hoists a championship trophy every season or whether it never breaks .500; whether the stadium is the site of mass merriment, uplift, and gold-medal performances or of heartbreak, political overreach,* and serious human tragedy†—the story of the venue will outgrow its confines, spilling into public consciousness, leaving an indelible mark on the city and its people.

When a stadium dies, that mark can feel more like a wound. The Silverdome is on its last legs and will doubtless soon be destroyed. The Apostolopoulos family must decide what's next. As of yet, nothing has been ruled out. In fact, they seem to be throwing everything at the wall. In 2015, Triple Investment Group held an international design competition for the property, worked up marketing materials for its possible redevelopment as a work/

---

* As former Salt Lake City mayor Rocky Anderson points out, stadium building and international athletic festivals are often used as pretexts for human and civil rights violations, as was the case ahead of the 2016 Rio Olympics, when tens of thousands of low-income Brazilian citizens were displaced from their homes to make way for Olympic infrastructure. Twenty years earlier Atlanta attempted to "clean up" its streets by offering homeless folks one-way bus tickets out of town. Anderson tells me he worked hard to make sure the games didn't "tread over people who are less fortunate" in Salt Lake.

† This was the case following a military coup led by General Augusto Pinochet, in late 1973, for example, when his junta used Estadio Nacional, in Santiago, Chile, as a detention center and torture camp, rounding up and interrogating thousands, while killing dozens. Today the venue remains in use for sporting competition.

live/play site, and even listed the land for sale—for $30 million—which created another big stink. "Right now our plan is to redevelop the site," Peter Apostolopoulos says, brushing off any talk of a sale. "We're still committed. It's not done. This is just a resting period."

Until the wrecking ball shows up and the construction crews roll in, there will be local anxiety over the fate of the Silverdome.* Mayor Waterman says the community is past the point of wanting the dome to return; they just want something to happen with it. She's been working hard to keep open the lines of communication between the city government and the stadium owners, but the relationship is fitful, weighed down by years of bitterness. Waterman says the owners have to be pushed to meet their maintenance obligations, and citizens often complain about the state of the site. Peter questions in what ways the Apostolopoulos family are failing in their duty as tax-paying property owners. Sure, the place is a bit messy, but it's not like they're expecting company. "There is no rush to tidy it up," he says, adding that there are some upkeep efforts.

Just ask Allard, who spends most of each week mowing the grass on the property's outer perimeter, only to start from scratch the following Monday. He used to take care of the weeds, which are veined throughout the parking lots, as well—but again, to what end? "I can only do so much when I'm by myself," he says as we exit the Silverdome, climbing into his rusted red pickup truck for a quick ride around the property. "Now you know why they complain about the weeds," he says, nodding toward the greenery. "But what am I supposed to do?"

There is something strangely beautiful about the way time and

---

* It was reported in late 2015 that demolition of the dome would begin the following spring. (It didn't.) In the summer of 2016 a Silverdome representative told me that sometime in 2017 was more likely.

nature have run their course around the Silverdome. It's not just the wild weeds. Huge spider webs are everywhere, of infinite complexity. "Spiders all over the place. They show up, and they love it. No one bothers them," says Allard, who tells me how they used to have a pet spider outside the guard shack, and about all the other critters that have made themselves at home. "Spiders, raccoons, groundhogs. We had a fox out here a couple times. In the spring, we get the geese. They like to hang out in the parking lot." One time, he says, when he was driving his motorcycle, the geese started flying at him. In retaliation, he got into his truck and chased the geese right back. "I chased them around the parking lot for a while," he says. "Chase *me*? I'm going to chase *you*!"

Allard is under no illusions when it comes to the Silverdome. He knows the stadium has outlived its usefulness, and he's ready to see it go, even though that might mean his job. "I'm ready," he says. "I'm ready for something different. I think we need to move on, get it over with."

As we motor around the parking lot, I notice some smaller birds balancing delicately along nearby power lines. Allard seems pensive, as our conversation turns to the inevitable end. He points to the birds. "We have a hawk that will fly out here. Red-tailed hawk. He is kind of cool," he says. "He will wait for the mice to run out. It's funny to watch." We see a few straggling geese up ahead. Allard smiles and steps on the gas. They fly off. He says, "The little birds will actually chase the big birds away. I've never understood that, why the big bird doesn't turn around and go, 'Hey, listen here!' The little birds always run the big birds out, for some reason." And with that, my tour guide turns silent. Perhaps wondering how long before he, too, will be gone. When there will be no one left to chase away the geese.

ACKNOWLEDGMENTS

A weird thing happens when a person spends his life in stadiums, watching everything but the game. I frequently heard a version of the following statement from operations crews, video board producers, groundskeepers, and countless other stadium staffers: "Sporting events are ruined for me."

They don't dislike the games; they're simply incapable of watching them, having been conditioned to train their eyes elsewhere—to the bald spots in the outfield grass, to the overhead lighting rigs, to the not-so-hidden HVAC ducts, or to the mustard stains on the concourse condiment carts. Spouses and friends call these people bores, insufferable, terrible dates. But they can't help it. Once you look away from the field of play, it can be hard to look back. Thank you to John Leas, Steve Wightman, George Toma, Dave Mellor, Mark Paluch, Adrienne Midgley, Doug Thornton, Jon Shestakofsky, David Newman, Brian Fisher, Kerry Graue, Mia Taravella, Barry Baum, Luke Shanno, Aaron Popkey, Bruce Speight, Kevin Saghy, Don Costante, and so many others who welcomed me into their worlds and showed me where to look.

While my research involved dozens of on-the-ground experiences and hundreds of supporting interviews, it also relied on a wide variety of sports- and stadium-related scholarship (much of which has been cited throughout) as well as a huge selection of articles and news clippings from publications like *Sports Illustrated*, *The New York Times*, *The Wall Street Journal*, *The Washington Post*, the *New Orleans Times-Picayune*, the *Los Angeles Times*, *The Nation*, *The Atlantic*, *The New Yorker*, *Smithsonian*, and *Sporting News*; websites and blogs like Deadspin, Grantland, Bloomberg, Cleveland.com, Field of Schemes, and Atlantic Yards/Pacific Park Report; and other outfits like ESPN, STMA, and SABR. A few of the books to which I most frequently turned for ideas and expertise include Mark Dyreson and Robert Trumpbour, eds., *The Rise of Stadiums in the Modern United States: Cathedrals of Sport* (New York: Routledge, 2010); John Bale and Olaf Moen, eds., *The Stadium and the City* (Keele, UK: Keele University Press, 1995); Allen Guttmann, *Sports Spectators* (New York: Columbia University Press, 1986); Allen Guttmann, *From Ritual to Record: The Nature of Modern Sports* (New York: Columbia University Press, 1978); Robert Trumpbour, *The New Cathedrals: Politics and Media in the History of Stadium Construction* (Syracuse, N.Y.: Syracuse University Press, 2007); Neil deMause and Joanna Cagan, *Field of Schemes: How the Great Stadium Swindle Turns Public Money into Private Profit*, rev. ed. (Lincoln: University of Nebraska Press, 2008); Michael Benson, *Ballparks of North America: A Comprehensive Historical Encyclopedia of Baseball Grounds, Yards and Stadiums, 1845 to 1988* (Jefferson, N.C.: McFarland, 2009); and Dave Zirin, *A People's History of Sports in the United States: 250 Years of Politics, Protest, People, and Play* (New York: New Press, 2009).

None of this would have been possible without the generosity of friends and family (and a few strangers-turned-friends) who opened their homes to me as I skittered across the country, armed with a notepad and a duffel bag. Your pullout couches and extra bedrooms were first-class accommodations. Thank you to Stephen and Marianne Garber, Doris Dozier, Sherrie Perkins, Don, Jessica, and Rachel Kohan, Jim Kohan, Judy Richonne, Stan, Paula, and Katherine Kohan, Marc Maxwell, Linda and Harold Schlozman, Charlotte and Jack Newman, Linda and Pat Mangan, Sara Landis, Adam Garber, Marc Fiedler, Mike, Wanda, and Bella Marquart, Frank and Mary Hart, Alan Jackson, Yosuke Miyashita, Jared Joiner, Michael Chasnow, Geetika Agrawal, Matt Klein, Katie Winter, and Eric and Naomi Sugar.

To Kathy Hunter, Jeff Duncan, Amy K. Nelson, Bob Remy, Bob White, Brad "Spider" Caldwell, Anthony Lubrano, Joe Stetson, Joanna Share, Leon Satz, John Diaz, Mark Acasio, Butch Leitzinger, Mike McCann, and Zach Bruch, thanks for offering insight, guidance, connections, and in some cases lots of booze. To Mike Ware, Tom McCarthy, Raymond Smith, Jimmy Downs, John Green, and Gary Borstelmann, I owe you an extra measure of appreciation. Thank you for sharing your stories.

So many friends and colleagues have contributed to this effort by offering encouragement, feedback, and counsel or by simply meeting me for a beer, providing a much-needed diversion. Thanks in particular to Sahar Ghaheri, Jordan Chamberlain, Cori Mattli, Luke Zaleski, Brendan Flaherty, Jon Fell, Matt Goldman, Jim Strouse, Lindsay and Demetri Yatrakis, Danny and Alexis Meyer, Hal Meyer, Mari Meyer, Daniel Silbert, Ben Ryder Howe, Paul Winner, Keith Newton, Scott Eden, Eric Leventhal, Adam Rubin, Temís Galindo, Geoffrey Warren-Boulton, Jessica Tainsh, Ken Kurson, Dave Levin, Eric Sobel, Jay Stolar, Joshua Weinstein, Noah Aronson, Bret Ratner, Jeremiah Glazer, Drew Morcheles, Devashish Kandpal, Malachi Handler, Alan Fell, Michael Cera, Stayton Bonner, Kira Henehan, Seth Klein, Tom Souhlas, Rachel Greengrass, and John Crary.

To my parents, Marilyn and Allen, thank you for a lifetime of support and for still lending me your car on occasion. To family members who didn't have me as a houseguest—Michal, Mike, and

Caleb; Noah and Elise; Talia and Scott; Eitan and Lauren; Jerry, Hedy, Sara, and Matt; Amy, Aaron, Anna, and Daniel; Aubrey and Jed—thank you for putting up with me in other ways and for letting me show up late to your weddings, when necessary. To Arielle, for whom I'm a permanent houseguest, thank you for believing in this project—and in me. And to the memory of Bob and Jane Weiner, of Mel and Bea Kohan, and of David Passer, thank you for taking me to my first ball games, for fanning my love of sports, and for buying me barbecue when I couldn't afford it.

To Steve Attardo, thanks for the excellent cover design.

To Gina Iaquinta, for fielding all my dumb questions.

To Peter Miller, for spreading the word.

To David Patterson, for being my advocate.

To Katie Adams, a brilliant editor whose interest in stadiums launched this whole adventure, for the opportunity.

Finally, to the fans who embraced me at their tailgates, taught me their traditions, fed me bratwurst and rag bologna, and generally sustained me during the journey, thanks for your charity and kindness—and for reminding me that being a fan can be downright fun. Unlike the stadium staffers, you never took the games for granted, and your passion provided a necessary counterbalance to the workaday detachment that threatened to dull my awe of these impressive and complicated buildings and the events therein. You also taught me the best way to watch a game—and it's not from the sidelines or a luxury suite. It's not even from the cheap seats. The best way to watch a game, I discovered, is alongside a true believer, with someone who deeply cares about the outcome. In other words: with a fan.

Personally, I can't wait to attend my next game, wherever that may be.

INDEX

Qatar, 358
Qualcomm Stadium, 198–99
Quick Change, 256*n*
Quicken Loans Arena, 82, 85, 86, 249
 digital ticketing platform at, 96, 97, 98, 110
 scalpers at, 82, 83, 85, 92, 95, 96, 97–101, 103–4, 110–11
Quinn, J. J., 305, 313–14

rabdouchoi ("truncheon-bearers"), 191
Rabinowitz, Seth, 281–82
RAC (Rutgers Athletic Center), 260–61, 267
racism, racial injustice, 237*n*, 323, 324, 325*n*
Raider Bandit, 189
Raider Nation, 174–78, 180–83, 184
 athletes targeted by, 185, 186, 187, 188
 bad reputation of, 175–76, 178, 180, 185, 189–90
 Black Hole section of, 176, 177, 181, 185–90, 201–2, 203–5
 community service by, 190
 cultural softening of, 187–88, 189
 as diverse, inclusive community, 183
 drinking in, 174, 176, 177, 178, 181, 197, 204
 fighting and violence of, 175, 186, 187, 189, 199, 204
 Gorilla Rilla of, 174–75, 176–78, 181, 183, 187, 201
 heckling by, 176, 188, 201, 204–5

 life-size dummy used by, 186–87, 188
 tailgating by, 174–75, 176–78, 181–82, 183, 187, 189, 197
 thrown objects by, 185
rape, rape culture, 120, 130, 184, 185, 214, 325
 see also sexual assault
Rasta (Packers fan), 6
Ratner, Bruce, 66, 67, 68, 69–70, 71, 75, 76
Raum, Brock, 243, 244, 245
Raymond, Dave, 241*n*
Raymond James Stadium, 158–59
Red Bull, 331
Redneck Riviera, 155
Red Panda, 256*n*
Reedus, Maurice "Sax Man," Jr., 101–2
Reid, Andy, 240
Remy, Bob, 118
Renaissance, 191
replays, video, 244–45
retractable roofs, 115
Revolt of the Black Athlete, The (Edwards), 323*n*
Rice, Carl, 28, 37
Rice-Eccles Stadium, 353
Richmond, Peter, 183
Riggs, Bobby, 324
Ringling Bros. and Barnum & Bailey Circus, 277
Rise of Stadiums in the Modern United States, The (Dyreson and Trumpbour, eds.), 314*n*
Rison, Andre, 187